FUNDAMENTALS OF INTERNATIONAL FINANCE

JOHN E. PIPPENGER

Department of Economics
University of California at Santa Barbara

PRENTICE-HALL, INC.
Englewood Cliffs, New Jersey 07632

Library of Congress Cataloging in Publication Data

Pippenger, John E.,
  Fundamentals of international finance.

  Includes bibliographies and index.
  1. International finance. I. Title.
HG3881.P52 1984   332'.042   83-22805
ISBN 0-13-340142-1

IN PERPETUUM MATER
AVE ATQUE VALE

Editorial/production supervision and interior design:
  Terry Soler and Fay Ahuja
Cover design: 20/20 Services, Inc.
Manufacturing buyer: Ed O'Dougherty

Printed in the United States of America

10 9 8 7 6 5 4 3 2 1

ISBN 0-13-340142-1

Prentice-Hall International, Inc., *London*
Prentice-Hall of Australia Pty. Limited, *Sydney*
Editora Prentice-Hall do Brasil, Ltda., *Rio de Janeiro*
Prentice-Hall Canada Inc., *Toronto*
Prentice-Hall of India Private Limited, *New Delhi*
Prentice-Hall of Japan, Inc., *Tokyo*
Prentice-Hall of Southeast Asia Pte. Ltd., *Singapore*
Whitehall Books Limited, *Wellington, New Zealand*

CONTENTS

iii

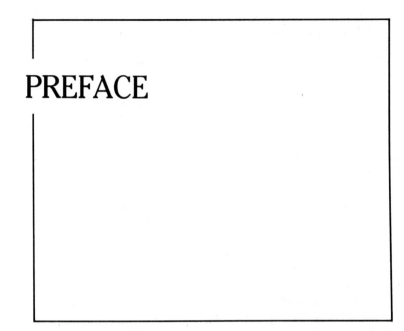

PREFACE

There are basically two reasons for writing a textbook: either for the money or because of dissatisfaction with existing textbooks. I prefer more money to less, but I wrote this text primarily because I have been dissatisfied for a number of years with existing textbooks in international finance. One problem is that most texts cover trade and finance. As a result, students in a class on international finance use only half the text. This text covers *only* international finance.

Another problem is that many texts are out of date. Only a few discuss Eurocurrencies, apply Fisherian capital theory to international finance, or develop the asset approach to exchange rates. None do all three. This text has a full chapter devoted to both Eurocurrencies and the asset approach. In addition, the analysis of international investment is developed from both a portfolio and Fisherian perspective.

I was also dissatisfied because most texts are written at a low level and none stress the role of price theory in international finance. Although it does not require calculus or a course in trade theory, this text assumes a solid background in intermediate micro- and macroeconomics. It is designed for either a quarter or semester upper-division course at a university or in an MBA program.

This text stresses price theory. For example, comparative advantage between present and future goods is used as a bridge between the pure theory of trade and international finance. In addition, the text develops a price theoretic explanation for how and why real shocks such as capital flows and changes in tastes introduce errors into Purchasing Power Parity. It also discusses the microeconomic aspects of international financial adjustment.

Perhaps most of all, I have been dissatisfied with a one-sided treatment of international finance. In spite of recent developments, the vast majority of texts analyze international adjustment and the transfer problem almost exclusively from a Keynesian perspective. Those texts that use a monetarist approach tend to be equally one-sided. I believe that any student who is taught international finance from only a Keynesian *or* monetarist perspective is shortchanged. This text provides a balanced treatment of both monetarist and Keynesian approaches to international adjustment. As a result, students develop a better understanding of both viewpoints because they have a framework for comparison.

A textbook is never a solo effort and a number of people have made substantial contributions to this one. I particularly want to thank J. David Richardson, Dennis Logue and Daniel Friedman for their extensive and useful comments. I would also like to thank the numerous students who made constructive comments and caught a variety of errors. My typist, Bee Hanson, has been a jewel. Without her this would have been a nightmare. The art work was done by Susan Robbins. Finally, I want to acknowledge my mentors: Armen Alchian, William Allen, Karl Brunner, and Jack Hirshleifer. If this book makes a contribution, it is largely because of what I learned from them.

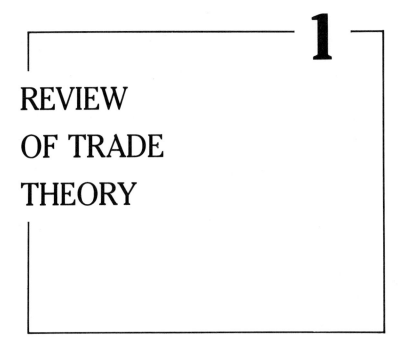

REVIEW
OF TRADE
THEORY

A major objective of this and the next chapter is to build a bridge between the pure theory of trade and international finance. The foundation of that bridge is the concept of comparative advantage.

Apart from a few hermits, none of us tries to be self-sufficient; we all specialize. We become architects, bakers, computer operators, dishwashers, or economists and exchange what we produce for the food, clothes, and other things we consume. The economic explanation for this behavior is that we are lured away from self-sufficiency by the benefits derived from trade and specialization based on comparative advantage. Our first project is to analyze comparative advantage, specialization, and trade in the context of two individuals. Then we apply the same ideas to the exchange of commodities between countries. In Chapter 2, we apply the same concepts to international investment.

TWO INDIVIDUALS

The two individuals are Alice Andersen and Bill Blake, and they produce two goods, wheat and cloth. In Figure 1.1(a) the production possibility frontier for Alice is $K_A K_A$ and her indifference curves appear as $I_0 I_0$ and $I_1 I_1$. The production possibility frontier for Bill is shown as $K_B K_B$ in Figure 1.1(b), and

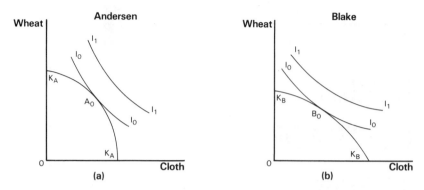

FIGURE 1.1   Production possibility frontiers and indifference maps for Andersen and Blake.

his indifference curves are also labeled I_0I_0 and I_1I_1. These production possibility frontiers show the maximum amount of wheat and cloth that can be produced per period, such as a month, given the individual's endowments and preferences for labor versus leisure. In the absence of exchange, the best Andersen and Blake can do is to move to points A_0 and B_0, respectively, where the indifference curve is tangent to the production possibility frontier. At each point, the marginal rate of substitution between wheat and cloth in production is just equal to the marginal rate of substitution in consumption.

Comparative Advantage

If, because of different tastes or different endowments, marginal rates of substitution between wheat and cloth are not the same at points A_0 and B_0, comparative advantage exists and there is a basis for mutually advantageous exchange. An examination of Figure 1.1 shows that at point A_0 more wheat "trades" for a given amount of cloth than at point B_0. This means Blake has a comparative advantage in cloth and Andersen a comparative advantage in wheat.

To illustrate the incentive for trade, the difference between marginal rates of substitution at points A_0 and B_0 in Figure 1.1 is exaggerated in Figure 1.2. At any rate of exchange of wheat for cloth that lies between the marginal rates of substitution at points A_0 and B_0, both individuals benefit by trading. For example, at the wheat price of cloth represented by the slope of the line PP in Figure 1.2, Alice and Bill both achieve a higher level of utility by moving to points A_1' and B_1', respectively.

In moving to point A_1', Andersen chooses the optimal level of production by increasing production of wheat and shifting along her production possibility frontier to A_1, where the marginal rate of substitution in production equals the slope of the price line PP. At that point she produces each

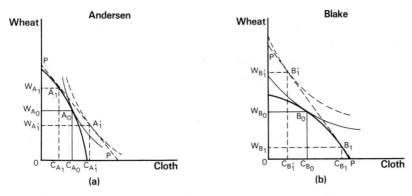

FIGURE 1.2   Production possibility frontiers and indifference maps for Andersen and Blake.

month $0C_{A_1}$ of cloth and $0W_{A_1}$ of wheat. Given the optimal level of production, she maximizes utility by moving along the price line PP to point A_1'. The move along the price line involves exchanging $W_{A_1'}W_{A_1}$ of wheat for $C_{A_1}C_{A_1'}$ of cloth. Blake, on the other hand, maximizes the value of his output by increasing the output of cloth and moving production to point B_1. His utility is maximized by exchanging $C_{B_1'}C_{B_1}$ of cloth for $W_{B_1}W_{B_1'}$ of wheat along the price line PP so that he consumes at point B_1'.

Let's try an arithmetic example. Andersen and Blake are shipwrecked on a desert island. They survive on coconuts and bananas that grow wild on the island. If they each work, say, 5 hours, Andersen can collect 100 bananas or 90 coconuts. Blake does not climb as well; he can pick 50 bananas or 80 coconuts in 5 hours. Suppose they do not specialize and each spends 2.5 hours picking coconuts and another 2.5 hours picking bananas. Their combined output is 75 bananas and 85 coconuts. By specializing based on comparative advantage, they can increase their production of both bananas and coconuts.

Even though Blake is less skillful, he is relatively less inept at collecting coconuts. As a result, he has a comparative advantage in coconuts even though he collects fewer per hour than Andersen. Suppose Blake spends the full 5 hours collecting coconuts and Andersen spends 1 hour picking coconuts and 4 hours collecting bananas. By utilizing comparative advantage, they produce 80 bananas and 98 coconuts instead of 75 bananas and 85 coconuts. With the extra bananas and coconuts they can set up a little still and begin to enjoy their stay on that desert island.

Figure 1.2 and our example illustrate the fundamental motive for abandoning self-sufficiency in favor of specialization and exchange. The incentive is mutual benefit based on comparative advantage. Andersen and Blake are *both* better off by increasing the production of the good in which they have a comparative advantage. If we are willing to treat exchange between

Andersen and Blake as though it took place in a competitive market, then we can go one step further and determine both the volume and terms of trade.

Volume and Terms of Trade

The first step is to go back to Figure 1.2 and derive the demand for and supply of cloth (or wheat) for Andersen and Blake. Begin with the price of cloth in terms of wheat, shown by the price line *PP*. At that price, Andersen produces (supplies) $0C_{A_1}$ of cloth per month and demands $0C_{A_1'}$. Each month Blake produces $0C_{B_1}$ of cloth and demands $0C_{B_1'}$. By choosing another price, we could use the same technique to determine the quantities supplied and demanded at that price. Following the same procedure for all prices in the relevant range yields the demand and supply schedules for cloth shown in Figure 1.3. In general, the schedules are not linear; indeed, it is possible for the supply schedule to be backward-bending. The schedules are shown here as straight lines because linear schedules are convenient.

The intersection of demand and supply in Figures 1.3(a) and (b) corresponds to points A_0 and B_0 in Figure 1.1. In the absence of trade, the best Andersen and Blake can do is to consume $0C_A$ and $0C_B$ of cloth. The marginal rates of substitution for Andersen and Blake in isolation appear in Figure 1.3 as $0\overline{P}_A$ and $0\overline{P}_B$, respectively. At any price between these two extremes, both individuals gain from trade, but only one price or terms of trade is consistent with competitive equilibrium.

With both individuals treated as though they were price takers in a competitive market, we can determine Andersen's demand to buy cloth (import schedule) and Blake's supply of cloth to Andersen (export schedule). At each price below $0\overline{P}_A$, the amount Andersen wants to buy each month from Blake is given by the horizontal distance between her total demand *DD* and domestic production *SS*. At each point above $0\overline{P}_B$, the horizontal distance between Blake's total demand for cloth *DD* and his production *SS* shows how much he is willing to export each month at that

FIGURE 1.3   Volume and terms of trade.

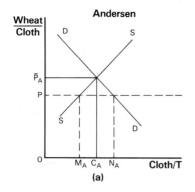
(a)

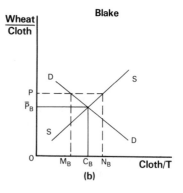
(b)

price. In Figure 1.3, those horizontal distances are equal at the price $0P$, where Andersen wants to buy $M_A N_A$ cloth and Blake wants to sell the same amount, which is shown as $M_B N_B$. At any other price there will be an excess demand for or an excess supply of cloth.

Figure 1.3 explicitly shows equilibrium in the cloth market. It also implicitly depicts equilibrium in the market for wheat. When Andersen demands $M_A N_A$ of cloth, that demand is made effective by an offer of wheat equal to $0P$ times $M_A N_A$. That is, for $M_A N_A$ of cloth, she is willing to pay or supply an amount of wheat equal to $0P$ times $M_A N_A$. Blake supplies $M_B N_B$ of cloth because at that price he wants to buy or import wheat equal to $0P$ times $M_B N_B$. Since $0P$ is the same in both cases and $M_B N_B$ equals $M_A N_A$, at the cloth price of wheat given by the reciprocal of the price $0P$, the quantity of wheat offered by Andersen equals the amount demanded by Blake. Walras's law, the sum of the excess demands is zero, holds. When one market in a two-market world clears, the other market must also clear.

It is appropriate to relate the equilibrium volume and terms of trade back to the production frontiers and indifference schedules shown in Figure 1.2. Assume the price PP in Figure 1.2 corresponds to the equilibrium price $0P$ in Figure 1.3. In that case, $0C_{A_1}$ in Figure 1.2(a) corresponds to $0M_A$ in Figure 1.3(a), $0C_{A_1'}$ corresponds to $0N_A$, and $0C_{B_1'}$ in Figure 1.2(b) corresponds to $0M_B$ in Figure 1.3(b), while $0C_{B_1}$ corresponds to $0N_B$. If you cannot see this correspondence, you should carefully derive Andersen's and Blake's demand and supply schedules from their production possibility frontiers and indifference curves.

In a course in microeconomics, the two-commodity model with two individuals reviewed above is extended to M commodities and N individuals in a straightforward way, using a mathematical model. That extension does not provide any new insights into the nature of exchange that are important for us, so we turn next to an analysis of trade between two countries.

TWO COUNTRIES

In international trade, the emphasis is on exchange between groups of people called countries, but these groups just as well could be called regions or states. The simplest model of international trade is the two-country, two-commodity model. Probably the most common way to develop the analysis is through the use of community indifference curves. With that approach, we interpret production possibility curves for Andersen and Blake as production possibility frontiers for countries A and B, and we interpret their indifference curves as community indifference curves.

Going from several production possibility curves to the production frontier for a group or nation is reasonably straightforward. Going from individual indifference curves to community indifference curves is another story. In order for community indifference curves to have the same properties as individual curves, we must place strong restrictions on the underlying individual utility functions.

Demand and Supply

There is an alternative approach that avoids community indifference curves. Consider one country, call it the United States, composed of Andersen and Blake. Given an understanding of Figures 1.2 and 1.3, we can obtain all the relevant information for the country by horizontally summing the demand and supply curves for Andersen and Blake. The individual demand and supply schedules and their horizontal summation are shown in Figure 1.4. With more than two people, exactly the same approach can be used to derive national demand and supply schedules.

Given production possibility frontiers and indifference maps for individuals in the second country, call it the United Kingdom, we can derive supply and demand schedules for that country in the same way. The demand and supply schedules for both the United States and the United Kingdom are shown in Figure 1.5. The diagram for the United States in Figure 1.5 is rotated 180 degrees on its vertical axis so that the diagrams for both countries share a common vertical axis. This facilitates the analysis here and in the next chapter. The only change is that now we measure quantity for the United States from right to left rather than from left to right.

In Figure 1.5 the United Kingdom has a comparative advantage in cloth and the United States a comparative advantage in wheat because, in the absence of trade, the wheat price of cloth is lower in the United Kingdom

FIGURE 1.4   Derivation of demand and supply for the United States.

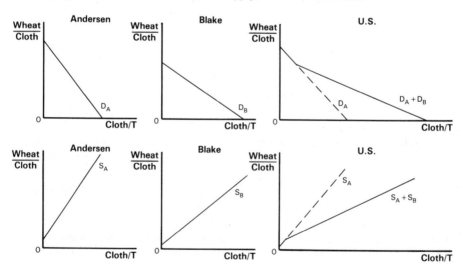

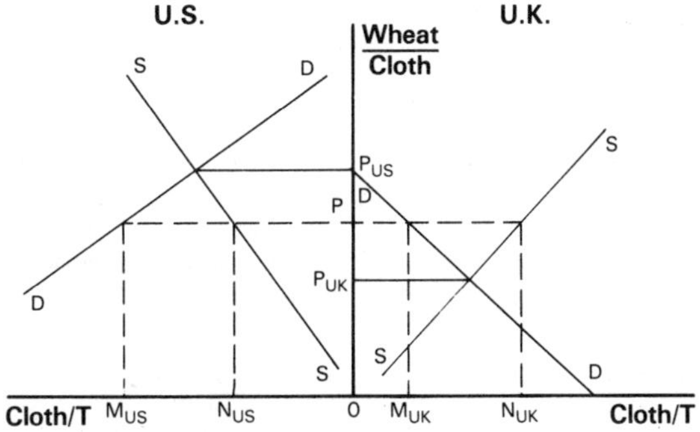

FIGURE 1.5
Exchange of cloth and wheat
between the United States and
the United Kingdom with no
impediments to trade.

than in the United States. That is, OP_{UK} is less than OP_{US}. With trade, the United States imports cloth and exports wheat. In the absence of transaction costs and other impediments to trade, imports and exports expand until market prices in both countries are equated at OP.

Excess Demand

In Chapters 5 and 6 we use excess demand and import demand schedules. Let's take this opportunity to review those concepts and use them to illustrate the determination of the volume and terms of trade. The demand for and supply of cloth in the United States are repeated in Figure 1.6(a). The excess demand schedule implied by these demand and supply schedules is given in Figure 1.6(b). It is obtained by subtracting domestic supply from domestic demand. At the price OP_{US} demand equals supply; excess demand is zero, and the excess demand schedule in Figure 1.6(b) intersects the vertical axis at the price OP_{US}. When the wheat price of cloth falls to OP, demand exceeds supply by $M_{US}N_{US}$ in Figure 1.6(a), which equals the excess demand OQ_{US} at that price in Figure 1.6(b). If the price rises above OP_{US}, the excess supply in Figure 1.6(a) is measured by the horizontal distance to the left of the vertical axis in Figure 1.6(b). That is, at any given price in Figure 1.6(b), the horizontal distance from the vertical axis to the schedule labeled SD measures the excess demand for cloth in the United States. Quantities to the right of the vertical axis represent positive excess demand, and quantities to the left negative excess demand or excess supply. The right-hand side of Figure 1.6(b) is the U.S. demand for imports. It shows how much the United States wants to import at each alternative price. The excess demand for cloth by the United States shown in Figure 1.6(b) implicitly defines an excess supply schedule for wheat. If you cannot determine the excess supply of or demand for wheat for each alternative price in Figure 1.6(b), go back and review the analysis underlying Figures 1.3 through 1.5.

Figure 1.6(c) shows the United Kingdom demand for and supply of cloth. If we horizontally subtract the quantity demanded from the quantity

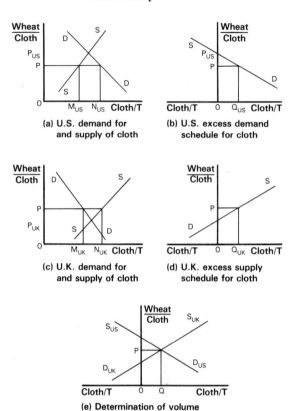

(a) U.S. demand for
and supply of cloth

(b) U.S. excess demand
schedule for cloth

(c) U.K. demand for
and supply of cloth

(d) U.K. excess supply
schedule for cloth

(e) Determination of volume
and terms of trade

FIGURE 1.6
Derivation of excess demand
and supply schedules.

supplied at each alternative price in Figure 1.6(c), we obtain the excess supply schedule shown in Figure 1.6(d). At the wheat price of cloth given by $0P_{UK}$, excess supply is zero. When the price rises to $0P$, the excess supply is $M_{UK}N_{UK}$, which equals $0Q_{UK}$ in Figure 1.6(d). If the price falls below $0P_{UK}$, demand exceeds supply and we are on the part of the excess supply schedule that lies to the left of the vertical axis in Figure 1.6(d). That is, at any given price in Figure 1.6(d), the horizontal distance from the vertical axis to the schedule labeled DS measures the excess supply of cloth in the United Kingdom. Quantities to the right of the vertical axis represent positive excess supply and quantities to the left negative excess supply or excess demand. The right-hand side of the excess supply schedule is the U.K. export supply schedule. It shows how much the United Kingdom is willing to export at each alternative price.

Figure 1.6(e) combines the excess demand schedule for the United States and the excess supply schedule for the United Kingdom. At the price $0P$, U.S. excess demand equals U.K. excess supply. At the price $0P$ in Figure 1.6(e), the United States wants to import $0Q$ per period and the

United Kingdom wants to export the same amount. The quantity $0Q$ in Figure 1.6(e) corresponds to $M_{US}N_{US}$ and $M_{UK}N_{UK}$ in Figure 1.5, and $0P$ is the same price in both.

PRICE DIFFERENTIALS

Differences in relative prices in the absence of trade (comparative advantage) provide the motivation for exchange. When there are no impediments to trade, the volume of imports and exports is maximized ($M_{US}N_{US}$ and $M_{UK}N_{UK}$) and relative price differentials are eliminated. Price differentials are the basis for exchange, but the effect of trade is to reduce price differentials. When there are transaction costs or other impediments to exchange, such as tariffs or trade controls, they reduce the volume of trade and create price differentials. Trade tends to equate relative prices, but transaction costs prevent complete equalization.

Consider Figure 1.7, where it is assumed that it costs some given quantity of wheat to ship each unit of cloth. The demand and supply schedules for both countries are the same as those shown in Figure 1.5. However, with trade the price of cloth in the United States now falls only to $0P_{US}'$ and it rises in the United Kingdom to only $0P_{UK}'$. The difference between the two prices $P_{UK}'P_{US}'$ reflects the cost of shipping cloth from the United Kingdom to the United States. Residents of the United States buy $N_{US}'M_{US}'$ cloth and pay $0P_{US}'$ times $N_{US}'M_{US}'$ in wheat for that cloth. In the United Kingdom, residents sell $M_{UK}'N_{UK}'$ cloth, which equals $N_{US}'M_{US}'$, but they receive only $M_{UK}'N_{UK}'$ times $0P_{UK}'$ in wheat. The difference, which equals the shaded area shown in Figure 1.7, is absorbed by the various activities involved in shipping cloth. If the "cost" is an import tariff, the shaded area is the tax collected by the U.S. government.

The effect of transactions costs is to prevent complete equalization of relative prices and to *reduce* the volume of trade. Given the schedules shown in Figure 1.7, if transaction costs rise, the price differential increases

FIGURE 1.7
Exchange of cloth and wheat between the United States and the United Kingdom with constant transaction costs.

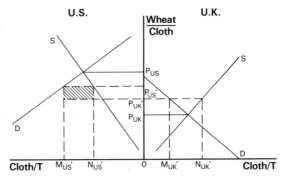

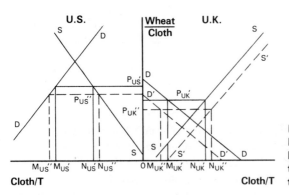

FIGURE 1.8
Exchange of cloth and wheat between the United States and the United Kingdom with rising transaction costs.

and the volume of trade decreases. In other words, given the demand and supply conditions, there is an *inverse* relation between *observed* price differentials and the volume of trade.

Suppose, however, that transaction costs per unit rise as trade increases. Let $P_{UK}'P_{US}'$ in Figure 1.8 represent the cost per unit when the volume of trade is $M_{UK}'N_{UK}'$. If demand and supply in the United Kingdom shift to $D'D'$ and $S'S'$, the volume of trade between the two countries increases, but transaction costs also increase, and the price differential becomes larger. Under these circumstances there is a positive relation between observed price differentials and the volume of trade. In Figure 1.8 the volume of trade increases to $M_{UK}''N_{UK}''$ and the price differential rises to $P_{UK}''P_{US}''$. The larger price differential, however, does not *cause* more trade. Trade volume increases because the underlying conditions of supply and demand change. The larger volume of trade causes transactions costs to rise, and price differentials increase because transactions costs are higher. If transaction costs fall rather than rise as trade increases, there is an inverse relation between the volume of trade and price differentials. As before, it is the change in underlying demand and supply conditions that is the driving force changing the volume of trade. With decreasing costs, transaction costs and price differentials fall because the volume of trade increases.

The analysis developed here is designed to make one basic point. Economic theory tells us that there is no simple causal relation between observed price differentials and the amount of some commodity that is imported or exported. As we will see in the next chapter, exactly the same argument applies to international investment. There is no simple causal relationship between interest rate differentials and international investment.

SUMMARY

Without trade, relative prices depend on domestic endowments and tastes. If domestic and foreign prices differ in the absence of trade, comparative advantage exists and there is a basis for trade that is mutually beneficial. When countries or individuals engage in trade, they tend to specialize in producing the commodities in which they have a comparative advantage. Although exchange is based on the existence of different relative prices, trade tends to equate relative prices. The volume and terms of trade depend on the import demand and export supply schedules, which in turn depend on endowments and tastes. What relationship—if any—exists between price differentials with trade and the volume of trade depends on the relationship between transaction costs and other impediments to trade, and the volume of trade. There is no causal relationship between observed price differentials and the volume of trade.

QUESTIONS FOR REVIEW

1. Define comparative advantage.
2. What determines the pattern of trade in our two-country world if both countries have identical production frontiers?
3. Describe the forces that, according to the pure theory of trade, determine the direction, composition, and volume of international trade.
4. Andersen's supply of cloth *is* a demand for wheat. Explain.
5. Even though differences in relative prices are the basis for trade, there is no reason to expect a systematic relation between observed price differentials and the volume of trade. Explain.
6. Draw the equilibrium volume and terms of trade for the wheat market implied by Figure 1.3 and discuss the relationship between the prices and amounts traded in the markets for wheat and cloth.
7. Suppose some workers in the U.S. are more suited for the cloth industry than the wheat industry. Some land is also more productive in cloth than wheat, and some physical capital is more suited for use in the cloth industry than it is for the wheat industry. Under these conditions, what groups do you think would advocate tariffs on cloth?
8. Some people claim that the deficit in the U.S. trade balance is the result of low productivity in the United States. Given the ideas developed in this chapter, is that possible?
9. Some claim that a "fair" tariff would just compensate for the productivity advantage a foreign country has in a domestic import. What would be the effect of imposing a "fair" tariff on all goods?
10. How does "learning by doing" affect the concept of comparative advantage?
11. Extend the two-commodity, two-country model to two commodities and three countries.
12. Discuss the equilibrium conditions for a model with N commodities and M countries. How will these conditions and production patterns change if

tastes change and one country demands more of one import and less of one export good? (*Suggestion:* Start with three commodities and three countries.)

ADDITIONAL READINGS

BHAGWATI, JAGDISH (ED.). *International Trade: Selected Readings* (Cambridge, Mass.: MIT Press, 1981).

HELLER, H. ROBERT. *International Trade: Theory and Empirical Evidence,* 2d ed. (Englewood Cliffs, N.J.: Prentice-Hall, 1973).

2

INTERNATIONAL
INVESTMENT

In Chapter 1 we developed an explanation for the composition and direction
of international trade in commodities. In this chapter we use the same basic
ideas to explain international investment. We do so by extending the earlier
analysis in two ways. First, we expand the concept of a commodity. Instead
of dealing with wheat and cloth, the commodities or objects of choice are
present wheat and future wheat, present cloth and future cloth—or, more
simply, present goods and future goods. Second, we introduce uncertainty.
In Chapter 1 there is an implicit assumption of certainty. Traders, for example, have no doubt about the prices at which they can sell commodities. In
the latter part of this chapter, investors also know the price at which they
can buy an asset, but yields on assets are uncertain.

FISHERIAN CAPITAL THEORY

Around the turn of the century, Irving Fisher developed a widely accepted
theory of capital. The essence of his approach is to use basic price theory but
to change the analysis from an exchange of wheat for cloth (present goods
for present goods) to an exchange of present goods for future goods.

Two Individuals and Two Periods

We begin the analysis with one commodity, cloth, two individuals, and two time periods, this year and next year. The two individuals remain Alice Andersen and Bill Blake. Each has an endowment of physical capital. Given this stock of capital, he or she can produce a certain amount of present and future goods. By increasing their stock of physical capital, they can increase their output of future goods. By not maintaining the capital stock, they can reduce future output and increase the amount available for present consumption.

An owner-operated farm is an example. Taking the work-leisure decision in both periods as given, a farmer can alter the amount of present and future wheat available in several ways. The most obvious way is by the amount of the present crop that is devoted to seed for next year, but there are others. For example, he can choose between weeding, which will help this year's crop, or spending time clearing land of trees and rocks, which will increase next year's crop. All businesses, including large corporations, face similar choices. How much time, effort, and resources should they devote to present production, and how much to future production? The simple explanation that we begin to develop in Figure 2.1 provides some important insights into these decisions.

The interpretation of Figure 2.1 is similar to that of Figure 1.1. Future goods C_1 are measured along the vertical axis and present goods C_0 on the horizontal axis. The production possibility curve KK describes how present goods can be converted into future goods. The curves labeled $I_i I_i$ represent alternative levels of utility. If Andersen and Blake are unable to trade, they maximize utility by producing and consuming at points A and B, respectively. The slopes of the indifference curves and production possibility frontiers at the tangencies A and B show the "domestic" rates of exchange between present and future goods for Andersen and Blake. We do not nor-

FIGURE 2.1   Production possibility frontiers and indifference maps for Andersen and Blake.

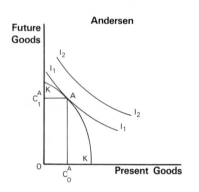
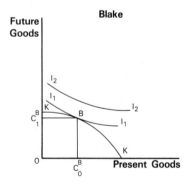

mally refer to rates of exchange between present and future goods as prices, but as interest rates. If at point A 1.2 units of future cloth exchange for one unit of present cloth, then the (real) interest rate is 20 percent. That is, the real interest rate is the price of this year's goods in terms of next year's goods, minus 1.

Comparative Advantage

In Figure 2.1 the rates of exchange between present and future goods are not equal at points A and B, and real rates of interest diverge. As a result, comparative advantage exists, and there is an incentive for trade. Since the slope at point A is steeper than at point B, the real interest rate in the absence of trade is higher for Andersen than for Blake. This means Andersen has a comparative advantage in future goods and Blake a comparative advantage in present goods. With exchange, Andersen exports future goods and imports present goods. Blake does the opposite. Inspection of Figure 2.1 reveals the direction but not the volume or terms of trade. To determine the volume and terms of trade, we need to develop saving and investment schedules.

Saving and Investment

Andersen's production possibility curve is redrawn in Figure 2.2. Underlying this production frontier is some level of technology, a labor decision, and a stock of physical capital. Taking the labor decision and technology in both periods as given, if the stock of physical capital is unchanged, $0Y_0$ of present goods and $0Y_1$ of future goods are produced. This combination of present and future goods is her endowment and appears as point E on the production possibility frontier. The endowment of present goods $0Y_0$ is Andersen's current income.

FIGURE 2.2
Saving and investment in isolation.

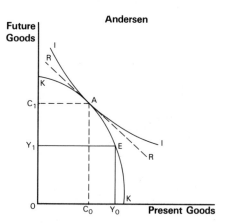

In isolation, Andersen maximizes utility by moving to point A on her production possibility frontier. As compared to her initial endowment at point E, she reduces the production of present goods by C_0Y_0 and increases future production by Y_1C_1. Since $0Y_0$ is current income and Andersen does not consume C_0Y_0, she saves C_0Y_0, which is also the amount of current income devoted to the production of future goods. That is, at the interest rate r corresponding to the price line RR in Figure 2.2, saving and investment by Andersen both equal C_0Y_0.

Given the assumption of isolation, saving and investment must be equal. If we drop that assumption and view Andersen as a price taker in a competitive market, we can derive her saving and investment schedules. The derivation is illustrated in Figure 2.3. Since Andersen has a comparative advantage in future goods, Figure 2.3 shows her saving and investment decisions for a lower interest rate r_1 corresponding to the flatter price line R_1R_1. Given this lower price for present goods in terms of future goods, she makes the optimum production decision by moving up and to the left along her production possibility frontier to point Q. This choice maximizes wealth, which is measured as $0W$. This level of wealth consists of $0Q_0$ in present goods and Q_0W which, given the interest rate r_1, is the present value of her production of future goods $0Q_1$. Given production at point Q, Andersen maximizes utility by trading future goods for present goods along the price line R_1R_1 until she reaches her highest indifference curve at point A in Figure 2.3, where she exchanges C_1Q_1 of future goods for Q_0C_0 of present goods. At the interest rate r_1, the production of present goods is reduced by Q_0Y_0 in order to increase the production of future goods by Y_1Q_1. The reduction in the production of present goods represents investment, so at interest rate r_1 Andersen invests Q_0Y_0. Since her income is $0Y_0$ and consumption is $0C_0$, she saves C_0Y_0.

By following a similar procedure, it is possible to determine how much Andersen or Blake save and invest at each alternative interest rate. The saving and investment schedules for Andersen and Blake shown in Figure

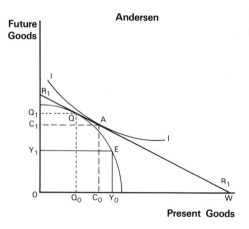

Future Goods

Andersen

Present Goods

FIGURE 2.3
Saving and investment with exchange.

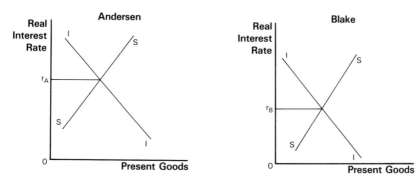

FIGURE 2.4   Saving and investment schedules for Andersen and Blake.

2.4 should be interpreted in terms of the decisions illustrated in Figures 2.2 and 2.3. (In general, saving and investment schedules are not linear; they are shown as linear only for convenience.)

The interest rates Or_A and Or_B in Figure 2.4 that equate saving and investment correspond to the marginal rates of substitution between present and future goods at points A and B, respectively, in Figure 2.1. At any interest rate below Or_A Andersen invests more than she saves, and at any rate above Or_B Blake saves more than he invests. At an interest rate between Or_A and Or_B, Blake reduces the production of future goods and increases the production of present goods, while Andersen does the opposite. Before going on, be sure you understand the relationship between the saving and investment schedules shown in Figure 2.4 and the reasoning developed in Figures 2.2 and 2.3. If the relationship is not clear, review the derivation of demand and supply schedules in Chapter 1.

The two panels of Figure 2.4 are combined into a single diagram in Figure 2.5. The diagram for Andersen is rotated 180 degrees on the vertical axis so that the quantity of present goods is measured from right to left. The two diagrams are then joined at the vertical axis. This simplifies the geometric determination of an equilibrium under the assumption that both individuals act as though they were price takers in a competitive market. In the absence of exchange, interest rates in Figure 2.5 are Or_A and Or_B. Since Or_A exceeds Or_B, Andersen has a comparative advantage in future goods. In the absence of any impediments such as risk, transaction costs, or trade controls, exchange equalizes relative prices, and both interest rates move to Or.

At the equilibrium rate Or in Figure 2.5, Andersen buys (imports) $N_A M_A$ of present goods, which she pays for by selling (exporting) $(1 + r) \times N_A M_A$ of future goods. Blake buys (imports) $(1 + r) \times M_B N_B$ future goods, which he pays for by selling (exporting) $M_B N_B$ in present goods. The amount of present goods bought by Andersen, $N_A M_A$, must equal the amount sold by Blake, $M_B N_B$.

In the terminology of international finance, Andersen has a balance of trade deficit financed by a surplus on capital account. She is a net buyer

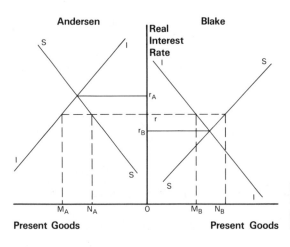

FIGURE 2.5
Exchange of present and future goods between Andersen and Blake.

(importer) of goods and a net seller (exporter) of securities or claims on future goods. Blake, on the other hand, finances a deficit on capital account with a surplus on trade account. He imports securities (claims on future goods), which he finances through an export of present goods. The difference between real rates of interest in the absence of trade provides the incentive for Blake to buy securities from Andersen and sell her goods. In the absence of transaction costs or other impediments, the exchange of present for future goods expands until real rates of interest are equalized.

Transaction costs and other impediments, of course, do exist. However, since risk in one form or another is one of the major obstacles to capital movements, an analysis of the effects of impediments to exchange is postponed until later in this chapter, where we take up risk.

So far we have dealt with two individuals. The analysis can be extended in a straightforward way to explain capital movements between regions or countries. One approach is to use regional or national production possibility frontiers and replace the individual indifference maps with community indifference curves. An alternative is to sum horizontally the saving and investment schedules for individuals (and firms) in each region or country. These regional or national saving and investment schedules can then be used to explain interregional and international capital movements, just as Figure 2.5 describes the exchange of assets for commodities between individuals.

TWO COUNTRIES OR REGIONS

Let's begin with aggregate investment and saving schedules for two regions, say, California and New York. For simplicity, assume California consists of two individuals, Andersen and Blake. The first two panels in Figure 2.6(a)

(a) Investment

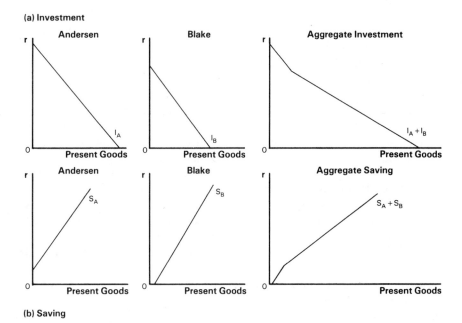

(b) Saving

FIGURE 2.6 Derivation of aggregate saving and investment schedules.

show their investment schedules from Figure 2.4. The third panel shows the horizontal summation, which is the investment schedule for California as a whole. The first two panels in Figure 2.6(b) show the saving schedules for Andersen and Blake. The third panel is the aggregate saving schedule, which is obtained by horizontally summing the individual saving schedules.

The aggregate saving and investment schedules are combined in Figure 2.7. In order to understand these schedules, we must understand how they

FIGURE 2.7
Aggregate investment and saving schedules for California.

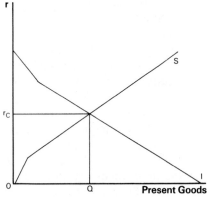

are related to the analysis described in Figures 2.1 through 2.5. For example, in Figure 2.7 investment and saving are equal when the real rate is $0r_C$. This rate corresponds to $0r$ in Figure 2.5, where Andersen borrows $N_A M_A$ of present goods from Blake in exchange for $N_A M_A \times (1 + 0r)$ of future goods. The aggregate investment and saving schedules shown in Figure 2.7 describe the production and saving decisions of two individuals, but the basic idea applies to investment and saving schedules summarizing the relevant decisions for any number of individuals. From now on, we deal with aggregate investment and saving schedules, but we must not forget the behavior of firms and individuals that underlies these schedules.

So far the analysis has been carried out in barter terms—an exchange of present goods for future goods. Barter, however, is quite rare. Even at swap meets, most transactions involve an exchange of money for goods. As we shift the analysis from individuals to regions and countries, we also shift from a barter to a money economy. The underlying motivation is still the exchange of present and future goods. Now, however, that is accomplished by exchanging money, an implicit claim on present goods, for financial assets such as stocks and bonds, which are explicit claims on future money and implicit claims on future goods.

Nominal Capital Flows

In order to avoid the complications introduced by exchange rates and to emphasize the point that the analysis of exchange between countries is not fundamentally different from the explanation of trade between regions, the approach is applied first to capital flows between New York and California. If you feel uncomfortable about the disappearance of the rest of the United States, you can consider these two states as symbols for the eastern and western parts of the United States.

By going back to Figures 2.1 through 2.7 and interpreting present and future goods as present and future money, we can derive traditional investment and saving schedules where investment is a demand for funds and a supply of financial assets, and saving is a demand for assets and a supply of funds. Summing these individual schedules horizontally for residents of New York and California yields two sets of regional saving and investment schedules. These schedules are shown in Figure 2.8, where the rate of interest is measured along the vertical axis and the quantity of dollars per unit of time along the horizontal axis. Price levels are not expected to change, so the interest rate is a real rate.

At interest rates below $0r_C$ in Figure 2.8, the horizontal distance between the investment and saving schedules for California represents that region's excess demand for funds (excess supply of financial assets). For interest rates above $0r_{NY}$, the horizontal distance between New York's saving and investment schedules describes its excess supply of funds (excess demand for financial assets). At interest rate $0r$, the excess demand for funds

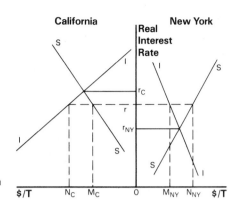

FIGURE 2.8
Determination of capital flows between California and New York.

by Californians, $M_C N_C$, equals the excess supply from New York, $M_{NY} N_{NY}$, and the combined capital markets clear.

By now the situation described in Figure 2.8 should seem like an old friend. In the absence of capital flows, real interest rates are different. Comparative advantage therefore exists, and there is an incentive for capital flows. Since California has the higher real rate in the absence of exchange, California exports future goods and imports present goods. Given competition and no impediments to exchange, California becomes a net importer of $M_{NY} N_{NY}$ worth of present goods from New York, which it pays for by exporting $M_C N_C$ worth of securities. The existence of transaction costs, risk, or other impediments to exchange of course reduces the capital flow and generates an interest rate differential.

Figure 2.8 describes capital movements between New York and California, but exactly the same reasoning applies to the United States and the United Kingdom or to one country and the rest of the world. If, in the absence of capital flows, real interest rates are different, comparative advantage exists and there is a basis for trade. The country with the relatively high real interest rate exports securities and imports goods, while the other country does the opposite. The amount of securities exchanged depends on the underlying excess demand and supply schedules (the difference between domestic saving and investment) and the extent to which transaction costs, risk, and other impediments to exchange prevent the full equalization of real rates of interest.

Additional Implications

So far we have concentrated on explaining the direction and magnitude of capital flows. The Fisherian approach, however, yields a number of other important insights. For example, it explains why capital sometimes flows from a country with a high interest rate to one with a low rate, and it can be extended to an analysis of the influence of capital flows on the term structure of interest rates.

Nominal yields   Consider capital flows between two countries, say, the United States and France. If, in the absence of exchange, real interest rates are higher in the United States, the United States becomes a net exporter of securities to France and a net importer of goods from France. If there are no impediments, this exchange results in the same real rate in both countries, say, r_E.

However, we do not see real rates of interest. What we observe are nominal rates. As a close first approximation, the nominal rate i can be expressed as the real rate r plus the expected rate of inflation $\dot{P}^e$. If trade equates real yields we can express the nominal rates in the two countries as follows:

$$i_{US} = r_E + \dot{P}_{US}^e$$
$$i_F = r_E + \dot{P}_F^e$$

where i_{US} and i_F are nominal rates in the United States and France, r_E is the real rate in both countries, and $\dot{P}_{US}^e$ and $\dot{P}_F^e$ are the expected rates of inflation in the United States and France, respectively. If trade tends to equate real interest rates, the nominal interest rate differential $i_F - i_{US}$ depends primarily on the expected rates of inflation in the two countries.

$$i_F - i_{US} = (r_E + \dot{P}_F^e) - (r_E + \dot{P}_{US}) = \dot{P}_F^e - \dot{P}_{US}^e$$

There is nothing abnormal about investment moving from a country with a high (nominal) interest rate to another with a low (nominal) rate. Suppose there is more inflation in France than in the United States. As a result, nominal yields tend to be higher in France, but France still imports securities from the United States because, in the absence of capital flows, *real* interest rates are higher in the United States.

Transaction costs and other impediments to exchange generate real interest rate differentials, but very large and persistent differences in observed yields usually are the result of large and persistent differences in rates of inflation. As an example, Table 2.1 shows nominal yields and annual rates of inflation using consumer price indexes for the United States and several other countries in 1979. The United Kingdom, Canada, and the United States have similar inflation rates and similar interest rates. In Brazil, Colombia, and Iceland, however, rates of inflation are much higher, and they also have much higher interest rates. On the other hand, Switzerland, West Germany, and Japan have both low interest rates and mild inflation.

Term structure   So far the analysis has been restricted to two periods, this year and next year, or the present and the future. The approach can be generalized to n periods in the same way that the analysis in Chapter 1 can

TABLE 2.1   Interest Rates and Rates of Inflation for 1979

COUNTRY	DISCOUNT RATE* (PERCENT PER YEAR)	INFLATION (PERCENT PER YEAR)
Switzerland	2.0%	3.6%
Germany	6.0	4.0
Japan	6.2	3.5
United States	12.0	11.3
Canada	14.0	9.1
United Kingdom	17.0	13.4
Greece	19.0	19.0
Iceland	26.0	44.0
Colombia	30.0	24.6
Brazil	33.0	52.6

* Discount rates are used because comparable market rates are not available for many countries. Discount rates, however, are often substantially below market rates.

Source: International Monetary Fund, *International Financial Statistics.*

be extended to n goods. Suppose we extend the analysis to 10 years. In the absence of trade, there would be an interest rate for each asset with a maturity from 1 to 10 years. One possible configuration for this pattern or term structure of interest rates is shown in Figure 2.9, where the interest rate is measured along the vertical axis and the maturity of the asset is shown on the horizontal axis. The solid lines *FF* and *UU* denote the pattern of (real) rates in the absence of exchange in France and the United States, respectively. For maturities of less than 5 years, real rates are higher in the United States, and for maturities beyond 5 years, real rates are higher in France. The interpretation of Figure 2.9 is that the United States has a comparative advantage in near-dated future goods and France has a comparative advantage in far-dated future goods.

FIGURE 2.9
Effect of capital flows on the term structure of real interest rates.

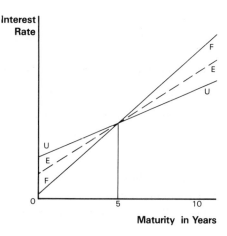

Since exchange tends to equate real rates, with unimpeded capital flows we would expect the term structure in both countries to resemble the broken line *EE*. Given the situation described in Figure 2.9, the United States would export securities with maturities under 5 years (capital inflow), and import assets with maturities over 5 years (capital outflow).

Limitations

Although Fisherian capital theory provides important insights, it also has serious limitations. The most obvious is that it ignores uncertainty and risk, an issue we consider later in this chapter. In addition, a Fisherian approach cannot explain cross hauling in assets; that is, the simultaneous import and export of assets of the same maturity. For example, it does not explain why the United States both exports and imports 20-year bonds. A third and much more subtle problem is the interpretation of equilibrium. The equilibria depicted here are conceptually different from those shown in Chapter 1.

Equilibria in price theory often depict long-run or steady-state situations. In the absence of changes in exogenous variables such as tastes or techniques of production, prices and quantities remain constant period after period. These equilibria are typical of the general equilibrium approach used in the pure theory of trade reviewed in the last chapter. Fisherian equilibria tend to be transitory. They have within them the seeds of their own destruction. When an individual or a society saves or dissaves, invests or disinvests, the resources it has available in the next period are different from those available earlier. As a result, prices and quantities that clear markets change. These conditions are typical of equilibria seen in short- and intermediate-run Marshallian analysis. They are also the kinds of equilibria underlying most macro models such as IS-LM.

In addition to their transitory nature, there is another aspect of Fisherian equilibria that we should understand. Let's reconsider Figure 2.2, where Andersen saves and invests C_0Y_0. The effect of investment is to move the production possibility curve for next year up and to the right. It is tempting to take this new production possibility curve and obtain the solution for next year by mechanically repeating the analysis used in Figure 2.2. Such a procedure, however, is illegitimate. Fisherian analysis is based on a very special approach. The following is an example of the kind of intellectual experiment underlying standard Fisherian capital theory. In George Bernard Shaw's play *Back to Methuselah*, after 21 years of incubation people hatch fully matured from eggs. Consider such an individual and assume that, on emerging from the egg, he or she knows with certainty the endowment of goods in each year of life and the prices that will prevail in each period. With certainty and no transaction costs, all markets, including futures markets, exist. As a result, when our newly hatched individual climbs out of the egg, he or she sits down and buys and sells present and future goods so as to maximize utility over his or her lifetime. Once this is done, the person simply marches through life executing the plans developed as he or she sat by the broken eggshell.

The point to this little story is that it illustrates the intellectual approach underlying Fisherian capital theory. There is no role for sequential decision making. Consumption, investment, and saving decisions for this year, next year, and all years are made simultaneously. The major reason for this characteristic is that the approach assumes certainty. Once we introduce positive information costs and therefore risk, sequential decision making becomes appropriate. Since you will know more about the future next year than you do this year, it is appropriate to make some decision now that you anticipate you will reconsider next year. Most of the remainder of this chapter concentrates on three aspects of risk: political risk, information costs, and portfolio diversification.

RISK

Political Risk

Political risk can arise from several sources. One is political instability. The threat of war or revolution can be a strong incentive to move funds to a safe place. The large movement of capital from Europe to the United States before the outbreak of World War II is one example. Political risk also exists because governments occasionally restrict the repatriation of earnings, principal, or both through capital controls or even confiscation. Although confiscation is rare in developed countries, capital controls are not. The result is that foreign owners of a given asset often face a higher risk of loss than do domestic owners of the same asset. It is this common form of political risk, rather than the threat of war or revolution, that we analyze here.

We can build on the Fisherian framework developed earlier to see how political risk influences international investment. The basic idea is that investors are willing to trade off risks of loss against rate of return. The higher the level of political risk, the higher the yield on foreign assets relative to domestic assets demanded by investors in order to compensate them for the increased possibility of loss.

It should not come as a surprise that political risk reduces international investment and creates differences in real yields. Consider Figure 2.10, which shows the investment and saving schedules for the United States and Brazil. The interest rate measured along the vertical axis is the real rate. Given the assumption of a fixed exchange rate, saving and investment in both countries can be measured in dollars along the horizontal axis. In the absence of capital flows, real yields are higher in Brazil. If there are no

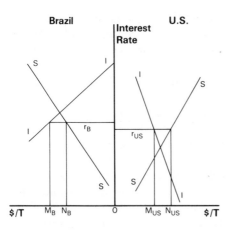

FIGURE 2.10
Capital flows with political risk.

political risks or other impediments, exchange equates *all* relative prices, including real interest rates.

If Americans investing in Brazil face political risk, they demand a risk premium. They will not buy a Brazilian asset unless it yields a higher return than a comparable American asset. As a result, there is less foreign investment in Brazil than there would have been in the absence of risk. Real interest rates in the United States rise to only $0r_{US}$, and in Brazil they fall to only $0r_B$. At these yields, the flow of capital into Brazil N_BM_B equals the capital outflow from the United States, $M_{US}N_{US}$. (Be sure you see what the yields and capital flow in Figure 2.10 would be in the absence of political risk or other impediments.)

The yield differential $r_{US}r_B$ in Figure 2.10 reflects the risk premium demand by American investors. If the risks were larger or Americans were more risk-averse, the capital flow would be smaller and the interest rate differential would be larger. That is, given the investment and saving schedules, there is an inverse relation between the size of the capital flow and the interest rate differential. Suppose the opportunities for investment in Brazil improve and the Brazilian investment schedule in Figure 2.10 moves to the left, as shown by the broken line $I'I'$ in Figure 2.11. If the risk premium remains unchanged, the flow of capital is larger and the interest rate differential remains unchanged. With a constant risk premium, there is no relation between the observed interest rate differential and the magnitude of the capital flow; a given differential is consistent with any capital flow.

Suppose, however, investors in the United States are reluctant to put more of their eggs in the Brazilian basket and therefore demand a higher risk premium as the proportion of Brazilian assets in their portfolios increases. The capital flow into Brazil still increases due to the shift in investment opportunities, but now the *increase* in the capital flow is smaller because the

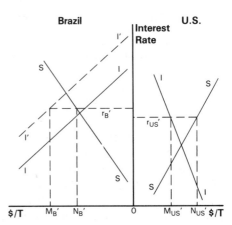

FIGURE 2.11
Capital flows with political risk.

risk premium and interest rate differential increase. In this case, there is a positive relationship between the size of the capital flow and the interest rate differential. It should, however, be clear that in no sense did the larger differential *cause* the larger capital flow.

The positive relation between the interest rate differential and capital flow can be seen by comparing Figures 2.10 and 2.11. The increased investment opportunities in Brazil are reflected in the new investment schedule $I'I'$ in Figure 2.11. Real yields rise in Brazil, which encourages additional foreign investment. If American investors require a greater risk premium as they put more of their eggs in the Brazilian basket, then both the new interest rate differential $r_{US}'r_B'$ and capital flow $N_B'M_B'$ (or $M_{US}'N_{US}'$) must be larger than $r_{US}r_B$ and N_BM_B (or $M_{US}N_{US}$) in Figure 2.10.

The last few paragraphs cannot be digested easily. Reread them and think your way through the analysis. When you have finished, you should understand the relation between (real) interest rate differentials and capital flows.

Although our analysis concentrates on political risk, exactly the same reasoning applies to any impediment to international investment, such as transaction costs. Impediments reduce capital flows and create real interest rate differentials. The relationship between capital flows and interest rate differentials, if any, depends on how foreign investment affects the impediment. If, for example, transaction costs fall with the level of capital flows, then the increased investment opportunities reflected in $I'I'$ in Figure 2.11 generate larger capital flows and a smaller interest rate differential.

Although political risk tends to reduce international investment, the desire to reduce ordinary risk through portfolio diversification can promote international investment. In order to see how, we need to understand the theory of portfolio management developed by James Tobin and Harry Markowitz.

The Tobin-Markowitz Model

A few paragraphs back we mentioned not putting all one's eggs in one basket. The Tobin-Markowitz model of portfolio diversification provides a formal explanation for that maxim. Before developing their model, however, let's consider a simple illustration. Suppose Andersen has a financial portfolio worth $100. She can invest in asset X or asset Y. For any given year, both assets have a 0.5 probability of yielding 20 percent and therefore have an expected yield of 10 percent. If she invests in all X or all Y, her expected return is $10 per year, with a 50 percent probability of either zero or $20. Suppose, however, she holds half of her portfolio in X and half in Y. The expected return remains $10, but the variability is reduced. With half of the $100 in each asset, there are three possible outcomes: zero when neither asset pays, $10 when one but not both pays, and $20 when both pay. If the returns are independent of each other, the probabilities for the three outcomes are 0.5 for $10 and 0.25 for both zero and $20. The crucial point of this example is that diversification reduces risk. By holding equal amounts of both assets, she has a 50-50 chance for $10 and a 25 percent chance for zero and $20, rather than a 50-50 chance for either zero or $20.

Model

Our formal analysis rests on several important assumptions. Investors' ideas about rates of return, their variances and covariances, are taken as given. The value of the portfolio is constant. Finally, yields are assumed to be normally distributed random variables, or utility functions are quadratic. The last assumption is necessary in order to evaluate alternative portfolio combinations in terms of only the means and variances in rates of return.

Let i_x and i_y be the actual returns from assets X and Y, respectively, including any capital gains or losses, and μ_x and μ_y be the expected yields from assets X and Y, respectively. The variances for returns on assets X and Y are $\sigma_{x,x}^2$ and $\sigma_{y,y}^2$, and the standard deviations are $\sigma_{x,x}$ and $\sigma_{y,y}$. The cross covariance between returns is $\sigma_{x,y}$ and the cross correlation is $\rho_{x,y}$, which equals $\sigma_{x,y}/\sigma_{x,x}\sigma_{y,y}$.

The expected return from a given portfolio μ is determined by the expected yields of the two assets and their relative proportions in the portfolio:

$$\mu = P_x\mu_x + P_y\mu_y \tag{2.1}$$

where P_x and P_y are the relative proportions of asset X and asset Y, respectively, in the portfolio, and $P_x + P_y = 1$.

The variance of the return from the portfolio σ^2 depends on three factors: the weights, P_x and P_y, the asset variances, $\sigma_{x,x}^2$ and $\sigma_{y,y}^2$, and the cross covariance, $\sigma_{x,y}$.

$$\sigma^2 = E[(P_x i_x + P_y i_y) - \mu]^2 = P_x^2 \sigma_{x,x}^2 + P_y^2 \sigma_{y,y}^2 + 2P_x P_y \sigma_{x,y} \qquad (2.2)$$

where E is the expectations operator. Since $\sigma_{x,y}$ equals $\rho_{x,y}\sigma_{x,x}\sigma_{y,y}$, we can rewrite equation (2.2) as follows:

$$\sigma^2 = P_x^2 \sigma_{x,x}^2 + P_y^2 \sigma_{y,y}^2 + 2P_x P_y \rho_{x,y}\sigma_{x,x}\sigma_{y,y} \qquad (2.3)$$

For the two-asset portfolio, Equation 2.3 describes how the variance of the portfolio depends on (1) the relative proportion of the two assets, (2) the variance of those assets, and (3) the correlation between assets.

We are now in a better position to see the incentive for portfolio diversification. Again consider a portfolio worth $100. Suppose asset X has an expected yield of 10 percent with a variance of 25, and asset Y has an expected yield of 9 percent and a variance of 36. If the returns are perfectly correlated, $\rho_{x,y} = 1$, including asset Y in the portfolio lowers the yield and raises the variance, so only a risk-lover would include Y. (Check this out for yourself.) If the correlation is sufficiently less than 1, including asset Y can lower the variance in the return on the entire portfolio and make asset Y attractive to someone who is risk-averse.

Suppose the correlation between the two yields is 0.5 and the portfolio is divided evenly between the two assets. In that case, the total yield is 9.5 percent, but the variance is less than 25.

$$\mu = 0.5 \times 0.1 + 0.5 \times 0.09 = 0.095$$
$$\sigma^2 = (0.5)^2 \times 25 + (0.5)^2 \times 36$$
$$+ 2 \times 0.5 \times 0.5 \times 0.5 \times 5 \times 6 = 22.75$$

If the correlation between returns is -0.5, the variance drops to 7.75.

$$\sigma = (0.5)^2 \times 25 + (0.5)^2 \times 36$$
$$+ 2 \times 0.5 \times 0.5 \times (-0.5) \times 5 \times 6 = 7.75$$

These two examples illustrate the incentive for portfolio diversification. They show why a rational investor might want to hold an asset that has both a low yield and high variance. These examples, however, do not show how an investor chooses an optimal portfolio. For simplicity, the choice of an optimal portfolio is illustrated in diagrams rather than mathematically.

Portfolio Choice

The choice of an optimal portfolio is illustrated in Figure 2.12. The vertical axis shows the standard deviation of the expected return; the horizontal axis measures the expected yield. The points A through E describe five assets. The curve NN shows the optimum portfolio frontier. That is, any

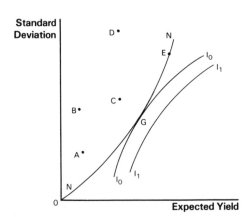

FIGURE 2.12
Optimal portfolio choice.

point on NN represents a combination of the assets that yields the highest possible expected rate of return for a given standard deviation. The curves I_0I_0 and I_1I_1 represent indifference curves showing the subjective tradeoff between risk and rate return. As one moves down and to the right in Figure 2.12, risk declines, rate of return increases, and the risk-averse investor moves to indifference curves with higher utility.

Given the asset menu described by points A through E and the resulting optimal frontier NN, the investor maximizes utility by choosing the point on NN that is tangent to the highest indifference curve. In general, the tangency is at a point such as G in Figure 2.12, where the investor holds a mixed portfolio. It is possible, however, for a portfolio with a single asset to lie on the efficient frontier. If the investor's indifference curve is tangent to the frontier at that point, E in Figure 2.12, he or she holds a specialized portfolio containing only one asset.

So far we have considered only a single individual. Now consider the case in which there are two individuals, each holding a single asset. In the absence of any exchange, each portfolio has an expected yield and variance. If the yields are not perfectly correlated, the two investors may benefit from an exchange of assets, because such an exchange may reduce the variance in *both* portfolios. The assumption of fixed portfolios, however, rules out the possibility of a net capital flow balanced by a net movement of goods.

The extension of the basic reasoning to two countries and more than two assets is simple. As long as yields in the two countries are not perfectly correlated, perhaps because business cycles are not perfectly correlated, there can be an incentive for an exchange of assets, because such an exchange can reduce the variance of returns for investors in *both* countries.

The incentive for holding foreign assets is illustrated in Figure 2.13. The solid curve labeled NN describes the optimal portfolio frontier when the portfolio is restricted to domestic assets. If yields on foreign assets are not perfectly correlated with returns from domestic securities, the optimal port-

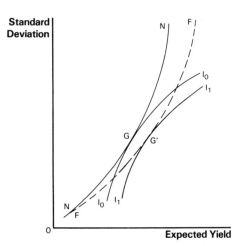

Figure 2.13
Optimal portfolio choice with domestic
and foreign assets.

folio frontier containing both domestic and foreign assets is likely to lie to the right of the optimal domestic frontier. In Figure 2.13, the frontier for the internationally diversified portfolio is labeled *FF*. In this case, an investor chooses the internationally diversified portfolio because he or she can move to the higher indifference curve, I_1I_1.

Although the Tobin-Markowitz approach does not explain net capital flows, it can explain cross hauling. That is, the approach can explain why the United States might export 90-day Treasury bills to Canada and also import 90-day Canadian Treasury bills. It also implies that assets move from a high to a low yield country, even if yields are real rather than nominal. Indeed, if real rates do differ and there is an exchange of similar assets, some assets must move from the country with a high yield to one with a lower yield. The Tobin-Markowitz approach takes as given subjective views about yields, their variances, and covariances. Dropping that assumption suggests that investors engage in both diversification and specialization.

INFORMATION COSTS
AND SPECIALIZATION

The introduction of risk and uncertainty into our analysis involves an implicit assumption that information is scarce—that is, costly—and therefore an economic good. If information were free, then we could know everything at zero cost and there would be no risk or uncertainty.

A main theme in Chapter 1 and the first part of this chapter is specialization based on comparative advantage. That theme can be extended to risk by treating the information that underlies subjective views about risk as an economic good. It is then natural to think in terms of comparative advantage in the "production" of information. In the framework of Tobin and Marko-witz, comparative advantage can be thought of as a relatively lower variance in expected returns for the same expenditure on the collection and evalua-tion of information about a given asset or class of assets.

Comparative advantage in the production of information implies that there are forces encouraging portfolio specialization. Consider an investor who can invest in firms in a variety of industries, such as automobiles, insurance, or chemicals. Suppose, as compared to the typical investor, this individual has a comparative advantage in information about the chemical industry. For a given expenditure on information, her ideas about variances in yields for firms in that industry are relatively low. As a result, she tends to invest more heavily in the chemical industry than the typical investor. Of course, in order to avoid risk, she diversifies within that industry and, since industry returns tend to move together, there also is an incentive to invest in other areas.

Two simple examples show how portfolio specialization can also pro-mote international investment. On the financial side, again consider the investor with a comparative advantage in information about the chemical industry. Since, as compared to the typical investor, her subjective ideas about the variance in yields are also lower for foreign chemical firms, there is an incentive for her to invest in those firms. Comparative advantage in information promotes portfolio specialization and encourages foreign invest-ment. Since the same reasoning applies to a foreign investor with the same comparative advantage (as compared to the typical investor), this approach provides another explanation for cross hauling in financial assets.

If we are willing to interpret the concept of information rather broadly, we can apply the same reasoning to direct investment. Consider a domestic oil firm such as Standard Oil of Indiana. It presumably has a comparative advantage in evaluating investment projects in the oil industry. Such a firm has a strong incentive to invest in an oil-related project abroad rather than diversify into some other domestic area such as fast foods. Since the same argument applies to a foreign firm such as Shell Oil, this approach also helps explain cross hauling in direct foreign investment.

The forces working toward specialization are consistent with incen-tives for diversification. The investor who has an incentive to specialize in chemical companies can also be risk-averse. In order to reduce risk, she diversifies within the chemical industry and also holds other assets such as Treasury bills. The fundamental point is that with positive informa-tion costs, we would expect portfolios to reflect both forces working to reduce risk through diversification and pressures encouraging specialization due to comparative advantage in the collection or evaluation of informa-tion. Finally, both diversification and specialization can promote foreign investment.

INSTITUTIONAL FACTORS

So far the discussion has ignored institutional influences and concentrated on what economic theory has to say about foreign investment. Economic forces, however, must work within an institutional framework, and this framework can both inhibit and encourage international investment. Laws discouraging or even prohibiting ownership of domestic assets by foreigners and prejudicial treatment of foreigners in courts tend to discourage foreign investment. But all institutional factors do not discourage foreign investment; and a few even encourage it.

In many developing countries, for example, capital markets are almost nonexistent. As a result, those who have money to invest and who want to hold financial assets are forced to turn to capital markets in developed countries. Actual or potential import duties and quotas can also encourage foreign investment. In the past, the American automobile industry has "leapt over" foreign tariffs on American cars by producing cars in foreign countries. Any imposition of restrictions on the import of foreign cars into the United States, or even the threat of such restrictions, provides a strong incentive for German and Japanese auto makers to build cars in the United States.

These are just a few examples of how institutional factors influence foreign investment; a complete catalog would take several volumes. The point is simply that the economic forces discussed earlier are only part of the story. The institutional framework is also a major factor in international investment. That part of the story, however, is best learned outside the classroom.

SUMMARY

If, in the absence of net capital flows, real interest rates differ between two regions or countries, then one region or country has a comparative advantage in present goods and the other has a comparative advantage in future goods. Given this comparative advantage, there is a basis for mutually beneficial exchange of present for future goods or net capital flow. The direction of the capital flow depends on who has the higher real interest rate in the absence of a net capital flow. The equilibrium real rate and size of the capital flow depend on the domestic investment and saving schedules. These schedules, in turn, depend on tastes and endowments.

Political risk and other impediments to exchange tend to reduce capital flows and increase observed interest rate differentials. The major cause of large and persistent interest rate differentials, however, is large differences in rates of inflation.

Unlike political risk, risk avoidance through portfolio diversification along the lines developed by Tobin and Markowitz can encourage foreign investment. If domestic and foreign yields are not perfectly correlated, holding foreign assets can reduce the variability in domestic portfolios, and risk averse investors tend to hold foreign assets.

Portfolio specialization based on comparative advantage in the collection and evaluation of information can also contribute to foreign investment. A firm or individual with a comparative advantage in information relevant to the oil industry is likely to view foreign oil investments as relatively less risky in the Tobin-Markowitz sense than the domestic fast food industry. A risk averse investor, therefore, would tend to invest in both the domestic and foreign oil industries.

Comparative advantage, portfolio diversification, and portfolio specialization are all complementary rather than competing explanations for foreign investment. Each theory helps us understand one facet of the complex process that determines international capital movements.

QUESTIONS FOR REVIEW

1. Given an endowment, a production possibility frontier, and a set of indifference curves, show how to derive the saving and investment function for an individual.

2. Use the production frontiers, price lines, and indifference curves for Andersen and Blake to describe the equilibrium shown in Figure 2.5.

3. Assume that there are two individuals and two assets. Initially each individual holds only one asset. Both individuals, however, hold the same views regarding the expected returns, variances, and covariances for the two assets.
   a. Using the Tobin-Markowitz approach, describe a situation in which there is an incentive for a one-time capital flow between them.
   b. Given the Tobin-Markowitz model, can there be a net capital flow? If so, how? If not, why not?

4. Use Fisherian capital theory to explain why college students typically spend more than they earn.

5. Discuss the limitations of Fisherian capital theory.

6. Compare and contrast the Tobin-Markowitz and Fisherian explanations for foreign investment.

7. If capital flows tend to eliminate interest rate differentials, how can we explain persistent and occasionally very large observed differentials?

8. After World War I, Germany had to pay a significant proportion of its income as a reparation payment to the Allies, particularly Britain and France. This payment created a famous debate between Keynes and Ohlin about whether or not the payment of money by Germany could be con-

verted into a transfer of goods. Use a Fisherian approach to explain how an individual or country would respond to a penalty or fine that was large relative to current income.

9. A variety of U.S. labor organizations and some corporations would like to restrict U.S. foreign investment. How might they gain from such restrictions? What groups would lose? What about consumers?

10. Marxists often claim that foreign investment by the United States and other industrialized countries in developing countries "exploits" the workers in developing countries. Given our Fisherian analysis, does capital or labor gain from capital flows into a country with a comparative advantage in future goods?

ADDITIONAL READINGS

BRYANT, R. "Empirical Research of Financial Capital Flows." In P. Kenen (ed.), *International Trade and Finance: Frontiers for Research* (Cambridge, Eng.: Cambridge University Press, 1975).

FIELEKE, NORMAN S. "International Lending in Historical Perspective." Federal Reserve Bank of Boston. *New England Economic Review* (November–December 1982).

GRUBEL, HERBERT G. "Internationally Diversified Portfolios: Welfare Gains and Capital Flows." *American Economic Review* (December 1968).

HAYNES, STEPHEN, AND JOHN PIPPENGER. "Discrimination among Alternative Models of International Capital Markets." *Journal of Macroeconomics* (winter 1982).

HIRSHLEIFER, J. *Investment, Interest, and Capital* (Englewood Cliffs, N.J.: Prentice-Hall, 1970).

HODJERA, ZORAN. "International Short-Term Capital Movements: A Survey of Theory and Empirical Analysis." *International Monetary Fund Staff Papers* (November 1973).

LEAMER, EDWARD E., AND ROBERT M. STERN. "Problems in the Theory and Empirical Estimation of International Capital Movements." In F. Machlup, W. S. Salant, and L. Tarshis (eds.), *International Mobility and Movement of Capital.* (New York: National Bureau for Economic Research, Columbia University Press, 1972).

SAMUELSON, PAUL. "The Transfer Problem and Transportation Costs." In R. Caves and H. Johnson (eds.), *Readings in International Economics* (Homewood, Ill.: Irwin, 1968).

3

BALANCE
OF PAYMENTS

The first part of this chapter considers the definition and organization of the balance of payments. The second discusses the interpretation of balance-of-payments statistics. In the final section, we review the history of the U.S. balance of payments.

DEFINITION

The balance of payments is a record of the value of all transactions between domestic and foreign residents over a given period of time, usually one year. It is based on the rule of double-entry bookkeeping. In principle, the value of every transaction is recorded as both a credit and a debit. In practice, however, many transactions are only partly recorded, estimated on the basis of surveys, or missed entirely. We will discuss some of the problems caused by incomplete recording of transactions after we examine the basic principles of balance-of-payments (BOP) accounting.

CREDITS AND DEBITS

Partial balance-of-payments statistics probably were first collected during the eighteenth century. Under the crude mercantilist doctrine, the immediate goal of international trade was the accumulation of treasure—that is, gold and silver. Since exports normally were paid for with gold or silver (or currencies convertible into gold or silver), exports were viewed as desirable and the export of anything was entered in the balance of payments as a plus or credit item. Imports normally required payment in gold or silver and were viewed as undesirable. They were entered in the balance of payments as a negative or debit item. Today, as in 1750, the purchase or import of anything from a foreign resident is recorded as a debit or minus entry in the balance of payments, and the sale or export of anything to a foreign resident is recorded as a plus or credit item.

Since exports are recorded as credits and balance-of-payments statistics follow the principle of double-entry bookkeeping, the payment we receive for exports must be recorded as a debit. Since imports are debits, the payment we make for imports must be recorded as a credit. That is, what we give up in every transaction is recorded as a credit and what we receive is entered as a debit. For example, brush aside the "veil of money" and think of the United States as importing Japanese TV sets and paying for them by exporting wheat. The value of the TV sets is entered on the debit side of the U.S. balance-of-payments account, and the value of the wheat we give up in order to obtain the TV sets is entered as a credit.

If debits and credits are shown independently in the form of a T-account, as in Table 3.2, then debits are usually shown on the right-hand side and credits on the left-hand side. This, of course, is the reverse of standard accounting procedure. In addition, although crediting sales and debiting purchases are consistent with standard accounting procedures, this approach conflicts with basic economic theory. From the point of view of economics, what we get (import) is the good or plus side of a transaction; what we give up (export) is the bad or minus side.

ORGANIZATION

Credits and debits are collected into subdivisions. These subdivisions vary between countries and over time. Using the format adopted by the Department of Commerce in 1976, Table 3.1 shows the balance-of-payments statistics for the United States from 1960 to 1981. The major subdivisions are (1) goods and services, (2) unilateral transfers, (3) assets, (4) allocation of special drawing rights, and (5) statistical discrepancy. These categories are discussed in general terms in this section. Anyone interested in more detail should consult the June 1976 issue of the *Survey of Current Business*.

Goods and Services

Lines 1 through 31 in Table 3.1 record the value of exports and imports of goods and services. Trade in goods is divided into military and nonmilitary. Services include tourist expenditures, transportation, payments of roy-

38   Balance of Payments

TABLE 3.1   U.S. International Transactions, 1960–1981 (In millions of dollars)

(Credit +; debits −)¹	Line	1960	1961	1962	1963	1964	1965	1966	1967	1968
Exports of goods and services ²	1	28,861	29,937	31,803	34,214	38,826	41,087	44,542	47,314	52,363
Merchandise, adjusted, excluding military ³	2	19,650	20,108	20,781	22,272	25,501	26,461	29,310	30,666	33,626
Transfers under U.S. military agency sales contracts	3	335	402	656	657	747	830	829	1,152	1,392
Travel	4	919	947	957	1,015	1,207	1,380	1,590	1,646	1,775
Passenger fares	5	175	183	191	205	241	271	317	371	411
Other transportation	6	1,607	1,620	1,764	1,898	2,076	2,175	2,333	2,426	2,548
Fees and royalties from affiliated foreigners	7	590	662	800	890	1,013	1,199	1,162	1,354	1,430
Fees and royalties from unaffiliated foreigners	8	247	244	256	273	301	335	353	393	437
Other private services	9	570	607	585	613	551	714	814	951	1,024
U.S. Government miscellaneous services	10	153	164	195	236	255	285	326	334	353
Receipts of income on U.S. assets abroad: Direct investment: Interest, dividends, and earnings of unincorporated affiliates	11	3,621	3,823	4,241	4,636	5,106	5,506	5,260	5,603	6,591
Reinvested earnings of incorporated affiliates	12	2,355	2,768	3,044	3,129	3,674	3,963	3,467	3,847	4,155
Other private receipts	13	1,266	1,055	1,197	1,507	1,432	1,543	1,793	1,756	2,440
Other private receipts	14	646	793	904	1,022	1,256	1,421	1,669	1,781	2,021
U.S. Government receipts	15	349	383	473	499	462	510	599	636	756
Transfers of goods and services under U.S. military grant programs, net	16	1,695	1,465	1,537	1,542	1,340	1,636	1,892	2,039	2,547
Imports of goods and services	17	−23,729	−23,591	−25,778	−27,047	−29,222	−32,301	−38,599	−41,606	−48,800
Merchandise, adjusted, excluding military ³	18	−14,758	−14,537	−16,260	−17,048	−18,700	−21,510	−25,493	−26,866	−32,991
Direct defense expenditures	19	−3,087	−2,998	−3,105	−2,961	−2,880	−2,952	−3,764	−4,378	−4,535
Travel	20	−1,750	−1,785	−1,939	−2,114	−2,211	−2,438	−2,657	−3,207	−3,030
Passenger fares	21	−513	−506	−567	−612	−642	−717	−753	−829	−885
Other transportation	22	−1,402	−1,437	−1,558	−1,701	−1,817	−1,951	−2,161	−2,157	−2,367
Fees and royalties to affiliated foreigners	23	−35	−43	−57	−61	−67	−68	−64	−62	−80
Fees and royalties to unaffiliated foreigners	24	−40	−46	−64	−51	−60	−67	−76	−104	−106
Private payments for other services	25	−593	−588	−528	−493	−527	−461	−506	−565	−568
U.S. Government payments for miscellaneous services	26	−313	−406	−398	−447	−535	−550	−644	−691	−760
Payments of income on foreign assets in the United States: Direct investment: Interest, dividends, and earnings of unincorporated affiliates	27	−394	−432	−399	−459	−529	−657	−711	−821	−876
Reinvested earnings of incorporated affiliates	28	−220	−194	−185	−223	−202	−299	−372	−381	−388
Other private payments	29	−174	−238	−214	−236	−327	−358	−339	−440	−488
Other private payments	30	−511	−535	−586	−701	−802	−942	−1,221	−1,328	−1,800
U.S. Government payments	31	−332	−278	−339	−401	−453	−489	−549	−598	−702
U.S. military grants of goods and services, net	32	−1,695	−1,465	−1,537	−1,542	−1,340	−1,636	−1,892	−2,039	−2,547
Unilateral transfers (excluding military grants of goods and services), net	33	−2,398	−2,834	−2,638	−2,754	−2,781	−2,854	−2,932	−3,125	−2,952
U.S. Government grants (excluding military grants of goods and services)	34	−1,672	−1,855	−1,916	−1,917	−1,888	−1,808	−1,910	−1,805	−1,709
U.S. Government pensions and other transfers	35	−214	−235	−245	−262	−279	−369	−367	−441	−407
Private remittances and other transfers	36	−423	−434	−477	−575	−614	−677	−655	−879	−836
U.S. assets abroad, net (increase/capital outflow (−))	37	−4,099	−5,538	−4,174	−7,270	−9,560	−5,716	−7,321	−9,757	−10,977
U.S. official reserve assets, net	38	2,145	607	1,535	378	171	1,225	570	53	−870
Gold	39	1,703	857	890	461	125	1,665	571	1,170	1,173
Special drawing rights	40									
Reserve position in the International Monetary Fund	41	442	−135	626	29	266	−94	537	−94	−870
Foreign currencies	42		−115	19	−112	−220	−346	−538	−1,023	−1,173
U.S. Government assets, other than official reserve assets, net	43	−1,100	−910	−1,085	−1,662	−1,680	−1,605	−1,543	−2,423	−2,274
U.S. loans and other long-term assets	44	−1,214	−1,928	−2,128	−2,204	−2,382	−2,463	−2,513	−3,638	−3,722
Repayments on U.S. loans ⁴	45	642	1,279	1,288	988	720	874	1,235	1,005	1,386
U.S. foreign currency holdings and U.S. short-term assets, net	46	−528	−261	−245	−447	−19	−16	−265	209	62
U.S. private assets, net	47	−5,144	−5,235	−4,623	−5,986	−8,050	−5,336	−6,347	−7,386	−7,833
Direct investment	48	−2,940	−2,653	−2,851	−3,483	−3,760	−5,011	−5,418	−4,805	−5,295
Equity and intercompany accounts	49	−1,674	−1,598	−1,654	−1,976	−2,328	−3,468	−3,625	−3,049	−2,855
Reinvested earnings of incorporated affiliates	50	−1,266	−1,055	−1,197	−1,507	−1,432	−1,543	−1,793	−1,756	−2,440
Foreign securities	51	−663	−762	−969	−1,105	−677	−759	−720	−1,308	−1,569
U.S. claims on unaffiliated foreigners reported by U.S. nonbanking concerns: Long-term	52	−40	−127	−132	162	−485	−88	−112	−281	−220
Short-term	53	−354	−431	−222	−5	−623	429	−330	−498	−982
U.S. claims reported by U.S. banks, not included elsewhere: Long-term	54	−153	−136	−126	−775	−981	−232	317	235	338
Short-term	55	−995	−1,125	−324	−781	−1,524	325	325	−730	−105
Foreign assets in the United States, net (increase/capital inflow (+))	56	2,294	2,705	1,911	3,217	3,643	742	3,661	7,379	9,928
Foreign official assets in the United States, net	57	1,473	765	1,270	1,986	1,660	134	−672	3,451	−774
U.S. Government securities	58	655	233	1,409	816	432	−141	−1,527	2,261	−769
U.S. Treasury securities ⁵	59	655	233	1,410	803	434	−134	−1,548	2,222	−798
Other ⁷	60			−1	12	−2	−7	21	39	29
Other U.S. Government liabilities ⁶	61	215	25	152	429	298	65	113	83	−15
U.S. liabilities reported by U.S. banks, not included elsewhere	62	603	508	−291	742	930	210	742	1,106	10
Other foreign official assets ⁷	63									
Other foreign assets in the United States, net	64	821	1,939	641	1,231	1,983	607	4,333	3,928	10,703
Direct investment	65	315	311	346	231	322	415	425	698	807
Equity and intercompany accounts	66	141	73	132	−5	57	86	258	319	
Reinvested earnings of incorporated affiliates	67	174	238	214	236	327	358	339	440	488
U.S. Treasury securities	68	−364	151	−66	−149	−146	−131	−356	−135	136
U.S. securities other than U.S. Treasury securities	69	282	324	134	287	−85	−358	906	1,016	4,414
U.S. liabilities to unaffiliated foreigners reported by U.S. nonbanking concerns: Long-term	70	1	50	3	−13	−38	29	180	85	715
Short-term	71	−91	176	−112	−23	113	149	296	499	759
U.S. liabilities reported by U.S. banks, not included elsewhere: Long-term ¹⁰	72	6	−5	5	53	88	241	188	158	72
Short-term ¹⁰	73	672	933	331	845	1,730	282	2,694	1,607	3,799
Allocations of special drawing rights	74									
Statistical discrepancy (sum of above items with sign reversed)	75	−1,019	−989	−1,124	−360	−907	−458	629	−205	438
Memoranda: Balance on merchandise trade (lines 2 and 18)	76	4,892	5,571	4,521	5,224	6,801	4,951	3,817	3,800	635
Balance on goods and services (lines 1 and 17)¹¹	77	5,132	6,346	6,025	7,167	9,604	8,285	5,963	5,708	3,563
Balance on goods, services, and remittances (lines 77, 35, and 36)	78	4,496	5,677	5,303	6,331	8,711	7,239	4,941	4,388	2,320
Balance on current account (lines 77 and 33)¹¹	79	2,824	3,822	3,387	4,414	6,823	5,432	3,031	2,583	611
Transactions in U.S. official reserve assets and in foreign official assets in the United States: Increase (−) in U.S. official reserve assets, net (line 38)	80	2,145	607	1,535	378	171	1,225	570	53	−870
Increase (+) in foreign official assets in the United States (line 57 less line 61)	81	1,258	741	1,118	1,558	1,362	69	−785	3,368	−759

For footnotes see page 40.

Source: Survey of Current Business, June, 1982.

1969	1970	1971	1972	1973	1974	1975	1976	1977	1978	1979	1980	1981	Line
57,522	65,674	68,838	77,495	110,241	146,666	155,729	171,630	184,337	220,137	286,772	342,102	372,892	1
36,414	42,469	43,319	49,381	71,410	98,306	107,088	114,745	120,816	142,054	184,473	224,237	236,254	2
1,528	1,501	1,926	1,364	2,559	3,379	4,049	5,454	7,351	7,973	6,549	8,306	9,747	3
2,043	2,831	2,534	2,817	3,412	4,032	4,697	5,742	6,150	7,183	8,441	10,058	12,168	4
450	544	615	699	975	1,104	1,039	1,229	1,366	1,603	2,156	2,582	2,991	5
2,652	3,125	3,299	8,579	4,465	5,697	5,840	6,747	7,264	8,399	10,028	11,497	12,168	6
1,533	1,758	1,927	2,115	2,513	3,070	3,543	3,531	3,883	4,705	4,980	5,780	5,867	7
486	573	618	655	712	751	757	822	923	1,059	1,100	1,185	1,386	8
1,160	1,294	1,546	1,764	1,985	2,321	2,920	3,584	3,848	4,296	4,396	5,412	5,340	9
343	532	347	357	401	419	446	489	557	520	520	362	426	10
7,649	8,169	9,160	10,949	16,542	19,157	16,595	18,999	19,673	25,458	38,183	37,150	31,873	11
4,819	4,992	5,983	6,416	8,384	11,379	8,547	11,303	13,277	14,115	19,219	20,133	18,894	12
2,830	3,177	3,177	4,532	8,158	7,777	8,048	7,696	6,396	11,343	18,965	17,017	12,978	13
2,338	2,671	2,641	2,949	4,830	7,356	7,644	8,955	10,881	14,944	23,654	32,987	50,407	14
925	907	906	866	936	1,074	1,112	1,332	1,625	1,843	2,292	2,549	3,665	15
2,610	2,713	3,546	4,492	2,810	1,818	2,207	373	263	236	465	631	602	16
-54,129	-60,050	-64,569	-79,435	-99,219	-137,357	-132,536	-162,248	-193,788	-229,880	-281,677	-333,800	-361,813	17
-35,807	-39,866	-45,579	-55,797	-70,499	-103,649	-98,041	-124,051	-151,689	-175,813	-211,819	-249,575	-264,143	18
-4,856	-4,855	-4,819	[12]-4,784	[12]-4,629	-5,032	-4,795	-4,895	-5,823	-7,352	-8,584	-10,777	-11,288	19
-3,373	-3,980	-4,373	-5,042	-5,526	-5,960	-6,417	-6,856	-7,451	-8,475	-9,413	-10,397	-11,460	20
-1,080	-1,215	-1,290	-1,596	-1,790	-2,095	-2,263	-2,568	-2,748	-2,896	-3,184	-3,607	-4,487	21
-2,455	-2,843	-3,130	-3,520	-4,694	-5,942	-5,888	-6,852	-7,874	-8,939	-10,457	-11,073	-11,611	22
-101	-111	-118	-155	-209	-160	-297	-293	-243	-393	-523	-514	-429	23
-120	-114	-123	-189	-176	-186	-186	-189	-196	-214	-241	-247	-264	24
-751	-827	-956	-1,043	-1,180	-1,262	-1,551	-2,006	-2,190	-2,573	-2,824	-3,065	-3,294	25
-717	-725	-746	-788	-862	-967	-1,044	-1,227	-1,358	-1,545	-1,718	-1,769	-1,930	26
-848	-875	-1,164	-1,284	-1,610	-1,331	-2,234	-3,110	-2,834	-4,211	-6,357	-9,470	-7,808	27
-417	-441	-621	-715	-699	-266	-1,046	-1,451	-1,248	-1,628	-2,402	-3,303	-3,708	28
-431	-484	-542	-569	-910	-1,065	-1,189	-1,659	-1,586	-2,583	-3,955	-6,167	-4,099	29
-3,244	-8,617	-2,428	-2,604	-4,209	-6,491	-5,788	-5,681	-5,841	-8,795	-15,481	-20,794	-28,352	30
-777	-1,024	-1,844	-1,844	-3,836	-4,262	-4,542	-4,520	-5,542	-8,674	-11,076	-12,512	-16,748	31
-2,610	-2,713	-3,546	-4,492	-2,810	-1,818	-2,207	-373	-263	-236	-465	-631	-602	32
-2,994	-3,294	-3,701	-3,854	-3,881	[12]-7,186	-4,613	-4,398	-4,617	-5,630	-5,541	-6,783	-6,808	33
-1,649	-1,736	-2,043	-2,173	-1,938	[12]-6,475	-2,894	-3,146	-2,787	-3,176	-3,550	-4,681	-4,504	34
-406	-462	-542	-572	-693	-694	-813	-934	-971	-1,066	-1,180	-1,303	-1,459	35
-989	-1,096	-1,117	-1,109	-1,250	-1,017	-906	-917	-859	-768	-832	-798	-645	36
-11,585	-9,337	-12,475	-14,497	-22,874	-34,745	-39,763	-51,269	-34,755	-61,130	-64,344	-86,026	-109,294	37
-1,179	2,481	2,349	-4	158	-1,467	-849	-2,558	-375	732	-1,133	-8,155	-5,175	38
-967	787	866	547					-118	-65			(*)	39
	-851	-249	-703		-172	-66	-78	-121	1,249	-1,136	16	-1,824	40
-1,084	389	1,350	153	9	-1,255	-466	-2,212	-294	4,231	-189	-1,667	-2,491	41
822	2,156	882	-1	182	-30	-317	-268	158	-4,683	257	-6,472	-861	42
-2,200	-1,589	-1,864	-1,568	-2,544	366	-8,474	-4,214	-3,693	-4,660	-3,743	-5,126	-5,137	43
-3,489	-3,293	-4,181	-3,819	-4,638	[12]-5,001	-5,941	-6,943	-6,445	-7,470	-7,676	-9,854	-9,710	44
1,200	1,721	2,115	2,086	2,596	4,826	2,475	2,596	2,719	2,941	3,908	4,459	4,370	45
89	-16	182	165	-802	[12]541	-9	133	33	-181	25	269	204	46
-8,206	-10,229	-12,940	-12,925	-20,388	-33,643	-35,380	-44,498	-30,717	-57,202	-59,469	-72,746	-98,982	47
-5,960	-7,590	-7,618	-7,747	-11,353	-9,052	-14,344	-11,949	-11,890	-16,056	-25,222	-19,238	-8,691	48
-3,130	-4,413	-4,441	-3,214	-3,195	-1,275	-6,196	-4,253	-5,494	-4,713	-6,258	-2,221	-4,297	49
-2,630	-3,177	-3,177	-4,532	-8,158	-7,777	-8,048	-7,696	-6,396	-11,343	-18,965	-17,017	-12,978	50
-1,549	-1,076	-1,113	-618	-671	-1,854	-6,247	-8,885	-5,460	-3,626	-4,726	-3,524	-5,429	51
-424	-586	-168	-243	-896	-474	-366	-42	-99	-53				52
298	-10	-1,061	-811	-1,987	-2,747	-991	-2,254	-1,841	-3,800	[14]-3,307	[14]-3,146	[14]-331	53
297	155	-612	-1,307	-933	-1,183	-2,857	-2,362	-751					54
-867	-1,122	-2,368	-2,199	-5,047	-18,333	-11,175	-19,006	-10,676	[15]-33,667	[15]-26,213	[15]-46,838	[15]-84,531	55
12,762	6,250	22,970	21,461	15,388	34,241	15,670	36,515	51,319	64,036	38,460	54,484	77,921	56
-1,301	6,908	26,879	10,475	6,026	10,546	7,027	17,893	36,816	33,678	-13,697	15,442	4,785	57
-2,343	9,489	26,570	8,470	641	4,172	5,563	9,892	32,538	24,221	-21,972	11,895	6,272	58
-2,269	9,411	26,578	8,213	59	3,270	4,658	9,319	30,230	23,555	-22,435	9,708	4,963	59
-74	28	-8	257	582	902	905	573	2,306	666	463	2,187	1,289	60
251	-456	-510	182	936	801	1,517	4,627	1,400	2,476	-73	561	-69	61
792	-2,075	819	1,638	4,126	5,818	-2,158	969	773	5,551	7,213	-159	-4,063	62
			185	323	254	2,104	2,205	2,105	1,430	1,135	3,145	2,665	63
14,002	-550	-3,909	10,986	12,862	23,696	8,643	18,826	14,503	30,358	52,157	39,042	73,136	64
1,263	1,464	367	949	2,800	4,760	2,603	4,347	3,728	7,897	11,877	13,666	21,301	65
832	1,080	-175	380	1,890	3,695	1,414	2,687	2,142	2,583	7,921	7,500	17,201	66
431	434	542	569	910	1,065	1,189	1,659	1,586	2,583	3,955	6,167	4,099	67
-68	81	-24	-89	-216	697	2,590	2,783	353	[16]2,178	[16]4,960	[16]2,645	[16]2,932	68
3,130	2,189	2,289	4,507	4,041	378	2,503	1,284	2,437	2,254	1,351	5,457	7,109	69
701	1,112	384	594	298	-90	406	-1,000	-847	-190				70
91	902	-15	221	737	1,934	-87	422	1,433	2,079	[14]1,362	[14]6,530	[14]532	71
160	23	-250	149	227	9	-280	231	373					72
8,726	-6,321	-6,661	4,605	4,475	16,008	906	10,759	6,346	16,141	32,607	10,743	41,262	73
	867	717	710							1,189	1,152	1,093	74
-1,516	-219	-9,779	-1,879	-2,654	-1,620	5,753	10,367	-2,465	11,866	35,312	25,870	25,909	75
607	2,603	-2,260	-6,416	911	-5,843	9,047	-9,306	-30,873	-33,759	-27,346	-25,338	-27,889	76
3,393	5,625	2,269	-1,941	11,021	9,309	22,893	9,382	-9,451	-9,743	-5,095	5,073	11,079	77
2,048	4,067	610	-3,622	9,078	7,599	21,175	7,531	-11,281	-11,597	3,063	6,202	8,975	78
399	2,331	-1,433	-5,795	7,140	2,124	18,280	4,384	-14,068	-14,773	-466	1,520	4,471	79
-1,179	2,481	2,349	-4	158	-1,467	-849	-2,558	-375	732	-1,133	-8,155	-5,175	80
-1,552	7,364	27,389	10,293	5,090	10,244	5,509	13,066	35,416	31,202	-18,624	14,881	4,854	81

Footnotes for Table 3.1

1. Credits, +: exports of goods and services; unilateral transfers to United States; capital inflows (increase in foreign assets (U.S. liabilities) or decrease in U.S. assets); decrease in U.S. official reserve assets.

Debits, −: imports of goods and services; unilateral transfers to foreigners; capital outflows (decrease in foreign assets (U.S. liabilities) or increase in U.S. assets); increase in U.S. official reserve assets.

2. Excludes transfers of goods and services under U.S. military grant programs (see line 16).

3. Excludes exports of goods under U.S. Military agency sales contracts identified in Census export documents, excludes imports of goods under direct defense expenditures identified in Census import documents, and reflects various other adjustments (for valuation, coverage, and timing) of Census statistics to balance of payments basis.

4. For all areas, amounts outstanding March 31, 1982, were as follows in millions of dollars: line 38, 29,944; line 39, 11,150; line 40, 4,306; line 41, 5,367; line 42, 9,121.

5. Includes sales of foreign obligations to foreigners.

6. Consists of bills, certificates, marketable bonds and notes, and nonmarketable convertible and nonconvertible bonds and notes.

7. Consists of U.S. Treasury and Export-Import Bank obligations, not included elsewhere, and of debts securities of U.S. Government corporations and agencies.

8. Includes, primarily, U.S. Government liabilities associated with military sales contracts and other transactions arranged with or through foreign official agencies.

9. Consists of investments in U.S. corporate stocks and in debt securities of private corporations and State and local governments.

10. Beginning with estimates for the second quarter of 1978, the distinction between short- and long-term liabilities is discontinued.

11. Conceptually, the sum of lines 79 and 74 is equal to "net foreign investment" in the National Income and Product Accounts (NIPA's). However, the foreign transactions account in the NIPA's (a) includes adjustments to the international transactions accounts for the treatment of gold, (b) excludes capital gains and losses of foreign affiliates of U.S. parent companies from the NIPA's measure of income receipts from direct investment abroad, and from the corresponding income payments, and (c) beginning with 1973-IV, excludes shipments and financing of military orders placed by Israel under Public Law 93-199 and subsequent similar legislation. Line 77 differs from "net exports of goods and services" in the NIPA's for the same reasons with the exception of the military financing, which is excluded, and the additional exclusion of U.S. Government interest payments to foreigners. The latter payments, for NIPA's purposes, are excluded from "net exports of goods and services" but included with transfers in "net foreign investment." A reconciliation table of the international accounts and the NIPA's foreign transactions account appears in the "Business Situation" in the SURVEY OF CURRENT BUSINESS, June 1982.

12. Includes return import into the United States, at a depreciated value of $21 million in 1972-IV and $22 million in 1973-II, of aircraft originally reported in 1970-III in line 3 as a long-term lease to Australia.

13. Includes extraordinary U.S. Government transactions with India. See "Special U.S. Government Transactions," June 1974 SURVEY, p. 27.

14. The maturity breakdown is available only on a limited basis.

15. The maturity breakdown is available only on a limited basis.

16. Includes foreign currency denominated notes sold to private residents abroad.

alties on patents, insurance premiums, and consulting services. Income from foreign assets held by residents of the United States represents payment for the export of capital services; interest and dividends paid to nonresidents reflect the import of the services of capital. The value of the export (import) of the services of capital is reported in lines 11 through 15 (27 through 31).

Unilateral Transfers

Normal transactions involve exchanges of equal value—for example, an exchange of goods for money. Gifts, by their very nature, are one-sided; there is no payment for a gift. In order to accommodate gifts in a system of double-entry bookkeeping, a special entry called unilateral transfers is introduced. This entry does not record the gift itself; that goes into the appropriate account. The entry in unilateral transfers records the value of what would have been the payment for the gift. In Table 3.1, net unilateral transfers are divided into military and nonmilitary transfers and reported in lines 32 through 36. For example, the entry of −6,608 on line 33 for 1981 means that in that year our gifts to foreigners (excluding military grants) exceeded gifts from foreigners by $6.608 billion.

Current Account

Although the format used by the Department of Commerce does not show the balance in current account, it is one of the most widely discussed items on the balance of payments. The balance on current account measures the combined balances on goods and services plus unilateral transfers.

Assets

The next major subdivision reports changes in claims generated by the import or export of assets. Changes in holdings of foreign assets by residents of the United States (line 37) are divided into three categories: official reserve assets, U.S. government assets, and private assets. Official reserve assets are the international reserves held by the Federal Reserve and United States Treasury. In addition to international reserves such as foreign exchange and gold, the United States government holds claims on foreigners arising from activities such as foreign assistance programs and financing of agricultural exports. Changes in these nonreserve claims are included in U.S. government assets (line 43). All claims on foreigners other than those of the U.S. government are treated as private.

Changes in foreign claims on the United States (line 56) are divided into two categories, foreign official assets and other foreign assets. Foreign official assets are direct dollar claims on the United States held by foreign monetary authorities—in particular, foreign central banks. All other direct claims on the United States are included in other foreign assets. Assets issued abroad but denominated in dollars, such as Eurodollar deposits, which are discussed in Chapter 14, are not direct claims on the United States and are not included in the balance of payments.

Short term and long term   Assets are divided into two classes, short term and long term. Claims such as demand and savings deposits, certificates of deposit, and bonds whose maturity *at time of issue* is one year or less are considered short term. Claims in the form of bonds of over one year maturity *at time of issue,* direct investment, and corporate stock are considered long-term assets.

Capital flows   In discussing trade in commodities, the tradition is to concentrate on what is bought or sold. In reporting the import and export of assets, the convention is to refer to the payment.

The import of a bond or any asset is a debit item in the capital account. Since the purchase of an asset results in U.S. residents paying out money or "capital," any debit entry in the asset account is called a *capital outflow*. On the other hand, the export of a bond means U.S. residents receive money or capital. Any credit entry in the asset account therefore is called a capital inflow. If an entry refers to a change in short-term claims, it is referred to as a short-term capital flow. Similarly, if an entry reports a change in long-term claims, it is called a long-term capital flow. For example, the export of a three-month U.S. Treasury bill is called a short-term capital inflow, and the import of common stock is referred to as a long-term capital outflow.

The following rule determines whether a capital flow is a credit or debit. If an entry in the balance of payments reflects an increase in foreign claims on the United States or a decrease in United States claims on foreigners, it is a capital inflow and a credit. If an entry is due to an increase in United States claims on foreigners or a decrease in foreign claims on the United States, it is a capital outflow and a debit. This rule is difficult enough to follow when it is read, and even more difficult to remember. Fortunately, the rule follows directly from the basic principle that all imports are debits and all exports are credits. Consider the import of a bond. It must be a debit. If it is a foreign bond, the import of the bond represents an increase in United States claims on foreigners. If it is a domestic bond, the import of the bond represents a reduction in foreign claims on the United States. Therefore, an increase in United States claims on foreigners, or a decrease in foreign claims on the United States, must be capital outflows and debit entries because they are the result of the import of a bond.

Consider the export of a bond. It must be a credit. If it is a foreign bond, the export of the bond represents a decrease in United States claims on foreigners. If it is a domestic bond, the export of the bond represents an increase in foreign claims on the United States. An increase in foreign claims on the United States or a decrease in United States claims on foreigners, therefore, must be credit entries and capital inflows, since they are the result of exporting bonds.

Special Drawing Rights

Special drawing rights (SDRs) in effect are lines of credit between central banks established through the International Monetary Fund (IMF). (For more information on SDRs, see Chapter 8). The initial allocation for the United States in 1970 was $867 million. This meant that the United States Treasury had a line of credit with the IMF that it could use to borrow up to $867 million worth of foreign currency. It also meant that the Treasury was obligated to lend $867 million to the IMF. The initial allocation of special drawing rights appears twice in the BOP. It is entered as a debit item in line 40, reflecting an increased claim on the IMF, and as a credit on line 74, because it is an increase in claims on the United States by the IMF. As the line of credit is used and our claims on the IMF change, the changes are recorded on line 40.

Statistical Discrepancy

The entry called statistical discrepancy is used in order to maintain the principle of double-entry bookkeeping. When all the numbers are collected and the sum of debits and credits is not equal, the difference is entered on the appropriate side of the balance of payments under the heading of statistical discrepancy. In other words, line 75 is the finagle factor.

Unlike normal double-entry bookkeeping, the numbers used to compile balance-of-payments statistics do not balance. Although many transactions are missed completely and cause the reporting to be incomplete, this does not create a statistical discrepancy. The problem arises because in some cases entries are based on estimates and in others only one side of a transaction is recorded. For example, an American tourist might use travelers checks to buy a watch in Tokyo. The checks move through the international banking system, where books do balance, and their value is recorded to the penny. Tourist expenditures, including the watch, however, are only estimated using sample surveys returned voluntarily by tourists. If the purchase of the watch is never recorded or is not reported accurately, the transaction contributes to the statistical discrepancy.

EXAMPLES

Some examples can help illustrate how transactions are recorded in the balance of payments. Each transaction considered here appears in Table 3.2 beside the number of the example. In example (1), a loan of $1 million for 10 years is made to France; that is, a U.S. resident buys a 10-year French bond

TABLE 3.2   U.S. Balance-of-Payments Account

	CREDITS (+)	DEBITS (−)	NET BALANCE
Goods and services	$1,000,000(2) 2,000(3) 10,000(5)	$ 2,000(4)	$1,010,000
Unilateral account		10,000(5)	−10,000
Asset account Short-term	2,000(4) 1,000,000(1)	2,000(3) 1,000,000(2)	
Long-term		1,000,000(1)	−1,000,000
Statistical discrepancy			
Total	$ 2,014,000	$ 2,014,000	0

for $1 million. Normally this would be paid for with a check in dollars which, again for simplicity, we assume is deposited by the French firm in a New York bank. The import of the bond represents an increase in U.S. long-term claims on foreigners and appears as a $1 million debit in the long-term capital account. The import of the bond is called a long-term capital outflow. The other side of the transaction, the payment for the bond, takes the form of an increase in foreign short-term claims on the United States. This side of the transaction appears as a $1 million credit entry in the short-term capital account, and it is called a short-term capital inflow.

In example (2), consider a $1 million sale of wheat to India. The export of wheat appears as a $1 million entry on the credit side of goods and services. If payment is made by check, then either foreign demand deposits in U.S. banks decline (foreign short-term claims on the United States decline) or our demand deposits in foreign banks increase (short-term claims on foreigners rise). Payment for the wheat therefore appears as a debit entry of $1 million in the short-term capital account and is called a short-term capital outflow.

Before going on with other examples, consider the net effect on the balance of payments of examples (1) and (2). Since the $1 million short-term capital inflow in example (1) just offsets the short-term outflow in example (2), the net result of examples (1) and (2) is that the United States has a credit balance of $1 million on goods and services and a debit balance on long-term capital of $1 million. That is, these two transactions taken together generate a $1 million credit on goods and services that is financed or offset by a $1 million long-term capital outflow. The United States exchanges $1 million in present goods for claims on future goods worth $1 million.

In example (3), a U.S. resident receives dividends from common stock held in a French corporation. The dividend check, worth $2,000, is deposited in a bank in Paris. U.S. short-term claims on foreigners increase by $2,000, which appears as a debit entry under short-term capital. The offsetting entry is a $2,000 credit under goods and services, which reflects the export of capital services to France. In example (4), the U.S. resident spends the $2,000 worth of French francs on a holiday in the south of Spain. The expenditures represent purchases of goods and services from nonresidents, and they are entered as a debit item in goods and services. The reduction in demand deposits at the French bank is a short-term capital inflow, and it is recorded as a credit item under short-term capital.

It is useful to consider the combined effects of examples (3) and (4). The short-term capital flows cancel each other, and there is no net effect on the short-term capital account. There is a debit entry for tourist expenditures and a credit entry under interest payments, so there is no net effect on goods and services.

In example (5), the U.S. government sends $10,000 worth of grain to a drought-stricken foreign country as a gift. The export of grain appears as a $10,000 entry on the credit side of goods and services, but in this case there is no payment. In order to maintain the system of double-entry bookkeeping, an entry of $10,000 is recorded on the debit side of the unilateral account. The wheat, of course, is the gift, but since there is no payment for a gift, the unilateral account is needed to maintain the rule that every transaction must appear on both the debit and credit sides of the balance of payments.

In published BOP statistics, credits and debits for each category often are not shown separately. A common practice is to subtract debits from credits and show only the net balance for each category. The far right column of Table 3.2 shows the net balance in each category for the five examples combined.

INTERPRETATION

As we have emphasized, the BOP is based on the principle of double-entry bookkeeping. Total debits must equal total credits, and it is impossible for the entire balance of payments to show either a deficit or surplus. The only way we can observe a difference between credits and debits is to select certain items out of the BOP and compare credits and debits for the given subset of items. Whatever subset we choose, the deficit (surplus) on that set of items must be matched by an identical balance with opposite sign on the remaining items. According to current usage, a line is drawn through the balance of payments; the items selected are placed "above the line," and the remaining items are put "below the line."

By placing certain items above and below the line, we define a deficit. Since all such definitions are in a sense correct, we must select between alternative measurements on the basis of their usefulness. No way of measuring a deficit is useful in isolation. In order to be meaningful, a deficit must be related through some theory to a relevant problem. In interpreting a given deficit, it is helpful to ask two questions. First, what problem or issue is this measurement supposed to help me understand? Second, what explicit (or implicit) theory underlies this particular definition of a deficit?

Over the years, the line has been drawn at many different places, and until recently, several different measures were reported by the Department of Commerce. At least two of these measures are commonly cited and discussed. They are (1) the basic balance and (2) the balance on official reserve transactions. Although we consider only one problem and theory for each way of measuring a deficit, there are other reasonable interpretations.

Basic Balance

Measurement   Using the basic balance, long-term capital flows (other than certain official long-term flows) and the balance on current account go above the line. All remaining items, statistical discrepancy, short-term capital flows, and changes in official claims go below the line as offsetting items.

Problem and theory   The basic balance is intended to serve as an indicator of basic or long-term trends in the balance of payments. The problem is whether or not the BOP is in equilibrium in the sense that a given situation can persist through time.

The following ideas appear to underlie the use of the basic balance. Under this approach, it is generally considered both possible and proper to finance a current account deficit by incurring long-term debt or to make long-term foreign investment by running a current account surplus. But it is considered neither proper nor possible to finance a persistent long-term capital outflow and/or a current account deficit by borrowing short term or reducing international reserves. This view assumes that there is only a limited pool of short-term capital and that these funds cannot be relied upon because they move from country to country in response to volatile expectations and temporary differences in net yields.

Given this view of the world, a deficit or surplus on current account plus long-term capital is only temporary. The short-term capital flow, statistical discrepancy, or official transactions financing the balance above the line are likely to disappear in response to changing international conditions. A deficit or surplus in the basic balance therefore represents a disequilibrium in the sense that this situation cannot be expected to continue.

Official Reserve Transactions

Measurement   In going from the basic balance to a balance based on official reserve transactions, private short-term capital flows and statistical discrepancy are moved above the line. This leaves changes in U.S. official reserve assets (line 38) and changes in foreign official assets in the United States (line 57 less line 61) below the line.

Problem and theory   Under a fixed or pegged exchange rate, the problem relevant for a balance on the basis of official reserve transactions is the amount of pressure on the official exchange rate in the foreign exchange market. Under a "dirty" float (flexible rates with official intervention), the relevant problem is the effect of official intervention on exchange rates. The theory underlying this approach is simple supply and demand.

Since the demise of pegged rates in 1973, the dollar value of most major currencies has been determined by a system of flexible rates with official intervention. The effect of that intervention is illustrated in Figure 3.1. Suppose initially an exchange rate of 2.5 deutsche marks per dollar just equates demand and supply for dollars in terms of marks without official intervention. There is then additional downward pressure on the dollar as private demand and supply shift to *D* and *S* in Figure 3.1 and the equilibrium exchange rate drops to 2.0 marks per dollar. If the Bundesbank (German central bank) or Federal Reserve intervenes and prevents the exchange rate from falling to the new equilibrium determined by *D* and *S*, the intervention generates a deficit for the United States on the basis of official reserve transactions.

In Figure 3.1, central banks moderate the fall in the value of the dollar by buying $100,000—that is, by selling $100,000 worth of marks. As a result of this intervention, the price of the dollar only falls to 2.20 marks per dollar. At that exchange rate, nonofficial residents of the United States buy $900,000 worth of goods, services, and assets from Germany per period while selling only $800,000. The excess of purchases over sales is $100,000, and this is the deficit recorded above the line. The matching item below the line is the increase in dollar assets held by the Bundesbank plus the decrease in mark assets held by the Federal Reserve.

FIGURE 3.1
Effect of official intervention under a dirty float.

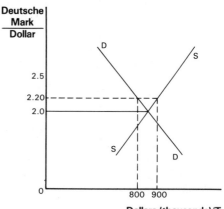

If the terminology used in discussing the balance of payments were consistent, the situation described in Figure 3.1 would be called a $100,000 deficit on nonofficial transactions. Unfortunately, such a deficit is commonly referred to as a $100,000 deficit on official reserve transactions. (Yes! The accounts measuring official reserve transactions show a credit balance of $100,000, but they are *below* the line.) In referring to most measures of a deficit (or surplus), the name used to describe the deficit refers to the items *above* the line. Here that custom is reversed. The name used to identify the deficit is associated with the items appearing *below* the line. A deficit measured on the basis of official reserve transactions means that the combined current account, nonofficial capital flows, and statistical discrepancy show a debit balance. Since the only items left are the official transactions themselves, they must appear below the line with a matching credit balance.

If private demand and supply in Figure 3.1 shift so as to raise the deutsche mark price of the dollar and central banks partially offset that movement, the monetary authorities sell dollars (buy marks), and their intervention creates a surplus in the balance of payments as measured on the basis of official reserve transactions.

When deficits or surpluses are based on the concept of transactions in official reserves, a surplus is an indication that over the period as a whole, central banks have been selling dollars in foreign exchange markets and, on balance, moderating a rise or contributing to a fall in the price of the dollar in terms of foreign currencies. A deficit indicates that central banks have been buying dollars in foreign exchange markets and thereby moderating the fall or adding to the rise in the price of dollars in terms of foreign currencies.

CAVEATS

Even if the problem and supporting theory for a given definition of a deficit are reasonably well understood, using the definition can be misleading. There are at least four reasons for this.

First, classification of items in the balance of payments can be highly arbitrary, and accounts often do not accurately reflect the corresponding theoretical concept. For example, long-term capital flows include the import and export of long-term bonds with only three months left until maturity. From a conceptual point of view, a three-month Treasury bill and a 20-year Treasury bond with three months left until maturity are essentially equivalent assets. In the BOP, however, one is reported as a short-term capital flow and the other as a long-term capital movement.

Second, the collection of BOP statistics is a difficult and complex task. Many transactions are only partially reported, estimated on the basis of surveys, or missed entirely. The entry under statistical discrepancy of over $25 billion for 1981 provides some idea of the potential for error in the statistics and suggests that balance-of-payments statistics should be taken with a grain of salt.

Third, in measuring a deficit, there is a tendency to think that the balance should be zero. In most cases, however, there is nothing inherently good about a zero balance. For example, a deficit according to official reserve transactions might be preferable to a zero balance enforced by strong trade and capital controls.

Fourth, in addition to unavoidable measurement problems, governments often engaged in practices (both deliberately and accidentally) that distort the statistics. For example, suppose a foreign central bank bought $1 billion in the foreign exchange market but deposited the dollars in a Eurodollar account in a London bank rather than depositing them in the United States or buying U.S. Treasury bills. The effect of the intervention in the foreign exchange market would not appear in the balance on official reserve transactions. The $1 billion would be reported as an increase in U.S. liabilities to foreign commercial banks, and the $1 billion entry would go above the line when measuring the deficit according to official reserve transactions.

HISTORICAL REVIEW
OF THE BALANCE OF PAYMENTS

Now that you have been duly warned about the reliability of the statistics, let's briefly review the history of the balance of payments for the United States. The first part of this review looks at the international investment position of the United States from a Fisherian perspective. In the second, we use the balance on official reserve transactions to examine the 1960s and 1970s.

International Investment

Table 3.3 shows that World War I was a major turning point in the international financial position of the United States. Before 1918, the United States was a debtor nation. That is, foreign claims on the United States exceeded United States' claims on foreigners. After World War I, the situation was reversed; claims on the rest of the world exceeded foreign claims on the United States.

During the 1800s, there were tremendous investment opportunities in the United States as immigrants poured in, the country grew, and the frontier rolled West. As compared to the more developed countries in Europe, real rates of return were relatively high, and the United States had a comparative advantage in future goods. Individuals, firms, and local governments in the United States financed factories, canals, railroads, and a wide variety of social overhead capital with funds borrowed from abroad. As a result, up to the early 1900s the United States generally had a deficit on both trade and

TABLE 3.3   International Investment Position of the United States, 1869 to 1960 ($ billions)

YEAR	U.S. INVESTMENT ABROAD	FOREIGN INVESTMENT IN THE U.S.	INTERNATIONAL INVESTMENT POSITION OF U.S. (NET CLAIMS)
1970	166.9	97.7	69.2
1960	85.6	40.9	44.7
1950	54.4	17.6	36.8
1940	34.3	13.5	20.8
1930	21.5	8.4	13.1
1919	9.7	3.3	6.4
1914 (June 30)	5.0	7.2	−2.2
1908	2.5	6.4	−3.9
1897	0.7	3.4	−2.7
1869	0.1	1.5	−1.4

Source: Historical Statistics of the United States: Colonial Times to 1970 (Washington, D.C.: U.S. Department of Commerce, 1975).

current accounts, matched by a net capital inflow. This situation is reflected in the growing net debtor position for the United States during the 1800s shown in Table 3.3. In 1869, the net debtor position was $1.4 billion, and by 1908 the net foreign debt had grown to $3.9 billion.

By the beginning of this century, the frontier had disappeared, the flood of immigrants turned to a trickle, and the United States matured from a developing nation to an industrialized giant. One effect of this metamorphosis was that the United States lost its comparative advantage in future goods and acquired a comparative advantage in present goods. In Table 3.3 this switch is reflected in the decline in the net debtor position from $3.9 billion in 1908 to $2.2 billion in 1914. World War I did not cause this metamorphosis, but it did accelerate and dramatize the change in the international investment position of the United States. During the war, England, France, and the other Allies sold off their investments in the United States in order to buy war material stamped "MADE IN U.S.A." Indeed, as a result of World War I, the United States paid off almost $4 billion of the foreign debt it had accumulated over the previous century. The roughly $4 billion decline in foreign claims on the United States from 1914 to 1919 plus an increase in United States's claims on foreigners over the same period of $4.7 billion transformed the 1914 debtor position of $2.2 billion to a net claim on foreigners of $6.4 billion in 1919. With very few exceptions, in each year since World War I the United States has increased its net foreign investment. By 1970, United States's claims on foreigners exceeded foreign claims on the United States by over $69 billion.

The balance-of-payments statistics for 1960 shown in Table 3.1 are a good example of the general pattern of the BOP from World War I through the early 1960s. In that year, the surplus on merchandise trade was about $5 billion and, when we exclude official assets, there was a net debit balance for assets of roughly the same amount. After the mid-1960s, the balance on merchandise trade tended to decline, and by 1971 there was a deficit which, with some exceptions, tended to grow throughout the 1970s. The net nonofficial capital outflow also faltered in the late 1960s and early 1970s, but it reappeared in the mid-1970s. In the late 1970s there were large foreign purchases of assets in the United States, but a substantial portion of these were bought by foreign central banks. For example, in 1978 there is a credit balance on line 56 of just over $64 billion. That is, net foreign purchases of assets in the United States were $64 billion. Of this total, however, about $33 billion were bought by foreign official institutions. With a total import of assets worth just over $61 billion (line 37) and a small sale of foreign official reserve assets (line 38), the United States in 1978 had a net nonofficial capital outflow of about $30 billion.

With growing deficits in merchandise trade, how was private foreign investment financed? We have already seen part of the answer. At times, the private imports of goods and assets were financed by selling securities to foreign central banks. That, however, is not the entire story. Another significant element is the growing *net* income from private foreign investment. In 1960, this net income was only about $3.5 billion. It grew to $6 billion by 1969 and exploded to over $45 billion by 1981.

If we are willing to abstract from the probable effects of official intervention in foreign exchange markets, the evidence suggests that the United States may have entered a new era. Instead of purchasing (net) foreign assets and financing these purchases with a surplus on merchandise trade, now the United States is becoming a net importer of both goods and assets, and is financing these imports with the income from earlier foreign investment. One popular explanation of our recent deficits in merchandise trade is the increasing cost of oil. Another is that the United States is losing its competitive advantage in world markets. Both explanations tend to be associated with pleas that the federal government ''do something'' to eliminate trade deficits. If the interpretation suggested here is correct, any effort to reduce or eliminate trade deficits would be a serious mistake. Our recent trade deficits simply reflect a new stage in the international investment position of the United States. Like the United Kingdom from the late 1800s to World War I, we are now a mature foreign investor, and we use our large and growing net income from foreign investment to buy goods, services, and more assets.

This section has used a Fisherian perspective to consider the role of capital flows in a historical review of the BOP. The next section reviews the BOP from 1960 through 1981 using the deficit as measured on the basis of official reserve transactions.

Official Transactions

Using official reserve transactions, Table 3.1 shows that, with the exception of small surpluses in 1966, 1968, and 1969, there was a deficit in the balance of payments from 1960 through 1978. From 1960 up to early 1973, deficits were primarily the result of central bank intervention required to maintain pegged exchange rates. (Pegged exchange rates are discussed in Chapter 7.) After early 1973, deficits reflect attempts by central banks to moderate short-run fluctuations in exchange rates under a managed or dirty float.

Regardless of the motive for the deficit, the effect was the same. The purchase of dollars by foreign central banks and the sale of foreign exchange by the Federal Reserve held down the dollar price of foreign exchange, particularly the German mark and Japanese yen, which encouraged imports and discouraged exports. The excess of imports of goods, services, and nonofficial assets over their export is the deficit above the line, which is financed by selling assets to foreign central banks (line 81) and reducing international reserves held by the Treasury and Federal Reserve (line 80).

The subsidy for private imports and investment dramatically reversed in 1979. In that year, foreign central banks reduced their dollar claims by over $13 billion, while international reserves held by monetary authorities in the United States rose by over $1 billion. In other words, in 1979 central banks spent approximately $14 billion propping up the dollar price of foreign currencies. By 1980, there was a small deficit again, which was replaced by an almost zero balance in 1981.

Whether or not 1979 is an aberration or the first sign of a new pattern for central bank intervention probably will depend on the underlying strength of the dollar. Central banks seem to be committed to moderating movements in exchange rates rather than defending certain rates or initiating changes. If this policy holds for the next few years, intervention by central banks will depend on the strength of the dollar. When market forces work to raise the price of the dollar in foreign exchange markets, central banks will tend to sell dollars and surpluses will tend to dominate. If, however, the pressure is for a continuing decline in the value of the dollar, official intervention will try to moderate this decline by buying dollars, which will generate deficits.

SUMMARY

The balance of payments is a product of double-entry bookkeeping, and total debits must equal total credits. What we receive in every transaction (import) is recorded as a debit, and what we give up in every transaction (export) is recorded as a credit. Imports and exports of assets or claims, such as stocks and bonds, are referred to as capital flows; the import of stocks and bonds is called a capital outflow and the export of these assets is called a capital inflow.

Balance-of-payments statistics may be interpreted in several ways. Since the BOP must balance, a particular way of measuring a deficit or surplus is a definition. Like all definitions, a definition of what is a deficit must be judged on its usefulness. In order to be useful, a particular way of measuring a deficit must be linked through some kind of theory to a relevant problem or issue. In order to interpret a given deficit, we must understand the underlying theory and recognize the problem or issue it is designed to illuminate.

The history of the balance of payments for the United States suggests that recent trade deficits are the result of our evolving into a mature foreign investor. The pattern of official intervention in the foreign exchange market shows a sharp reversal in 1979 from deficit to surplus. Whether or not intervention will follow the newer pattern of holding down the price of the dollar probably depends on the strength of the dollar in foreign exchange markets.

QUESTIONS FOR REVIEW

1. Each of the following transactions generates two entries in the BOP. Describe both entries. Where appropriate, determine whether the entry reflects a capital inflow or outflow and whether it is short term or long term. *Example:* An American sells wheat to a Swiss firm and is paid with a check on a Swiss bank. That is a credit on current account and a debit on short-term capital. The entry in the capital account is a short-term capital outflow.
    a. An American tourist buys a meal in Paris and pays with a travelers check in dollars.
    b. The U.S. government gives wheat to India.
    c. A British resident buys stock in General Motors from a U.S. resident. He pays with a check drawn on a bank in New York.
    d. A British resident receives a dividend check from General Motors. The check is written on a bank in Detroit.
2. Why does an export of wheat that is a gift generate a debit entry under unilateral transfers?
3. Use the balance-of-payments format developed by the Department of Commerce and shown in Table 3.1 to describe your transactions over the last week.
4. How can there be a balance-of-payments surplus or deficit when, except for accounting errors, total credits must equal total debits?
5. Pick one year out of those shown in Table 3.1 and calculate the deficit or surplus in the current account, on the basic balance, and according to official reserve transactions.

6. Choose one commonly used definition of a balance-of-payments deficit or surplus. Would you recommend that a country with a deficit according to this measure take steps to eliminate the deficit? If so, why? If not, why not?

7. If total recorded debits in the BOP equal total recorded debits, then the BOP statistics are free from any errors. Agree or disagree, and explain why.

8. Describe the balance of payments for California and New York, as shown in Figure 2.8.

9. Do you think the United States is likely to have a trade deficit next year? If so, why? If not, why not?

10. Suppose the productivity of capital rises in the United States—that is, the United States becomes relatively more efficient in the production of future goods. Would that increase in productivity tend to increase or decrease the U.S. trade deficit?

11. The pure theory of trade explains the equilibrium composition of the trade account in the absence of capital flows. In a similar way, Fisherian capital theory provides an explanation for the equilibrium composition of the balance of payments. Explain.

ADDITIONAL READINGS

The Balance of Payments Statistics of the United States—A Review and Appraisal. Report of the Review Committee for Balance of Payments Statistics to the Bureau of the Budget (Washington: U.S. Government Printing Office, 1965).

"Report of the Advisory Committee on the Presentation of Balance of Payments Statistics." *Survey of Current Business* (June 1976).

COOPER, RICHARD N.   "The Balance of Payments in Review." *Journal of Political Economy* (August 1966).

KEMP, DONALD S.   "Balance-of-Payments Concepts—What Do They Really Mean?" Federal Reserve Bank of St. Louis *Review* (July 1975).

KINDLEBERGER, C. P.   "Measuring Equilibrium in the Balance of Payments." *Journal of Political Economy* (November–December 1969).

SALTER, SIR ARTHUR.   "Britain's Experience as a Creditor Country." An excerpt from *Foreign Investment*, Princeton Essays in International Finance, pp. 2–10 (February 1951), reprinted in W. and C. Allen, *Foreign Trade and Finance* (New York: Macmillan, 1959).

4

FOREIGN EXCHANGE MECHANICS

Most of us become involved with foreign exchange as tourists. On a trip to France or Mexico, we exchange currency or travelers checks for francs or pesos. Often it is done in a hotel, gift shop, or restaurant. Tourist expenditures, however, are only a small part of the total demand for and supply of foreign exchange generated by the import and export of goods, services, and securities. In this chapter we consider the organization of the foreign exchange market and some of the transactions that lie behind that market. This review will help us understand the more formal analysis of foreign exchange markets in the next two chapters.

We start with a typical transaction. An American firm imports wine from France. After reviewing the major aspects of this transaction, we see how the search for the cheapest way to finance the goods in transit generates a form of covered interest rate arbitrage, a topic that we discuss in more detail in Chapter 5. We go on to a brief discussion of spot and forward exchange, and finish with a description of the retail and interbank markets for foreign exchange.

EXAMPLE

Consider the following example. An importer in Denver wants to buy wine from a French vineyard in Bordeaux. The wine is worth 500,000 francs, which at an exchange rate of 10 cents per franc comes to $50,000. Both parties agree to the transaction in principle; now they must work out the details of the contract.

Delivery

The negotiations take place in June, and the delivery date is set as on or about November 1. This delivery date requires that the French vineyard ship the wine by September 17. It first must be put on a train and sent to a French port, where it will be loaded on a freighter. The ship sails through the St. Lawrence Seaway and is unloaded in Chicago. The wine is then transferred to a train or truck and shipped to Denver.

The time in transit between Bordeaux and Denver, about 45 days, raises an important issue that must be settled in the contract. Is payment made when the wine is shipped by the exporter or when the importer receives it? If payment is at time of shipment, the importer pays for the goods more than six weeks before they arrive. With payment on delivery, the exporter does not receive payment until 45 days after the goods are shipped. Neither the importer nor the exporter normally wants to tie up operating capital by financing the goods in transit.

In similar domestic transactions the time in transit is much shorter, and the seller usually gives the buyer 30 days to pay after the goods are shipped. The seller may finance this trade credit by using accounts receivable as collateral for a bank loan. Goods in transit between countries, however, are usually financed directly by borrowing from a third party with the goods as collateral. After considering two other aspects of the contract, we will return to the financing of the transaction.

Currency Used

Another important feature of the contract is whether payment is in dollars or francs. If payment is in francs, the U.S. importer is exposed to the risk that the price of francs might rise between the time the contract is signed and payment is made. With payment in dollars, the franc value of the contract can change and the French exporter bears the risk. Since most transactions involving the United States are denominated in dollars, we assume the contract calls for payment in dollars on September 17.

Since payment is in dollars, the exporter is uncertain of the price in francs. This uncertainty can be eliminated by using the forward (or futures) market. In forward markets, currencies are bought and sold for delivery at a specific time in the future at a price agreed upon today. With payment due in dollars, the French exporter can guarantee the franc value of those dollars by selling them forward. In June, when the contract is signed, the exporter enters into a forward contract with a bank to deliver (sell) $50,000 on September 17 at a price of, say, 10 francs per dollar. The forward contract eliminates any uncertainty about the *franc* value of the wine. Regardless of what the spot exchange rate is on September 17, the exporter can use the $50,000 it receives to buy 500,000 francs. By entering into a forward contract to sell dollars on the date they are due from the importer, the exporter avoids any uncertainty due to changes in the exchange rate between June and September.

CIF or FOB?

Another issue is who is responsible for the transaction costs? These include transport and insurance costs, and costs associated with obtaining the appropriate documents. If the contract price is CIF (certificates, insurance, and freight), these costs are the responsibility of the exporter. If it is FOB (free on board), the costs are the responsibility of the importer. In either case, like the cost of financing the goods in transit, these costs are part of the price of doing business. Ultimately, consumers pay them. In the discussion that follows, we assume the price is CIF.

Financing

As mentioned earlier, the wine in transit between Bordeaux and Denver is usually financed by borrowing. Now we want to see what determines who borrows and where.

Where   The importer agreed to pay $50,000 when the wine was shipped. Now it is September 17, and it must come up with $50,000. Since the importer is not in the finance business, it prefers to borrow the money rather than tie up working capital. The question is, where is the cheapest place to borrow the money, New York or Paris?

Suppose the importer borrows $50,000 for 45 days in New York. When the wine is delivered on November 1, it must pay $50,000 $\times$ $(1 + i_{US})$, where i_{US} is the interest rate for 45 days in the United States. For example, suppose the annual interest rate in the United States is 10 percent. The rate for 45 days is approximately 1.232 percent [0.10(45/365)]. In that case, the importer has to pay about $50,616 when the loan is due and the wine is delivered. An alternative is to borrow francs and use them to buy dollars spot. How much that costs depends on the 45-day interest rate in France, i_F, and the relation between the spot dollar price of the franc S and the 45-day forward rate for the franc, F.

In order to raise $50,000, the importer must borrow francs equivalent to $50,000 $(1/S)$. At the end of 45 days, a payment is due in francs of $50,000$(1/S)(1 + i_F)$. In order to avoid risk due to changes in the exchange rate between September and November, the importer enters into a forward contract on September 17 to buy this amount of francs in the forward market for delivery on November 1. The dollar price of the francs in the forward contract is the forward rate, F. The dollar cost of borrowing \$50,000 in Paris for 45 days therefore is $\$50,000(1/S)(1 + i_F)F$ or $\$50,000(1 + i_F)(F/S)$.

Consider the following example. The spot exchange rate is \$0.10/F1.00. In order to obtain \$50,000, the importer must borrow F500,000. Suppose the interest rate in Paris also is 10 percent per year, so that the rate for 45 days is about 1.232. The importer knows that 506,164 francs are due on November 1 (F500,000 × 1.01232). To avoid the risk of an adverse movement in the exchange rate, the importer buys this amount of francs forward. On September 17, the 45-day forward rate for francs is \$0.0999 per franc. The importer can buy 506,164 francs in the forward market for \$50,565.

In our two examples, interest rates in France and the United States are both 10 percent, yet it is cheaper to borrow in France—\$50,616 versus \$50,565. France is cheaper because the importer sells the francs it borrows for a higher spot price, \$0.10/F1, than it pays to buy them back in the forward contract, \$0.0999/F1. Note that the level of the spot and forward rate does not affect the cost of borrowing in France. Spot and forward rates can both double or halve, and nothing changes. For example, suppose the spot rate is \$1/F1 and the forward rate is \$0.999. It still costs \$50,565 to borrow in Paris: $\$50,000(1 + 0.01232)(0.999/1.00) \approx \$50,565$. When the loan is negotiated in New York, the importer pays $\$50,000(1 + i_{US})$ when the goods are delivered. If the funds are borrowed in Paris, the cost is $\$50,000$ $(1 + i_F)(F/S)$. Whether the goods are financed in New York or Paris therefore depends on whether $(1 + i_{US})$ is greater or less than $(1 + i_F)(F/S)$.

Who   In our example, we assumed that the importer arranged the loan. That approach involved an implicit assumption that the importer is better known and has easier access to both domestic and foreign credit markets than the exporter. If the situation were reversed, there is an incentive for the exporter to arrange for the loan.

When neither firm has a clear advantage in terms of borrowing in both markets, who borrows tends to be determined by where the cost of funds is lowest. If the firms are of roughly equal standing, then each tends to face relatively lower transaction costs when operating in the domestic market. There is therefore an incentive for the firm in the country where borrowing is relatively cheap to arrange for the loan to cover the cost of the goods in transit.

Trader Arbitrage

The incentive to minimize costs applies whichever firm borrows to finance goods in transit. The result is pressure to equate the effective cost of funds in various countries.

Consider the following example. Initially interest rates in both countries are 1 percent for 45 days, or about 8.11 percent per year, and spot and forward rates are 10 francs per dollar. The cost of borrowing in the United States, $(1 + i_{US})$, equals the cost in France $(1 + i_F)(F/S)$. As an extreme example, suppose a tight monetary policy in France drives the interest rate toward 4 percent for 45 days and borrowing to cover goods in transit becomes cheaper in New York. As traders shift their borrowing to New York, they put pressure on both interest rates and exchange rates. The spot price of francs, S, rises and the forward rate, F, declines. The spot price of francs rises because U.S. importers find it cheaper to borrow in the United States and so they stop selling spot francs that they were borrowing in Paris. As a result, the supply of spot francs falls and the price rises.

The supply of forward francs increases because borrowing shifts from French importers borrowing in Paris to U.S. exporters borrowing in New York. When French importers borrowed in Paris, they sold francs spot and paid at time of shipment. When financing shifts to New York, they pay on delivery and cover the exchange risk by selling francs forward. The shift in borrowing also tends to moderate the rise in French interest rates and to put pressure on U.S. rates. Less trader borrowing in Paris reduces credit demand there, and more trader borrowing in the United States increases the demand for funds in New York.

The pressure on interest rates and exchange rates works toward equating the effective cost of funds in the two countries. For example, as a result of switching toward the low-cost source of funds, interest rates in Paris might rise to 3 rather than 4 percent for 45 days, and interest rates in New York might rise from 1 to 2 percent. If the reduced supply of spot francs and the decreased demand for francs forward drives the spot dollar price of the franc to about \$1.004/F1 and the forward rate to about \$0.9943/F1, the cost of borrowing is the same in both countries because 1.02 approximately equals $(1.03)(0.9943/1.004)$. That is, $(1 + i_{US})$ approximately equals $(1 + i_F)(F/S)$.

The incentive for traders to minimize costs of borrowing is only one of the forces tending to equate $1 + i_{US}$ and $(1 + i_F)(F/S)$. As we will see in Chapters 5 and 6, other mechanisms work in the same direction.

Credit Instruments

Borrowing has played a key role in our discussion. Now it is time to see how this takes place. In this example, the U.S. importer pays in dollars on delivery. The exporter obtains all the shipping and insurance documents and writes a *letter of credit* stating the value, quantity, and other details of the shipment and draws up a *draft*. The draft orders the importer to pay the contract price in dollars on November 1 to some third party, perhaps bearer.

When the importer accepts the draft, it becomes a legal obligation of the importer and is called a *trade acceptance*. If the importer is not well known, the contract probably requires that the importer's bank also accept the draft. When, for a fee, the bank accepts the draft, it becomes a *banker's acceptance*. The draft is still a legal obligation of the importer, but now if for some reason the importer does not pay the amount due, the bank is obligated to do so. This guarantee increases the marketability of the instrument.

The exporter combines the banker's acceptance with the appropriate shipping and insurance documents that support it and sells the acceptance at a discount for francs, normally to its own commercial bank. Using a correspondent bank in New York, the French bank sells the acceptance in the New York money market. The good name of the firm and/or bank accepting the draft makes it a negotiable security. There are active markets for acceptances in all major financial markets. You might check *The Wall Street Journal* for the current rate on prime banker's acceptances. Note what has happened in this example. The importer pays in November, the exporter is paid in September, and a third party finances the goods in transit.

THE MARKET FOR FOREIGN EXCHANGE

Now that we have an idea of the nuts and bolts of importing and exporting, let's take a look at the organization of the foreign exchange market. First we consider different types of foreign exchange: spot, forward, and futures. Then we look at the retail and wholesale sides of the market.

Spot

Spot transactions take several forms. A tourist might buy peso travelers checks or currency for a trip to Acapulco. The importer in Denver might buy French francs to pay for the wine. The importer has several choices. One is a telegraph or cable transfer. In that case, the bank from which it buys the francs cables instructions to its Paris correspondent to deposit the francs in an account for the exporter. Another is for the importer to buy a draft or check in francs written on the correspondent bank in Paris that it can mail to the exporter. It also can have the bank send a draft.

Normally the price is slightly higher for both currency and telegraph transfers. Currency is more difficult to handle and drafts normally do not clear for several days, so that a bank has the use of the money in the meantime. In the wholesale market that we will look at shortly, there is a brief grace period. If First City Bank buys German marks from First National Bank, First City has two business days to pay and First National has two days to deliver the marks. Same-day transactions are possible, but spot normally means two business days to deliver and pay.

Forward and Futures

There are two ways to buy or sell foreign exchange for delivery at some future date at a price agreed upon today. One is to enter into a contract with a bank or even another individual. That transaction is a *forward contract* and the price is a *forward exchange rate*. The contract stipulates what will be traded, where the transaction will take place, who the buyers and sellers are, and the price that will be paid. With a forward contact, there is no middleman. The bank, for example, agrees to sell 10,000 marks in 90 days at 41 cents per mark, and we agree to buy them.

The alternative is to buy or sell a *futures contract* in an organized futures market. In a futures market we deal with an organized exchange. We buy or sell a futures contract in German marks for next June just as we would buy or sell a futures contract for wheat or frozen fryers for next June. In the case of wheat or frozen fryers, the futures contract probably would be with the Board of Trade in Chicago. For a foreign currency, it would be with the International Money Market (IMM) in Chicago. There is an active futures market in only a few currencies. Table 4.1 shows the currencies, delivery dates, and prices on the IMM for Friday, December 3, 1982, as reported by *The Wall Street Journal*. (See Table 4.2 for some examples of forward rates in the interbank market.)

TABLE 4.1   Futures Prices and Contracts, International Money Market, Friday, December 3, 1982

	Open	High	Low	Settle	Change	Lifetime High	Low	Open Interest
BRITISH POUND (IMM)—25,000 pounds; $ per pound								
Dec	1.6415	1.6450	1.6360	1.6435	− .0025	1.9350	1.5830	9,018
Mar83	1.6395	1.6455	1.6350	1.6425	− .0040	1.8500	1.5850	9,373
June	1.6400	1.6470	1.6395	1.6450	− .0035	1.7550	1.5870	492
Sept	....	....	....	1.6490	− .0050	1.6360	1.6050	182
Dec	....	....	....	1.6520	− .0050	1.6425	1.6350	100
Est vol 7,062; vol Thur 10,223; open int 19,165, −1,538.								
CANADIAN DOLLAR (IMM)—100,000 dlrs.; $ per Can $								
Dec	.8078	.8096	.8065	.8072	+ .0002	.8350	.7618	5,691
Mar83	.8045	.8066	.8031	.8036	....	.8174	.7282	12,938
June	....	....	....	.8016	+ .0001	.8148	.7810	479
Sept	....	....	....	.7995	+ .0005	.8105	.7960	5
Est vol 4,568; vol Thur 5,417; open int 19,113, +727.								
JAPANESE YEN (IMM) 12.5 million yen; $ per yen (.00)								
Dec	.4040	.4066	.4035	.4048	+ .0006	.4505	.3596	7,330
Mar83	.4070	.4098	.4064	.4078	+ .0005	.4400	.3622	15,516
June	.4105	.4120	.4100	.4105	+ .0005	.4120	.3650	237
Est vol 10,891; vol Thur 14,802; open int 23,083, +1,133.								
SWISS FRANC (IMM)—125,000 francs-$ per franc								
Dec	.4783	.4837	.4782	.3806	+ .0018	.5920	.4486	8,350
Mar83	.4863	.4915	.4860	.4884	+ .0014	.5680	.4546	17,636
June	.4951	.4986	.4944	.4955	+ .0013	.5069	.4616	178
Sept	....	....	....	.5042	+ .0030	.5012	.4635	2
Dec	....	....	....	.5110	+ .0030	.5030	.4815	12
Est vol 17,421; vol Thur 17,836; open int 26,178, +666.								
W. GERMAN MARK (IMM)—125,000 marks; $ per mark								
Dec	.4099	.4128	.4094	.4117	+ .0010	.4675	.3853	6,474
Mar83	.4140	.4166	.4127	.4150	+ .0003	.4228	.3882	17,049
June	.4168	.4194	.4165	.4190	+ .0013	.4450	.3915	137
Est vol 10,784; vol Thur 13,348; open int 23,660, +2,428.								

TABLE 4.2   Interbank Foreign Exchange Rates

Foreign Exchange

Friday, December 3, 1982
The New York foreign exchange selling rates below apply to trading among banks in amounts of $1 million and more, as quoted at 3 p.m. Eastern time by Bankers Trust Co. Retail transactions provide fewer units of foreign currency per dollar.

Country	U.S. $ equiv. Fri.	Currency per U.S. $ Fri.
Argentina (Peso) ..	.000024	41640
Australia (Dollar)	.9630	1.0384
Austria (Schilling)	.0585	17.09
Belgium (Franc)		
Commercial rate	.0210	47.57
Financial rate	.0205	48.85
Brazil (Cruzeiro)	.00429	232.99
Britain (Pound) 1.6435		.6085
30-Day Forward 1.6444		.6081
90-Day Forward 1.6445		.6081
180-Day Forward 1.6449		.6079
Canada (Dollar)	.8089	1.2362
30-Day Forward	.8075	1.2384
90-Day Forward	.8056	1.2413
180-Day Forward	.8038	1.2441
Chile (Official-Rate) ...	.0152	66.00
China (Yuan)	.5136	1.9471
Colombia (Peso)	.0144	69.36
Denmark (Krone)	.1166	8.5750
Ecuador (Sucre)	.0302	33.15
Finland (Markka)	.1863	5.3690
France (Franc)	.1452	6.8850
30-Day Forward	.1441	6.9375
90-Day Forward	.1421	7.0350
180-Day Forward	.1386	7.2150
Greece (Drachma)	.0143	70.15
Hong Kong (Dollar) ...	.1515	6.5985
India (Rupee)	.1041	9.6100
Indonesia (Rupiah)	.0015	684.75
Ireland (Punt) 1.3760		.7267
Israel (Shekel) 0323		30.87
Italy (Lira)	.00071	1411.00
Japan (Yen)	.004057	246.50
30-Day Forward	.004064	244.05
90-Day Forward	.004082	244.99
180-Day Forward	.004113	243.15
Lebanon (Pound)	.2449	4.0825
Malaysia (Ringgit)	.4228	2.3650
Mexico (Peso)	z	z
Netherlands (Guilder)	.3745	2.6700
New Zealand (Dollar)	.7250	1.3793
Norway (Krone)	.1439	6.9480
Pakistan (Rupee)	.0786	12.7298
Peru (Sol)	.00115	870.05
Philippines (Peso)	.1124	8.8950
Portugal (Escudo) 0111		90.10
Saudi Arabia (Riyal) .	.2908	3.4385
Singapore (Dollar)	.4577	2.1850
South Africa (Rand) ..	.9152	1.0927
South Korea (Won)	.0013	745.30
Spain (Peseta)	.0085	117.58
Sweden (Krona)	.1362	7.3430
Switzerland (Franc) ...	.4824	2.0730
30-Day Forward	.4850	2.0620
90-Day Forward	.4900	2.0410
180-Day Forward	.4969	2.0125
Taiwan (Dollar)	.0246	40.58
Thailand (Baht)	.0435	23.00
Uruguay (New Peso)		
Financial ....z		z
Venezuela (Bolivar) ...	.2329	4.2938
W. Germany (Mark) ..	.4122	2.4260
30-Day Forward	.4133	2.4198
90-Day Forward	.4153	2.4080
180-Day Forward	.4187	2.3882

— — —

Table 4.1 illustrates one of the major differences between forward and futures contracts. Futures contracts are only for certain months. In addition, settlement can take place at various times during that month. For forward contracts, there are standard maturities—30, 60, 90, and 180 days—but if you need pound sterling in 58 days, it is available.

Retail

Almost every commodity has a wholesale and retail market, and foreign exchange is no different. The retailers are primarily local banks that sell to businesses and tourists. Their prices, however, reflect rates set in the interbank market plus a small retail markup.

Interbank

The wholesalers are the foreign exchange departments of large banks in the major financial centers around the world, including New York, London, Tokyo, and Singapore. There is no physical location where dealers meet; the market is a worldwide network of phone and telex lines linking all the important financial centers. During normal business days, the market is open 24 hours a day. By the time London closes, New York is operating. After New York closes, currencies are traded in San Francisco for another three hours. Then come Tokyo and Singapore, and back to London.

The turnover is tremendous. In April 1977, the Federal Reserve Bank of New York surveyed 44 American banking institutions. Their trading volume for that month alone was over $100 billion, or about $5 billion per business day. Because of the large number of institutions and countries involved, there are no reliable statistics on the total volume of foreign exchange transactions. A small clue is provided by an estimate of overall world imports and exports for 1977, which was over $2 trillion.

Although institutional details differ between various countries, the two most important trading centers, New York and London, are similar. In both cities, a relatively small number of large banks have foreign exchange departments where traders regularly buy and sell foreign currencies. These operations may run from only a couple of traders to a dozen or more. Some of these banks are willing to buy or sell a given currency to another bank on request. They are said to "make the market" in that currency. We will concentrate on these market banks.

In the last example in the first section, the exporter sells a dollar banker's acceptance to a French bank for francs. That bank sells the acceptance in New York through its correspondent bank there. The French bank probably uses the dollars it receives to buy francs. The foreign exchange department of a major New York bank now has fewer francs and more dollars. That may be what the trader responsible for francs wants. The francs might even be sold at a favorable rate in order to realign the bank's holdings of foreign currencies. If that is the case, there are no immediate repercussions. There is, however, a strong possibility that the trader quoted a competitive rate in order for the bank to maintain a reputation as a market-making bank. A bank that does not readily quote competitive rates finds customers going elsewhere. Since banks make their money on the spread between buying and selling rates, that means a loss of revenue.

Suppose the trader responsible for francs in the foreign exchange department of the New York bank decides the bank is holding fewer spot francs and more dollars than is appropriate. What are the options? One is to buy spot francs with dollars in the interbank market. This can be done either directly or through a broker. Although the trader would like to buy francs at a lower price than he or she sold them, if there is pressure to realign the books quickly, the trader might simply call a broker and ask for the best available rate.

Brokers neither buy nor sell; their specialty is bringing buyers and sellers together. Until a deal is struck, neither bank knows with whom it is trading. Either side, however, may question the broker about the credit standing of the other. When the deal is struck, each bank sends the other written confirmation of the details, and the broker earns a commission on the transaction. (In Canada, brokers are hired by the chartered banks and are paid a salary rather than commission.)

If the decision is to trade directly, the trader contacts either a local or foreign market bank. (Recently, brokers have begun arranging deals between foreign and domestic banks.) When contacting the other bank, the trader typically does not reveal whether the bank is a potential buyer or seller. He or she simply requests a quote on francs and is told both the buying and the selling rate. The response may also include a limit to the amount the other bank is willing to buy or sell at that price. Within those limits, if any, our trader is free to buy or sell. This decision must be made immediately. If there is any delay, there is no obligation to trade at the quoted rates.

Buying francs in the spot market, however, may not be the best strategy. Other less direct ways of altering the bank's position can be more profitable. If interest rates in New York or on Eurodollars are relatively attractive, the decision could be to invest the dollars and buy francs forward. In that case, the trader substitutes forward for spot francs. A currency swap is another possibility. A swap consists of a simultaneous spot purchase (sale) and forward sale (purchase) of a currency. If the books show the bank is low in spot francs but heavily committed to buy francs forward, simultaneously buying francs spot and selling them forward improves the bank's position in both directions.

So far we have considered some of the ways an individual market bank might respond when actual and desired holdings of a currency are not in balance. If holdings of a currency for market-making banks as a group are in balance, transactions such as these simply reallocate holdings between market banks. In that case, there normally is little or no pressure to change exchange rates. When market banks as a group face similar portfolio imbalances, the drive to realign portfolios changes exchange rates. If market banks in general want to increase their holdings of francs and reduce dollar holdings, competition forces up the dollar price of the franc.

As an example of interbank exchange rates, Table 4.2 shows selling rates for most currencies in New York at 3:00 P.M. on Friday, December 3, 1982. These rates are reported every business day in *The Wall Street Journal*. The rates are quoted both as the dollar price of foreign exchange and the foreign price of the dollar. The Austrian schilling, for example, is quoted as 0.0585 dollars per schilling and 17.09 schillings per dollar. Several types of rates are quoted. If there is no designation, the quote is the normal spot rate for delivery in two days. There are also forward rates for several of the more widely traded currencies.

Belgium has two spot exchange rates. The commercial rate is for the official or regulated market. Most current transactions are settled with commercial francs, and only authorized banks can carry out transactions in that market. Most capital transactions take place in the financial market, which is free. Foreign exchange acquired in one market may not be sold in the other.

Chile shows an official spot rate rather than an interbank rate. The exchange rate for the Chilean peso is set by the Central Bank of Chile. The central bank may apply an exchange differential of up to 0.5 percent of the official rate on purchases and sales. Exchange rates for currencies other than the U.S. dollar are not quoted officially. Anyone interested in the details of the restrictions on the Chilean peso or any other currency should consult the *Annual Report on Exchange Arrangements and Exchange Restrictions* published by the International Monetary Fund.

SUMMARY

The contract between importer and exporter must cover several points. These points include the delivery and payment dates, the currency used for payment, and whether the transaction is CIF or FOB. Although the payment date determines who is responsible for the financing, where the goods in transit are financed depends on where the cost of funds is the lowest. These costs depend on both interest rate differentials and the relationship between spot and forward exchange rates.

Like almost all markets, the market for foreign exchange has a retail and wholesale level. The retail level consists primarily of smaller banks that buy and sell foreign exchange to individuals and firms. In the spot market these transactions include currency, telegraph transfers and drafts. Forward contracts at the retail level normally are made with these banks while futures contracts are traded in the International Money Market in Chicago.

The wholesale market consists primarily of a worldwide network of large market making banks that do most of their business with other banks, either directly or through brokers. Most of the transactions in this market are by telex or phone with two business days allowed for delivery and payment in the spot market.

QUESTIONS FOR REVIEW

1. If one Australian dollar costs 0.963 U.S. dollars, what is the Australian price of U.S. dollars? After you calculate the answer, turn to Table 4.2 to see if you are right.

2. Given the spot and 90-day forward price of pound sterling in Table 4.2, what interest rate differential would roughly equate the cost of borrowing in the United States and Great Britain?

3. You are a U.S. importer and you have an obligation to pay a German exporter 250,000 marks in 90 days. One way you can avoid any exchange risk is to buy the marks forward or in a futures market. Describe an alternative way to cover this forward commitment that does not involve a forward or futures contract.

4. The existence of a forward or futures market in foreign exchange can reduce the risk faced by both exporters and importers. Explain.

5. You are a German importer who has a commitment to pay 150,000 Canadian dollars in 180 days. You want to cover this commitment, but suppose there is no active forward or futures market for Canadian dollars in terms of German marks. How can you use forward or futures contracts to cover your commitment and avoid any exchange risk? (Remember, there is an active forward and futures market between U.S. dollars and both Canadian dollars and German marks.)

6. You own a flour mill in Bilbao, Spain. A customer calls and wants you to quote a price for 5 tons of wheat flour to be delivered in 90 days. You know what it will cost to mill the flour, but not how much wheat will cost in pesetas in 90 days. (1) How can you find out a price for the wheat in pesetas that you can use to calculate a quote for the flour? (2) Suppose there is no futures market for wheat in Spain. What might be an alternative?

ADDITIONAL READINGS

KUBARYCH, ROGER M. *Foreign Exchange Markets in the United States* (New York: Federal Reserve Bank of New York, 1978).

PITHER, RAYMOND. *A Manual of Foreign Exchange*, 7th ed. (London: Pitman, 1975).

WALKER, TOWNSEND. *A Guide for Using the Foreign Exchange Market* (New York: Wiley, 1981).

5

DETERMINATION OF EXCHANGE RATES IN THE SHORT RUN

Now it is time to analyze the determination of exchange rates in the short run. The perspective is Keynesian in the sense that financial markets clear continuously, but unemployment exists because information and transaction costs or other impediments seriously inhibit the rapid reallocation of resources. Since real income and price levels are held constant, we are analyzing responses that are relatively short compared to the time it takes a Keynesian multiplier to operate. In Chapter 9 we extend this approach to include changes in output and employment.

Our first job is to derive demand and supply schedules for foreign exchange from the underlying import and export schedules for goods and services. After that, we see how exogenous changes in imports and capital flows influence exchange rates. Then we analyze spatial, cross-rate, and covered interest rate arbitrage. Finally, we consider the role of speculation.

DEMAND FOR FOREIGN EXCHANGE

In addition to constant income and price levels, our derivation of demand and supply schedules for foreign exchange assumes infinitely elastic supply schedules for exports. The supply schedule is horizontal, and changes in the volume of exports do not alter prices. The last assumption greatly simplifies

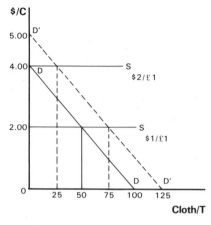

FIGURE 5.1
U.S. dollar demand for and British dollar supply of cloth.

the exposition and makes the analysis more consistent with the Keynesian approach analyzed in Chapter 9.

For simplicity, suppose the United Kingdom exports cloth and the price of cloth is 2 pounds per unit, or £2/C. For each alternative exchange rate, we know the dollar price of cloth. If the exchange rate is 2 dollars per pound, $2/£1, then the price of cloth, $/C, is 4 dollars per unit ($2/£1) × (£2/C). Given the dollar and pound prices of cloth, the American demand for imports determines the quantity and pound value of U.S. imports.

As an example, let's assume the following import demand for cloth, where C/t is the quantity of cloth demanded per unit of time, such as a month:

$$C/t = 100 - 25(\$/C)$$

TABLE 5.1   Derivation of Demand for Pounds

(1) DOLLAR PRICE OF POUND ($/£)	(2) POUND PRICE OF CLOTH (£/C)	(3) DOLLAR PRICE OF CLOTH ($/C) = ($/£)(£/C)	(4) QUANTITY OF CLOTH DEMANDED PER MONTH $C/t = 100 - 25$ ($/C)	(5) QUANTITY OF POUNDS DEMANDED PER MONTH £/t = (£/C) (C/t)	(6) QUANTITY OF DOLLARS SUPPLIED PER MONTH $/t = ($/C) (C/t)
$2.00	£2.00	$4.00	0	£ 0	$ 0
1.75	2.00				
1.50	2.00	3.00	25.00	50.00	75.00
1.25	2.00	2.50	37.50	75.00	93.75
1.00	2.00	2.00	50.00	100.00	100.00
0.75	2.00	1.50	62.50	125.00	93.75
0.50	2.00				
0.25	2.00	0.50	87.50	175.00	43.75
0.00	2.00	0.00	100.00	200.00	0.00

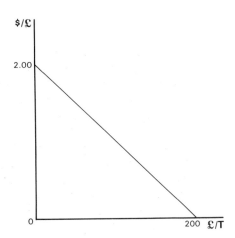

FIGURE 5.2
Demand for pound sterling.

This demand schedule is shown as *DD* in Figure 5.1. The solid lines in Figure 5.1 trace the quantity of cloth imported and pounds demanded for two alternative exchange rates. At $2.00/£1.00, a unit of cloth costs $4, and the supply schedule in Figure 5.1 is infinitely elastic at $4/*C*. No cloth is imported and no pounds demanded. When the exchange rate drops to $1/£1, the supply schedule is infinitely elastic at $2/*C*. Fifty units are imported and $100 are spent on imports per month. In order to import 50 units of cloth, British exporters must be paid £2 per unit, or £100. At $1/£1, the quantity of pounds demanded therefore is £100 per month.

Table 5.1 shows the derivation of the demand for pound sterling for these and several other exchange rates when the U.S. demand for imports corresponds to *DD* in Figure 5.1 and the U.K. supply of exports is infinitely elastic at £2 per unit. This demand schedule is shown in Figure 5.2. Several of the entries in Table 5.1 are blank. If you cannot fill them in, go back and review the last three paragraphs.

American demand for British goods generates a demand for pounds in the foreign exchange market and a supply of dollars. It follows, therefore, that the British demand for American goods generates a demand for dollars and supply of pound sterling.

SUPPLY OF FOREIGN EXCHANGE

Table 5.2 and Figure 5.3 illustrate how the supply of pounds and demand for dollars depend on the U.K. demand for imports and the U.S. supply of exports. In this example, the supply of exports by the United States is

TABLE 5.2 Derivation of Supply of Pounds

(1) DOLLAR PRICE OF POUND ($/£)	(2) POUND PRICE OF DOLLAR (£/$)	(3) DOLLAR PRICE OF WHEAT ($/W)	(4) POUND PRICE OF WHEAT (£/W)	(5) QUANTITY OF WHEAT DEMANDED (W/t)	(6) QUANTITY OF DOLLARS DEMANDED ($/t)	(7) QUANTITY OF POUNDS SUPPLIED (£/t)
$ 0.833	£1.20	$1.25	£1.500	0	$ 0	£ 0
1.000	1.00	1.25	1.250	37.50	46.87	46.87
1.250	0.80	1.25	1.000	75.00	93.75	75.00
1.666	0.60	1.25	0.750	112.50	140.625	84.37
2.000		1.25				
5.000	0.20	1.25	0.250	187.50	234.37	46.87
10.000		1.25				
100.000	0.01	1.25	0.012	223.12	278.90	2.78
	0.00	1.25	0.000	225.00	281.25	0

infinitely elastic at $1.25 per unit of wheat. The British demand to import wheat is given by the following equation, which is drawn as *DD* in Figure 5.3:

$$W/t = 225 - 150(£/W)$$

Let's start at the top of the British demand for wheat shown in Figure 5.3. An exchange rate of $0.833/£1 implies that a dollar costs approximately £1.20. At that exchange rate, the supply schedule for wheat in terms of pounds is infinitely elastic at £1.50/W because £1.20/$1 times $1.25/W is £1.50/W. No wheat is demanded or pounds supplied. When the dollar price of the pound rises to $1/£1, the pound price of the dollar falls to £1/$1, and the supply schedule for wheat facing the United Kingdom is infinitely elastic at £1.25/W. At that price, the United Kingdom imports 37.5 units of wheat per month, which costs $46.87. Given an exchange rate of $1/£1, $46.87 costs £46.87 and British residents supply 46.87 pounds to the foreign exchange market each month. In Figure 5.3, the 46.87 pounds supplied appears as the tall, partially shaded rectangle whose height is £1.25/W and whose width is 37.5 W/t.

As the dollar price of the pound rises, the pound price of the dollar falls and wheat becomes cheaper to British residents. A linear demand schedule is elastic above its midpoint, unitary elastic at the midpoint, and inelastic below the midpoint. Demand is elastic when a given percentage change in price elicits an even larger percentage change in quantity purchased, so that expenditure rises as the price falls. It is inelastic when a given percentage change in price generates a smaller percentage change in the quantity bought. In that case, expenditure falls as the price falls. Unitary elasticity means that price and quantity change by the same percentage, so that expenditure is constant.

Let's consider next the midpoint of the demand for wheat, where the elasticity is unity. At approximately $1.666/£1, the pound price of a dollar is

FIGURE 5.3
British pound demand for wheat and U.S. supply of wheat in pounds.

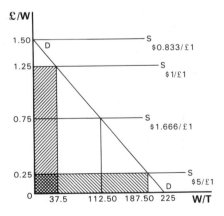

£0.60/$1.00 and the supply schedule in Figure 5.3 falls to £0.75/W. The United Kingdom imports 112.5 units, which costs $140.62 or £84.37. At an exchange rate of $1.666/£1, British residents demand $140.62 in the foreign exchange market per month and supply £84.37. In Figure 5.3, the quantity of pounds supplied appears as the almost square rectangle with height £0.75/W and base 112.50 W/t.

As the price of the pound rises and we move down the elastic part of the import demand schedule, the quantity of pounds supplied rises with an increase in the dollar price of the pound. However, as the exchange rate continues to rise and we move down the inelastic part of the import demand schedule, the quantity of pounds spent on imports falls and the amount of pounds supplied to the foreign exchange market falls as the dollar price of the pound rises. As an example, suppose the exchange rate rises to $5/£1. The supply schedule for wheat in Figure 5.3 shifts down to £0.25/W, where 187.5 units are demanded. The quantity of pounds spent on imports per month and supplied to the foreign exchange market at $5/£1 is shown in Figure 5.3 as the short wide rectangle with height £0.25/W and width 187.5 W/t. The area of this rectangle (£46.87/t) is definitely less than the almost square rectangle (£84.37/t), and the quantity of pounds spent on imports falls as the exchange rate rises from $1.666/£1.00 to $5/£1.

A more complete derivation of the supply of pounds is shown in Table 5.2. Once again, several entries are blank. If you cannot fill in these blanks, go back and review the last few paragraphs. The pound supply schedule is drawn in Figure 5.4. The distorted S shape probably seems strange, but it shouldn't. Every linear demand schedule implies an expenditure or supply schedule that bends back on itself. In the elastic range, a decline in price results in an increase in expenditure. Expenditure is at a maximum where the elasticity of demand is unitary and expenditure falls to zero as price goes to zero.

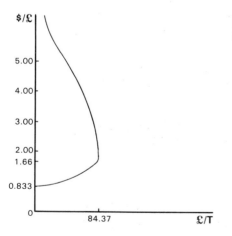

FIGURE 5.4
Supply of pound sterling.

As the exchange rate increases in Figure 5.4 and we move up the vertical axis, the pound price of wheat declines and we move down the British demand schedule for imports. The inverse relation between the exchange rate and the pound price of wheat gives the supply schedule its distorted S shape. The supply schedule asymptotically approaches the vertical axis as the exchange rate goes to infinity, because as the dollar price of the pound goes to infinity, the pound price of the dollar and the pound price of wheat go to zero.

A careful comparison of Figures 5.3 and 5.4 reveals a simple relation between the elasticity of demand for imports and the elasticity of supply for pound sterling. The range over which the elasticity and slope of the supply schedule for pounds are positive corresponds to the elastic part of the demand for imports. The vertical point on the supply for pounds, where elasticity is zero and the quantity supplied is at a maximum, corresponds to the point on the demand for imports where elasticity is unitary. The backward-bending part of the supply schedule, where elasticity of supply is negative, is the result of an inelastic demand for imports.

By now it should be clear that the backward-bending supply schedule for pound sterling is the result of assuming a linear demand for a single good or fixed bundle of goods. Although such an assumption is common because it greatly simplifies the analysis, the assumption can be misleading. As long as we are concerned about demand and supply schedules for foreign exchange around market clearing prices, the assumption of linear schedules does not raise any serious problems. They can be viewed as linear approximations of the true demand and supply schedules for imports and exports in the neighborhood of the quantities and prices actually traded. However, once we move very far from equilibrium prices and quantities, the assumption breaks down.

In deriving the demand for and supply of foreign exchange, we assume that the United States exports wheat and Great Britain exports cloth. The assumption of a single good or fixed bundle of goods is the standard approach, and it makes a linear demand for imports appear reasonable. The world, however, contains a variety of goods and services, and international adjustment involves not only changes in the quantity of goods traded, but also changes in the kind of goods imported and exported. As exchange rates change in our experiment, goods switch from exports to nontraded goods or even to imports.

As an illustration, take today's dollar price of the pound and the pattern of goods and services traded between the two countries. Suppose the dollar price of the pound were half of its current value, with price levels and real income the same in both countries. Prices of British goods in dollars would be so low that not only would we buy more of what we originally imported, but we would also begin to import some new commodities. Indeed, at one-half the current price of the pound, it probably would be profit-able to buy wheat in Great Britain and export it to the United States.

In order to drive the point home, let's take our experiment one step further. Suppose the dollar value of the pound fell to one one-thousandth of its current value. With the price level the same in the United Kingdom, that exchange rate would make Americans millionaires when they spend their income in the United Kingdom. It literally would be cheaper to fly to London for a weekend of first-class hotels and restaurants than to go to a local McDonald's for a hamburger and shake. Once we recognize that adjustment involves both the quantities and the types of goods imported and exported, a linear import schedule becomes inappropriate. Whether or not the short-run supply schedule for foreign exchange is backward-bending is an empirical question, not an implication of theory. Experience seems to indicate that a linear supply schedule probably is more appropriate than one that bends back on itself.

The change in the composition of the bundle of goods being imported and exported raises another conceptual problem. It is a common procedure to relate the elasticity of the demand and supply schedules for foreign ex-change to the elasticity of the underlying demand and supply schedules for imports and exports. Although the elasticity of demand and supply for a single good or fixed bundle of goods is clearly defined, the concept of elastic-ity is not applicable to a bundle of goods whose composition is changing.

Do not throw the baby out with the bath water: The procedure we used to derive the demand for and supply of foreign exchange provides important insights, and the discussion of the limitations of the approach is designed to help us use those insights in a judicious way.

EXOGENOUS SHOCKS

In order better to understand this approach to the determination of exchange rates, let's consider the effects of some exogenous shocks. A typical experi-ment is to examine the effects of an autonomous increase in the demand for imports. Later we will see how a change in capital flows affects exchange rates.

Autonomous Increase in Imports

We begin with the demand and supply schedules derived earlier. They are shown in Figure 5.5 as solid lines that yield an equilibrium rate of $1.25/£1. Next we wave our magic wand, and preferences in the United States shift away from domestic and toward foreign goods. The U.S. demand for imports in Figure 5.1 shifts to the right to $D'D'$, and at each exchange rate more British goods and pound sterling are demanded. In Figure 5.5, the

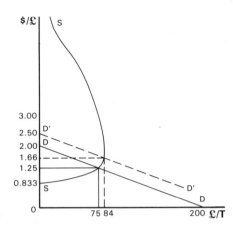

FIGURE 5.5
Demand for and supply of pound sterling.

demand schedule for pounds moves to the right to $D'D'$ and the exchange rate rises.

What about the supply schedule for pounds? Does it shift? If we maintain the assumption that domestic and foreign incomes and price levels are constant, under this approach there is no shift in the supply schedule for pounds and no forces moderate the initial increase in demand for British goods. Equilibrium is restored by an increase in the dollar price of the pound, which alters the terms of trade, encourages exports, and discourages imports. As we will see in the discussion of the Keynesian adjustment mechanism in Chapter 9, changes in output can also play an important role in this adjustment process.

Capital Flows

So far we have ignored capital flows. How do they influence exchange rates? We again begin the analysis by assuming that the equilibrium exchange rate is $1.25/£1, as shown in Figure 5.6, but this time for simplicity we use linear demand and supply schedules. Initially there are no capital flows. Then investment demand and long-term interest rates rise in the United Kingdom, and the United States begins to import long-term claims. For simplicity, we assume that the pound value of those assets is unaffected by the exchange rate. The increased demand for pounds generated by the import of British assets shifts the demand schedule in Figure 5.6 to the right from DD to $D'D'$, and the exchange rate rises to $1.40/£1. The transfer of present goods and services from the United States to the United Kingdom needed to finance the import of assets is accomplished by an increase in the exchange rate.

Before the capital flow, exports and imports in Figure 5.6 are both $0Q$. The trade balance is zero, and the exchange rate is $1.25/£1. The increased demand for pounds to pay for British assets shifts the pound demand to

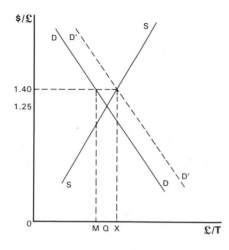

FIGURE 5.6
Demand for and supply of pound sterling.

$D'D'$, and the exchange rate rises to $1.40/£1. In the short run the demand and supply schedules for pounds generated by commodity imports and exports do not change because neither output nor tastes have changed. These demand and supply schedules are still DD and SS. As a result, the rise in the exchange rate reduces imports to $0M$ and raises exports to $0X$. The surplus in the trade balance, MX, generated by the rise in the exchange rate just equals the long-term capital outflow, which is the horizontal distance between DD and $D'D'$.

In the absence of gifts or government intervention in the foreign exchange market, a net capital flow requires an offsetting transfer of goods and services. With flexible exchange rates and no reallocation of resources, that transfer is achieved through a change in the exchange rate. When we expand this analysis in Chapter 9 and allow employment to change, we will see that alterations in output can also play an important role in the transfer process.

ARBITRAGE

Our discussion of exchange rates has ignored both time and space. We have considered only spot exchange rates and treated that market as though it operated like the New York Stock Exchange. Now it is time to see how arbitrage links markets across space and through time. We start with arbitrage between two currencies and two locations, expand to arbitrage between three currencies, and finish with arbitrage over time.

Spatial Arbitrage

As we saw in Chapter 4, the foreign exchange market does not have a central location like the New York Stock Exchange. It consists of a network of brokers and market banks in the major financial centers of the world. It is effective arbitrage between these financial centers that allows us to treat the foreign exchange market as though it operated like the New York Stock Exchange.

Arbitrage is one of the basic forces at work in our economy. It brings oranges from California to New York and bananas from Costa Rica to Illinois. The basic idea of arbitrage is simple. Buy something where its price is relatively low and sell it where the price is higher—provided, of course, that the price spread more than covers the transportation costs. Arbitrage is the driving force in the model of international trade developed in Chapter 1. A price differential in the absence of trade provides an incentive for profitable arbitrage, and the effect of arbitrage is to reduce or eliminate price differentials.

As a concrete example of spatial arbitrage in foreign exchange, let's consider New York and London and the dollar price of pounds. Suppose at some time during the day, when both markets are open, there is a surge in the demand for pounds in the United States. In London, the exchange rate is $1.50/£1, but the increased demand in the United States starts to drive the price in New York toward $1.52/£1. As a price differential emerges, arbitrage moderates the pressure on the pound in New York by transferring part of that pressure to London. When transaction costs are as low as they are in a highly organized market like the foreign exchange market, we expect arbitrage quickly to eliminate price differentials and effectively integrate London and New York into a single market.

As an example of how arbitrage works, consider a large bank in London. Over the telex, the head of the dollar section in the foreign exchange department sees the dollar price of pounds spurt up in New York. Here is a chance to make some money, but not for very long; arbitrage in one form or another quickly closes the gap. In order to exploit the situation, the arbitrager does two things immediately and almost simultaneously. First, he or she contacts a broker or a correspondent bank in New York and sells, say, 5 million pounds. At almost the same instant, he or she buys the same amount of pounds in London. If the arbitrager does not buy and sell at almost the same instant the spread appears, there is a risk of missing the opportunity—or even worse, of buying high and selling low because market conditions reverse.

The sale of pounds in New York, where their price is high, and the repurchase in London, where the price is low, contributes to eliminating the price differential. As others, including importers and exporters, respond to the opportunity to buy pounds cheaply in London and/or sell dollars at a favorable rate in New York, arbitrage quickly eliminates significant price differentials. As a result, New York and London are effectively integrated into a single market, and we can talk about "the" market for pound sterling.

Cross-Rate Arbitrage

Spatial arbitrage integrates London and New York into a single market for exchanging pounds and dollars. Cross-rate arbitrage links all the financial centers and foreign exchange markets. Since it is the simplest possible example, we consider three currencies, British pounds (£), American dollars ($), and German marks (DM), and three cities, London, New York, and Frankfurt. Exactly the same reasoning applies to any number of currencies and locations.

Let's start with a set of inconsistent cross rates and profitable arbitrage. Suppose initially the three rates are as follows: in New York $1.50/£1; in Frankfurt $0.50/DM1; and in London DM4/£1. If such an opportunity ever arose, with a few million dollars we could get rich. Take 3 million dollars and buy 2 million pounds. Use the pounds to buy 8 million marks. With the marks, buy 4 million dollars. That makes a 1-million-dollar gross profit. Fierce competition in international financial markets prevents such opportunities from occurring. Since millions or even billions of dollars and other currencies can be bought or sold in a matter of minutes, even very small opportunities for cross-rate arbitrage are usually quickly exploited and eliminated.

Our transactions and those of other arbitragers put pressure on the three exchange rates. The dollar price of the pound tends to rise; the mark price of the pound falls; and the mark price of the dollar rises. Each of these movements works toward establishing consistent cross rates. How far do the exchange rates move? If we ignore problems generated by bid-ask spreads and other transaction costs, there is a simple answer. The rates move until any return from cross-rate arbitrage is eliminated and the following condition is reached:

$$(\$/DM)(DM/£)(£/\$) = 1.0$$

How much each exchange rate changes as arbitrage funds move depends on what financial commentators call the breadth and depth of the three markets. In terms of economics, that translates into the relative elasticities of the excess demand schedules in the three markets. Assuming that the pound/mark market is relatively thin—that is, less elastic—the movement of arbitrage funds has more impact on the pound price of the mark than on the other two rates. With that assumption, the following is a set of consistent cross rates that might evolve out of the initially inconsistent cross rates: $1.52/£1, $0.5092/DM1, and £0.335/DM1.

Given the role of the dollar as the key currency, in many cases it is more appropriate to express the condition for consistent cross rates slightly differently. Trade between, say, Costa Rica and Venezuela is very small, and there probably is no active market between the Venezuelan bolívar (B) and Costa Rican colón (C). If we are in Costa Rica and we go to a bank to buy bolívars with colóns, the bank quotes the price on the basis of the dollar price of the two currencies. As a result, in many cases it is more appropriate to write the condition for consistent cross rates in a slightly different form.

$$C/B = (\$/B)(C/\$)$$

The colón price of the bolívar is determined by the dollar price of the bolívar and colón.

Implications for Demand and Supply

Earlier in the chapter we derived demand and supply schedules for pound sterling from the underlying demand for and supply of goods and services between the United States and United Kingdom. That exercise tends to suggest that the exchange rate between each pair of countries is determined in isolation. Cross-rate arbitrage, however, implies that all foreign exchange markets are interrelated. As a result, elasticities of demand and supply for a given currency are larger than what is implied by the commodity import and export schedules for two countries in isolation.

As an example, suppose we start with the consistent cross rates cited above, \$1.52/£1, \$0.5092/DM1, and £0.335/DM1. Now there is an increased demand for British goods. It pushes up the dollar price of the pound and creates inconsistent cross rates. Arbitragers respond by buying marks with dollars, pounds with marks, and then selling the pounds for dollars. Arbitrage moderates the rise in the dollar price of the pound by increasing the supply of pounds in New York.

The increased demand for British goods must be financed. As long as we exclude capital flows, that leaves changes in trade patterns. The most obvious way to finance increased imports from the United Kingdom is to increase exports to that country, but that is not the only possibility. Another is to increase exports to and/or reduce imports from other countries such as Germany. The increase in the dollar price of the mark due to arbitrage generates a surplus in the U.S. balance of trade with Germany that can help offset increased imports from Great Britain.

But how do we get pounds from an export surplus with Germany? Remember, cross-rate arbitrage also pushes up the mark price of the pound, which generates a trade surplus for Germany with the United Kingdom. The excess pounds generated by this trade surplus are bought with the marks obtained from the U.S. trade surplus with Germany. These pounds help finance the increase in U.S. imports from the United Kingdom. The net result is that the increased demand for British goods is financed not only by an increase in U.S. exports to the United Kingdom, but also by a change in trading patterns between the United States and Germany, and Germany and the United Kingdom. This example considers only three countries. But when we see how cross-rate arbitrage works for three countries, we can appreciate how cross-rate arbitrage moderates the impact of a real shock to a single exchange rate by involving all trading partners and currencies in the adjustment process.

Exactly the same forces are at work when the exchange rate between two currencies is effectively determined by the dollar prices for them. Suppose, for example, Costa Rica demands more Venezuelan oil. Costa Ricans buy dollars and use them to buy oil from Venezuela. The colón price of the bolívar rises because the colón price of the dollar and dollar price of the bolívar both rise. (Note that the colón price of the pound and mark as well as the pound and mark price of the bolívar also rise.) Costa Rica may sell a few more bananas or some more coffee to Venezuela, but it pays for the increased oil imports primarily by selling more coffee and bananas to the United States and Europe. These countries, in turn, buy less coffee and oil from Venezuela. Higher oil imports by Costa Rica are paid for primarily by more Costa Rican exports to the United States and Europe and fewer imports by those countries from Venezuela, rather than by Costa Rica selling more bananas and coffee to Venezuela.

Covered Interest Rate Arbitrage

We already have seen one form of covered arbitrage. In Chapter 4, we saw how the response by traders to relative costs of borrowing in different countries tends to equate those costs. In Chapter 13, we will see another version. Here we examine covered interest rate arbitrage from a third perspective.

We start with an American bank or large corporation that has $1 million worth of Treasury bills which have just matured. The problem is, where to reinvest the money? Although there are many alternatives available, we concentrate on just two, 90-day Treasury bills issued by the American and British governments. In order for the two investments to be comparable with respect to risk, we assume that the purchase of a British Treasury bill is covered with a forward contract so there is no risk of loss due to fluctuations in exchange rates.

If the money is invested in the United States, at the end of 90 days the investor receives one plus the 90-day yield in the United States, $(1 + i_{US})$ times $1 million, or $1,000,000 \times (1 + i_{US})$. For example, if the 90-day yield on American Treasury bills is 1.97 percent, then in 90 days the investor receives $1,019,700. If the funds are invested in British Treasury bills, then the dollar return depends on British interest rates and the spread between the spot and forward exchange rates. In order to buy British T-bills, the investor first must buy $1 million worth of pound sterling at the spot price of the pound, S, which is an amount of pounds equal to $\$1,000,000 \times (1/S)$. For example, if the spot rate, S, is $\$1.25/\pounds1$, then $1/S$ is $\pounds1/\$1.25$ or $\pounds0.80/\$1$. One dollar is worth 0.80 pounds, and $\$1,000,000$ buys $\pounds800,000$.

How many riskless dollars these $\pounds800,000$ buy in 90 days depends on the British Treasury bill rate, i_{UK} and the 90-day forward dollar price of the pound, F. Suppose the 90-day yield on British Treasury bills is 3.0 percent and the forward rate is $\$1.2375/\pounds1$. At the end of 90 days, the investor receives $\pounds824,000$ ($\pounds800,000 \times 1.03$). When these pounds are sold forward at a rate of $\$1.2375/\pounds1$, the investor receives $\$1,019,700$, which is the same 1.97 percent yield returned by 90-day Treasury bills in the United States.

This example illustrates an important point. In covered interest rate arbitrage, the yield from a foreign asset depends on both the foreign interest rate *and* the relation between spot and forward rates. The interest rate in the United Kingdom is 3.0 percent for 90 days, but the arbitrager receives only 1.97 percent because buying pounds at $\$1.25/\pounds1$ and selling them for only $\$1.2375/\pounds1$ generates a loss of 1.03 percent.

Notice that the level of exchange rates has no influence on the return. Both F and S can double or halve, and it does not alter the dollar return from the investment. What does alter the profitability is the forward rate relative to the spot rate. Other things being equal, the higher the dollar price of the forward pound as compared to the spot pound, the more profitable is a covered British asset.

Equilibrium A little reflection reveals that the yield on a covered British asset is $(1 + i_{UK})(F/S)$. One dollar buys $1/S$ in pounds. When the investment of $1/S$ in pounds matures, it pays $(1/S)(1 + i_{UK})$. When these pounds are sold forward, they are worth $(1/S)(1 + i_{UK})F$ in dollars.

When the domestic yield and covered foreign yield are the same, as they are in the example used above, an investor is indifferent between holding domestic or covered foreign assets. This equality can be expressed in two ways. In one, the difference between covered foreign and domestic yields, which is called the *net covered yield*, is zero:

$$(1 + i_{UK})\frac{F}{S} - (1 + i_{US}) = 0$$

In the other, the interest rate differential equals the forward premium:

$$\frac{1 + i_{US}}{1 + i_{UK}} = \frac{F}{S}$$

In these equilibrium or parity conditions, the two interest rates and the forward exchange rate must be for the same maturity, and domestic and foreign assets must be comparable. It would be inappropriate to use 90-day Treasury bill rates for the United States and rates on 90-day banker's acceptances in the United Kingdom because a banker's acceptance is more risky than a Treasury bill and therefore commands a higher yield. Finally, exchange rates and interest rates must all be for identical times. The analysis does not apply to interest rates at 11:00 A.M. and exchange rates at noon.

Market integration Spatial arbitrage integrates markets across space. Cross-rate arbitrage weaves different foreign exchange markets into an interactive network. Covered interest rate arbitrage combines foreign exchange and short-term capital markets into an interdependent system. In order to see how covered arbitrage links capital and foreign exchange markets, we start our example with no incentive for covered arbitrage. Interest rates are the same in both countries, and there is no forward discount or premium. Interest rates of 10 percent in both countries and exchange rates of $1/£1 in both spot and forward markets may not be realistic but they are easy to work with, so let's use them. The initial situation, with no incentive for arbitrage, is depicted by the solid excess demand schedules labeled *SD* for the four relevant markets shown in panels (1) to (4) in Figure 5.7. These schedules describe the excess demands in each market for all participants other than those engaged in some form of covered interest rate arbitrage. They are labeled *SD* because to the left of the vertical axis they describe excess supply, and to the right they describe excess demand.

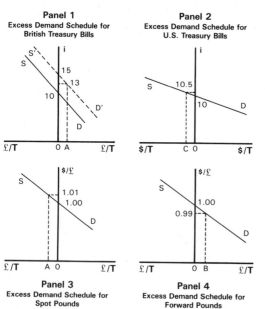

Panel 1
Excess Demand Schedule for
British Treasury Bills

Panel 2
Excess Demand Schedule for
U.S. Treasury Bills

FIGURE 5.7
Covered interest rate arbitrage between Treasury bills.

Panel 3
Excess Demand Schedule for
Spot Pounds

Panel 4
Excess Demand Schedule for
Forward Pounds

In order to be consistent with the demand and supply schedules for foreign exchange derived earlier, each of these markets is shown as a flow excess demand for pounds or dollars, even though arbitragers have a stock demand for assets. We can avoid some difficult problems involved in the interaction of stocks and flows by making the time period of our flow demand schedules correspond to the maturity of the assets demanded by arbitragers. Since a desired stock of, say, 90-day Treasury bills must be rolled over every 90 days, we can express a stock demand for these assets as a flow over 90-day intervals. This approach also helps emphasize that we are dealing with comparative static equilibria, not dynamics.

Now consider an exogenous increase in the demand for credit in the United Kingdom. The excess demand schedule for Treasury bills in Figure 5.7(a) shifts up to $S'D'$. In the absence of covered arbitrage, exchange rates and the Treasury bill rate in the United States are unchanged, but the yield on British Treasury bills rises to 15 percent. There now is a net covered yield in favor of London because $(1 + i_{UK})(F/S)$ is greater than $1 + i_{US}$. As arbitrage responds to the net covered yield, it moderates the pressure on interest rates in Great Britain by increasing the supply and reducing the demand for credit in London. In the process, part of the initial shock is transmitted to the foreign exchange market and part is absorbed by capital markets in the United States.

Figure 5.7 illustrates how covered arbitrage combines the four markets into an interactive system. In (1) the increased demand for credit in the United Kingdom shifts the excess demand schedule from SD to $S'D'$. In the absence of covered arbitrage, the yield on Treasury bills would rise to 15 percent. The movement of $0A$ in arbitrage funds from New York to London absorbs part of the shock, and yields on British T-bills rise to only 13 percent. In order to buy $0A$ worth of British Treasury bills, arbitragers must buy $0A$ pounds in the spot market. Spot rates in Figure 5.7(3) rise to $1.01/£1. As they buy $0A$ pounds spot, arbitragers sell $0B$ pounds forward, where $0B$ equals $0A \times (1 + 0.13)$. The forward sale drives the forward rate in Figure 5.7(d) to $0.99/£1. The movement of $0C$ arbitrage funds ($0C = 0A \times$ $1.01/£1$) out of New York drives U.S. Treasury bills in (b) up to 10.5 percent.

After the movement of arbitrage funds shown in Figure 5.7, there is still a slight net covered yield in favor of London. However, if enough arbitrage funds move, the net covered yield disappears and there is no incentive for any *additional* covered arbitrage. Whether or not that happens, arbitrage transmits part of the initial shock to the United States and both interest rates rise, but the rise is greater in the United Kingdom because the movement of arbitrage funds puts upward pressure on spot pounds and reduces forward rates. As an exercise, you should analyze the effects of an exogenous shift in each of the other three markets.

Impediments to Covered Arbitrage

Spatial and cross-rate arbitrage are highly effective. Exchange rates are essentially identical in different cities, and deviations from consistent cross rates are small. As we will see in Chapter 14, covered interest rate arbitrage between Eurocurrencies is also highly effective. The premium on 90-day pounds, F/S, almost continuously equals the interest rate differential between 90-day Eurodollars in London and 90-day Europounds in Paris. Outside Eurocurrency markets, however, large net covered yields persist for weeks or even months. As an example, Table 5.3 shows large and persistent net covered yields between the United States and Canada and Great Britain.

On the surface, large and persistent net covered yields appear to be inconsistent with wealth maximization on the part of banks and others with the liquid assets, international connections, and information necessary for effective covered arbitrage. At present there is no consensus as to why large net covered yields exist and persist. There are, however, a number of potential explanations. They include transaction costs, portfolio choice, liquidity, and political risk.

Transaction costs   When Keynes formulated the theory of covered interest rate arbitrage in the 1920s, he recognized that some positive yield from arbitrage is necessary to cover transaction costs. Through the entire discussion we have ignored bid-ask spreads and other transaction costs borne by arbitragers. Between World Wars I and II, the consensus was that these costs ran about ½ of 1 percent. As a result, for net covered yields of less than ½ of 1 percent, there was no incentive to move arbitrage funds. Since the 1950s, these costs appear to have fallen to ⅛ or even 1⁄16 of 1 percent. Transaction costs therefore can explain only a small part of the net covered yields shown in Table 5.3.

Portfolio balance   The Tobin-Markowitz model of portfolio balance discussed in Chapter 2 can also explain net covered yields. Under portfolio balance, investors have subjective ideas about expected yields and their variances and covariances. Given this information and attitudes concerning risk, each arbitrager has some optimal portfolio that may contain both domestic and covered foreign assets. If yields on domestic and comparable covered foreign assets are not perfectly correlated, in order to induce an arbitrager to substitute a covered foreign asset for a comparable domestic asset, the covered yield on foreign assets must rise relative to the return from comparable domestic assets. The relative rise in returns from covered assets is necessary to compensate the arbitrager for moving to a more specialized and therefore more risky portfolio.

Conceptually this explanation is similar to the case of rising transaction

TABLE 5.3 Weekly Arbitrage Data on 90-Day Treasury Bills

DATE 1974	TREASURY BILL RATES (% PER YEAR)			PREMIUM (+) OR DISCOUNT (−) ON FORWARD POUND (% PER YEAR)	NET COVERED YIELD IN FAVOR OF LONDON (% PER YEAR)	TREASURY BILL RATES (% PER YEAR)			PREMIUM (+) OR DISCOUNT (−) ON FORWARD CANADIAN DOLLARS (% PER YEAR)	NET COVERED YIELD IN FAVOR OF CANADA (% PER YEAR)
	U.K.	U.S.	SPREAD IN FAVOR OF LONDON			CANADA	U.S.	SPREAD IN FAVOR OF CANADA		
Jan. 4	12.04%	7.38%	4.66%	− 7.44%	−2.78%	6.13%	7.38%	−1.25%	−0.60%	−1.85%
11	12.04	7.75	4.29	− 7.30	−3.01	6.10	7.75	−1.65	−0.22	−1.87
18	11.88	7.75	4.13	− 7.69	−3.56	6.10	7.75	−1.65	−0.18	−1.83
25	11.86	7.92	3.94	− 8.82	−4.88	6.08	7.92	−1.84	0.0	−1.84
Feb. 1	11.82	7.42	4.40	−10.00	−5.60	6.04	7.42	−1.38	−0.04	−1.42
8	11.80	6.99	4.81	−10.95	−6.14	5.99	6.99	−1.00	−0.20	−1.02
15	11.75	7.00	4.75	−10.09	−5.34	5.95	7.00	−1.05	−0.35	−1.40
22	11.66	6.94	4.72	− 8.54	−3.82	5.95	6.94	−0.99	−0.33	−1.32
Mar. 1	11.77	7.51	4.26	−12.46	−8.20	5.92	7.51	−1.59	−0.20	−1.79
8	11.77	7.66	4.11	− 9.81	−5.70	5.97	7.66	−1.69	−0.08	−1.77
15	11.75	7.74	4.01	− 9.64	−5.62	6.01	7.74	−1.73	0.25	−1.48
22	11.80	8.02	3.78	− 8.32	−4.54	6.17	8.02	−1.85	0.49	−1.36
29	11.82	8.34	3.48	− 7.24	−3.76	6.36	8.34	−1.98	0.42	−1.56

Source: Federal Reserve Bulletin (April 1974), p. A85.

costs discussed in Chapters 1 and 2. In Chapter 1, an increased demand for imports increases the volume of trade. Since transaction costs rise with the volume of trade, both the price differential and the volume of trade increase. If yields on domestic and comparable covered foreign assets are not perfectly correlated, the Tobin-Markowitz model suggests that, beyond some point, arbitragers require an increasing risk premium as they commit a larger proportion of their portfolio to covered assets. If that is the case and the aggregate wealth of arbitragers is roughly constant, then beyond some point the covered foreign yield must rise relative to comparable domestic yields as the volume of covered arbitrage increases.

As an example, start with an initial equilibrium in which a 0.2 percent net covered yield in favor of London just compensates the marginal arbitrager for holding covered foreign assets. Now there is upward pressure on interest rates in the United Kingdom, and our arbitrager moves funds to London. A larger proportion of the portfolio is now committed to covered foreign assets. If yields are not perfectly correlated, more covered assets means a more risky portfolio, and the relative yield on covered foreign assets must rise to offset the increased risk. More arbitrage requires a higher net covered yield, say 0.3 percent in favor of London, to compensate arbitragers for the increased risk involved in holding more covered foreign assets.

Incomplete markets and liquidity   A 90-day U.S. Treasury bill and a covered 90-day British Treasury bill are both claims on dollars in 90 days. If we ignore any remote possibility of default on the forward contract or by the two governments, both assets are certain claims on a given amount of dollars in 90 days. From the point of view of an American investor, however, they are not equally liquid.

There is an active market in U.S. Treasury bills, but there is no such market for covered foreign assets as a package. Suppose an investor wants to sell U.S. Treasury bills. He or she simply calls a broker. Since there is no active market for covered foreign assets, sale of a covered British Treasury bill involves three steps. First, sell the British T-bill. Second, use the pounds to buy dollars spot. Third, cover the forward contract by an offsetting purchase of forward pounds. These transactions absorb time and involve additional bid-ask spreads, which makes the covered British Treasury bill less liquid than the U.S. Treasury bill.

Capital controls   Capital controls can also explain net covered yields. Governmental restrictions delay or limit repatriation of interest or capital. Interest paid to or received from foreigners can be taxed. These restrictions and taxes distort international financial markets in the same way that quotas and tariffs disrupt international commodity markets. Even if capital controls do not exist, the threat of such controls creates a form of political risk that can inhibit covered arbitrage.

Political risk is a popular explanation for observed net covered yields because it is consistent with the observed pattern in such yields. As we saw in Table 5.3, covered interest rate arbitrage often is not very effective for assets such as Treasury bills. As mentioned earlier, however, arbitrage effectively eliminates net covered yields between Eurocurrencies—see, for example, Table 14.3.

Political risk can explain this pattern. The British government, for example, has imposed capital controls on pound sterling in the past and may impose or change them at any time. That government, however, has never imposed such controls on nonsterling loans within the United Kingdom and is not likely to do so in the future. One reason is that borrowing or lending dollars in London has no direct effect on the British money supply or financial markets. In addition, the British authorities know that if they do impose controls on such activity, it will simply move to a more hospitable country. Similarly, the French government may be concerned about how capital flows affect the French money supply and financial markets, but it has little reason to be concerned about borrowing or lending dollars, pounds, or marks in Paris. The French authorities also know that restrictions will only reduce the participation of French banks as the market shifts its transactions to London or Singapore. As a result, there is essentially no political risk involved in arbitrage between Eurodollars in London and Europounds in Paris. There is, however, political risk for arbitrage between pound assets in the United Kingdom and dollar assets in the United States because governments are concerned about the effect of capital flows on domestic markets, and they can effectively control domestic capital movements.

Political risk also provides an explanation for why net covered yields in Table 5.3 are so much larger between the United States and United Kingdom than between the United States and Canada. For most of the last 30 years, Great Britain has used various types of capital controls. Short-term capital flows between the United States and Canada, however, have been almost completely free of controls. As a result, there is very little, if any, political risk between the United States and Canada.

These explanations for net covered yields should be viewed as complements. Each gives us some additional insight into the operation of covered interest rate arbitrage. With further research, we should be able to develop a better idea of the relative importance of these influences and perhaps discover other explanations for why covered interest rate arbitrage at times permits what appear to be opportunities for profitable covered interest rate arbitrage.

Market Conventions

If you didn't take a close look at Table 5.3 earlier do so now, because it uses some conventions associated with covered arbitrage. The interest rate differential is approximated by a simple difference, such as $(i_{US} - i_{UK})$, rather than $(1 + i_{US})/(1 + i_{UK})$, and the forward premium is reported as $(F - S)/S$ rather than F/S. In addition, interest rate differentials and forward premiums are measured on an annual basis.

In the financial community, interest rates are discussed and reported on an annual basis. Take a Treasury bill that costs $100 and pays $103 in 90 days. In *The Wall Street Journal* the yield on this treasury bill is reported as 12.17 percent. The 3.0 percent yield for 90 days is converted to an annual rate by multiplying by 365/90. The conversion factor for a 60-day asset would be 365/60. Since this convention also holds for interest rate differentials, the forward premium must be converted to an annual rate by a similar procedure.

The simple difference $i_{US} - i_{UK}$ is easy to calculate and it is usually a reasonable approximation for $(1 + i_{US})/(1 + i_{UK})$ minus 1. As a result, the covered arbitrage equation is usually written as follows:

$$i_{US} - i_{UK} = (F - S)/S$$

In order to see how this expression is related to the equilibrium condition used earlier, let's write the expression

$$(1 + i_{US}) = (1 + i_{UK})(F/S)$$

as

$$1 + i_{US} = F/S + i_{UK}(F/S)$$

Now let p equal $i_{UK}[(F/S - 1)]$. Since $(1 - S/S)$ is zero, we can express $i_{UK}(F/S)$ as p plus i_{UK} plus 1 minus S/S. We now can write $i_{UK}(F/S)$ as $p + i_{UK} + 1 - (S/S)$. If we substitute $p + i_{UK} + 1 - (S/S)$ for $i_{UK}(F/S)$ in the last equation and simplify, we get the following result:

$$i_{US} - i_{UK} = (F - S)/S + p$$

The term p is the product of two terms that are normally less than 1, and it tends to be small relative to other terms in the equation. It therefore is ignored, and the equilibrium condition for covered arbitrage is often written as follows:

$$i_{US} - i_{UK} = (F - S)/S$$

For example, using annualized data, suppose i_{US} is 12.2 percent, i_{UK} is 10 percent, and $(F - S)/S$ is 1 percent. In that case, if we compute the exact net covered yield in favor of the United States, it is 1 percent.

$$\frac{(1 + 0.122)}{(1 + 0.10)} - 1.01 = 0.01$$

An arbitrager earns 1 percent more by investing in the United States. Now let's compute the same net covered yield using the approximation:

$$(0.122 - 0.10) - 0.01 = 0.012$$

The approximation is off by two-tenths of 1 percent.

SPECULATION

When people engage in international arbitrage, they borrow where yields, including forward cover, are low and lend where interest rates are relatively high. By simultaneously borrowing, lending, and entering into a forward contract, they avoid any risk that yields might move against them. When people speculate, they in effect make a bet that yields or prices will move in their favor. When an importer must pay in a foreign currency on delivery and does not cover that obligation with a forward contract, the firm is specu- lating or betting that, when it must pay, the spot exchange rate will be lower than the current forward rate.

It is often convenient to talk about speculators and arbitragers as though they were different people, but in fact the same individuals and firms do both. An exporter may cover some transactions and not others. A bank may cover forward obligations in some currencies but not others. In the remainder of this chapter we consider some current ideas about speculation. We will analyze some of the effects of speculation in Chapter 13.

Views of the Role of Speculation

Ideas about the role of speculation in foreign exchange markets tend to reflect prevailing views about the nature of speculation in general. Over the last 20 years, there has been a revolution in economists' attitudes about speculation. Before the early 1960s, most economists, businesspeople, and politicians thought of speculation as perverse and socially counterproduc- tive. The irrationality of speculation in financial markets is an important theme in Keynes's *General Theory,* and the view still influences Keynesian economics. In the foreign exchange market, this attitude crystallized into the belief that speculation is destabilizing. Although the term "destabilizing speculation" has a variety of interpretations, probably the most common is that speculation tends to amplify short-run movements in exchange rates.

Suppose that, in the absence of speculation, some event such as a dock strike or bad harvest increased the domestic price of foreign exchange.

Then, according to this view, speculators interpret the initial price rise as evidence of a further increase in the price of foreign exchange. They buy foreign exchange and drive up the price even further. At some point, exchange rates start back down to the long-run equilibrium determined by economic fundamentals, and the whole process works in reverse. Price declines lead to speculative sales, and the exchange rate is temporarily driven below its long-run equilibrium.

The idea that speculation is destabilizing or in some other way perverse is a common one. Many of those involved in the day-to-day operation of foreign exchange and other financial markets see speculation as being at least partially irrational or perverse. References during turbulent periods in foreign exchange markets to the "gnomes of Zurich" is one example of such beliefs. Periodic congressional investigation of speculative markets and strong opposition to the establishment of new futures markets reflect widespread distrust of speculation.

Most economists now reject the idea that speculation is systematically perverse or counterproductive because empirical and theoretical work begun in the 1950s appears to be inconsistent with that view. Careful and extensive examination of month-to-month, week-to-week, and day-to-day changes in prices in futures and other speculative markets does not show the systematic patterns implied by destabilizing and other forms of perverse speculation. Instead, prices appear to behave as though they were *random walks*. That is, today's price change is uncorrelated with all previous changes, and past price changes give us no economically useful information about future price changes.

This empirical evidence motivated a reformulation of ideas about the role and function of speculative markets. The essence of the new approach is that organized speculative markets are effective mechanisms for collecting and evaluating information. The idea was first applied to futures markets, so let's use a futures market for foreign exchange to examine alternative responses to information.

Take the futures price for pound sterling for next August. Between now and the next business day, new information emerges and the price of the pound changes. Suppose that information is favorable to the pound, and its price rises. If the market overestimates the ultimate impact of that information, the initial price rise is ultimately followed by price decreases as the market corrects the initial overresponse. If the market underresponds to the new information, the initial rise in the price of pounds is repeated as the market absorbs the information.

The third alternative is that the market correctly evaluates the full impact of this information. In that case, there is no tendency for subsequent price increases or decreases. Since the next price change is the result of *new* information, it must be uncorrelated with the initial price change. Suppose good news tended to be followed by more good news. The market would recognize this pattern in its response to the initial good news, and only the unpredictable element in the subsequent news would be *new* information and have any impact on the price.

Destabilizing speculation   In the first type of response, speculation is destabilizing because the market systematically overresponds to new information. Speculation amplifies short-run fluctuations in prices, and price changes tend to be negatively correlated. Price rises tend to be followed by price declines, and the reverse. This destabilizing speculation can result from speculators who buy on a price rise because they think a price increase is a signal for more price increases.

Stabilizing speculation   In the second example, speculation is stabilizing. By underresponding to new information, speculators reduce short-run fluctuations in prices and tend to introduce positive serial correlation into price changes. A price increase (decrease) one day tends to be followed by subsequent price increases (decreases). This kind of stabilizing speculation might come from speculators who think price rises are temporary and sell as prices rise.

Efficient market   In the third example, the market does not over- or underrespond to new information. This behavior corresponds to what is commonly called an *efficient market*. In such a market, speculation reflects rational expectations. In an efficient market with rational expectations, the futures price quoted today for next August fully reflects all information currently available to the market. In other words, the futures price is the best available estimate of what the spot price will be next August. If the current futures price reflects all available information, no information that is available to the market today can be used to predict the next price change. Information about past price changes is available, and so future price changes must be uncorrelated with past price changes. If speculative markets are efficient and expectations are rational, price changes for given futures contracts should be uncorrelated. In addition, if expectations are rational and people are risk-neutral, forward or futures prices should be unbiased predictors of the relevant spot prices.

What about the empirical evidence? Which view does it support? If we restrict our choice to three simple alternatives: speculation is systematically destabilizing; speculation is systematically stabilizing; or expectations are rational, then the choice is clear. The vast majority of the analysis of price behavior in speculative markets suggests market efficiency and rejects both stabilizing and destabilizing speculation.

Reliably anticipatory expectations   Even though efficient markets and rational expectations are more consistent with the empirical evidence than the other two alternatives, many—and perhaps even most—economists are not willing to accept the hypothesis that speculative prices always fully reflect all available information. For one thing, that position assumes zero information costs. With positive information costs, it is inefficient to collect all information. The value of some information is smaller than its cost. In addition, there is the possibility that speculation could be either stabilizing or destabilizing under certain conditions even though neither operates under normal circumstances. Given these reservations, the following view of speculation is a reasonable one. Speculative markets may make mistakes, but they do not *systematically* overrespond or underrespond to new information. This position corresponds to what one of the pioneers in this area, Holbrook Working, called "reliably anticipatory expectations."

SUMMARY

The short-run demand for and supply of foreign exchange can be derived from the demand for imports and supply of exports. When we use these demand and supply schedules for foreign exchange to analyze the effects of an increase in import demand and capital flows, they imply depreciation. However, restricting the analysis to only two countries tends to exaggerate the amount of depreciation because part of the adjustment takes place through changes in trade with third countries.

Even though the foreign exchange market consists of a network of banks scattered around the world, we can analyze it as though it were located in a single location, such as the New York Stock Exchange, because spatial and cross-rate arbitrage effectively integrate this network of banks into a single market for foreign exchange. In a similar way, covered interest rate arbitrage integrates markets across space and time by establishing links between spot, forward, and capital markets.

There are three common views about the nature of speculation in foreign exchange markets. It is stabilizing, destabilizing, or efficient and rational. Given the empirical evidence concerning the behavior of prices in speculative markets, it is difficult to accept the view that speculation is systematically stabilizing or destabilizing. However, the idea that markets fully reflect all available information probably is too strong. The idea that speculation is reliably anticipatory in the sense that speculation does not systematically over- or underrespond to information appears to be a reasonable alternative.

QUESTIONS FOR REVIEW

1. Assume the supply of British exports is infinitely elastic at £3 per unit and the U.S. demand for those imports is given by the following equation:

    $Q/t = 150 - 30(\$/Q)$

    a. Draw the U.S. demand for pounds. Clearly label where quantity supplied is greatest and where it is zero.

    b. Draw the U.S. supply of dollars. Clearly label the points where quantity supplied is greatest and where it is zero.

    c. Relate the elasticity of the demand for imports to the elasticity of supply for dollars.

2. Discuss why the approach used in (1) tends to overemphasize the likelihood of an inelastic demand for foreign exchange.

3. Suppose the price level doubles in the United States and the U.S. demand for imports shifts to

$$Q/t = 150 - 15(\$/Q)$$

If U.K. exports remain infinitely elastic at £3/Q, how does the rise in the U.S. price level shift the demand for pound sterling?

4. The first law of economics is that quantity demanded decreases as price increases. The second law is that elasticity is a positive function of time. The longer the time period, the larger the response to a change in price. What does the second law imply about our derivation of the demand for and supply of foreign exchange? In particular, how does it relate to the idea that a devaluation can temporarily worsen the trade balance?

5. Go back to Table 4.2. If cross-rate arbitrage was effective, what were the following exchange rates: Argentinian peso/Australian dollar, Costa Rican colon/Venezuelan bolivar, Saudi Arabian riyal/Spanish peseta?

6. The following exchange rates, $2.69/£1, $0.20/F1, and F12/£1 (F stands for French franc) represent a set of inconsistent cross rates. As an arbitrager, how would you take advantage of this inconsistency? How would your arbitrage and that of others tend to affect these rates?

7. Suppose, in the absence of covered arbitrage, 90-day (not annual) interest rates are 3 percent in both the United States and the United Kingdom. The spot price of the pound is $1/£1, and the forward price is $1.01/£1. Which way will arbitrage funds tend to move? How will this movement of funds tend to affect interest rates in the United States and United Kingdom, and exchange rates in the spot and forward markets? Finally, is arbitrage likely to eliminate the net covered yield? If so, why? If not, why not?

8. Pick some stock in the New York Stock Exchange and follow the price for two weeks. Based on this sample, develop some strategy of buying and selling that would have allowed you to make a profit over that two weeks greater than simply buying and holding or going short over the two weeks. Now apply the same strategy to an entirely different two-week period for the same stock. Did you still make money? What about broker's fees? Does your little experiment support or reject the idea that markets are efficient?

9. Is the adjustment mechanism summarized in Figure 5.6 consistent with the analysis developed in Chapter 1? If so, explain why. If not, explain why not.

10. Compare and contrast the transfer mechanism—the mechanism that converts a capital flow into an offsetting trade balance—developed in this chapter with the one developed in Chapter 2.

ADDITIONAL READINGS

BRANSON, WILLIAM H.   "The Minimum Covered Interest Differential Needed for International Arbitrage Activity." *Journal of Political Economy* (November–December 1969).

BURT, JOHN, FRED R. KAEN, AND G. GEOFFREY BOOTH.   "Foreign Exchange Market Efficiency under Flexible Exchange Rates." *Journal of Finance* (September 1977).

CORNELL, W. BRADFORD.   "Spot Rates, Forward Rates and Exchange Market Efficiency." *Journal of Financial Economics* (August 1977).

———, AND J. KIMBALL DIETRICH.   "The Efficiency of the Market for Foreign Exchange under Floating Exchange Rates." *Review of Economics and Statistics* (February 1978).

GEWEKE, JOHN, AND EDGAR FEIGE.   "Some Joint Tests of the Efficiency of Markets for Forward Foreign Exchange." *Review of Economics and Statistics* (August 1979).

HANSEN, LARS P., AND ROBERT J. HODRICK.   "Forward Exchange Rates as Optimal Predictors of Future Spot Rates: An Econometric Analysis." *Journal of Political Economy* (October 1980).

ISARD, PETER.   *Exchange-Rate Determination: A Survey of Popular Views and Recent Models*. Princeton Studies in International Finance, No. 42, May 1978.

KOHLHAGEN, STEVEN W.   *The Behavior of Foreign Exchange Markets—A Critical Survey of the Empirical Literature*. New York University, Graduate School of Business Administration, Solomon Brothers Center for the Study of Financial Institutions, Monograph 1978–3.

LEVICH, RICHARD M.   "On the Efficiency of Markets for Foreign Exchange." In R. Dornbusch and J. Frenkel (eds.), *International Economic Policy: Theory and Evidence* (Baltimore: Johns Hopkins University Press, 1979).

MARSTON, RICHARD C.   "Interest Arbitrage in Euro-Currency Markets." *European Economic Review* (January 1976).

McCALLUM, B. T.   "The Role of Speculation in the Canadian Forward Exchange Market: Some Estimates Assuming Rational Expectations." *Review of Economics and Statistics* (May 1977).

OFFICER, LAWRENCE H., AND THOMAS D. WILLETT.   "The Covered-Arbitrage Schedule: A Critical Survey of Recent Developments." *Journal of Money, Credit and Banking* (May 1970).

PIPPENGER, JOHN.   "Interest Arbitrage between Canada and the United States: A New Perspective." *Canadian Journal of Economics* (May 1978).

6

LONG-RUN DETERMINANTS OF EXCHANGE RATES

This chapter discusses the long-run determination of exchange rates. Impediments such as information and transaction costs are ignored, and the homeostatic mechanism that Adam Smith called the "invisible hand" operates effectively. As a result, markets are fully integrated, and there is no unemployment. We start our long-run analysis by developing the theory of purchasing power parity (PPP). Then we use PPP to examine how exogenous shocks such as an increased demand for imports and changes in capital flows affect exchange rates when markets effectively allocate resources, and there is no unemployment. In the final section, we review the standard objections to purchasing power parity and see how these objections become relevant when there are transaction costs.

PURCHASING POWER PARITY

Theory

The basic idea behind purchasing power parity is simple. A currency should be able to buy the same bundle of goods at home and abroad. That is, the purchasing power of a dollar should be the same whether we spend it in Chicago, Los Angeles, or Copenhagen.

In order to understand the theory fully, we need to consider its theoretical foundations. The long-run analysis in this chapter initially assumes competition and zero transaction costs. When we add these assumptions to the usual assumptions of price theory, they imply PPP as an equilibrium condition.

Absolute   Given competition and zero transaction costs, the law of one price must hold, and the dollar price of any good q_i must equal its pound price times the dollar price of the pound.

$$(\$/q_i) = (\$/£)(£/q_i)$$

If this condition does not hold, it is possible to buy the good, say coal, in one country and sell it in the other at a profit.

Since this condition holds for *every* good, it also holds for any bundle of goods, Q. Take any arbitrary bundle of goods, say a bushel of apples, a gallon of milk, and a barrel of oil. Since $(\$/q_i)$ equals $(\$/£)(£/q_i)$ for each of these goods, it follows that the same condition holds for the bundle Q.

$$(\$/Q) = (\$/£)(£/Q)$$

Rewriting this expression slightly yields what is called the absolute version of purchasing power parity:

$$(\$/£) = \frac{(\$/Q)}{(£/Q)}$$

If a given bundle of goods costs \$10 in the United States and five pounds in the United Kingdom, then according to the absolute version of purchasing power parity the exchange rate should be \$2/£1.

PPP also applies within a country. Instead of the United States and Great Britain, let's substitute New York and Los Angeles. Since the dollar price of a dollar is 1, the absolute version of purchasing power parity implies that the dollar price of a given bundle of goods is the same in both cities. When we apply the idea to large cities it works reasonably well, but between large cities and small towns, say the Big Apple and Muncie, Indiana, the theory clearly has some problems. Since a similar situation holds between countries, the absolute version of PPP is usually abandoned in favor of the relative version.

Relative   Consider two time periods, zero and some later time t. According to the absolute version of PPP, the following two conditions hold at time t and time zero.

$$(\$/£)_t = (\$/Q)_t/(£/Q)_t$$
$$(\$/£)_0 = (\$/Q)_0/(£/Q)_0$$

Dividing the first condition by the second and doing a little rearranging yields the relative version of purchasing power parity:

$$(\$/£)_t/(\$/£)_0 = \frac{(\$/Q)_t/(£/Q)_t}{(\$/Q)_0/(£/Q)_0} = \frac{(\$/Q)_t/(\$/Q)_0}{(£/Q)_t/(£/Q)_0}$$

Since $(\$/Q)_t/(\$/Q)_0$ is simply a price index for the United States using the weights implicit in the bundle Q and $(£/Q)_t/(£/Q)_0$ is the corresponding price index for the United Kingdom, we can rewrite the relative version in its more common form:

$$R_t/R_0 = P_D/P_F$$

In this equation R is the domestic price of foreign exchange and P_D is the domestic and P_F the foreign price index. In order to be consistent with the underlying theory, the two price indexes must have period zero as their base, and both must use the same weights.

The relative version of PPP has a different message from the absolute version. It says that the *change* in the exchange rate from one period to another equals the change in the relative purchasing power of the two currencies. For example, it predicts that if over the next two years prices go up by 115 percent in Argentina while they go up only 15 percent in the United States, two years from now the dollar price of the Argentinian peso will be about half of what it is now.

The relative version of PPP is used more than the absolute version because it is more consistent with what we observe in foreign exchange markets. It also works better within countries. Applied to the United States, the relative version implies that inflation is the same in all parts of the country. The price of a gallon of milk or loaf of bread may not be the same in New York and Muncie, but when the price doubles in one city, it usually also about doubles in the other.

Causality

In the analysis we have just done, there is no causal relationship between price levels and exchange rates. PPP is simply an equilibrium condition. The theory, however, has been advocated most strongly by economists associated with monetarism and it has acquired a causal interpretation in which changes in relative price levels drive or ''cause'' changes in exchange rates.

Whether one is a Keynesian or a monetarist, both exchange rates and price levels are endogenous variables. For Keynesians, real and nominal variables tend to affect each other. For monetarists, however, at least in the long run, real factors influence nominal prices, but money does not affect real variables such as relative prices and real output. As a result, monetarists tend to view price levels as essentially a monetary phenomenon and often speak as though price levels drive exchange rates. This approach, however, tends to distort the monetarist position and has generated some misunderstanding. Within the monetarist tradition, a more appropriate interpretation of the relation between relative price levels and exchange rates is that they are both essentially monetary phenomena. We will have a better idea about what that means after Chapter 11, where we compare and contrast Keynesian and monetarist views about the international adjustment mechanism.

EXOGENOUS SHOCKS

We can use PPP to analyze the long-run effects of various exogenous shocks. As in the last chapter, let's consider two shocks: an increase in the demand for imports and an increase in capital flows.

Imports

Consider a shift in consumer preferences away from cars built in Detroit toward cars built in Japan. Doesn't the increased demand for Toyotas raise the demand for Japanese yen and cause the dollar to depreciate? According to PPP, the answer is "no." Depreciation of the dollar requires an increase in the U.S. price level relative to the Japanese price level. The shift toward Japanese products may alter relative prices, but there is no reason to expect that the shift toward imports will alter relative price *levels*.

The increased demand for Japanese cars is a decreased demand for American cars. As output declines in Detroit, capital and labor are released to work in other areas, and American production of exports and import of competing goods increases. The shift in the pattern of production in the United States comes about because the price of American cars falls not only in relation to Datsuns and Toyotas, but also in relation to other domestic products such as airplanes and wheat. With the price system working smoothly, there is no reason to expect changes in *relative* prices to alter the general level of prices. In Japan, the increased production of cars draws resources away from other industries, reducing the supply of other exports and increasing the demand for imports. Once again there is no reason that this shift in the pattern of production should change the price level in Japan. Of course, the shift in preferences generates real changes. Relative prices and patterns of production change, but according to purchasing power parity there is no reason to expect the dollar price of the yen to increase unless the change in *relative* prices is associated with an increase in the price *level* in the United States relative to Japan.

What's going on here? In Chapter 5, an autonomous increase in imports caused the domestic currency to depreciate, but here the same shock leaves the exchange rate unchanged. The primary reason for the different results is that in Chapter 5 Adam Smith's invisible hand has a broken thumb, whereas here the price mechanism works perfectly.

The decision to buy more foreign goods has two sides. If people plan to spend more of their income on foreign goods, they plan to spend less on something else. In other words, the increased demand for imports reduces demand elsewhere. If the price mechanism works, resources released by the reduced demand for domestic cars are used to produce exports and/or import substitutes. Just as in Chapter 1, the increased demand for imports *is* an increased supply of exports. As a result, in the long run both demand and supply schedules for foreign exchange shift to the right. When the price system works, adjustment is achieved through a change in relative prices, and there is no need for exchange rates to change.

There are two ways to interpret the short-run model developed in Chapter 5. The first emphasizes transitional unemployment. Shifting resources from the production of cars to airplanes is expensive and takes time. Under that interpretation, the short run used in the last chapter refers to periods that are relatively short as compared to the time it takes to shift resources between industries or regions. Since output in export and import competing industries does not expand immediately, the supply schedule for foreign exchange is fixed in the short run. An increased demand for imports therefore shifts the demand for foreign exchange to the right before it shifts the supply.

There is another, more Keynesian, interpretation of the short-run model. In a Keynesian world, the price mechanism breaks down and output is limited by aggregate demand. The reduced demand for Fords does not lead to increased production of airplanes and wheat, it creates involuntary unemployment in Detroit. The increased demand for Toyotas increases the demand for foreign exchange, but there is no increased supply of exports to increase the supply of foreign exchange. Instead, there is unemployment in Detroit and dollar depreciation. With this interpretation, the short-run model we used in Chapter 5 refers to the interval before the Keynesian multiplier has time to reduce output.

Foreign Investment

Suppose initially there are no capital flows, but then a technological breakthrough encourages investment in the United Kingdom and real returns rise on British assets. Americans buy British stocks and bonds, increasing the demand for pound sterling. Given the level of real income, the decision to buy British assets is a decision to buy less of something else. Most likely American investors buy fewer dollar assets and perhaps save more—that is, buy fewer commodities.

Reduced investment and/or increased saving in the United States reduces domestic demand for goods and services, including imports, and releases factors of production for employment in industries producing exports and commodities that compete with imports. At the same time, increased investment in the United Kingdom increases the British demand for commodities. With full employment, that increased demand must spill over into an increased demand for imports. We are back in the Fisherian analysis of Chapter 2. An increase in investment opportunities in the United Kingdom generates a supply of assets to the United States and a demand for American goods. The purchase of British assets by Americans creates an export surplus by reducing commodity imports and increasing exports. All this adjustment is accomplished through the price mechanism, without any change in the exchange rate.

The adjustment requires changes in relative prices. Domestic and foreign real interest rates rise. Increased investment in the United Kingdom increases demand for some commodities, and reduced investment in the United States combined with less consumption in the United States and Great Britain reduces demand for other commodities. From this perspective, there is no presumption that the terms of trade move against the United States or that the American price level rises relative to the British price level. Given the reasoning underlying purchasing power parity, depreciation is not necessary to bring current and capital accounts into equilibrium.

At this point, all we can say is that there is no need for depreciation. We cannot determine how the exchange rate does change because we do not yet have enough tools to determine the response of the price levels in the United Kingdom and the United States. As we will see in Chapter 10, higher interest rates reduce the quantity of money demanded in both countries, and both price levels rise. But the change in relative price levels and, therefore, the change in the exchange rate depends on the relative interest elasticities of the demand for and supply of money. From this perspective, the exchange rate plays no role in the adjustment mechanism associated with capital flows.

In Chapter 5, capital flows systematically altered exchange rates. In the short run, depreciation is necessary to create the trade surplus required to balance a capital outflow. The reason for the difference in results is essentially the same as it was for imports. In the short-run analysis, the price mechanism fails. As a result, we ignore the effects of the reduced demand in the United States and increased demand in the United Kingdom associated with a purchase of British assets.

FORWARD RATES
AND INTEREST RATE
DIFFERENTIALS

Purchasing power parity also applies to forward rates and, when combined with simple Fisherian capital theory, yields implications about long-run relationships between spot exchange rates, forward rates, and interest rate differentials.

If we ignore the complications introduced by uncertainty, PPP suggests that the expected change in the exchange rate equals the expected change in relative price levels. Suppose we expect the price level in Argentina to double over the next year while the price level in the United States remains constant. If we believe that the relative version of purchasing power parity holds, then we have to expect that the dollar price of the peso will fall by about 50 percent over the next year.

Let $R_{90}{}^E$ be the dollar price of the foreign currency that is expected to prevail in 90 days. The expected change in the exchange rate therefore is $R_{90}{}^E/R_0$. The idea that the expected change in the exchange rate depends on the difference in expected rates of inflation can be written as follows:

$$R_{90}{}^E/R_0 = \frac{P_D{}^E}{P_F{}^E}$$

In this expression, $P_D{}^E$ and $P_F{}^E$ are the domestic and foreign price levels expected to prevail in 90 days. Both have the same weights and period zero as the base.

In order to link purchasing power parity and Fisherian capital theory, it is useful to express the expected change in the price level as 1 plus the expected rate of inflation $\dot{P}^E$, or $(1 + \dot{P}^E)$. For example, if we expect prices to rise by 15 percent over the next year, then the expected price level P^E equals 1 plus 0.15, or 1.15. Given this change in notation, we can write the relation between expected changes in exchange rates and relative price levels as follows:

$$R_{90}{}^E/R_0 = (1 + \dot{P}_D{}^E)/(1 + \dot{P}_F{}^E)$$

where $\dot{P}_D{}^E$ and $\dot{P}_F{}^E$ are, respectively, the expected rates of domestic and foreign inflation.

Given the assumption of certainty used to develop Fisherian capital theory in Chapter 2, the 90-day forward rate $R_{90}{}^F$ and the spot rate expected to prevail in 90 days, $R_{90}{}^E$, must be equal. This equality implies that the forward premium (or discount) over the spot rate $R_{90}{}^F/R_0$ also equals the difference in expected rates of inflation over the next 90 days.

$$R_{90}{}^F/R_0 = (1 + \dot{P}_D{}^E)/(1 + \dot{P}_F{}^E)$$

The right-hand side of the last equation should jog your memory. In Chapter 2 it is pointed out that Fisherian capital theory implies that, if trade equates real interest rates, nominal interest rate differentials depend on differences in expected rates of inflation.

$$\frac{(1 + i_D)}{(1 + i_F)} = \frac{(1 + \dot{P}_D^E)}{(1 + \dot{P}_F^E)}$$

In this expression the expected rates of domestic and foreign inflation $\dot{P}_D^E$ and $\dot{P}_F^E$ must refer to the same time period as the maturity of domestic and foreign interest rates, i_D and i_F.

The combination of Fisherian capital theory and purchasing power parity therefore implies that, in the long run, forward premiums R_{90}^F/R_0 tend to equal interest rate differentials $(1 + i_D)/(1 + i_F)$ because both tend to equal the difference in expected rates of inflation $(1 + \dot{P}_D^E)/(1 + \dot{P}_F^E)$.

$$R_{90}^F/R_0 = (1 + \dot{P}_D^E)/(1 + \dot{P}_F^E) = (1 + i_D)/(1 + i_F)$$

Note that in this long-run approach the equality between forward premiums and interest rate differentials does not depend on the effectiveness of covered interest rate arbitrage.

TRANSPORTATION COSTS AND THE LONG RUN

Even in the long run, the assumption that all transaction costs are zero probably is not appropriate. This assumption has been adopted because it helps illustrate a number of theoretical points. The approach corresponds to first learning about the operation of certain laws in physics, such as the law of gravity, while ignoring the effects of friction.

In this section, we consider the effects of one type of transaction cost, transportation costs. Like most other forms of transaction costs, these costs decline with the length of the run. It is cheaper to haul wheat from Buenos Aires to Hamburg when you have six months than it is when you have only six weeks. The transportation costs considered here are the minimum costs relevant for the long run.

Transportation costs range from economically insignificant for items such as diamonds and Rembrandt paintings to prohibitive for commodities such as concrete and haircuts. A continual gradation of transportation costs, however, is difficult to work with analytically. For simplicity, we analyze the effects of transportation costs in two stages. In the first, costs are the same percentage of the price for all goods. Transportation costs behave like an ad valorem tax. In the second step, commodities are divided into two groups. In the first group, transportation costs are treated as though they were zero. In the second, the costs are so high the goods are excluded from international trade. The first group is referred to as *traded goods,* and the second as *nontraded.*

Identical Costs

One effect of transaction costs is to generate a neutral band around PPP within which the market rate of exchange can move. Let the cost of shipping any good between two countries be ε times the domestic price—for example, $\varepsilon \times (\$/q_i)$. With effective arbitrage, the upper limit for the pound price of any commodity q_i is $(\$/q_i)(1 + \varepsilon)(£/\$)$. The pound price cannot exceed the dollar price plus the transaction costs, $\$/q_i(1 + \varepsilon)$, converted into pounds at the going exchange rate, £/\$. The pound price cannot fall below the domestic price minus the transaction costs converted into pounds at the current exchange rate, $\$/q_i(1 - \varepsilon)£/\$$.

Since, by assumption, transaction costs for every commodity are the same percentage of the price, these limits apply to any arbitrary bundle of goods, Q. The pound price of the bundle Q has an upper limit of $(\$/Q)(1 + \varepsilon)(£/\$)$ and a lower limit of $(\$/Q)(1 - \varepsilon)(£/\$)$. This condition can be expressed as follows:

$$£/Q = (\$/Q)(1 \pm \varepsilon)(£/\$)$$

Rewriting this equation slightly yields a modified form of the absolute version of PPP:

$$\$/£ = \frac{\$/Q}{£/Q}(1 \pm \varepsilon)$$

Suppose ε is 5 percent (0.05) and $(\$/Q)/(£/Q)$ is \$2/£1. Then any exchange rate between \$2.10/£1 and \$1.90/£1 is consistent with purchasing power parity.

For the relative version of PPP, transaction costs generate a much wider neutral band. Given transaction costs, the relative version can be written as follows:

$$\frac{(\$/£)_t}{(\$/£)_0} = \frac{[(\$/Q)_t/(£/Q_t)](1 \pm \varepsilon)_t}{[(\$/Q)_0/(£/Q_0)](1 \pm \varepsilon)_0}$$

$$= \frac{[(\$/Q)_t/(\$/Q_0)](1 \pm \varepsilon)_t}{[(£/Q_t)/(£/Q_0)](1 \times \varepsilon)_0} = \left(\frac{P^D}{P^F}\right)\frac{(1 \pm \varepsilon)_t}{(1 \pm \varepsilon)_0}$$

where P^D and P^F are the domestic and foreign price indexes, respectively. In the relative version of the theory, transaction costs of only 5 percent generate a neutral range of *20 percent*. Suppose price levels in both countries remain constant, so that P^D/P^F equals 1.0. In that case, with ε equal to 0.05 (5 percent), the exchange rate can rise by 10 percent and still be consistent with PPP.

$$\frac{(\$/\pounds)_t}{(\$/\pounds)_0} = (1.0)\frac{1.05}{0.95} = 1.10$$

A 10 percent decline in the exchange rate is also consistent with constant price levels.

$$\frac{(\$/\pounds)_t}{(\$/\pounds)_0} = (1.0)\frac{0.95}{1.05} = 0.90$$

This example illustrates an important point. Even moderate transaction costs can introduce a wide neutral range into the relative version of PPP.

Differential Costs

Now let's consider the effects of differential transaction costs. The bundle of goods Q is divided into two groups, traded goods Q_1 with zero transaction costs, and nontraded goods Q_2 with prohibitive costs. Both the absolute and relative versions of PPP hold for price indexes based only on traded goods. The interesting question is, under what conditions does PPP hold for a broadly based price index containing both traded and nontraded goods? The answer for the absolute version is when relative prices between traded and nontraded goods are the same in both countries.

For simplicity, consider only three goods: an import good, TV sets, an export, wheat, and a nontraded good, haircuts. For purposes of exposition, TV sets are labeled TV, wheat is W, and haircuts, H. With zero transaction costs, the dollar price of traded goods is the same in both countries, and PPP holds for bundles restricted to traded goods. In order for the absolute version to hold for more broadly based indexes, relative prices between traded and nontraded goods must be the same at home and abroad. If H/TV and H/W are not the same in both countries, then the dollar price of haircuts is not the same at home, $\$/H$, and abroad, $(\$/\pounds)(\pounds/H)$, and PPP does not hold for a bundle containing both traded and nontraded goods.

The relative version of PPP, however, does not require that relative prices for traded and nontraded goods be equal. Suppose relative prices between traded and nontraded goods are different but remain constant. If the price of TV sets and wheat rises 10 percent at home, then domestic haircuts also rise by 10 percent. In that case, even a broadly based domestic price index rises by 10 percent. If prices for TV sets and wheat remain constant abroad, then in order for the *relative* price of haircuts to remain unchanged, the nominal price of haircuts must also be unchanged. Regardless of relative prices, the foreign price index does not change. With relative prices constant, the change in price levels is unambiguous, and the relative version of PPP holds.

Why does the relative version of PPP fail? It fails primarily because relative prices between traded and nontraded goods change. In order to illustrate this point, consider the following example. Using the same three goods, consider a country that is too small to affect the terms of trade. The wheat price of TV sets is fixed in the world market. Now there is an increased domestic demand for haircuts. If the domestic price level remains constant, the price of haircuts rises, and prices for wheat and TV sets fall. Since the price of traded goods falls, the domestic price of foreign exchange falls even though the broadly based measure of the domestic price level remains constant. Purchasing power parity fails to hold because relative prices between traded and nontraded goods change. We will see this process at work again in the next section and in Chapter 11.

OBJECTIONS

Standard objections to PPP fall into three broad classes. The first raises the problem of appropriate price indexes; the second concerns the choice of a base period; and the third considers the effects of real shocks such as changes in tastes, capital flows, or productivity.

Price Indexes

In the abstract world of pure theory, where we can ignore transaction costs and product differentiation, there is no problem about appropriate price indexes. Any index is appropriate as long as the weights are identical for both countries. When we move from theory to application, price indexes become a serious problem. Theory requires identical weights, but identical weights are difficult to construct when goods differ. The bread we buy in supermarkets hardly compares to the bread of France, and German and American beer are certainly not identical. As a result of product differentiation, in practice we can only approximate the ideal of identical weights.

In addition to identical weights, we would like indexes that are reasonable measures of inflation. Such indexes would have to be broadly based, containing both traded and nontraded goods. Unfortunately, no serious attempt has been made to develop broadly based indexes with comparable weights for different countries. As a result, empirical work has been forced to rely on consumer and wholesale price indexes or GNP deflators. All three of the standard indexes are flawed because they use different weights in different countries. In addition, consumer and wholesale indexes are often based on a narrow range of goods. Consumer indexes usually are dominated by nontraded goods such as food and rent, whereas wholesale indexes primarily reflect the prices of raw materials such as copper and oil, almost all of which have active international markets. These weighting patterns have caused some economists to claim that consumer indexes are inappropriate because they are dominated by nontraded goods, and that wholesale indexes are not appropriate because they are dominated by traded goods.

Base Period

The choice of a base period poses another practical problem. Ideally, a base period should be free of any transitory influences such as dock strikes or political crises. Unfortunately, there is nothing so rare as normalcy. A normal period free of transitory shocks is about as easy to find as the normal or average family with two and one-third children.

Real Shocks

The major objection to PPP, however, is that real shocks, such as changes in capital flows, tastes, or productivity, introduce systematic errors. One way this can happen is when the calculations are based on price indexes with different weights. Real shocks tend to alter relative prices, and even when relative prices are the same in the two countries, introduce measurement errors into calculations of PPP when weights differ. Even if appropriate price indexes are used, when trade does not fully equate relative prices, real shocks can alter price ratios between traded and nontraded goods and introduce errors. In Chapter 11, we will see an example of how real shocks introduce errors into purchasing power parity.

Bela Balassa has suggested a modification of PPP that is based on a systematic pattern of relative prices between traded and nontraded goods. The essence of Balassa's argument is that productivity systematically influences relative prices for traded and nontraded goods and therefore introduces a predictable bias into purchasing power parity.

Balassa's Modification

Balassa argues that most nontraded goods, particularly services, are characterized by only small international differences in production techniques and labor requirements. Barbers are an excellent example. Throughout the world, barbers rely primarily on a chair, a pair of scissors, and a comb. About the only difference is that in developed countries the chair is adjustable and the clippers electric. Competition, however, tends to equate wages paid to barbers and others employed in the nontraded sector with wages paid to workers in the sector producing traded goods, where productivity differentials between countries can be substantial.

If this argument is correct, we would expect price ratios of traded and nontraded goods to be related systematically to differences in productivity and per capita real income. Consider a simple example with TV sets and haircuts between, say, the United States and Mexico. In both countries a barber might, on average, cut 20 heads of hair a day. In the United States it takes 4 work-days to produce a TV set, and in Mexico 8 work-days. The higher productivity in the United States has two effects. It makes per capita real income higher in the United States and makes haircuts relatively expensive. One TV set buys 160 haircuts in Mexico, but only 80 haircuts in the United States.

This differential in relative prices introduces a predictable error into PPP. Assume the price of a TV set in Mexico and the United States is 40,000 pesos and 400 dollars, respectively. Given the prices for TVs, the price of haircuts must be $5 ($400/80) in the United States and P250 (P40,000/160) in Mexico. If we calculate PPP using a bundle containing only traded goods, such as two TV sets, the theory predicts that one peso costs one cent, which is correct.

$$\frac{\$0.01}{P1.00} = \frac{2.0TV \times (\$400/TV)}{2.0TV \times (P40,000/TV)} = \frac{\$800}{P80,000}$$

Now let's add nontraded goods to the bundle, say 80 haircuts, and reduce the TVs to 1. This change keeps the dollar price of the bundle constant, but it lowers the peso price because haircuts are relatively cheap in Mexico. At one cent per peso, a Mexican TV costs $400 but a Mexican haircut costs only $2.50. Adding haircuts to the bundle therefore lowers our measure of the Mexican price level relative to the U.S. price level.

$$\frac{\$0.0133}{P1.00} = \frac{1.0TV \times (\$400/TV) + 80.0 \text{ haircuts } (\$5.00/\text{haircut})}{1.0TV \times (P40,000/TV) + 80.0 \text{ haircuts } (P2.50/\text{haircut})}$$
$$= \frac{\$800}{P60,000}$$

In this example, replacing traded with nontraded goods lowers our measure of the Mexican price level by about 25 percent. As a result, PPP overpredicts the dollar price of the peso. In general, according to this argument, the greater the productivity differential and the more heavily weighted nontraded goods, the more purchasing power parity overpredicts the price of the currency of the less developed country.

When this reasoning is applied to the relative version of PPP, it implies that *changes* in relative levels of per capita real income introduce systematic errors into predicted changes in exchange rates. For example, if productivity and per capita real income rise faster in the United States than Mexico, PPP overpredicts the rise in the dollar price of the peso.

EVALUATION OF PPP

There is a strong tendency to view a theory as either right or wrong. The philosophy of science, however, suggests an approach that might be summarized as follows: All theories are wrong, but some are less wrong than others. The great advantage of this approach is that it forces us to evaluate a theory not against some ideal of perfection, but against available alternative explanations.

Given that perspective, our choice must be purchasing power parity. The theory has not always worked very well, but no other explanation has been as successful in predicting exchange rates under many different conditions and for a wide variety of countries. We must, however, recognize that PPP wins largely by default. With the possible exception of the modification suggested by Balassa, which has not yet been tested for a wide variety of countries and time periods, there are no serious alternatives to PPP as an explanation of the long-run determination of exchange rates.

Even after we accept a theory, there is the question of how much confidence we should have in it. Table 6.1 gives some insight into the accuracy of purchasing power parity. It shows what are commonly called "real exchange rates" between the United States and Canada, Japan, and the United Kingdom for the early 1920s. Real exchange rates are simply actual exchange rates divided by the rates implied by purchasing power parity. For example, suppose the actual rate between the United States and the United Kingdom is $/£. The rate predicted by purchasing power parity is $(P_{US}/P_{UK})(\$/£)_0$, where P_{US} and P_{UK} are U.S. and U.K. price indexes and $(\$/£)_0$ is the exchange rate in the base period. In this case, the following ratio gives the real exchange rate:

$$(\$/£)/[(P_{US}/P_{UK})(\$/£)_0]$$

The real exchange rate is a measure of the predictive error. When the ratio is unity, actual and predicted exchange rates are identical. If the ratio is 1.05, then the actual rate is 5 percent above the predicted rate.

The reason we use data from the early 1920s, when rates were flexible, is that then central banks did not intervene in foreign exchange markets and governments did not impose trade or capital controls in order to influence exchange rates. Table 6.1 uses wholesale price indexes with 1913 as the base. Since all the countries were on a gold standard in 1913, mint par is the base period exchange rate. (For a definition of mint par, see Chapter 7.)

TABLE 6.1   Real Exchange Rates: Wholesale Indexes and 1913 Mint Par

YEAR AND MONTH	ENGLAND	CANADA	JAPAN	AVERAGE
1920				
1	0.93	0.88	1.22	1.01
2	0.90	0.87	1.21	0.99
3	1.00	0.89	1.18	1.02
4	1.01	0.91	1.02	0.98
5	1.00	0.93	0.94	0.95
6	1.05	0.93	0.88	0.95
7	1.02	0.95	0.90	0.96
8	1.00	0.95	0.90	0.95
9	0.98	0.95	0.88	0.94
10	0.99	0.99	0.95	0.98
11	1.01	1.01	1.02	1.01
12	1.04	1.00	1.02	1.02
1921				
1	1.12	1.04	1.02	1.06
2	1.15	1.06	1.06	1.09
3	1.13	1.06	1.07	1.09
4	1.14	1.08	1.13	1.12
5	1.13	1.04	1.16	1.11
6	1.08	1.03	1.17	1.09
7	1.01	0.99	1.18	1.06
8	1.00	1.02	1.18	1.07
9	1.02	0.97	1.27	1.09
10	1.03	0.94	1.33	1.10
11	1.00	0.91	1.31	1.07
12	1.03	0.95	1.31	1.10
1922				
1	1.04	0.96	1.29	1.10
2	1.03	0.98	1.20	1.07
3	1.03	0.99	1.18	1.07
4	1.02	1.00	1.15	1.06
5	0.99	0.96	1.10	1.02
6	0.96	0.94	1.11	1.00
7	0.95	0.92	1.13	1.00
8	0.93	0.90	1.08	0.97
9	0.92	0.88	1.05	0.95
10	0.90	0.88	1.02	0.93
11	0.93	0.90	1.02	0.95
12	0.96	0.89	1.03	0.96
1923				
1	0.95	0.88	1.04	0.96
2	0.98	0.90	1.07	0.98
3	0.99	0.90	1.06	0.98
4	0.98	0.90	1.06	0.98
5	0.99	0.91	1.10	1.00
6	0.99	0.91	1.12	1.01
7	1.00	0.92	1.13	1.02
8	0.97	0.92	1.10	1.00
9	0.94	0.89	1.14	0.99
10	0.95	0.89	1.18	1.01
11	0.94	0.87	1.18	1.00
12	0.97	0.86	1.19	1.01
1924				
1	0.96	0.87	1.13	0.99
2	0.98	0.88	1.12	0.99
3	0.99	0.89	1.08	0.99
4	1.02	0.88	1.04	0.98
5	1.02	0.90	1.03	0.98
6	1.00	0.93	1.01	0.98
7	1.00	0.94	1.02	0.99
8	1.01	0.94	1.03	0.99
9	1.01	0.94	1.03	0.99
10	1.01	0.93	1.03	0.98
11	1.04	0.92	1.01	0.99
12	1.04	0.90	0.98	0.97

For some months, predictive errors for individual countries are quite large. They occasionally exceed 30 percent for Japan. Errors for Canada and the United Kingdom are as large as 12 and 13 percent. Large deviations, however, appear to be temporary. In most cases, the predictive error shrinks to 4 or 5 percent within a few months. Canada shows some tendency for PPP to systematically overpredict the exchange rate, but for the United Kingdom and Japan, the real exchange rate appears to be centered around unity. The systematic overprediction for Canada suggests an inappropriate base period.

The average predictive error for the three countries is also shown in Table 6.1. The largest average error is 10 percent. For the last year shown in Table 6.1, 1924, the monthly average error is only 1 or 2 percent. That is not a bad performance; not many theories in economics can predict that accurately over such a long period of time.

SUMMARY

Purchasing power parity provides a theory of the long-run determination of exchange rates. In the relative version of PPP, which is the most commonly used, the theory implies that changes in exchange rates depend primarily on relative changes in the purchasing power of domestic and foreign money. A major assumption of PPP is that the price mechanism effectively allocates resources. As a result, adjustment to real shocks takes place primarily through changes in relative prices and the composition of production, rather than through changes in exchange rates.

When we combine purchasing power parity with Fisherian capital theory, we obtain a long-run explanation for the equality between forward premiums and interest rate differentials. According to this explanation, the two tend to be equal because both reflect differences in expected rates of inflation.

In an ideal world with zero information and transaction costs, purchasing power parity holds exactly. In our world, such costs introduce errors into PPP. They introduce a margin of error into the predictions of PPP similar to the gold points discussed in Chapter 7. In addition, these costs generate errors because they allow price ratios between traded and non-traded goods for different countries to diverge. But in spite of its imperfections, purchasing power parity is the best available theory of the long-run determination of exchange rates.

QUESTIONS FOR REVIEW

1. Discuss the theoretical foundations of purchasing power parity.
2. Distinguish between the absolute and relative version of PPP.

3. What are the basic assumptions underlying the theory of purchasing power parity?

4. What are some of the problems involved in choosing an appropriate price index?

5. Look up the foreign exchange market in your local newspaper. Find the three exchange rates that have changed the most and the least over the last year. Compare the change in relative price levels vis-à-vis the United States for the two groups of countries.

6. How do real shocks such as changes in tastes, technology, capital flows or income introduce errors into PPP?

7. Using price indexes with different weights introduces a form of measurement error into PPP. Explain.

8. Chapter 5 described one mechanism that worked toward equating forward premiums and interest rate differentials. This chapter has developed another. Compare and contrast the two mechanisms.

9. Compare and contrast the response of exchange rates to an exogenous increase in imports developed in this chapter and the last chapter.

10. Compare and contrast the response of exchange rates to a change in capital flows developed in this chapter and the last chapter.

11. Suppose Chapter 5 contains a reasonable explanation for the determination of exchange rates in the short run and this chapter a reasonable theory for the long-run determination. Describe the dynamic reactions of the exchange rate to the two exogenous shocks analyzed in the two chapters. How would "efficient" or "rational" expectations influence this dynamic behavior?

ADDITIONAL READINGS

BALASSA, BELA. "The Purchasing-Power Parity Doctrine: A Reappraisal." *Journal of Political Economy* (December 1964).

FRENKEL, JACOB A. "The Collapse of Purchasing Power Parities during the 1970's." *European Economic Review* (May 1981).

GAILLIOT, HENRY J. "Purchasing Power Parity as an Explanation of Long-Term Changes in Exchange Rates." *Journal of Money, Credit and Banking* (August 1970).

OFFICER, LAWRENCE H. "The Purchasing-Power-Parity Theory of Exchange Rates: A Review Article." International Monetary Fund *Staff Papers* (March 1976).

PIPPENGER, JOHN. "Purchasing Power Parity: An Analysis of Predictive Error." *Canadian Journal of Economics* (May 1982).

ROLL, RICHARD. "Violations of Purchasing Power Parity and Their Implications for Efficient International Commodity Markets." In *International Finance and Trade*, Vol. 1. M. Sarnat and G. P. Szegö (eds.) (Cambridge, Mass.: Ballinger, 1979).

"A Symposium on Purchasing Power Parity." *Journal of International Economics* (May 1978).

7

ALTERNATIVE INTERNATIONAL MONETARY SYSTEMS

Foreign exchange markets can operate within a variety of institutional frameworks. In this chapter we review some of the most common international monetary systems. First we look at flexible rates and the current managed float; then we examine a gold standard. The gold standard is a steppingstone to our analysis of the operation and demise of pegged exchange rates.

FLEXIBLE EXCHANGE RATES

No Intervention

Under freely flexible exchange rates, there is no direct official intervention. Neither central banks nor treasuries buy or sell foreign exchange in order to influence rates. Exchange rates are determined entirely by the market forces considered in the last two chapters.

For the first few years just after World War I, most major currencies operated under a system of freely fluctuating exchange rates. Today, exchange rates between the United States and most of its major trading partners are ultimately determined by market forces, but central banks frequently intervene to reduce what they perceive to be unwarranted short-run fluctuations. This arrangement is usually referred to as a *managed* or *dirty float*.

Managed Float

Under a managed or dirty float, central banks do not try to defend some level of exchange rates. Instead, they attempt to moderate what they perceive to be unwarranted short-run fluctuations. Although intervention is based on many factors, we can describe the basic thrust and some of the effects of intervention with a rather simple model.

Under a managed or dirty float, central banks tend to "lean against the wind." That is, they sell as prices rise and buy as prices fall. To get an intuitive feel for the effect of leaning against the wind, consider Figure 7.1. The initial private excess demand schedule is the solid line *SD*. There is no intervention, and the exchange rate is $1.50/£1. Now the excess demand schedule rises to the broken line labeled *S'D'*. If the authorities do not intervene, the rate rises to $1.60/£1.

Suppose, however, the central bank leans against the wind. As the rate increases, it sells *OM* pounds that day and the rate rises to only $1.55/£1. If there is no intervention the next day, the rate rises another nickel to $1.60/£1. However, as the rate rises, the central bank sells some more pounds, say *ON*, and the rate rises to $1.58/£1. If the excess demand schedule stays at *S'D'* and the central bank continues to intervene, the exchange rate rises and eventually reaches $1.60/£1. Suppose, however, that after one day the excess demand schedule returns to *SD*. In that case, the rate rises and falls 10 cents without intervention, but intervention limits the change to only 5 cents.

This example illustrates how leaning against the wind influences exchange rates. It converts a single large, permanent change in exchange rates into a series of smaller changes, but does not prevent the rate from being determined ultimately by market forces. Intervention also reduces transient or temporary fluctuations in exchange rates.

Why do central banks intervene? There are a variety of reasons, but

FIGURE 7.1
Leaning against the wind.

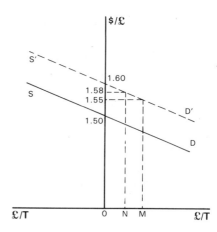

the most important probably is that politicians and central bankers tend to distrust the price mechanism in general and speculation in particular. As we noted in Chapter 5, there is a widespread belief that speculation in foreign exchange markets is destabilizing, that it tends to cause prices to over-respond to new information. By leaning against the wind, central banks can offset some or all of the overresponse. Another motivation for intervention is the belief that reducing short-run fluctuations in exchange rates promotes international trade and capital flows.

If one believes speculation is destabilizing or that fluctuations in exchange rates discourage international trade and capital flows, then leaning against the wind is reasonable behavior for a central bank. But what if expectations are reliably anticipatory or even rational? In that case, intervention causes the market to underrespond to new information. The information conveyed by exchange rates becomes distorted, and intervention tends to disrupt international commodity and capital markets.

Although there is disagreement about the role of speculation under flexible rates, there is a general consensus that speculation contributed to the smooth operation of the gold standard. In the next section, we analyze an idealized gold standard between the United States and Great Britain.

GOLD STANDARD

Gold standards come in a variety of sizes and shapes. They range from a full-bodied gold standard to a gold exchange standard. Under a full-bodied gold standard, money is gold coin or banknotes and deposits backed 100 percent by gold. Under a gold exchange standard, there is a fractional reserve monetary system, and foreign currencies convertible into gold, rather than gold itself, are used as reserves for the banking system.

In spite of institutional variations, all effective gold standards share three basic characteristics. (1) There must be an official domestic price for gold, and the central bank or treasury must buy and sell gold on demand at the official price. (2) The government cannot restrict the importation or exportation of gold. (3) Most important of all, the domestic money stock must be linked to gold reserves. When the monetary gold stock decreases, the stock of money must decrease.

Under a gold exchange standard, foreign currencies convertible into gold replace gold. This substitution does not alter the basic nature of the adjustment process that is the essential feature of a gold standard. The adjustment process does not depend on gold. As we will see, it operates within the United States without any reference to gold.

To illustrate the operation of a gold standard, we assume that both the United States and Great Britain have a central bank and monetary systems with fractional reserves. The official price of gold for Great Britain is £100 per ounce and for the United States, it is $200 per ounce.

Mint Par

The official prices for gold establish a mint par rate of exchange between the two currencies. If 1 ounce of gold buys either 100 pounds or 200 dollars, then in the absence of transaction costs, £100 must trade for $200 and the exchange rate must be $2/£1. This exchange rate, which is determined by the gold content of the two currencies, is called *mint par*.

Gold Points

Transaction costs, however, are not zero, so market rates can deviate from mint par. How far they can deviate depends on the costs associated with shipping gold between countries. Suppose it costs $2 to ship 1 ounce of gold from New York to London. The upper limit for the spot exchange rate is $2.02/£1 and the lower limit $1.98/£1. No one pays over $2.02/£1 because it is possible to use $200 to buy 1 ounce of gold from the Fed, ship the gold to London at a cost of $2, and sell it to the Bank of England for £100. The total cost is $202, or $2.02 per pound sterling.

A similar process sets the lower limit at $1.98/£1. Anyone with pounds to sell is reluctant to accept less than $1.98 per pound. One hundred pounds buys 1 ounce of gold in London. In New York, the gold is worth $200. After paying the $2 it costs to ship the gold to New York, the return from selling the pounds is $198, or $1.98/£1. The higher price, $2.02/£1, is referred to as the *upper gold point* and the lower price, $1.98/£1, is the *lower gold point*.

The Price-Specie-Flow Mechanism

In the late 1700s David Hume, the philosopher and economist, wrote a few paragraphs that revolutionized our ideas about international finance. The language is a bit archaic—"specie" for example, means precious metals, especially gold—but the argument is still lucid.

> Suppose four-fifths of all the money in Great Britain to be annihilated in one night, and the nation reduced to the same condition, with regard to specie, as in the reigns of the Harrys and Edwards, what would be the consequence? Must not the price of all labour and commodities sink in proportion, and everything be sold as cheap as they were in those ages? What nation could then dispute with us in any foreign market, or pretend to navigate or to sell manufactures at the same price, which to us would afford sufficient profit? In how little time, therefore, must this bring back the money which we had lost, and raise us to the level of all the neighbouring nations? Where, after we have arrived, we immediately lose the advantage of the cheapness of labour and commodities; and the farther flowing in of money is stopped by our fulness and repletion.

Again, suppose, that all the money of Great Britain were multiplied fivefold in a night, must not the contrary effect follow? Must not all labour and commodities rise to such an exorbitant height, that no neighbouring nations could afford to buy from us; while their commodities, on the other hand, became comparatively so cheap, that, in spite of all the laws which could be formed, they would be run in upon us, and our money flow out; till we fall to a level with foreigners, and lose that great superiority of riches, which had laid us under such disadvantages?

The process Hume describes is known as the price-specie-flow mechanism. When we translate his analysis into the language of contemporary economics, the price-specie-flow mechanism rests on four basic propositions. First, there is a stable supply function for money that depends on the stock of monetary gold. Second, there is a stable demand for real money balances that depends on real income. Third, at least for purely monetary shocks, purchasing power parity holds. Fourth, in the long run, there is full employment.

Model   These propositions can be formalized as follows. In both countries the stock of money, M, depends on a reasonably stable money multiplier, m, and the monetary base, B.

$$M = mB$$

Although the monetary multiplier m depends on legal reserve ratios, interest rates, and portfolio decisions by households and commercial banks, changes in the multiplier do not entirely offset changes in the monetary base. The monetary base may contain elements other than gold, but the gold stock must dominate movements in the base and stock of money.

In both countries the demand for real money balances, M/P, depends on real income, y, and nominal interest rates, i, where P is an appropriate domestic price index.

$$M/P = f(y,i)$$

The demand for real balances is directly related to real income and inversely related to interest rates. There may be less than full employment in the short run, but in the long run there is full employment, and a country's endowments and labor force determine the level of real income. In Hume's day international capital markets were not well developed, and he justifiably ignored the effects of capital flows and interest rates. Initially we do the same.

The final idea is purchasing power parity:

$$(\$/£)_t/(\$/£)_0 = \frac{P_{US}'}{P_{UK}'}$$

For PPP, the price indexes for the United States and United Kingdom, P_{US}' and P_{UK}', must have the same weights. The U.S. and U.K. price indexes used to deflate nominal money balances to obtain real balances normally do not have the same weights. These weights depend on production and consumption patterns in the two countries, and there is no reason to presume that these are the same.

To build an internally consistent model with these two kinds of price indexes, we would have to specify how alterations in relative prices alter the relationship between the indexes appropriate for purchasing power parity and the domestic consumer price indexes or GNP deflators used to deflate nominal money balances. In addition, we would need to know how every shock altered relative prices, which would require a specification of the entire microeconomic substructure. Such a project is far beyond our limited objectives. We therefore follow the usual procedure of ignoring the complications generated by different price indexes and assume that the indexes used to deflate money correspond to those used for purchasing power parity.

This assumption buys us a lot in terms of simplicity, and it does not distort the basic story of how a gold standard operates. Of course we pay a price for simplicity, and it is that our results are deceptively precise. For example, given our assumption and ignoring the effects of gold points, the model implies that from one equilibrium to another, price indexes for both countries move exactly proportionately. Even under ideal conditions, where the price indexes used for PPP move exactly proportionately, there is no reason to believe that domestic consumer indexes, GNP deflators, or other welfare measures of inflation in the two countries should move in lock step.

The model we have just developed describes equilibrium states. It does not contain the equations of motion that describe how the system gets from one equilibrium to another. In the next section we examine the adjustment process.

Operation

The operation of the price-specie-flow mechanism is illustrated in Figures 7.2(a) and (b). In both, the upper and lower gold points are, respectively, $2.02/£1 and $1.98/£1. In Figure 7.2(a), the initial demand and supply schedules intersect within the upper and lower gold points, and there are no gold flows. For now we ignore capital flows, so that the demand and supply schedules for pounds are based entirely on commodities.

Commodities   Suppose, like Hume, we wave our magic wand and part of the monetary gold stock in Great Britain disappears. The decline in the British gold stock reduces the British monetary base and, according to our money supply equation, the stock of money in the United Kingdom falls. As a result, real money balances decline. Given the initial level of real income and interest rates, there is an excess demand for money. The price of

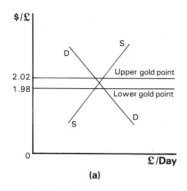
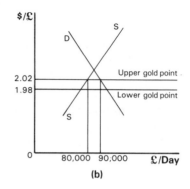

FIGURE 7.2   The price-specie-flow mechanism.

money rises; that is, the price level falls. Output also may fall in the short run. Given PPP, the fall in the British price level pushes the intersection of private demand and supply for pounds upward, as shown in Figure 7.2(b).

In the absence of gold flows, the exchange rate would rise to, say, $2.05/£1, where the value of British exports of goods and services equals the value of imports. Gold flows, however, prevent the exchange rate from rising above the upper gold point at $2.02/£1. In Figure 7.2(b), Americans buy £90,000 worth of goods and services per day from Great Britain, but they sell only £80,000. In the foreign exchange market, British residents supply £80,000 per day and Americans demand £90,000. The gap of £10,000 per day is filled by individuals who take $20,000 per day to the Fed and buy 100 ounces of gold. They ship the gold to London and sell it to the Bank of England for £10,000. The United States imports British goods and services worth £90,000 per day. The imports are paid for by exporting goods and services worth £80,000 and by transferring from the Federal Reserve to the Bank of England 100 ounces of gold per day worth £10,000.

The increase in the British gold stock increases the British money supply and reduces the downward pressure on British prices. The reduction in the monetary base for the United States reduces the stock of money in the United States, and the American price level starts to chase the British price level downward. As long as the British price level has fallen by more than the American, the intersection of demand and supply for pounds tends to be above the upper support point, and gold flows from the United States to the United Kingdom. The movement of gold moderates the decline in British prices and puts downward pressure on prices in the United States. This process continues until price levels in both countries have fallen proportionately and, according to PPP, the demand and supply schedules intersect within the upper and lower support points, as shown in Figure 7.2(a). At that point, equilibrium is reestablished and the gold flow stops.

In this example, the reduction in the British stock of gold reduces the world price level. British and American prices fall. Output in both countries also may fall in the short run, but in the new equilibrium there is full employment. The reason for the price decline is that we implicitly assumed the initial shock reduced the world stock of monetary gold. If we had transferred the British gold to the United States, the story would be a little different. As an exercise, work that one out for yourself.

Hume's price-specie-flow mechanism works through relative price levels and the current account. It is primarily a long-run adjustment mechanism and ignores capital flows, which were unimportant when Hume wrote in the late 1700s. During the 1800s, international capital markets developed rapidly and became an important factor in the market for foreign exchange. This development provided a short-run adjustment mechanism through short-term capital flows.

Reinforcing capital flows   Once again we start with the demand and supply schedules intersecting between the upper and lower gold points, as shown in Figure 7.2(a). Again part of the gold stock in Great Britain disappears, and the stock of money and bank credit contracts. This time, however, we recognize that the reduction in loans and investments by commercial banks in the United Kingdom puts temporary upward pressure on short-term interest rates in London. The rise in short-term rates makes British short-term assets relatively attractive to both British and American residents, and the United Kingdom tends to develop a surplus in the short-term capital account. In the short run, there is an increased demand for pound sterling by Americans buying British assets and a reduced supply of pounds as U.K. residents switch from American to British assets. The intersection of the demand and supply schedules for pounds shifts upward.

When the intersection rises above the upper support point, gold starts to flow from the United States to the United Kingdom, and the adjustment process described earlier begins to work. The initial decline in the stock of money and prices in the United Kingdom is moderated by gold movements induced by capital flows, which immediately transfer part of the downward pressure on prices to the United States. We do not have to wait for changes in relative price levels to influence commodity imports and exports. Because of their relatively low information and transaction costs, financial markets tend to respond almost instantaneously to upward pressure on British interest rates.

In this example, short-term capital flows reinforce trade flows and speed up the adjustment process. These same capital flows, however, can act as shock absorbers and reduce gold flows associated with temporary shifts in the demand for or supply of foreign exchange.

Offsetting capital flows   Consider a different kind of shock, a shift in preferences by Americans away from domestic goods toward imports. According to the analysis developed in Chapter 5, this shock increases the demand for pounds in the short run, and the dollar price of the pound tends to rise. (As we will see in the next chapter, output also may fall.) In the absence of capital flows, the simple price-specie-flow mechanism implies that in the short run gold flows from the United States to the United Kingdom in order to prevent a rise in the exchange rate. According to Chapter 6, this gold eventually must flow back to the United States in order to prevent a permanent change in relative price levels. Short-term capital flows tend to moderate these gold flows.

Let's go back to Figure 7.2(a) and (b). Once again, the initial condition is described by Figure 7.2(a). Now Figure 7.2(b) shows the demand and supply schedules for pounds in the short run after the increased demand for imports. In the absence of capital flows, the import surplus for the United States must be financed by an export of gold to the United Kingdom. The movement of gold, however, tends to reduce money and bank credit in the United States and increase them in the United Kingdom. As a result, short-term interest rates tend to rise in New York relative to London, and the United States develops a surplus on short-term capital account. Suppose the net export of short-term securities by the United States rises to £5,000. In that case, the trade deficit for the United States of £10,000 is financed by exporting £5,000 worth of gold and £5,000 worth of short-term assets. The short-term capital flow acts as a substitute for the temporary gold flow. Less gold initially flows into Great Britain, and so less returns later to the United States.

The Bank of England

So far we have treated central banks as responding passively to gold flows. That was not always the case. In the heyday of the gold standard from about 1876 until World War I, several central banks took actions that sometimes reinforced and at other times inhibited the adjustment mechanism. In this section we discuss how the Bank of England tried to influence capital flows around the turn of the century. By convention, the Bank of England is commonly referred to simply as "the Bank."

Before World War I, London was the primary international financial center, and pound sterling was the most important currency in foreign exchange markets. In addition, London was the primary market for world trade in gold. This position placed Great Britain and the Bank of England at the center of the operation of the gold standard.

The problem was that the British banking system operated on a very slim gold reserve. Most commercial banks held little or no gold beyond the coins needed for day-to-day operations. They held their liquid reserves primarily in the form of overnight loans in the London money market and deposits at the Bank of England. Under the Bank Charter act of 1844, beyond a limited fiduciary issue, which was backed up by government securities, notes issued by the Bank of England were covered 100 percent by gold. But there was no legal requirement for a gold reserve against deposits at the Bank of England.

As custodian for the British gold reserve, the Bank of England at times attempted to reduce gold flows, particularly gold losses, by influencing short-term rates in London relative to short-term rates in other financial centers. Suppose the Bank started to lose gold or was afraid it might do so. It would raise the discount rate and other rates at which it lent funds in London. It might even borrow short-term funds or sell government securities to push up British interest rates. The rise in short-term rates in London generated a short-term capital inflow that helped reduce the loss of gold. How effective this tactic was is open to question, but at the time it was thought to be very effective. One banker claimed that a 7 percent Bank rate would bring gold from Antarctica.

Updated Hume   If Hume were alive today, he undoubtedly would update his price-specie-flow story. It might run something like this. Suppose four-fifths of all the monetary gold in England should disappear over night. The Bank of England must contract the supply of money and bank credit. Interest rates rise, output declines, and prices start to fall. The rise in interest rates in London attracts short-term investments, and gold moves toward London. As lower British prices encourage U.K. exports and discourage imports, the country also develops a surplus on trade account, which attracts even more gold. As gold flows in, upward pressure on British interest rates disappears. British prices stop falling and start to rise toward those in the rest of the world. Rising prices, falling interest rates, and a trade surplus work toward eliminating any unemployment. The gold inflow eventually restores the original relationship between relative price levels and interest rates, and the gold flow stops.

Intranational Adjustment

The gold standard adjustment mechanism is usually applied to countries, but the same mechanism works within a country. Following Hume, suppose part of the money stock in California disappeared overnight. Prices, and in the short run probably output, decline, and short-term interest rates rise. Goods produced in California become cheap, and sales to other states rise. Purchases by Californians from other states decline. The pressure on short-term interest rates in California leads to a net sale of short-term securities to residents in other states. As a result, California becomes a net exporter of goods, services, and securities.

In order to see how this net outflow of goods, services, and securities is financed, let's consider the sale of a $1,000 Treasury bill to a resident of New

York City. The person buying the Treasury bill writes a check for $1,000 and gives it to the Californian selling the T-bill. The Californian deposits the check in a bank in Los Angeles. That bank credits his or her account and collects the check by sending it to the Federal Reserve Bank in San Francisco. From there, the check is shipped to the Federal Reserve Bank in New York, where it is deducted from the account at the Fed of the bank on which the check is written. The Fed forwards the check to the bank on which it is written, and the $1,000 is deducted from the account of the individual who bought the Treasury bill. The end result is that reserves held by commercial banks in New York move to California in exactly the same way that gold moves from the United States to the United Kingdom when part of the British gold stock disappears.

This shift in bank reserves sets in motion an adjustment mechanism that is identical to the price-specie-flow mechanism. The adjustment mechanism under a gold standard works so that price levels in different countries move together. The same process, but with reserve flows substituting for gold flows, is what keeps price levels moving together in different parts of the same country. Indeed, lower transaction costs, absence of trade and capital controls, and greater labor mobility make the analysis more relevant for adjustment between regions within a country than between countries.

Balance-of-Payments Deficits

Under a gold standard, deficits in the balance of payments usually were measured by putting flows of monetary gold and short-term capital below the line and all other transactions above the line. The relevant problem for this approach is whether or not the international monetary system is in equilibrium. If there is a deficit or surplus with this measure, then the existing set of relative price levels and/or pattern of trade and capital flows must change.

The adjustment process we have just reviewed is part of the theory underlying the measure. There also is the belief that it is possible and proper to finance current account balances with long-term capital flows. The stock of long-term capital is seen as stable, large, and growing. However, it is not appropriate to finance a balance on combined current and long-term capital accounts with a short-term capital flow. The supply of internationally mobile short-term capital is viewed as limited and not very dependable. As a result, net flows of both monetary gold and short-term capital imply a state of the world that cannot persist.

International Liquidity

Before we go on to pegged exchange rates, we need to consider how a gold standard solves the problem of growth in international reserves as the world economy expands. The reason this is important is that inadequate growth in international gold reserves and excessive growth in dollar reserves were important factors in the collapse of pegged exchange rates in the early 1970s.

Assume an initial equilibrium with a given gold stock, price levels, and real incomes. Now consider what happens if real income doubles in both the United States and United Kingdom. Desired real money balances go up in both countries. If there are no open market purchases by central banks or other actions to increase the money supply and no change in the stock of gold, price levels must fall. If necessary, gold flows ensure that price levels fall proportionately in the two countries.

The increase in world real income increases world trade in real terms and tends to increase the size of balance-of-payment deficits and surpluses that must be financed by gold flows. The decline in the price level, however, increases the real value of gold and moderates the increase in the nominal value of deficits and surpluses generated by the larger volume of trade in real terms. In addition, the gold standard has a built-in mechanism for long-run price stability. As the price level declines, the cost of mining gold declines and gold production becomes more profitable. New mines open, and production in old mines expands. As the stock of monetary gold expands, price levels rise, and the profitability and rate of gold production move back toward what they were originally. As a result, in both the long run and the short run the real value of the stock of monetary gold grows with real income and trade.

Rejection of Fixed and Flexible Rates

If the gold standard worked so well, why wasn't it reestablished after World War II? The primary reason was a shift in priorities. Under an effective gold standard, the balance of payments dominates domestic monetary policy. Faced with rising unemployment and a persistent loss of gold, a country on an effective gold standard must reduce the money supply even if that means more unemployment. Even before World War I, a number of countries altered mint par or temporarily suspended the gold standard when faced with a domestic crisis. After the massive unemployment of the Great Depression in the 1930s, economists, businesspeople, and politicians all recognized that internal objectives of full employment and price stability were more important than fixed exchange rates and balance-of-payments equilibrium.

If that was the case, then why not adopt flexible exchange rates after World War II? Flexible rates were not popular for several reasons. One was that large variations in exchange rates when they were freely flexible in the early 1920s convinced most economists, businesspeople, and politicians that speculation under flexible rates was destabilizing. In addition, the era of the gold standard from about 1876 to World War I was one of rapid growth in real income, trade, and international investment. The stable exchange rates provided by the gold standard were widely believed to be an important factor in promoting prosperity through worldwide economic integration.

Because of the general dissatisfaction with both fixed and flexible exchange rates, during World War II representatives of the Allies developed plans for a new international monetary system based on pegged but adjustable exchange rates. It was designed to promote trade and foreign investment through stable exchange rates, but did not require countries to subordinate internal objectives of full employment and price stability to the balance of payments. The system was based on the Articles of Agreement of the International Monetary Fund. On paper it was an ingenious plan, and it worked reasonably well for about 20 years. Then it fell apart. Chapter 8 reviews the establishment and evolution of the International Monetary Fund. In the next section, we examine the operation and demise of pegged exchange rates.

THE ADJUSTABLE PEG

An *adjustable peg* is an attempt to get the benefits of a gold standard without paying the price. As with the gold standard, exchange rates are kept within a narrow band around a par or official exchange rate. Unlike under the gold standard, monetary policy under an adjustable peg is dominated by internal objectives such as price stability and full employment. The basic philosophy underlying a system of pegged exchange rates is that temporary surpluses or deficits in the balance of payments should be financed by central banks, but a prolonged or "fundamental disequilibrium" should be eliminated by changing the par or official exchange rate.

Our first job is to understand the mechanics of pegged exchange rates. Then we can analyze the adjustment mechanism and see why the system failed. A system of pegged exchange rates can vary in a number of institutional details. Our discussion is based on the system that operated from the late 1950s through the early 1970s, but it ignores complications introduced by the secondary reserve requirements for commercial banks that existed in some countries.

Official Rates

Under the adjustable peg, other countries set an official or par exchange rate between their currency and the U.S. dollar. This implicitly established a par value for each currency in terms of every other currency through the logic of consistent cross rates (discussed in Chapter 5). The United States, in turn, adopted an "official" price for gold. Except for purchases of newly mined gold, monetary gold was not bought from or sold to individuals, only to official institutions such as foreign central banks.

Until the summer of 1971, the Federal Reserve, acting for the U.S. Treasury, bought and sold gold at $35 per ounce. As part of the agreements reached between the major industrial countries at the Smithsonian Meetings in December 1971, the official price of gold was raised to $38 an ounce. Gold, however, was no longer bought and sold freely at that price. About three months before the effective collapse of pegged rates in March 1973, the price of gold was raised to $42.20 an ounce.

Intervention

Foreign central banks were obligated to keep the dollar price of their currencies within a narrow band around the official rate. Before December 1971, the band was plus or minus 1 percent of the official rate. Later it was plus or minus 2.25 percent.

The following example illustrates how intervention by central banks keeps exchange rates within a narrow band around the par or official rate. Suppose the official rate for pound sterling is $2/£1. With a range of plus or minus 1 percent, the upper limit is $2.02/£1 and the lower limit is $1.98/£1. These are the upper and lower support points shown in Figure 7.3.

If private demand and supply schedules for pounds intersect between these support points, the Bank of England can sit on its hands. Suppose, however, an expansionary monetary policy in the United States drives the intersection above the upper support point, as shown by *DD* and *SS* in Figure 7.3. The Bank of England prevents the rate from rising above $2.02/£1 by selling pounds and buying dollars. Under the conditions described in Figure 7.3, the Bank of England sells 1 million pounds sterling per week. In doing so, the Bank buys $2,020,000. When the demand and supply schedules intersect below the lower support point, the Bank of England buys enough pounds (sells enough dollars) to keep the rate from falling below the lower

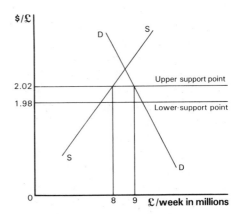

FIGURE 7.3
Mechanics of pegged exchange rates: selling pound sterling.

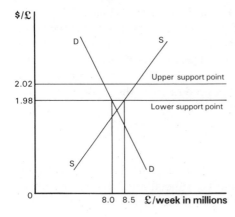

FIGURE 7.4
Mechanics of pegged exchange rates:
buying pound sterling.

support point. This possibility is illustrated in Figure 7.4, where the Bank of England buys a half-million pounds sterling per week in order to keep the rate from falling below $1.98/£1.

Up to this point, pegged rates are similar to a gold standard. The major difference is that direct intervention by central banks rather than gold flows keeps exchange rates within a narrow band around the par rate. The similarity could have been even closer. The gold standard adjustment mechanism could have operated under an adjustable peg.

No Sterilization

In the absence of offsetting open market operations, intervention in foreign exchange markets influences domestic and foreign money supplies and credit conditions. In order to see how this works, consider the second example, where the Bank of England buys pounds and sells dollars. When the Bank buys pounds with dollars, it normally receives a check in pounds written on a British commercial bank. It collects the check by reducing the commercial bank's account at the Bank of England, which reduces the legal reserves of the British banking system. As the central bank for Great Britain, all commercial banks have deposits at the Bank of England, and those deposits are part of the legal reserves of the British banking system. In other words, a sale of dollars by the Bank of England under a pegged rate has the same effect on the British money supply and credit markets that a sale of gold has under a gold standard.

Intervention can also affect money and credit in the United States. When the Bank of England buys pounds, it pays the foreign exchange dealer with a check in dollars, which the dealer deposits in an American bank. If the check is written on the Bank's account at the Federal Reserve Bank in New York, the U.S. commercial bank sends the check to the Fed for collection.

The Fed credits the account of the commercial bank and debits the account of the Bank of England. Reserves of the U.S. banking system rise, and the stock of money and credit expands. In this case, intervention in the foreign exchange market by the Bank of England has the same effect on credit markets and the stock of money in the United States as a gold flow from the United Kingdom to the United States.

If central banks do not use open market operations to prevent their intervention in foreign exchange markets from influencing money and credit, then the gold standard adjustment mechanism operates under pegged exchange rates. For example, in Figure 7.4 demand and supply initially intersect below the lower support point, and the Bank of England buys pound sterling. These purchases reduce the British money stock and contract bank credit. In the United States, the opposite takes place. In the short run, interest rates in London tend to rise relative to New York, and in the long run the British price level tends to fall relative to the American price level. There is, therefore, both a short-run and long-run adjustment mechanism at work pushing the intersection of demand and supply in Figure 7.4 up toward the lower support point.

Sterilization

Central banks, however, sterilized reserve flows through offsetting open market operations that insulated domestic financial markets from the effects of their purchases or sales of foreign exchange. Sterilization was quite natural. One of the major reasons for adopting pegged rates was to avoid the monetary discipline of the gold standard. Sterilization accomplished that by breaking the link between reserves and the stock of money and bank credit.

When the Bank of England purchases pounds in the foreign exchange market, it reduces British bank reserves. A purchase of government securities by the Bank increases those reserves. The Bank of England therefore offsets the domestic effects of selling dollars by buying an equivalent amount of British government securities in the open market. Since selling pounds (purchasing dollars) in the foreign exchange market increases reserves of commercial banks, the Bank sells British Treasury bills as it sells pounds in the foreign exchange market. These offsetting open market operations tend to insulate British financial markets from the effects of intervention, but they do not insulate American financial markets. Offsetting open market operations by the Fed would have been necessary to insulate the American money stock and credit markets, if it were not for a special arrangement between the Federal Reserve Bank in New York and many foreign central banks.

Foreign central banks keep operating balances at the Federal Reserve. In most cases, however, they have an arrangement with the Fed to keep their checking accounts at or near some predetermined level. When the

Bank of England sells pounds and acquires dollars, the transaction tends to raise the Bank's deposits at the Fed. To prevent the Bank's deposits from becoming too large, the New York Fed has the authority to buy U.S. Treasury bills and hold them for the Bank of England. This purchase of Treasury bills automatically returns the reserves to the commercial banking system in the United States. A sale of pounds leaves the reserves of American commercial banks unchanged, because the Bank of England usually uses the dollars it receives to buy U.S. Treasury bills. Of course, the whole thing works in reverse when the Bank buys pounds. In that case the New York Fed sells U.S. Treasury bills it holds for the Bank of England in order to restore the Bank's checking account to the desired level.

Sterilization not only insulates money stocks and credit markets from the effects of intervention, it also short-circuits the gold standard adjustment mechanism. Take the example associated with Figure 7.4. The Bank of England buys pounds, but it also buys British Treasury bills and sells U.S. Treasury bills. Nothing happens to money or bank credit in either country, and there is no market mechanism at work to shift the intersection of demand and supply up toward the lower support point. As a result, there is no automatic market mechanism at work to reestablish equilibrium in the balance of payments.

Fundamental Disequilibrium

Sterilization under pegged rates is not an accident; it is an inherent part of avoiding the monetary constraints imposed by a gold standard. The gold standard adjustment mechanism, however, must be replaced with something else. Under an adjustable peg, the idea is to finance temporary disequilibria and to use discrete changes in exchange rates to remove persistent or fundamental disequilibria.

The basic idea is illustrated in Figure 7.5. In that diagram, the vertical axis measures the exchange rate and the horizontal axis depicts time. The wavy line labeled *RR* represents the movement of the intersection of demand and supply for foreign exchange over time. That is, *RR* shows what the

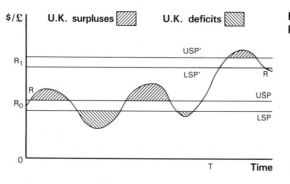

FIGURE 7.5
Fundamental disequilibrium.

exchange rate would be at each point in time in the absence of intervention by central banks. From some initial time zero until T, the free market rate oscillates around the original par rate, R_0. When RR is above the original upper support point USP, Britain has a surplus in its balance of payments; and when RR is below the original lower support point LSP, there is a deficit. As long as surpluses and deficits are temporary and roughly offset each other, Britain can finance deficits with the dollars it acquires during surpluses, and no adjustment is required.

At time T in Figure 7.5, a basic shift takes place, and the market rate depicted by RR fluctuates around a new higher level. At the initial par rate R_0, Britain runs a chronic surplus in the balance of payments. This situation corresponds to what is called a "fundamental disequilibrium in the balance of payments." Under an adjustable peg, the appropriate response is to appreciate the pound by establishing a new par value at R_1. The automatic adjustment mechanism of a gold standard is replaced with a political decision to appreciate pound sterling.

If decisions to revalue a currency were made promptly, revaluations would probably be an effective substitute for the price-specie-flow mechanism. Unfortunately, in practice decisions to revalue are postponed until the threat of a financial crisis forces a change. At least two kinds of pressures appear to work toward postponing currency revaluations: One is political, and the other is technical.

Identification The technical problem is to identify a "fundamental disequilibrium." If there is a deficit on the basis of official reserve transactions, without a crystal ball how do we tell whether it is temporary and should be financed, or permanent and requires devaluation? The natural reaction is to wait and see if the problem goes away on its own. By the time it is obvious that there is a fundamental disequilibrium, the time for action is long overdue.

Political pressures The political pressures for delay are a bit more subtle. For devaluation, two factors probably dominate. First, devaluation tends to be interpreted as evidence that the government's policies have failed, and any politician is reluctant to admit failure. Failure does not win elections. The second factor is that devaluation tends to increase inflation in the short run by releasing suppressed inflationary pressures. To see how this works, consider the following example. The initial par exchange rate is $2/£1, and no central bank intervention is required to keep the rate between the upper and lower support points. Suppose the British government finances a large budget deficit by selling government securities to the Bank of England. The British money supply and stock of bank credit expand. British prices rise, interest rates tend to decline, and Britain starts to run a deficit in the balance of payments. However, the Bank of England sterilizes the effects of selling dollars, and there is no downward pressure on money, bank credit, or prices, and no upward pressure on interest rates. There is a fundamental disequilibrium in the balance of payments that must be removed by devaluation.

Devaluation, however, is politically unattractive because maintenance of the official exchange rate partially insulates domestic prices from the initial expansionary monetary policy and also subsidizes British residents. Intervention by the Bank of England prevents the pound price of the dollar from rising, which temporarily holds down the price of imports, including raw materials used to produce goods domestically. A constant exchange rate and rising prices in Great Britain make British goods more expensive to foreigners, and foreign demand for British exports declines, which also moderates the rise in British prices.

The deficit in the balance of payments is a subsidy from the British government to British residents. In Figure 7.4, the pound value of all private British imports is one-half million pounds per week greater than the value of private British exports of goods, services, and securities. The difference is a subsidy financed by a reduction in international reserves held by the Bank of England. Depreciation of pound sterling removes the subsidy to British consumers and allows British prices to respond fully to the initial monetary expansion. Depreciation is not the cause of British inflation; it is, however, associated with a rise in prices and a reduction in real income in Great Britain, and that makes depreciation as politically unattractive as it is economically necessary.

If depreciation under pegged rates is so difficult, then appreciation should be easy. Unfortunately, it doesn't work that way. It is a fair breeze indeed that doesn't harm someone. Let's take West Germany as an example. Throughout most of the 1960s and early 1970s, German prices tended to rise more slowly than American prices. As a result, Germany tended to run balance-of-payments surpluses and periodically increased the dollar price of the mark. Between these periodic appreciations, intervention by the West German central bank tended to keep the dollar price of the mark artificially low and the mark price of the dollar artificially high. The low dollar price for the mark encouraged exports to the United States, and the high mark price for the dollar discouraged German imports. The subsidy to exports and protection from imports promoted the overexpansion of German export and import competing industries. That subsidy is part of the reason we see all those old VW bugs running around.

Effective appreciation of the mark became increasingly difficult because it meant removing the subsidy to German exports and protection for import competing industries, which would create at least temporary if not prolonged unemployment in these industries. Since unemployment also does not win elections, the government tended to postpone appreciation as long as possible. Delay, however, compounded the problem by reinforcing the allocative distortions and making the necessary readjustment even more painful. When Germany finally abandoned pegged rates in 1973, Volkswagen almost went bankrupt.

The result of the identification problem and political pressures was that the adjustable peg was left without an effective adjustment mechanism. Sterilization short-circuited the price-specie-flow mechanism, while political pressures and the inability to identify fundamental disequilibria prevented prompt currency revaluations. Instead of a series of frequent, small, and uneventful revaluations for individual currencies, the system tended to experience occasional crises associated with relatively large revaluations for many currencies. This pattern opened the door to a form of speculation that compounded the problem and often precipitated the crisis.

One-Way Options

Let's go back to Figure 7.4. Britain has a persistent deficit, and the pound should be devalued. The British government, however, hopes the deficit is only temporary. Britain does not devalue the pound, and the Bank of England sterilizes the effects of intervention. The demand and supply schedules stay where they are, and so does the deficit. As the deficit persists for months or even years, it becomes increasingly obvious that the probability of a significant increase in the value of the pound is almost zero. The pound can move in only one direction—down. It is only a question of when the British government will make the political decision to depreciate pound sterling. In this situation, speculators have a one-way option. When they sell pounds short, there is almost no fear of a significant loss due to a rise in the dollar value of pounds and a very good chance that the pound will be devalued. It is like betting on a horse race and knowing that every other jockey but yours is trying to lose. In this situation, speculators not only sell pounds in the forward market, they borrow pounds in London, sell them for dollars, and invest the dollars in New York. If interest rates in London are higher than in New York, the interest rate differential discourages speculation. In some cases, however, the rates are higher in New York, so there is an additional incentive to move speculative funds to New York.

The rush out of pounds into dollars is not restricted to speculators. Sound business practice dictates that companies must protect themselves from losses due to revaluation. Suppose you are the comptroller for the international division of Ford Motor Company. The company has plants, working balances, and other assets in the United Kingdom. Pound devaluation means all those assets are going to have to be written down in dollar value, a potentially huge loss for Ford. An important part of your job is to protect Ford from that loss. How do you do it? First, you sell off every liquid asset you hold in the United Kingdom and bring any working balances in British banks down to an absolute minimum. Next, you might borrow in

London to cover the remaining working balances and sell the pounds for dollars. Finally, if you are convinced that devaluation is imminent, you might even sell pounds in the forward market to help cover the loss incurred in writing down the dollar value of Ford plant and equipment due to devaluation. Of course, if you are the comptroller of a British firm doing business with or in the United States, you move as many of your liquid assets as possible from London to New York, and you keep any dollars earned in the United States in New York. All this activity shifts the supply of pounds in Figure 7.4 to the right, the demand to the left, and increases the deficit.

The story, however, does not stop there, because the one-way options also affect the demand and supply for pounds generated by trade flows. The demand for pounds dries up. British exporters want to be paid in dollars. They do not cover and buy pounds in the forward market because there is little or no chance that the price of pounds will rise, but it may fall substantially. The supply of pounds from trade, however, tends to expand. American exporters want payment on delivery in dollars and British importers want to buy dollars while they are cheap, increasing the spot demand for dollars and the supply of pounds generated by commodity flows. These leads and lags, as they are called, further aggravate the deficit. The demand and supply schedules in Figure 7.4 shift downward further and the deficit becomes even larger.

Exactly the same story works in reverse when a country postpones appreciation too long, as the Germans did in the 1960s and early 1970s. During the winter of 1970–71, for example, it became increasingly clear that the mark would be appreciated to eliminate a persistent surplus in the German balance of payments. The Federal Reserve *Bulletin* for October 1971 provides the following description of how speculation, prudent management, and leads and lags finally swamped the German central bank's attempt to defend an undervalued mark:

> On April 30, German reserves stood at $16.7 billion, representing a gain of nearly $3.0 billion for the first 4 months of 1971, while the forward dollar contracts of the German Federal Bank had risen to $2.7 billion. Over the same period, German corporations had raised close to $4 billion abroad, representing roughly half of their total credit needs.
>
> On Monday, May 3, the main German economic research institutes issued a report calling for a prompt floating or revaluation of the mark. Sympathetic reactions to this report by high-ranking German officials persuaded the market that some such move would soon be forthcoming. In holding the spot rate at the ceiling, the German Federal Bank was accordingly flooded with offers of dollars against marks. Over the 2 days May 3 and 4, the bank had to absorb more than $1 billion, and on the morning of Wednesday, May 5, a further $1 billion was taken in within the first 40 minutes of trading. At that point the German Federal Bank suspended its market operations. Although German banks were legally free to continue to deal if they wished, there was no official fixing, and trading virtually ceased in the Frankfurt market for the rest of the week.

Although the absence of an effective adjustment mechanism proved to be the Achilles heel of pegged exchange rates, another problem also plagued the system. Technically, gold was the ultimate international reserve. Each currency was pegged in terms of the dollar, and dollars were tied to gold. The value of the world monetary gold stock, however, failed to grow with the volume of world trade, and the U.S. stock of gold systematically declined.

Inadequate Gold and Excess Dollars

We saw earlier how international reserves grew with trade under a gold standard. Under pegged rates, international reserves grew in primarily two ways. Foreign central banks could hold more dollars or gold, and the monetary authorities in the United States could hold more gold. Table 7.1 shows estimates for the monetary stock of gold for non-Communist countries, official dollar reserves for these countries, and the monetary gold stock for the United States. The data are for five-year intervals from 1950 through 1970. The patterns are quite clear. The world stock of monetary gold grows slowly until the mid-1960s and then declines. Dollar holdings rise rapidly, and the U.S. gold reserve steadily declines.

The total world gold stock grew slowly because gold production was not very profitable. The official $35 an ounce price for gold was set in 1934. By the 1960s the general price level and cost of mining gold had more than doubled, but the price of gold was still the same as in 1934. With essentially no growth in the world stock of monetary gold, growth in international reserves meant that foreign central banks held more dollars. Not only did official dollar claims on the United States increase as the United States followed an expansionary monetary policy, but some central banks also

TABLE 7.1   Gold and International Reserves: 1950 to 1970

YEAR	TOTAL WORLD MONETARY GOLD STOCK ($ MILLIONS)	U.S. STOCK OF MONETARY GOLD ($ MILLIONS)	OFFICIAL LIQUID CLAIMS ON THE U.S. ($ MILLIONS)	RATIO OF LIQUID CLAIMS TO U.S. GOLD STOCK
1950	$35,380	$22,820	$ 5,147*	0.22
1955	38,000	21,753	8,834*	0.40
1960	40,540	17,804	11,078	0.62
1965	43,300	13,806	19,922	1.44
1970	41,275	11,072	20,057	1.81

* Short-term liabilities to international institutions and foreign governments reported by banks in the United States.

Source: Federal Reserve *Bulletin*, various issues.

wanted to hold more gold, so the U.S. gold stock declined. As a result, as is shown in the fourth column of Table 7.1, the ratio of official dollar claims on the United States to the U.S. stock of monetary gold steadily increased.

The combination of steadily increasing foreign official holdings of dollars due to deficits in the U.S. balance of payments and a steadily decreasing American gold stock put the system in an impossible situation. About the only way the stock of international reserves could grow was for the liquidity position of the United States to deteriorate. The United States was like a commercial bank whose reserve ratio is continually declining. At some point, the depositors become concerned about their money and there is a run on the bank. An increase in the dollar price of gold might solve the problem temporarily, but it could never be a permanent solution.

The basic problems for pegged exchange rates were interdependent. The absence of an effective adjustment mechanism prolonged balance of payments disequilibria and increased the amount of reserves needed to run the system. Inadequate reserves encouraged speculation against weak currencies. The slow growth in monetary gold, however, forced the system to rely on increased dollar reserves. Even under the best of conditions, a continual increase in foreign official claims on the United States relative to the American stock of monetary gold was bound to cause periodic scrambles for gold that would force a series of increases in the dollar price of gold. This inherent problem was aggravated by inflation in the United States and deficits that pumped dollars into foreign central banks, particularly in Germany and Japan.

The reserve problem could have been resolved by switching to a single reserve asset, either dollars, gold, or some new form of international reserves created by international agreement. Governments, however, were not willing to accept the constraints of a gold standard. Under a dollar standard, foreign monetary policy would be dominated by U.S. monetary policy, and in the absence of gold, there would be no external restraint on American monetary policy. Foreign countries would not tolerate that alternative. Some feared imported inflation, others were concerned about maintaining full employment, and pride was an element for everyone.

As the system of pegged rates crumbled, there was a flurry of interest in creating some form of reserve asset, a kind of paper gold that could be generated by international agreement. As we will see in the next chapter, these efforts made some progress, but not enough to provide the system with a new form of international reserve. In the end, the system of pegged rates among major industrial countries broke down and was replaced with a dirty or managed float.

The IMF

Those of you who read the financial pages or are familiar with international financial markets probably are puzzled about the lack of references to the International Monetary Fund in our discussion of pegged rates. Technically, the articles of agreement of the IMF served as the legal foundation for pegged exchange rates, and the IMF played and plays an important role in international finance. From an economist's point of view, however, it does not deserve top billing. On a day-to-day basis, pegged rates were run by the central banks of major industrialized countries, and all important decisions were made by their governments. The IMF did not tell Great Britain or France or any large country when to revalue its currency; governments made their decisions and then informed the IMF. Although the relatively small amount of resources available to the IMF does not give it much leverage over larger countries, it can influence smaller countries by putting important conditions on loans. The IMF also serves as an important framework for international discussion and cooperation.

SUMMARY

Under a system of freely flexible rates, exchange rates are determined by the forces discussed in the two previous chapters. When countries adopt a managed or dirty float, central banks "lean against the wind," which moderates short-run fluctuations in exchange rates while allowing market forces to determine long-run movements. Whether or not intervention is appropriate depends primarily on the nature of speculation and the effect of short-run fluctuations in exchange rates on trade and capital flows.

With a gold standard, gold flows associated with balance-of-payments deficits or surpluses set in motion market forces that eventually eliminate imbalances by shifting demand and supply schedules for foreign exchange. The same mechanism distributes bank reserves within a country and causes price levels to move together in different regions of the same country.

Pegged but adjustable exchange rates were an attempt to get the best of both flexible rates and a gold standard. They provided the freedom for monetary policy of flexible exchange rates and, in principle, the rate stability of a gold standard. Although a variety of factors contributed to the demise of pegged rates, two probably dominated. First was the lack of an effective adjustment mechanism. Sterilization short-circuited the gold standard mechanism, while technical problems and political pressures prevented timely revaluations. Second, the system suffered from an inherent conflict in the growth of international reserves; dollars expanded too rapidly and gold too slowly.

QUESTIONS FOR REVIEW

1. Define mint par and gold points.
2. Briefly summarize Hume's price-specie-flow mechanism. How does the existence of well-developed capital markets modify Hume's analysis?

3. "Under an international gold standard, when the exchange rate is at one of the gold points, some gold almost certainly will flow." How much gold is some, and why is the movement of gold only "almost" certain?

4. The United States or any large country provides an excellent example of the adjustment mechanism under a gold standard. Explain.

5. Under both a gold standard and pegged exchange rates, market rates moved within a narrow band around a par rate of exchange. Describe the mechanism that kept market rates within the band under both systems.

6. Under pegged exchange rates, countries systematically sterilized the effects of their intervention in the foreign exchange market.
   a. How is sterilization carried out?
   b. Why did countries sterilize?
   c. What effect did sterilization have on the adjustment process or lack of it?

7. Why were countries under pegged exchange rates usually so slow to appreciate and depreciate their currencies?

8. Use Table 3.1 to answer the following question. Did the U.S. balance of payments contribute to a slow and steady increase in international reserves under pegged rates?

9. The system of pegged rates suffered from several problems: an inadequate adjustment mechanism, one-way speculation, and both excessive and inadequate liquidity. Explain how these problems are interrelated.

10. Suppose there is a gold standard and an exogenous real shock, such as the increased demand for imports discussed in Chapters 5 and 6. How does the price-specie-flow mechanism work then? Does it make any difference if you base your analysis on the ideas developed in Chapter 5 or 6? If it does make a difference, explain what that difference is and why there is a difference.

11. In the absence of official intervention, changes in flexible exchange rates appear to be essentially uncorrelated. If so, what kind of correlation would we expect under a managed float? Choose the exchange rate for some major currency and compute the daily percentage change in the rate over 50 business days. Now calculate the autocorrelation coefficient for this series for up to five lags. Is there evidence of leaning against the wind by the authorities?

ADDITIONAL READINGS

BLOOMFIELD, ARTHUR I.   *Monetary Policy under the International Gold Standard: 1880–1914* (New York: Federal Reserve Bank of New York, 1959).

BROWN, WILLIAM A.   *The International Gold Standard Reinterpreted, 1914–34* (New York: AMS Press, 1970).

HAWTREY, RALPH G.   *The Gold Standard in Theory and Practice* (London: Longmans, Green, 1927).

PIPPENGER, JOHN, AND LLAD PHILLIPS. "Stabilization of the Canadian Dollar: 1952–1960." *Econometrica* (September 1973).
"Treasury and Federal Reserve Foreign Exchange Operations." Semiannual report published in the Federal Reserve *Bulletin* in the spring and fall.
TREZISE, PHILIP H. (ED.). *The European Monetary System: Its Promise and Prospects* (Washington, Brookings Institution, 1979).
TRIFFIN, ROBERT. "The Gold Standard: Myths and Realities: 1815–1913." In *Our International Monetary System: Yesterday, Today and Tomorrow* (New York: Random House, 1968).

8

THE INTERNATIONAL
MONETARY FUND:
ORIGINS AND
EVOLUTION

The International Monetary Fund or IMF institutionalized a movement toward international monetary cooperation that started in the early 1920s. We begin this chapter with a brief review of the early attempts at cooperation and then take up the objectives, organization, and development of the IMF. An appendix lists some of the major events in international finance beginning with 1919.

EARLY COOPERATION

Cooperation between countries on international monetary problems was rare before World War I. The price-specie-flow mechanism was widely accepted, and central bankers understood their role in making that process work. There was little incentive for cooperation during the early 1920s because exchange rates were flexible, and there was very little intervention. Flexible rates, however, were viewed as temporary. There was a general consensus that countries would return to a gold standard and that the return would require international cooperation.

The 1920s

The Genoa Conference   The first major push for international monetary cooperation came at the Genoa Conference in 1922. This conference was part of a series called by Britain, France, Italy, Belgium, and Japan to try to deal with the economic and financial problems that followed World War I. A major objective was to restore the gold standard. The conference adopted proposals that contained three key elements. (1) Central bank operations should prevent large fluctuations of domestic prices in terms of gold. (2) Central banks should continuously cooperate. (3) There should be center countries that hold reserves entirely in gold and peripheral countries that hold reserves partly in gold and partly in the currencies of the center countries. Items (2) and (3) emerged later as important concepts in the operation of the IMF. Failure to follow the first principle, however, opened the door to worldwide inflation.

Return to gold   The Genoa Conference established the principle of cooperation. That principle was put into effect when Britain returned to gold early in 1925. During the early 1920s Montague Norman, director of the Bank of England, and Benjamin Strong, president of the Federal Reserve Bank of New York, had developed a solid friendship. Both believed that monetary policy must be dominated by domestic objectives, and both supported cooperation between central banks. Their friendship and common objectives contributed to a cooperative effort between the Federal Reserve and the Bank of England to help Britain return to and stay on the gold standard. As part of that effort, Norman and Strong agreed to three major points. (1) The Federal Reserve would not try to raise or lower prices in the United States. (2) The Fed would attempt to hold interest rates in New York below those in London. (3) The United States would provide the United Kingdom with a credit of $300 million to help back the pound when convertibility into gold was restored. In an age of billions and trillions, $300 million might not seem very large, but it was over half of the Federal Reserve's open market portfolio, which seldom exceeded $500 million during this period.

Britain's return to gold at prewar mint par was premature. Even after several years of declining prices in the United Kingdom, British prices were still relatively high as compared to the United States. In order to defend the old mint par, the Bank of England had to continue the deflationary policies that had reduced prices and created widespread unemployment in Britain during the early 1920s. Britain's return to gold was part of a general movement. By the end of 1926, France was the only major country that had not stabilized its currency in terms of gold, and it was in the process of doing so. The return to convertibility, however, did not restore the prewar gold standard. The growing commitment to domestic objectives, particularly full employment, was inconsistent with the fairly automatic adjustment mechanism that operated before World War I. Like the adjustable peg, this system required international cooperation and coordination, and it broke down under pressure. In September 1931 Britain was forced off gold, and over the next few years most European countries followed.

The 1930s

Breakdown   Several factors contributed to the breakdown in cooperation. First, and by far the most important, the Great Depression put intolerable strains on the international monetary system. Second, Montague Norman, Emile Moreau, president of the Bank of France, and Hjalmar Schacht, president of the Reichsbank, could not avoid being drawn into the frequently acrimonious debate over German reparations payments. In addition, the determination of Washington to stay out of the reparations controversy reduced the Federal Reserve's involvement in European monetary affairs. Finally, Strong's death in 1928 and an ensuing power struggle within the Federal Reserve further reduced the Fed's ability to cooperate with other central banks.

By the early 1930s, cooperation turned into beggar thy neighbor. Several countries, including the United States, tried to export unemployment by devaluation. The United States also raised tariffs to new highs under the infamous Smoot-Hawley Act. Even communication and consultation between central banks almost disappeared. The next tentative steps toward cooperation did not begin until 1936.

The Tripartite Agreement   After extended negotiations, on September 25, 1936, the British, French, and U.S. governments issued almost identical statements announcing a devaluation for the French franc, which was still tied to gold. London and Washington "welcomed" the "readjustment." The statements went on to promise avoiding disturbing responses to the readjustment, to reject competitive devaluations, and to call for relaxation of trade and exchange restrictions. Other countries were urged to join this Tripartite Monetary Agreement, and a few did.

As part of the agreement, the three countries later worked out a system to stabilize exchange rates. The United States agreed to buy and sell gold to the other two countries at $35 per ounce. Technically this price could be changed daily, but Washington chose to hold the price constant. France and Great Britain agreed to work together to stabilize dollar, pound, and franc exchange rates on a day-by-day basis. But pressure on the franc continued, and France adopted a floating rate in June 1937.

The Tripartite Agreement was not only the first step on the road back to international monetary cooperation, it was also a forerunner of the IMF. Like the IMF, the Tripartite Agreement emphasized cooperation, recognized the need to avoid competitive devaluations, and stressed reductions in trade and exchange controls. In addition, the dollar was the key currency. The United States fixed the dollar price for gold, and other countries stabilized exchange rates.

In October 1939, Hitler invaded Poland, and World War II began in earnest. Unlike the Depression, war did not stop the move toward international monetary cooperation. While losing ground in the Pacific and North Africa, the Allies were developing plans for the international monetary system they would establish after they won the war. These plans bore fruit in 1944, when President Roosevelt invited delegates from 44 member countries of the United Nations to develop an international monetary system. The meeting opened in July at the Mount Washington Hotel in Bretton Woods, New Hampshire, with 730 delegates. After three weeks of negotiations, they agreed to the establishment of the International Monetary Fund and what is now the World Bank. By the end of 1945 a sufficient number of governments had ratified the agreements, and the first meeting of the IMF took place in 1946.

ARTICLES OF AGREEMENT
OF THE IMF

Negotiations at Bretton Woods were dominated by the United States and Great Britain. The British delegation, led by Keynes, advocated an ambitious plan that included something very close to a world central bank. The American delegation, headed by Harry Dexter White, had more limited objectives.

Keynes's Plan

Keynes wanted a system that met the following objectives: (1) There must be a cooperative mechanism for determining exchange rates that prevents competitive devaluations and exchange and trade controls. (2) The system should be able to create a stock of international reserves that would grow with world trade. These reserves should be expanded and contracted to offset both insufficient and excessive world aggregate demand. (3) Pressure must be applied to both surplus and deficit countries to restore equilibrium. (4) Interference with internal national policies must be kept to a minimum.

The centerpiece of the proposal was an International Clearing Union that could create an international money called *bancor*. Bancor would be fixed, but not unalterably, in terms of gold. Central banks of all member countries would hold an account with the Union through which they would settle their exchange balances with one another at par values defined in terms of bancor. Countries with debit balances could draw on overdraft facilities to cover their deficits, and countries with surpluses would acquire credit balances. To encourage adjustment, deficit and surplus countries paid interest on both credit and debit balances. The stock of reserves would be altered by adjusting available overdraft facilities. Since no credits are transferred outside the Clearing Union, only within it, the Union could always honor any checks written on it.

The International Clearing Union was a world central bank in the sense that it could create international reserves out of thin air. The task of the Union was to make sure the members played by the rules and that advances to members were prudent and beneficial for the Union as a whole. Under the rules of the Union, exchange rates could fluctuate within plus or minus 5 percent of the par or official exchange rate, and par rates were adjusted easily.

White's Plan

White's proposal was more limited. It provided for an International Stabilization Fund, with a modest increase in total international reserves. There was more emphasis on exchange rate stability, more willingness to put pressure on deficit countries, and no pressure on surplus countries. The objectives of the stabilization fund were outlined as follows: (1) Stabilize exchange rates. (2) Shorten the duration and lessen the magnitude of balance-of-payments disequilibrium. (3) Promote international trade and productive capital flows. (4) Facilitate the effective utilization of blocked foreign balances accumulated in some countries during the war. (5) Reduce foreign exchange restrictions, bilateral clearing arrangements, and discriminatory foreign exchange practices.

Differences

The two plans differed on four major points. The United States opposed the larger amount of liquidity that would be provided by the Union. The United States also wanted more stable exchange rates. Instead of rates flexible within plus or minus 5 percent of a par rate that was easily adjustable, the United States proposed a narrower range and a par rate that could be changed only with the consent of 80 percent of the votes in the Fund. Unlike the Union, in the Fund there was no pressure on the surplus country to adjust, presumably because the United States was certain to be the major surplus country immediately after the war. The final disagreement was over national autonomy. The Union minimized interference in domestic policies because Keynes was more concerned about price stability and full employment than stable exchange rates. Interference, however, was implicit in the U.S. position.

Although Keynes was able to modify White's plan in several ways, the Articles of Agreement worked out at Bretton Woods were based on the U.S. proposal. In the following sections, we review the key provisions of the articles as they were developed at Bretton Woods. We start with the structure of the Fund, review the common objectives of Keynes and White, and then see how the conflict between the United States and Great Britain was resolved.

Structure

Article XII establishes a board of governors, executive directors, and a managing director. Each member of the Fund appoints one governor and one alternate. All powers of the Fund are vested in the board of governors. A governor can cast the number of votes alloted under Section 5 of Article XII to the member that appoints him or her.

According to Section 5, each member has 250 votes plus one additional vote for each $100,000 of its quota. These votes are adjusted by the addition (subtraction) of one vote for each $400,000 of net sales (purchases) of a country's currency by the Fund. The initial quotas are shown in Table 8.1.

The executive directors are responsible for the conduct and general operations of the Fund. The articles establish at least twelve directors. Initially, five executive directors were appointed by the five members with the largest quotas, and seven were elected. By 1983, the number of executive directors was twenty-two. Six were appointed, and sixteen elected. Each appointed director casts the number of votes allotted to the member appoint-

TABLE 8.1   Schedule of Initial Quotas (In millions of U.S. dollars)

Australia	200	India	400
Belgium	225	Iran	25
Bolivia	10	Iraq	8
Brazil	150	Liberia	0.5
Canada	300	Luxembourg	10
Chile	50	Mexico	90
China	550	Netherlands	275
Colombia	50	New Zealand	50
Costa Rica	5	Nicaragua	2
Cuba	50	Norway	50
Czechoslovakia	125	Panama	0.5
Denmark	*	Paraguay	2
Dominican Republic	5	Peru	25
Ecuador	5	Philippine Commonwealth	15
Egypt	45	Poland	125
El Salvador	2.5	Union of South Africa	100
Ethiopia	6	Union of Soviet	
France	450	Socialist Republics	1,200
Greece	40	United Kingdom	1,300
Guatemala	5	United States	2,750
Haiti	5	Uruguay	15
Honduras	2.5	Venezuela	15
Iceland	1	Yugoslavia	60
		Total	8,800

* The quota for Denmark was determined later.

Source: Articles of Agreement of the International Monetary Fund (Schedule A).

ing him or her, and elected directors cast the number of votes by which they are elected.

The managing director runs the staff and conducts the day-to-day business of the Fund. Although the managing director cannot be either a governor or an executive director, he or she is chair of the executive directors, but without a vote. The articles also establish the United States as the home office for the Fund. The location and voting structure reflect the dominance of the United States at Bretton Woods.

Common Objectives

Keynes and White had a number of common objectives. Most of these are spelled out in Article I, which states the purposes of the Fund:

> The purposes of the International Monetary Fund are:
>
> (i)   To promote international monetary cooperation through a permanent institution which provides the machinery for consultation and collaboration on international monetary problems:
>
> (ii) To facilitate the expansion and balanced growth of international trade, and to contribute thereby to the promotion and maintenance of high levels of employment and real income and to the development of the productive resources of all members as primary objectives of economic policy:
>
> (iii) To promote exchange stability, to maintain orderly exchange arrangements among members, and to avoid competitive exchange depreciation.
>
> (iv) To assist in the establishment of a multilateral system of payments in respect of current transactions between members and in the elimination of foreign exchange restrictions which hamper the growth of world trade.
>
> (v)   To give confidence to members by making the Fund's resources available to them under adequate safeguards, thus providing them with opportunity to correct maladjustments in their balance of payments without resorting to measures destructive of national or international prosperity.
>
> (vi) In accordance with the above, to shorten the duration and lessen the degree of disequilibrium in the international balances of payments of members.
>
> The Fund shall be guided in all its decisions by the purposes set forth in this Article.

Item (iv) is reinforced by Article VIII, which requires members to avoid restrictions on current payments and discriminating currency restrictions. That article also states that countries must supply the Fund with a variety of economic and financial data.

Although the Fund strongly opposed restrictions on current account, it allowed and even encouraged capital controls. According to Article VI, "A member may not make use of the Fund's resources to meet a large or sustained outflow of capital, and the Fund may request a member to exercise controls to prevent such use of the resources of the Fund." In addition, "Members may exercise such controls as are necessary to regulate international capital movements. . . ." This attitude toward capital flows was the result of large speculative capital flows in the thirties and the general belief that speculation was destabilizing.

Resolution of the Conflict

As mentioned earlier, the proposals by Keynes and White conflicted on four major points. The Keynes plan had relatively wide bands and easily adjustable par rates because he wanted minimum interference with domestic policy. The White proposal stressed relatively rigid exchange rates and narrow bands, which required more interference. The U.S. plan penalized only deficit countries, but the British plan penalized both surplus and deficit countries. Keynes's proposal, in effect, set up a world central bank, whereas White's plan provided only for a modest increase in reserves.

Autonomy and rigidity The issues of national autonomy and exchange rate rigidity are interrelated. More of one implies less of the other. When Britain returned to gold in 1925, it sacrificed employment for a fixed exchange rate. Keynes did not want Britain or any other country to repeat that experience. If full employment and price stability conflict with the exchange rate, the exchange rate must give. As a result, the British plan emphasized wide bands around par rates that could be easily changed. The White plan, however, stressed rigid exchange rates. A country could not devalue without formal approval by the Fund, and exchange rates were kept within a narrow band around par. This position implicitly implied that coordination dominated autonomy.

The original articles clearly resolve only one issue in this debate. They state that exchange rates must be kept within a narrow band around par, plus or minus 1 percent. The inherent conflict between stable exchange rates and independent domestic policies is sidestepped; nothing spells out the conditions under which par values can be changed. Instead of a formal approval of a change in par values by a large majority of the Fund, the articles simply say that members can change a par value "only after consultation with the Fund." The only condition is that "A member shall not propose a change in the par value of its currency except to correct a fundamental disequilibrium." The term "fundamental disequilibrium" is never defined, undoubtedly so that the British and the Americans could each interpret it as they wished.

Without any effective guidelines in the articles, practice and precedent resolved the conflict between national autonomy and rigidity of exchange rates. Large, industrialized countries revalued whenever they wished, but they systematically postponed revaluations and often sacrificed domestic goals to a stable exchange rate. That is, they were free to follow the Keynes plan, but chose to follow White's.

Although the resources available through the Fund were not large enough to give it much clout over large, industrialized countries, they were important for smaller and/or less developed countries. As a result, for these countries the Fund filled the role of international policeman implicit in the White proposal.

Burden of adjustment   Keynes's concern that surplus and deficit countries should share the burden of adjustment is reflected in Article VII. That clause allows the Fund to declare a currency scarce and permits countries to impose restrictions on a scarce currency. Article VII, however, has never been invoked. Even during the early years of the IMF, when there was a severe "dollar shortage," the dollar was not declared a scarce currency. On this issue, Keynes won on paper but lost in practice.

Liquidity   The Articles of Agreement did not establish a world central bank. Instead of bancor, each country had a quota of gold and its own currency that it contributed to the Fund. These contributions gave the Fund a pool of currencies that it could lend to a deficit country.

Suppose, for example, France needs $1 billion in reserves to cover a temporary deficit and avoid depreciation. If the loan is approved, the Bank of France would buy dollars, pounds, and German marks from the IMF with French francs. France would repay the loan by selling $1 billion worth of dollars, pounds, and marks to the Fund for francs. Today loans are denominated in special drawing rights or SDRs, which we discuss later in the chapter.

Initially each member paid in gold either 25 percent of its quota, called the *gold tranche,* or 10 percent of its official holdings of gold and U.S. dollars, whichever was smaller. The rest was paid in domestic currency. There also was a provision in the articles to review and adjust quotas every five years. A four-fifths majority of total votes, however, was necessary to adjust quotas, and no individual quota could be changed without the member's consent. In spite of these conditions, quotas did grow over time. Table 8.2 shows the schedule of quotas and percentage voting power for all members as of September 1982. Because of its large quota, the United States still holds over 19 percent of the votes.

TABLE 8.2 Quotas, Voting Power, and Exchange Arrangements

MEMBER	CURRENCY	QUOTA IN MILLIONS OF SDRs AS OF SEPTEMBER 1982	PERCENTAGE VOTING POWER AS OF SEPTEMBER 1982	EXCHANGE ARRANGEMENTS AS OF JUNE 1982
Afghanistan	Afghani	67.50	0.14	F
Algeria	dinar	427.50	0.70	BSKT
Antigua and Barbuda	East Caribbean dollar	3.60	0.04	$
Argentina	peso	802.50	1.28	F
Australia	dollar	1,185.00	1.87	F
Austria	schilling	495.00	0.80	BSKT
Bahamas	dollar	49.50	0.12	$
Bahrain	dinar	30.00	0.08	LF
Bangladesh	taka	228.00	0.39	BSKT
Barbados	dollar	25.50	0.08	$
Belgium	franc	1,335.00	2.10	EMS
Belize	dollar	7.20	0.05	$
Benin	franc	24.00	0.08	FF
Bhutan	ngultrum	1.70	0.04	OC
Bolivia	peso	67.50	0.14	F
Botswana	pula	13.50	0.06	BSKT
Brazil	cruzeiro	997.50	1.58	F
Burma	kyat	109.50	0.21	SDR
Burundi	franc	34.50	0.09	$
Cameroon	franc	67.50	0.14	FF
Canada	dollar	2,035.50	3.18	F
Cape Verde	escudo	3.00	0.04	BSKT
Central African Republic	franc	24.00	0.08	FF
Chad	franc	24.00	0.08	FF
Chile	peso	325.50	0.54	F
China, People's Republic of	yuan	1,800.00	2.82	OC
Colombia	peso	289.50	0.49	F
Comoros	franc	3.50	0.04	FF
Congo	franc	25.50	0.08	FF
Costa Rica	colón	61.50	0.13	F
Cyprus	pound	51.00	0.12	BSKT
Denmark	krone	465.00	0.76	EMS
Djibouti	franc	5.70	0.05	$
Dominica	East Caribbean dollar	2.90	0.04	$
Dominican Republic	peso	82.50	0.17	$
Ecuador	sucre	105.00	0.20	$
Egypt	pound	342.00	0.57	$

TABLE 8.2 (*continued*)

MEMBER	CURRENCY	QUOTA IN MILLIONS OF SDRs AS OF SEPTEMBER 1982	PERCENTAGE VOTING POWER AS OF SEPTEMBER 1982	EXCHANGE ARRANGEMENTS AS OF JUNE 1982
El Salvador	colón	64.50	0.14	$
Equatorial Guinea	ekwele	15.00	0.06	OC
Ethiopia	birr	54.00	0.12	$
Fiji	dollar	27.00	0.08	BSKT
Finland	markka	393.00	0.65	BSKT
France	franc	2,878.50	4.49	EMS
Gabon	franc	45.00	0.11	FF
Gambia, The	dalasi	13.50	0.06	OC
Germany, Federal Republic of	deutsche mark	3,234.00	5.04	EMS
Ghana	cedi	159.00	0.28	LF
Greece	drachma	277.50	0.47	F
Grenada	East Caribbean dollar	4.50	0.05	$
Guatemala	quetzal	76.50	0.16	$
Guinea	syli	45.00	0.11	SDR
Guinea-Bissau	peso	5.90	0.05	SDR
Guyana	dollar	37.50	0.10	LF
Haiti	gourde	34.50	0.09	$
Honduras	lempira	51.00	0.12	$
Hungary	forint	375.00	0.62	BSKT
Iceland	króna	43.50	0.11	F
India	rupee	1,717.50	2.69	F
Indonesia	rupiah	720.00	1.15	LF
Iran	rial	660.00	1.06	SDR
Iraq	dinar	234.10	0.40	$
Ireland	pound	232.50	0.40	EMS
Israel	shekel	307.50	0.51	F
Italy	lira	1,860.00	2.91	EMS
Ivory Coast	franc	114.00	0.21	FF
Jamaica	dollar	111.00	0.21	$
Japan	yen	2,488.50	3.88	F
Jordan	dinar	45.00	0.11	SDR
Kampuchea, Democratic	riel	25.00	0.08	—
Kenya	shilling	103.50	0.20	SDR
Korea	won	255.90	0.43	F
Kuwait	dinar	393.30	0.65	BSKT
Lao People's Democratic Republic	kip	24.00	0.08	$

TABLE 8.2 *(continued)*

MEMBER	CURRENCY	QUOTA IN MILLIONS OF SDRs AS OF SEPTEMBER 1982	PERCENTAGE VOTING POWER AS OF SEPTEMBER 1982	EXCHANGE ARRANGEMENTS AS OF JUNE 1982
Lebanon	pound	27.90	0.08	F
Lesotho	maloti	10.50	0.05	OC
Liberia	dollar	55.50	0.12	$
Libya	dinar	298.40	0.50	$
Luxembourg	franc	46.50	0.11	EMS
Madagascar	franc	51.00	0.12	BSKT
Malawi	kwacha	28.50	0.08	SDR
Malaysia	ringgit	379.50	0.63	BSKT
Maldives	rufiyaa	1.40	0.04	LF
Mali	franc	40.50	0.10	FF
Malta	pound	30.00	0.08	BSKT
Mauritania	ouguiya	25.50	0.08	BSKT
Mauritius	rupee	40.50	0.10	SDR
Mexico	peso	802.50	1.28	F
Morocco	dirham	225.00	0.39	F
Nepal	rupee	28.50	0.08	$
Netherlands	guilder	1,422.00	2.24	EMS
New Zealand	dollar	348.00	0.58	F
Nicaragua	córdoba	51.00	0.12	$
Niger	franc	24.00	0.08	FF
Nigeria	naira	540.00	0.87	F
Norway	krone	442.50	0.72	BSKT
Oman	rial Omani	30.00	0.08	$
Pakistan	rupee	427.50	0.70	F
Panama	balboa	67.50	0.14	$
Papua New Guinea	kina	45.00	0.11	BSKT
Paraguay	guarani	34.50	0.09	$
Peru	sol	246.00	0.42	LF
Philippines	peso	315.00	0.53	LF
Portugal	escudo	258.00	0.44	LF
Qatar	riyal	66.20	0.14	LF
Romania	leu	367.50	0.61	$
Rwanda	franc	34.50	0.09	$
St. Lucia	East Caribbean dollar	5.40	0.05	$
St. Vincent and the Grenadines	East Caribbean dollar	2.60	0.04	$
São Tomé and Príncipe	dobra	3.00	0.04	SDR
Saudi Arabia	riyal	2,100.00	3.28	LF
Senegal	franc	63.00	0.14	FF

TABLE 8.2 (*continued*)

MEMBER	CURRENCY	QUOTA IN MILLIONS OF SDRs AS OF SEPTEMBER 1982	PERCENTAGE VOTING POWER AS OF SEPTEMBER 1982	EXCHANGE ARRANGEMENTS AS OF JUNE 1982
Seychelles	rupee	2.00	0.04	SDR
Sierra Leone	leone	46.50	0.11	SDR
Singapore	dollar	92.40	0.18	BSKT
Solomon Islands	dollar	3.20	0.04	BSKT
Somalia	shilling	34.50	0.09	$
South Africa	rand	636.00	1.02	F
Spain	peseta	835.50	1.33	F
Sri Lanka	rupee	178.50	0.31	F
Sudan	pound	132.00	0.24	$
Surinam	guilder	37.50	0.10	$
Swaziland	lilangeni	18.00	0.07	OC
Sweden	krona	675.00	1.08	BSKT
Syrian Arab Republic	pound	94.50	0.18	$
Tanzania	shilling	82.50	0.17	BSKT
Thailand	baht	271.50	0.46	LF
Togo	franc	28.50	0.08	FF
Trinidad and Tobago	dollar	123.00	0.23	$
Tunisia	dinar	94.50	0.18	BSKT
Turkey	lira	300.00	0.50	F
Uganda	shilling	75.00	0.15	F
United Arab Emirates	dirham	202.60	0.35	LF
United Kingdom	pound	4,387.50	6.82	F
United States	dollar	12,607.50	19.52	F
Upper Volta	franc	24.00	0.08	FF
Uruguay	new peso	126.00	0.23	F
Vanuatu	vatu	6.90	0.05	SDR
Venezuela	bolívar	990.00	1.57	$
Viet Nam	dong	135.00	0.25	SDR
Western Samoa	tala	4.50	0.05	F
Yemen Arab Republic	rial	19.50	0.07	$
Yemen, People's Democratic Republic of	dinar	61.50	0.13	$
Yugoslavia	dinar	415.50	0.68	F
Zaïre	zaïre	228.00	0.39	SDR
Zambia	kwacha	211.50	0.37	SDR
Zimbabwe	dollar	150.00	0.27	BSKT

Source: International Monetary Fund, *Annual Report 1981/82.*

The articles are rather vague about the conditions for borrowing—that is, buying foreign exchange from the Fund with domestic currency. According to Article V, Section 3, a member in good standing can do so as long as "the proposed purchase would not cause the Fund's holdings of the purchasing member's currency to increase by more than twenty-five percent of its quota during the period of twelve months ending on the date of the purchase nor to exceed two hundred percent of its quota, ..." Practice, however, established a format for borrowing, which we will discuss in the next section.

Quotas failed to provide adequate reserve growth. One problem is the restrictions put on increases in quotas. Another is that there is no active market for the currency of many members, so their contribution is useless. As we will see in the next section, as the Fund evolved, it was able to develop a variety of schemes to increase its resources.

DEVELOPMENT OF LENDING FACILITIES

By 1946, the Fund was prepared to begin exchange transactions. Under Article XX, it was obligated to call for the establishment of par rates of exchange, even though the world was still recovering from the shock of World War II. At that time, most countries simply chose their existing exchange rates. Given the economic situation, neither the Fund nor new exchange rates could solve the basic problem.

World War II had left Japan and most of Europe destitute. Damage to factories, transportation systems, and homes varied from country to country, but it was severe almost everywhere. Imports were needed to supply food and shelter for survival, and to rebuild factories. With production at a standstill, there was almost nothing to export. Economic problems were compounded by the threat of political instability, and few could forget that Hitler rose to power on the shoulders of economic chaos. The United States and Canada were untouched by the war; their agricultural and industrial capacity was greater than ever. War-torn countries looked to North America for the food and other supplies they needed. As a result, U.S. exports rose rapidly. By 1947, the export surplus was almost $10 billion, which was more than 4 percent of U.S. GNP. Lend-lease, however, ended in 1945 and, despite attempts at relief by the United Nations Relief and Rehabilitation Administration (UNRRA) and other agencies heavily supported by North America, foreign exchange reserves fell rapidly in Europe and Japan.

The IMF was not designed to meet this kind of problem; neither was any other international institution. In June 1947, the United States responded with the European Recovery Program, better known as the Marshall Plan. For four years, the United States supplied loans and grants to finance economic recovery. Between mid-1948 and mid-1952, the United States provided Europe with $11.6 billion in grants and $1.8 billion in loans. For Japan, grants came to $950 million and loans to $275 million. Although this aid paid for one-fourth of Europe's total imports of goods and services from 1947 to 1950, it amounted to no more than 10 percent of European production. The Marshall Plan helped, but reconstruction was primarily a European and Japanese effort, and it was impressive. For the countries participating in the European Recovery Plan, industrial production rose 39 percent from 1948 to 1952. Exports more than doubled, while imports increased by about one-third. By 1952 the balance on goods, services, and private remittances for these countries showed a small surplus, and the trade surplus of the United States had fallen to $2.6 billion.

As the Marshall Plan began to take hold, the activities of the IMF fell to a low level. In 1947, members drew $468 million. That fell to $208 million in 1948 and $101 million in 1949; and there were no drawings in 1950. Even in 1949, when pressure on the pound sterling and several other currencies created an international financial crisis, the Fund did not play an effective role. On September 17 the British devalued, and in three days 15 other countries followed. No financing apparently was arranged, and the British and other governments simply informed the Fund of their decision.

Lending Procedures

The 1949 episode reinforced the Fund's search for a way to implement the vague language in the articles with regard to borrowing. The roadblock was that, following Keynes, the United Kingdom and most other members wanted unconditional borrowing, whereas the United States maintained its original position and insisted on strong conditions and definite time limits. The relatively large U.S. quota at the time, about 30 percent, gave the United States a powerful voice.

In February 1952, the executive directors hammered out the framework for the Fund's financial operations. With respect to term, loans normally are paid in three years and cannot exceed five years. Countries can borrow the gold tranche, now the reserve tranche, without conditions. Additional borrowings involve conditions. The use of progressively stronger conditions at each step became formal policy in 1959. It is impossible to provide any details about these conditions, because negotiations are confidential and conditions vary from case to case. For a detailed discussion of conditionality, see the *IMF Survey: Special Supplement on the Fund*, November 1982.

Standby Arrangements

In February 1952, the executive board also approved the principle of the standby arrangement. This arrangement, in effect, allows countries to establish a line of credit with the Fund. It guarantees that they can draw up

TABLE 8.3   Standby Arrangements Effective during Financial Years Ended April 30, 1953–1982 (In millions of SDRs)

YEAR	NUMBER	AMOUNT	YEAR	NUMBER	AMOUNT
1953	2	55.00	1968	32	2,352.36
1954	2	62.50	1969	26	541.15
1955	2	40.00	1970	23	2,381.28
1956	2	47.50	1971	18	501.70
1957	9	1,162.28	1972	13	313.75
1958	11	1,043.78	1973	13	321.85
1959	15	1,056.63	1974	15	1,394.00
1960	14	363.88	1975	14	389.75
1961	15	459.88	1976	18	1,188.02
1962	24	1,633.13	1977	19	4,679.64
1963	19	1,531.10	1978	18	1,285.09
1964	19	2,159.85	1979	14	507.85
1965	24	2,159.05	1980	24	2,479.36
1966	24	575.35	1981	21	5,197.93
1967	25	591.15	1982	19	3,106.21

Source: IMF Annual Report for 1981/2.

to some given amount for a specified period of time. Table 8.3 shows the development of these arrangements from 1953 through 1982.

General Arrangements to Borrow

In the early 1960s, the resources of the Fund consisted of the quotas of the members. Twenty-five percent were in gold and the rest in members' currencies. The gold was not available for intervention to help peg exchange rates, and many currencies were not widely traded and therefore not appropriate for intervention. As a result, the Fund began to run short of currencies that countries wanted to borrow. Claims on the IMF by the United States posed the immediate problem. By November 1961, drawings of dollars had raised potential U.S. claims on the IMF to $5.8 billion, which far exceeded the Fund's effective resources.

To solve this problem, in 1962, 10 major industrial countries agreed to lend to the IMF under certain specified conditions. This general arrangement to borrow increased the Fund's effective resources by $6 billion. The original arrangement was for four years, but it has been extended and increased. In April 1980, it was extended for another five years and expanded to SDR 6.4 billion, or about $7.1 billion.

Special Lending Facilities

As the general resources of the Fund expanded through increases in quotas and arrangements to borrow, the IMF also developed a series of special lending facilities. In general, these facilities are designed to respond to a variety of factors that have created balance-of-payments problems, particularly for less developed countries.

Compensatory financing   The IMF established a compensatory financing facility in 1963 and liberalized it in 1966. The objective of this facility is to help members of the Fund which depend heavily on exports and experience low export earnings, particularly when these are due to weather or other natural disasters. Reduced earnings from travel and workers' remittances are included. A shortfall is determined relative to a five-year average. Earnings for the current year plus the two previous years are averaged with projections for the next two years. The Fund makes the projections under two guidelines: The average for the forecast cannot exceed the initial two years by more than 10 percent and should not be below the current year. A country must meet more conditions than low earnings from an important export. If high returns from one export offset low returns from another, the country is ineligible. The situation must be short term and essentially beyond the control of the country. In addition, the Fund may require measures to improve a country's overall balance-of-payments situation.

Under this facility, a country can draw up to 100 percent of its quota. For drawings over 50 percent, a country must convince the Fund that it has been trying to solve its balance-of-payments problems. Countries pay interest and normally must repay the loan within three to five years. The use of this facility does not reduce a member's access to regular drawings from the Fund. By 1982, 32 countries had made 57 drawings totalling about $1.25 billion. Outstanding drawings were equal to about half that amount.

In May 1981, the Fund extended similar assistance to members with balance-of-payments problems caused by a temporary rise in the cost of cereal imports. An excess is calculated in a manner similar to the shortfall. The limit on drawings is also similar to the limit on shortfalls, but there is a limit on combined borrowings of 125 percent. The new facility will operate until May 1985, with a review by the executive board no later than June 30, 1983.

Buffer stock facility   There are several international buffer stock agreements designed to stabilize prices of primary products. If participants in these agreements have trouble meeting their obligation because of balance-of-payments problems they can, under appropriate conditions, borrow from the Fund to meet those obligations. Drawings cannot exceed 50 percent of quota, and the Fund can waive the 200 percent limit on its holding of a member's currency. The buffer stock facility was established in June 1969, and by 1979 the Fund had authorized loans in connection with tin, cocoa, and sugar.

Oil facility   In August 1974, the Fund established a special oil facility to assist members to meet the effect on their balance of payments of the rapid increases in oil prices due to OPEC. The major conditions were that the country was expected to cooperate with the Fund to solve its balance-of-payments problems, and that it avoid competitive devaluation and escalation of restrictions on trade and payments. Loans under this facility were for three to seven years. The resources were provided by a number of oil-exporting countries.

The oil facility was terminated in March 1976. Total borrowings under this facility amounted to SDR 6.9 billion.

Extended facility   In September 1974, the Fund established an extended financing facility. Under this facility, the IMF can help cover balance-of-payments deficits due to social or structural problems that require longer periods and larger amounts in relation to quotas then under normal conditions. Loans are in addition to those made under credit tranche policies.

The borrowing country is expected to present a program setting forth the objectives and policies for the whole period of the extended arrangement and a detailed statement of the policies it will follow in each 12-month period. Drawings can take place over a period of three years. Outstanding purchases may not exceed 140 percent of the member's quota nor raise the Fund's holdings of that currency above 265 percent of the member's quota, excluding holdings related to compensatory, buffer stock, and oil facilities. Table 8.4 shows the extended loans approved during the IMF's fiscal year 1981–82.

TABLE 8.4   Extended Funding Arrangements: 1981–1982 (In millions of SDRs)

MEMBER	DATE OF INCEPTION	DATE OF EXPIRATION	TOTAL AMOUNT OF ARRANGEMENT
Costa Rica	6/17/81	6/16/84	276.75
Guyana (extension)	7/25/80	7/24/83	50.00
India	11/9/81	11/8/84	5,000.00
Jamaica	4/13/81	4/12/84	241.30
Pakistan	12/2/81	11/23/83	919.00
Sierra Leone	3/30/81	2/22/84	22.30
Zaïre	6/22/81	6/21/84	912.00
Zambia	5/8/81	5/7/84	800.00
Total			8,221.35

Source: IMF Annual Report for 1981/82.

Supplementary financing facility   In August 1977, the executive board created a supplementary financing facility. This facility is designed for countries facing serious payments imbalances that are large compared to their quotas. The use of this facility is subject to the usual conditions, phasing, and performance criteria. The original funds for this facility, about $11 billion, came from contributions by 15 countries.

When these funds were exhausted, the IMF replaced the supplementary financing facility with the enlarged access policy. The general objectives are the same as for supplementary financing. Guidelines for assistance can change over time. As of November 1982, there was a limit of 150 percent of quota annually or 450 percent over a three-year period. There also was a limit of 600 percent of quota on the cumulative use of Fund resources net of scheduled repurchases. These limits, which may be exceeded in exceptional circumstances, exclude drawings under the compensatory and buffer stock financing facilities or outstanding drawings under the oil facility.

CHALLENGE AND REFORM

During the 1960s the United States lost about $4.5 billion in reserves, mostly gold, while foreign official claims on the United States rose by about $5 billion. In 1970 and 1971, this modest deficit turned into an avalanche. In those two years alone, U.S. official reserves fell by almost $5 billion while foreign official claims increased by over $34 billion (see Table 3.1).

A major crisis in the spring of 1971 forced the mark and several other currencies to float. In August of 1971, President Nixon responded to the U.S. inflation and international situation with a famous speech in which he announced the cessation of official gold sales by the United States, no official intervention in foreign exchange markets, a 10 percent surcharge on most dutiable imports, and wage and price controls. All without prior consultation with the IMF. Over the next three months the Group of Ten, not the IMF, took the initiative to restore par values. (The Group of Ten consists of Belgium, Canada, France, West Germany, Italy, Japan, the Netherlands, Sweden, the United Kingdom, and the United States.) Their negotiations led to meetings at the Smithsonian Institution in December 1971. At these meetings, the Group of Ten agreed to widen bands (plus or minus 2.25 percent) and to set new official exchange rates. These changes were accepted by the Fund.

At the time, several participants proclaimed the Smithsonian Meetings a great success. History, however, had another verdict. In 1972 official claims on the United States rose by another $10 billion. In June 1972, Britain was forced to float, which precipitated a rush into other European currencies, and several markets were closed for about five days. By early 1973, the official rates established at the Smithsonian could no longer be defended, and the system of pegged but adjustable rates collapsed. With floating rates between the United States and most developed countries, the Fund appeared obsolete. Rumors of the Fund's demise, however, proved premature; continued intervention and reform gave it new life.

Managed Float

In a world of freely floating exchange rates, an important function of the IMF evaporates because there is no need for official intervention. Most major industrialized countries, however, did not let rates fluctuate freely in terms of dollars. They intervened to prevent what they saw as unwarranted short-run movements.

The U.S. balance on official reserves transactions for the late 1970s gives some insight into the magnitude of this intervention because, under a flexible rate, these balances are primarily the result of intervention. From 1973 to 1979, annual balances ran from about $5 billion to over $35 billion (see Table 3.1).

Continued Pegging

In 1973, most developed countries stopped pegging their currencies to the dollar, but that did not lead to a world of generalized floating. Many less developed countries continued to peg in terms of dollars, and many developed countries pegged in terms of other currencies.

The right-hand column in Table 8.2 shows the exchange rate arrangements for members of the IMF as of June 30, 1982. The symbols $, £, FF, SDR, and OC mean that a currency is pegged, respectively, to the U.S. dollar, pound sterling, French franc, Special Drawing Rights, or another currency. EMS denotes a member of the European Monetary System and BSKT indicates that a currency is pegged to some other basket of currencies. LF means there is limited flexibility, and F stands for a free or managed float. Only 31 countries, including the United States, have a free or managed float; 102 currencies are pegged.

Reform of the IMF started before the challenge of the early 1970s began. By the mid-1960s, pressure began to build to replace gold with something like bancor. The result, which was only a first step, was the first amendment to the articles, which created Special Drawing Rights.

Special Drawing Rights

As world trade grew in the late 1950s and through the 1960s, the need for international reserves increased. The ideal solution would have been for the world monetary gold stock and dollar reserves to rise together with the increase in trade. Unfortunately, that is not what happened. With inflation and the price of gold fixed at $35 an ounce, world gold production tended to decline, and after the mid-1960s monetary gold stocks fell as speculation and industrial demand outstripped production. Total reserves actually fell from

1965 to 1970 as increases in dollar reserves failed to match gold losses. The key role for gold put the system in an intolerable position because, as the stock of foreign official claims on the United States rose, U.S. gold reserves fell (see Table 7.1). The United States was acting as a world banker, but it was becoming increasingly illiquid. Under these conditions, there could be a run on the bank at any time.

There were several possible solutions. One was to raise the dollar price of gold. That would raise the value of the U.S. gold stock and temporarily spur gold production. But it would only be a matter of time before the same problem would appear and the dollar would have to be devalued again. Another was simply to break the link with gold and make dollars the reserve asset. That alternative implies that the growth of international reserves depends on the U.S. balance of payments, which Table 3.1 shows can swing unpredictably from surplus to deficit and back to surplus. Another solution was to go back to the Keynes plan and try to create an international reserve asset, and that was what the IMF started to do with *special drawing rights,* or *SDRs.*

The basic outline for the system of SDRs was developed within the Group of Ten and approved at the IMF's annual meeting in Rio de Janeiro, Brazil, in September 1967. Creation of SDRs was authorized in 1968 by the First Amendment to the Articles of Agreement of the IMF. The first allocation of special drawing rights, $3.5 billion, took place in 1970. Table 8.5 shows the growth of SDRs since 1970.

The SDR originally was defined as equivalent to 0.888671 grams of fine gold, the official gold content of one U.S. dollar when the price of gold was $35. In 1974, after generalized floating, the valuation was changed. The SDR

TABLE 8.5 Net Cumulative Allocations of Special Drawing Rights (In millions of SDRs)

YEAR	AMOUNT
1970	3,414.045
1971	6,363.286
1972	9,314.835
1973	9,314.835
1974	9,314.835
1975	9,314.835
1976	9,314.835
1977	9,314.835
1978	9,315.125
1979	13,347.560
1980	17,380.836
1981	21,433.330
1982	21,433.330
1983	21,433.330

Source: *IMF Annual Report,* various issues.

was defined in terms of a basket of currencies, with the weights roughly depending on the relative importance of each country in world trade. That scheme, however, was too complicated, and in 1981 the Fund cut the number of currencies from 16 to 5, the U.S. dollar (42 percent), the German mark (19 percent), and the French franc, Japanese yen, and pound sterling (13 percent each).

To see how SDRs work, let's take a simple example. One million in SDRs is allocated to France. This allocation imposes an obligation on both France and the IMF. On the one hand, if the Fund requests them, the French central bank is obligated to supply French francs to the Fund up to an amount equal to twice France's allocation, the franc equivalent of 2 million in SDRs. The Fund buys the francs by crediting France's SDR account at the IMF. If France wants to borrow foreign currencies from the IMF, the Fund is obligated to supply them up to the equivalent of 1 million in SDRs. In that case, France pays for the foreign currencies with SDRs that it holds with the Fund.

Members who buy foreign exchange from the IMF are expected to use the currencies only for balance-of-payments needs or to restore total reserves. Drawings are not subject to prior challenge by the IMF on this expectation, but if it is not met, the Fund can direct other countries' drawings to that currency. Purchases do not have to be reversed, but a country must maintain an average of 30 percent of its past cumulative allotments of SDRs over any five-year moving period. A participant with holdings of SDRs over its allocation receives interest on the excess. One with holdings below the allocation pays a charge on the deficiency. The rate of interest and charges are based on a formula that uses a weighted average of short-term interest rates in the United States, the Federal Republic of Germany, the United Kingdom, France, and Japan.

The beauty of SDRs is in the eye of the beholder. Some see the SDR as a first and major step toward the creation of a new international reserve asset, a version of bancor that can be created by a stroke of the IMF's pen. Others see it as largely a charade—just an institutionalized swap agreement under which central banks agree to borrow and lend their currencies to each other through the IMF. Whoever proves right about SDRs, they did not come in time to save the system from the onslaught of dollars and pressures on exchange rates that swamped pegged rates in the early 1970s.

Committee of Twenty

As mentioned earlier, 1971 rocked the IMF to its foundations. In July 1972, the board of governors of the IMF appointed an ad hoc Committee of Twenty to develop a plan for international monetary reform. The committee consisted of a representative from each country or group of countries that appointed or elected an executive director.

The committee convened that September in Washington with the intention of rebuilding the system of pegged rates so that it would work effectively through the rest of the twentieth century. The effort began with a broad consensus on several issues. The new system must treat deficit and surplus countries more symmetrically; exchange rates must be more flexible; and SDRs should replace dollars as the principal reserve asset. There also was very little agreement on a number of important issues, including balance-of-payments adjustment, settlement of payments imbalances, the composition and level of reserves, and support for developing countries. Over the next two years the committee worked on these and other problems, but with little success. The dollar floated in early 1973, and the OPEC oil embargo and price increases started in October 1973. The problems caused by OPEC doomed pegged rates. For the foreseeable future, no country would be willing to commit itself to an official or par exchange rate.

Under these conditions, the committee dropped its goal of reform in favor of an evolutionary approach. It finished its work in June 1974, and issued a final report and an outline of reform. Except for two items, one of them obvious, very little came out of the committee's efforts. The obvious result was a recommendation that "countries may adopt floating rates in particular situations, subject to Fund authorization, surveillance, and review." The original articles did not provide for floating, and this proposal simply recognized existing practice. The other recommendation was for the establishment of a Council of the Governors to "supervise the management and adaptation of the international monetary system."

The outline of reform paragraph 31 describes the council as follows:

A permanent and representative Council, with one member appointed from each Fund constituency, will be established. The Council will meet regularly, three or four times a year as required, and will have the necessary decision-making power to supervise the management and adaptation of the monetary system, to oversee the continuing operation of the adjustment process, and to deal with sudden disturbances which might threaten the system.

The Committee of Twenty also recommended an interim committee patterned on the council. The interim committee would have "an advisory role in those areas in which the Council . . . will have decision-making powers." The board of governors of the Fund established a 22-member interim committee in October 1974, and the committee guided the drafting of the Second Amendment to the Articles of Agreement, which became effective April 1, 1978.

Second Amendment

The second amendment initially was intended merely to adapt the articles to a temporary period of floating rates pending adoption of a reformed system of pegged but adjustable rates outlined by the Committee of Twenty. As it became clear that floating was not temporary, the emphasis shifted to adapting the articles to prolonged floating. The amendment covers six major topics: gold, technical changes, SDRs, simplification and expansion of financial operations, establishment of the council, and exchange arrangements. It also reverses the philosophy of the original articles. At Bretton Woods, pegged rates were seen as a contribution to economic stability. In the second amendment, economic stability is viewed as a prerequisite for pegged exchange rates.

Gold   The second amendment reflects the consensus to downgrade gold; it is eliminated as the common denominator for currencies and replaced by SDRs. The link between gold and SDRs is broken. Members can deal freely in gold both between themselves and in the market. Requirements for payment in gold to or by the Fund are eliminated. The Fund is obligated to sell 50 million ounces of gold and can dispose of the remainder in various ways.

Technical changes   Provisions for the election of executive directors are updated to reflect the 15 elected directors. Several activities are renamed. The General Account is renamed the General Department, and the Special Drawing Account is relabeled the Special Drawing Rights Department. The General Department is given three separate accounts. The General Resources Account holds the general resources of the Fund. A Special Disbursement Account holds the profits from the sale of gold. The Investment Account holds the resources earmarked for investment and the profit from investments.

SDRs   When the SDR was created, it was restricted in a number of ways. To a large extent, these restrictions reflected disagreement about whether SDRs should be something like bancor, a kind of international money, or simply a credit instrument. Among the restrictions were limitations on each member's obligation to accept and hold SDRs, obligations to reconstitute SDR holdings, a requirement to show a balance-of-payments "need" before using SDRs, and a requirement that the IMF designate members eligible to receive SDRs and approve SDR transfers.
 The second amendment modifies these constraints only slightly. It deletes the requirement for Fund approval for transactions between members, and it allows the executive directors to make other decisions about the use of SDRs with smaller majorities than before.

Financial operations   The most important change in financial operations ensures that all the Fund's currency holdings are usable. As mentioned earlier, a large proportion of the Fund's resources were tied up in currencies that were not used in international settlements. Since, under the original articles, members chose the currencies they bought from the Fund, a large proportion of the Fund's resources were useless. The amended articles allow the Fund to specify the currencies that will be sold to or repurchased by a member. If the Fund sells a currency that is not "freely usable," the country issuing the currency must exchange it for one that is freely usable.

The amendment extends the Fund's authority in two areas. It has more discretion to permit transactions under special policies, such as the buffer stock facility, without affecting a member's position in the reserve tranche. The Fund also has the authority to invest in marketable securities issued by international financial organizations or members.

Council   The amendment empowered the board of governors to establish the council discussed earlier. A provision, however, requires approval by 85 percent of the voting power in the Fund. In cases such as this one, where there is strong support and strong opposition, the requirement for a high approval rate may simply be a political ploy. It gives supporters a symbol of victory, but allows opponents an effective veto. Whatever the motivation, it seems unlikely that the council will ever be established. Given the success of the interim committee and the fact that it, unlike the council, is not a political threat to the executive directors, it is likely that the temporary interim committee, or some variant, will become a permanent fixture of the Fund.

Exchange arrangements   The bottom line on exchange arrangements is that the second amendment allows each country to choose its own system of exchange rates. Countries, however, must live up to certain obligations and are subject to surveillance by the Fund.

SUMMARY

The principle of international monetary cooperation was established at the Genoa Conference and was put into practice when England returned to gold in 1925. The Great Depression wiped out the first steps toward cooperation as countries turned to competitive devaluations. The Tripartite Agreement reestablished international monetary cooperation and set the stage for the International Monetary Fund.

At Bretton Woods, the British delegation led by Keynes advocated a system of stable but easily adjustable exchange rates, based on a Clearing Union that could create international reserves. The U.S. delegation, led by Harry Dexter White, proposed a system with less flexibility and only a modest increase in international reserves through an International Stabilization Fund. Although there was some compromise, the U.S. view dominated the Articles of Agreement of the IMF.

The articles failed to resolve at least two crucial issues. They did not spell out the rules for borrowing from the Fund, and they never defined "fundamental disequilibrium," the one condition cited for changing par rates of exchange. Practice established the concept of conditionality for borrowing, but the idea of a fundamental disequilibrium was never made operational.

As the Fund gained experience, it increased its resources through the general arrangements to borrow and introduced a series of special lending facilities. In 1970, the Fund took the first step toward Keynes's Clearing Union by establishing special drawing rights.

The adoption of floating rates in the early 1970s was not as great a threat to the Fund as it initially appeared. Intervention under floating rates, the European Monetary System, and continued pegging by many less developed countries created a demand for international reserves which the OPEC oil crisis reinforced.

The adoption of the second amendment legitimized the Fund's operations under floating rates and in general brought the Articles of Agreement up to date. At this point it is not clear where international monetary reform will lead us; the existing mixture of pegged and floating rates seems likely to persist into the next century.

QUESTIONS FOR REVIEW

1. Discuss the development of international monetary cooperation between the two world wars.
2. Compare and contrast the American and British proposals at Bretton Woods.
3. How were the differences between Keynes and White resolved?
4. Describe the structure of the IMF.
5. What were the basic flaws in the original Articles of Agreement?
6. Briefly discuss the development of special lending facilities.
7. What kind of international monetary reform would you advocate, and why?

ADDITIONAL READINGS

CHANDLER, LESTER V. *Benjamin Strong* (Washington, D.C.: The Brookings Institution, 1958).

CHRYSTAL, K. ALEC. *International Money and the Future of the SDR*. Princeton Essays in International Finance, No. 128, (June 1978).

CLARKE, STEPHEN V. O.   *Exchange-Rate Stabilization in the Mid-1930's: Negotiating the Tripartite Agreement.* Princeton Studies in International Finance No. 41 (September 1977).

————.   *Central Bank Cooperation 1924–31* (New York: Federal Reserve Bank of New York, 1967).

CLAY, HENRY.   *Lord Norman* (London: Macmillan, 1957).

COHEN, BENJAMIN J.   *The European Monetary System: An Outsider's View.* Princeton Essays in International Finance, No. 142 (June 1981).

DAM, KENNETH W.   *The Rules of the Game: Reform and Evolution in the International Monetary System* (Chicago: University of Chicago Press, 1982).

DE VRIES, MARGARET G.   *The International Monetary Fund 1966–1971: The System under Stress* (Washington, D.C.: International Monetary Fund, 1976).

HORSEFIELD, J. KEITH.   *The International Monetary Fund 1945–1965* (Washington, D.C.: International Monetary Fund, 1969).

International Monetary Fund Survey: Supplement on the Fund, September 1979 and November 1982.

MEIER, GERALD M.   *Problems of a World Monetary Order,* 2d ed. (New York: Oxford University Press, 1982).

MOGGRIDGE, DONALD.   *The Return to Gold, 1925* (Cambridge, Eng.: Cambridge University Press, 1969).

MURPHY, J. CARTER.   *The International Monetary System: Beyond the First Stage of Reform* (Washington, D.C.: American Enterprise Institute, 1979).

SOLOMON, ROBERT.   *The International Monetary System, 1945–1976: An Insider's View* (New York: Harper & Row, 1977).

TEW, BRIAN.   *The Evolution of the International Monetary System 1945–77* (New York: Halsted Press, 1977).

TREZISE, PHILIP H. (ED.).   *The European Monetary System: Its Promise and Prospects* (Washington, D.C.: The Brookings Institution, 1979).

APPENDIX
Chronology of Important Financial Events, 1919–1983

June 28, 1919: Versailles Treaty is signed by the Allies and Germany but never ratified by the United States.

January 16, 1920: The League of Nations holds its first meeting in Paris, but the United States never joins.

May 11, 1921: German total reparation obligation set at $33 billion by the Allied Supreme Council meeting in London.

August 25, 1921: German-American Peace Treaty signed in Berlin.

May 19, 1922: Genoa Conference approves 12 resolutions, which include calling a central bankers' meeting and establishing a gold exchange standard.

January 11, 1923: French and Belgian troops occupy the Ruhr, after Reparation Commission declares Germany in default on reparation payments.

November 15, 1923: German currency is stabilized at 1 rentenmark equal to 1 trillion paper marks.

January 14, 1924: Dawes Committee begins work to determine ways of balancing Germany's budget and reinforcing stabilization of German currency.

September 1, 1924: Dawes Plan for payment of German reparations begins.

April 28, 1925: Britain returns to gold standard at pre-World War I mint par in terms of dollars.

July 31, 1925: French and Belgian troops evacuate the Ruhr.

January 30, 1926: British forces evacuate Cologne.

July 12, 1926: Churchill and Caillaux sign British-French war debt agreement, which becomes effective on July 27, 1929.

June 25, 1928: France legally stabilizes the franc at one-fifth the 1914 parity and establishes a gold standard.

February 11, 1929: Committee of Experts, headed by Young, develops plan for German reparation payments.

September 20, 1929: Hatry stock scandal in Great Britain occurs as New York stock market prices begin to weaken.

October 24, 1929: New York stock market panic starts.

May 17, 1930: Young Plan goes into operation, Bank for International Settlements is established, and Dawes Plan ends.

June 17, 1930: Smoot-Hawley Act raises United States tariffs to new highs.

November 6, 1930: Oustric stock scandal in France ruins several banks and many small investors.

May 11, 1931: Credit-Anstalt, with 70 percent of assets and liabilities of all Austrian banks, reports heavy losses. Episode is the start of an international financial chain reaction.

June 20, 1931: Hoover proposes a year's moratorium in intergovernmental debt payments.

July 13, 1931: Macmillan Report reveals large foreign short-term claims on London.

July 13, 1931: Danat Bank in Berlin closes, followed by closing of Berlin bourse and exchange controls in Germany.

September 1931: Britain leaves gold standard.

September 25, 1936: Tripartite Agreement announced. International monetary cooperation resumes.

June 30, 1937: The French franc floats.

May 4, 1938: The French franc is stabilized against pound sterling. This stabilization lasts until the outbreak of World War II.

August 25, 1939: British Exchange Equalization Account withdraws from market and pound sterling drops from $4.68 to $4.40 in one day. By the end of August, it is at $4.27.

September 4, 1939: After declaring war on the third, England imposes exchange control and pegs the pound at $4.06 to $4.02.

July 1–22, 1944: Articles of Agreement of the Fund and those of the World Bank formulated at the International Monetary and Financial Conference, held at Bretton Woods, New Hampshire, U.S.A.

December 27, 1945: Fund's Articles of Agreement enter into force upon signature by 29 governments representing 80 percent of original quotas.

March 8–18, 1946: Inaugural meeting of board of governors of IMF held in Savannah, Georgia; the by-laws are adopted, it is agreed that the Fund's headquarters will be in Washington, and the first executive directors are elected.

May 6, 1946: IMF executive directors hold inaugural meeting in Washington.

July 6, 1946: Canada revalues to parity with U.S. dollar.

September 27–October 5, 1946: First annual meetings of the IMF are held in Washington.

March 1, 1947: IMF begins operations.

May 8, 1947: First drawing from the Fund takes place.

November 1947: Canada imposes severe restrictions on imports from and travel in the United States and other countries.

September 1949: Canada devalues 10 percent against the U.S. dollar.

September 18–29, 1949: European countries devalue, ranging from 30.5 percent for pound sterling to 12.3 percent for Belgian franc.

September 30, 1950: After a heavy influx of funds into Canada, Canadian authorities float the Canadian dollar.

December 14, 1951: After 14 months of progressive relaxation, Canada abolishes exchange control. This action makes it the first country to give up the "transitional-period" exchange controls authorized by the IMF.

October 1, 1952: Executive board of IMF approves proposals for standardized standby arrangements.

August 12, 1957: France devalues by 16.7 percent.

December 29, 1958: France devalues by 14.8 percent.

January 5, 1962: IMF executive board adopts terms and conditions of the general arrangements to borrow.

May 2, 1962: After over a year of semi-pegging, Canada adopts an official par rate of 92.5 U.S. cents per Canadian dollar.

February 27, 1963: Fund's compensatory financing facility is established.

September 29, 1967: Board of governors of IMF approves outline of a plan to establish special drawing rights (SDRs).

November 17, 1967: Bank of England sells more than $1 billion to support pegged rate.

November 18, 1967: Britain devalues pound from $2.80 to $2.40.

March 16–17, 1968: Gold pool dissolved and replaced with two-tier gold market.

April 30–May 9, 1969: German central bank buys $4 billion to peg exchange rate.

June 25, 1969: Buffer stock financing facility is established by IMF.

July 28, 1969: First Amendment to the Articles of Agreement, establishing a facility based on the SDR, goes into effect.

August 8, 1969: France devalues by 11.1 percent.

October 24, 1969: Germany appreciates mark by 9.3 percent.

January 1, 1970: First allocation of SDRs.

June 1, 1970: Canada refloats.

April 1971: German central bank acquires $3 billion in pegging rate.

May 4, 1971: Bundesbank absorbs another $1 billion.

May 5, 1971: Bundesbank buys $1 billion in first hour of trading and withdraws from market. Start of German float.

August 15, 1971: Nixon suspends convertibility of dollar into gold, imposes temporary surcharge on imports, along with wage and price controls. Dollar floats.

August 16–20, 1971: Bank of Japan buys $2 billion in attempt to hold exchange rate.

August 23–27, 1971: Bank of Japan absorbs $2 billion more and decides to let yen float.

December 17–18, 1971: Group of Ten meets at Smithsonian Institution in Washington. They restore pegged rates with wider bands and substantial changes in parities. Dollar devalued relative to most currencies and gold. New gold price is $38 per ounce. U.S. import surcharge also removed.

March 7, 1972: EEC adopts narrow margins for their currencies, creating EEC "snake" in Smithsonian "tunnel."

June 13, 1972: Britain sells $2.6 billion in six days and authorities announce that the pound will float "for a temporary period." When sterling floats, there is a rush into other snake currencies, and most European markets are closed until June 28.

July 26, 1972: Board of governors of IMF adopts a resolution establishing a Committee on Reform of the International Monetary System and Related Issues known as the Committee of Twenty.

February 5–9, 1973: Bundesbank buys $5 billion to hold new Smithsonian rate.

March 1, 1973: European central banks absorb more than $3.6 billion and stop official transactions until March 19. Market effectively closed.

March 11, 1973: Belgium, Denmark, France, Germany, Luxembourg, and the

Netherlands announce a joint float against the dollar effective March 16. Sweden and Norway also join float. Era of floating dollar begins.

October–December 1973: OPEC raises oil prices fourfold and imposes a selective oil embargo.

November 12, 1973: Two-tier gold market ends. Central banks can value and sell gold at free market price.

June 12–13, 1974: Committee of Twenty concludes its work, agreeing on a program to help the monetary system evolve.

September 13, 1974: Fund sets up an extended facility for medium-term assistance to members with special balance-of-payments problems due to structural economic changes.

October 3, 1974: Interim Committee holds its inaugural meeting, following its establishment on October 2.

April 4, 1975: Executive board establishes an oil facility.

January 7–8, 1976: Interim Committee, meeting in Kingston, Jamaica, agrees on IMF quota increases and legalization of floating.

May 5, 1976: Executive directors establish a trust fund to provide balance of payments assistance to developing members with the profits from the sale of gold as approved by the board of governors.

June 2, 1976: Fund holds its first auction of gold.

February 4, 1977: Fund makes first loan disbursements under the trust fund.

August 29, 1977: Executive directors establish supplementary financing facility, with commitments to total SDR 7.78 billion.

April 1, 1978: Second Amendment of Articles of Agreement of the IMF enters into force.

November 1978: U.S. Treasury and Federal Reserve use massive intervention to support dollar. Intervention financed by borrowing from Germany, Japan, Switzerland, the IMF, and official gold sales.

December 13, 1978: Fund announced 50 percent increase in quotas under the seventh general review of quotas and calls for the allocation of SDR 12 billion in 1979–81. Increase accepted by members on December 1, 1980.

February 23, 1979: Supplementary financing facility enters into force.

January 1, 1981: Fund begins to use simplified basket of five currencies to determine daily valuation of the SDR. At the same time, the Fund allocates SDR 4,052.5 million to members, the third and final allocation under which allocations of SDR 4 billion were also made in 1979 and 1980.

March 13, 1981: Fund institutes policy of enlarged access to its resources following the full commitment of resources from the supplementary financing facility.

May 7, 1981: The managing director of the IMF and the governor of the Saudi Arabian Monetary Agency (SAMA) sign agreement under which the Fund can borrow up to the equivalent of SDR 8 billion from SAMA, and its policy of enlarged access becomes operational.

May 13, 1981: Fund reaches an agreement with the monetary authorities of 13 industrial countries under which they will make available the equivalent of SDR 1.1 billion over a period of two years to help finance the Fund's policy on enlarged access.

September 8, 1981: Saudi Arabia's quota increase to SDR 2.1 billion becomes effective.

January 15, 1982: First payments from supplementary financing facility's subsidy account are made to 21 eligible low-income developing member countries.

December 20, 1982: Mexico adopts a three-tier exchange rate: a floating rate and two controlled rates.

January 18, 1983: Group of Ten agree to expand general arrangements to borrow from $7.1 billion to about $19 billion.

March 7, 1983: Australia devalues its dollar by 10 percent.

March 8, 1983: New Zealand devalues its dollar by 6 percent.

March 14, 1983: Belgium imposes emergency exchange controls.

March 21, 1983: Currencies in the European monetary system are realigned. The French franc, Italian lira and Irish pound are devalued and the other five currencies appreciate.

9

INTERNATIONAL ADJUSTMENT FROM A KEYNESIAN PERSPECTIVE

There are many variations to the Keynesian theme, but all Keynesian models contain one common element. At some crucial point, the effective coordination of markets and the efficient allocation of resources breaks down. The economy gets stuck inside the production possibility frontier. If there are market forces working to push the economy toward the frontier, they are weak and unreliable. As a result, output is limited by aggregate demand and, in the absence of effective government intervention, there is chronic involuntary unemployment.

In order to get a feel for this approach, suppose there is a bumper crop of potatoes. Farmers have more potatoes to sell, but aggregate demand is unchanged, so no one buys the potatoes and they rot in the fields. For most of us, that scenario seems a bit strange. Farmers may complain that prices are "too low," but they can sell all they have at the going price. People who lived through the 1930s, however, remember a different world. The price mechanism broke down. In New York, potatoes were rotting on Long Island while people in Brooklyn were unemployed and hungry. The unemployed would have been willing to work for the farmers in exchange for potatoes, but the farmers never saw their demand for potatoes because it took the form of a supply of labor rather than a supply of money.

The primary objective of this chapter is to see what this Keynesian view implies about international adjustment. In order to concentrate on basic adjustment mechanisms, we follow Robert Mundell and J. Marcus

Fleming and use a conventional *IS-LM* model for a small, open economy to analyze the effects of monetary and fiscal policy under fixed and flexible exchange rates. The appendix develops a large-country model, and the Takayama article in the additional readings includes several variations of this model.

Our development of an *IS-LM* model for a small open country assumes familiarity with the *IS-LM* approach for a closed economy. If you are not familiar with *IS-LM,* track down your old macro text and review the model before you try to read the rest of this chapter. If you can't find your old text or want to try another, Chapter 2 in Martin Bailey's *National Income and the Price Level* provides a compact and lucid development of *IS-LM.* Two other popular texts are *Macroeconomics* by Robert Gordon, and *Macroeconomics* by Rudiger Dornbusch and Stanley Fischer.

THE IS-LM MODEL

As in most simple Keynesian models, the price level is constant. Product prices depend on factor prices plus a markup. With unemployed capital and labor, factor prices do not rise as output and employment increase. However, some external shock, such as a rise in oil prices, can drive up production costs and prices. For simplicity, our country is too small to affect output or interest rates in the rest of the world. Foreign income, prices, and interest rates are all exogenous. We also ignore political risk and other impediments to capital flows. Domestic assets are perfect substitutes for foreign assets, and the domestic interest rate depends on the world interest rate, i_W. Later in the chapter, we will relax some of these assumptions.

Consumption

We begin with a standard Keynesian consumption function, where total consumption, C, depends on income, Y.

$$C = a_0 + a_1 Y$$

The term a_0 measures autonomous consumption, and a_1 is the marginal propensity to consume with respect to income. As long as we ignore shocks like OPEC, the price level is constant and we can interpret consumption, C, and income, Y, as either nominal or real.

Saving

In a Keynesian framework, desired saving is what remains from income after consumption. Desired saving, S, therefore is income minus desired consumption:

$$S = Y - C$$

After substituting $a_0 + a_1 Y$ for C and rearranging, saving depends on income, as follows:

$$S = -a_0 + (1 - a_1)Y$$

The term $-a_0$ describes autonomous saving and $1 - a_1$ is the marginal propensity to save with respect to income, or MPS.

Investment

Our open economy has a conventional investment equation where investment, I, depends on the interest rate, i.

$$I = b_0 - b_1 i$$

With a constant price level, I is either nominal or real investment, and i is either the nominal or the real interest rate. The marginal propensity to invest with respect to the interest rate is given by $-b_1$, and b_0 is the level of autonomous investment.

Government Expenditure

Government expenditure, G, is a policy variable. For simplicity, we ignore taxes and treat all government expenditure as though it were financed by a sale of bonds.

So far all our behavioral equations look like their counterparts for a closed economy. Now we have to open up our model by introducing trade and capital flows. We start with imports.

Imports

With domestic and foreign prices constant, we are back in Chapter 5. For a given level of income, imports, IM, depend on the domestic price of foreign exchange, π. As that price rises, foreign goods become more expensive and imports normally fall. Like the demand for commodities in general, the demand for imports depends on income. An increase in income increases imports, and an increase in the domestic price of foreign exchange reduces imports.

$$IM = n_0 + n_1 Y - n_2 \pi$$

The term n_0 determines the level of autonomous imports, n_1 is the marginal propensity to import with respect to income, and $-n_2$ is the marginal propensity to import with respect to the exchange rate.

Exports

Domestic exports, X, are foreign imports. Symmetry requires that exports for our small country depend on income in the rest of the world, $\overline{Y}$, and the exchange rate. Exports rise with increases in both exchange rates and foreign income.

$$X = x_0 + x_1\overline{Y} + x_2\pi$$

The term x_0 measures the level of autonomous exports, x_1 is the foreign marginal propensity to import with respect to foreign income, and x_2 is the foreign marginal propensity to import with respect to the exchange rate.

Commodity Equilibrium

As in a closed economy, equilibrium in commodity markets requires that aggregate demand equal output. In an open economy, domestic consumption, investment, government expenditure, and exports constitute the demand for domestic goods. Since total domestic expenditure, $C + I + G$, includes imports, IM, the equilibrium condition for the commodity market is written as follows:

$$Y = C + I + G + X - IM$$

Balance-of-Payments Equilibrium

Here and in the next three chapters, equilibrium in the balance of payments means that the central bank is not gaining or losing international reserves through intervention in the foreign exchange market. With that interpretation, our equilibrium condition for commodity markets implies balance-of-payments equilibrium. Since desired saving, S, equals $Y - C$, the commodity market equilibrium can be written as follows:

$$IM - X = I + G - S$$

The term IM minus X describes the desired trade deficit. The amount of new securities the government and domestic firms want to sell is I plus G, and the value of new securities domestic households want to buy is S. The desired net export of securities or net capital inflow is therefore given by $I + G - S$. For simplicity, we ignore items such as interest payments and gifts. The balance of payments is in equilibrium and international reserves are unchanged when the desired trade deficit, $IM - X$, equals the desired net capital inflow, $I + G - S$.

IS Schedule

Now that we have the behavioral equations and equilibrium conditions for commodity markets and the balance of payments, we can derive the *IS* schedule for a small, open economy. We start by substituting the behavioral equations for C, I, X, and IM into the equilibrium condition for commodity markets. This substitution yields the following equation:

$$Y = (a_0 + a_1 Y) + (b_0 - b_1 i) + G + (x_0 + x_1 \overline{Y} + x_2 \pi)$$
$$- (n_0 + n_1 Y - n_2 \pi)$$

The next step is to rearrange the equation so that income, Y, is expressed as a function of the interest rate and other factors influencing aggregate demand:

$$Y = \frac{1}{1 - a_1 + n_1} [(a_0 + b_0 + x_0 - n_0) + x_1 \overline{Y} + G + (x_2 + n_2)\pi - b_1 i]$$

This equation is the *IS* schedule for our small, open economy. It describes the position of the schedule, its slope, and how it shifts in response to changes in exchange rates and changes in autonomous or policy components of aggregate demand. You should take the time to work through this derivation for yourself.

Closed economy   To see how this *IS* schedule is related to the usual schedule for a closed economy, let's drop all the elements that refer to imports or exports. That leaves us with the following equation, which should be familiar. If it isn't, look in the macro text again.

$$Y = \frac{1}{1 - a_1} [(a_0 + b_0) + G - b_1 i]$$

The terms a_0 and b_0 are, respectively, the levels of autonomous consumption and investment, and G is a policy variable describing government expenditure. The simple income multipliers with respect to autonomous and government expenditure are $1/(1 - a_1)$. Since $1 - a_1$ is the marginal propensity to save or MPS, we can express the simple income multiplier with respect to autonomous or government expenditure as $1/MPS$.

For a closed economy, the logic of the simple income multiplier runs as follows. Given a constant interest rate, a one-dollar increase in exogenous expenditures must raise income by enough to increase saving by exactly one dollar. Suppose, for example, the marginal propensity to consume is 0.8, which implies that the marginal propensity to save is 0.2. We start with an initial equilibrium where aggregate demand equals output. Then government expenditure rises by 1 dollar. In order to reestablish equilibrium, saving must rise by 1 dollar, so that $I + G$ once again equals S. With an MPS of 0.2, income must rise by 5 dollars, or $1/0.2$. The simple income multiplier is 5, and each unit of increase in autonomous or government expenditure shifts the IS curve to the right by 5 units.

The response of income to the interest rate, i, is given by $-b_1/(1 - a_1)$. A unit increase in the interest rate reduces investment by b_1. To restore equilibrium, saving also must fall by b_1, which means that income falls by b_1/MPS. Since the IS-LM graph has the interest rate on the vertical axis, the slope of the IS schedule is given by the reciprocal of $-b_1/(1 - a_1)$. The term $-(1 - a_1)/b_1$ measures the change in the interest rate associated with a unit change in income.

Comparison   Now let's compare IS schedules. The basic interpretation of the IS schedule is the same for open and closed economies. In the closed economy there is one leakage, saving, and the basic multiplier is 1 over the marginal propensity to save. In the open economy there are two leakages, saving and imports, so the multiplier is 1 over the marginal propensity to save plus the marginal propensity to import.

Consider a unit increase in any autonomous expenditure, perhaps investment, b_0. Income must rise by enough so that saving plus imports rise by 1 unit. That is, income must rise by $1/(1 - a_1 + n_1)$, or 1 over the marginal propensity to save, $(1 - a_1)$, plus the marginal propensity to import, n_1. Suppose the marginal propensity to save is 0.2 and the marginal propensity to import is 0.3. With a constant interest rate, a 1-dollar increase in an autonomous expenditure increases income by 2 dollars, because when income rises by 2 dollars, saving plus imports rise by 1 dollar, and equilibrium is restored between aggregate demand and output. The simple income multiplier with respect to government expenditure, G, autonomous consumption, a_0, investment, b_0, and exports, x_0, is therefore $1/(1 - a_1 + n_1)$, rather than $1/(1 - a_1)$. Since a unit increase in imports reduces expenditure on domestic output by 1 unit, the simple income multiplier with respect to autonomous imports, n_0, is $-1/(1 - a_1 + n_1)$.

A unit increase in foreign income, $\overline{Y}$, increases domestic exports by x_1, so a unit increase in foreign income shifts the IS curve to the right by $x_1/(1 - a_1 + n_1)$. A unit increase in the exchange rate π increases exports by x_2 and reduces imports by n_2, so the simple income multiplier for the exchange rate is $(x_2 + n_2)/(1 - a_1 + n_1)$. The size and sign of x_2 plus n_2 depend on the elasticities of demand and supply for imports and exports discussed in Chapter 5. We assume a normal response to the exchange rate, so that x_2 plus n_2 is positive. Since the basic multiplier now is $1/(1 - a_1 + n_1)$ rather than just $1/(1 - a_1)$, a unit increase in the interest rate lowers income by $b_1/(1 - a_1 + n_1)$, and the slope of the IS schedule is $-(1 - a_1 + n_1)/b_1$.

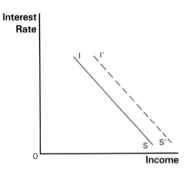

FIGURE 9.1
The *IS* schedule and exchange rates.

IS schedules for open and closed economies are conceptually similar. They both show the combination of income and interest rate for which aggregate demand equals output. The major difference in terms of the *IS-LM* graph is that for an open economy with flexible exchange rates, there is a whole family of *IS* schedules, one schedule for each alternative level of the exchange rate, π. Take, for example, some initial *IS* schedule such as the solid line labeled *IS* in Figure 9.1. This *IS* schedule implicitly assumes certain values for all the parameters and right-hand variables in the following equation:

$$Y = \frac{1}{(1 - a_1) + n_1} [(a_0 + b_0 + x_0 - n_0) + x_1 \overline{Y}$$
$$+ G - b_1 i + (x_2 + n_2)\pi]$$

Now let the domestic price of foreign exchange rise by 1 unit. Imports fall by n_2, exports rise by x_2, and the *IS* schedule shifts to the right by $(x_2 + n_2)/[(1 - a_1) + n_1]$. This new *IS* schedule is labeled *I'S'* in Figure 9.1.

Under pegged exchange rates, π is a policy variable like the level of government expenditure. Policy decisions to alter the exchange rate shift the *IS* schedule, but the *IS* schedule does not shift as part of the adjustment to some exogenous shock.

LM Schedule

For both an open and a closed economy, the *LM* schedule shows the combinations of income and interest rate for which money demand equals money supply. In our simple model, the demand for nominal money balances, M, is a linear function of nominal income, Y, and the interest rate, i.

$$M = kY - \lambda i$$

Increases in income increase the quantity demanded, and increases in interest rates reduce it.

The supply of nominal money balances depends positively on the stock of high-powered money or monetary base, B, and the interest rate, i.

$$M = m_1B + m_2i$$

In this formulation, m_1 depends on factors such as the public's preferences for cash relative to demand deposits and legal reserve requirements. The term m_2 reflects how bank demands for excess reserves respond to interest rates.

The monetary base, B, consists of the currency issued by the government plus the deposits of commercial banks at the central bank. We assume that these monetary liabilities of the government are equal to the domestic securities, D, and international reserves, R, held by the central bank.

$$B = D + R$$

We obtain the *LM* schedule by setting money demand equal to money supply.

$$kY - \lambda i = m_1B + m_2i$$

In standard interpretations of Keynesian models, the interest rate is the price that clears the demand for and supply of money. We therefore solve this equation for the interest rate:

$$i = [k/(m_2 + \lambda)]Y - [m_1/(m_2 + \lambda)]B$$

The slope of the *LM* schedule is $k/(m_2 + \lambda)$. Given the monetary base, B, a unit increase in income requires a rise in the interest rate equal to $k/(m_2 + \lambda)$ in order to restore monetary equilibrium.

A unit increase in the monetary base lowers the interest rate by $m_1/m_2 + \lambda)$ or shifts the *LM* schedule to the right by m_1/k. Consider Figure 9.2. The solid line labeled *LM* shows the initial *LM* schedule associated with a

FIGURE 9.2
The *LM* schedule and international reserves.

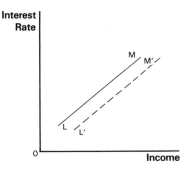

certain level of domestic securities, D, and international reserves, R, held by the central bank. If international reserves rise to R' and the central bank does not sterilize the reserves by selling securities, the monetary base rises and the LM schedule in Figure 9.2 shifts to $L'M'$. The horizontal shift in the LM schedule equals $(m_1/k)(R' - R)$. This shift represents the increase in income that is necessary to restore monetary equilibrium at a given interest rate.

Under a flexible exchange rate and no intervention, the level of international reserves, R, is constant. In that case, the monetary base is a policy variable determined by open market operations, and the LM curve does not shift as part of the adjustment process. When exchange rates are fixed or pegged, open market operations still take place and D is a policy variable, but the level of international reserves is endogenous due to reserve flows. As a result, both the monetary base and the LM schedule can shift as part of the adjustment process.

Notice how our interpretation of the LM and IS curves changes. Under flexible rates, the IS curve can shift as part of the adjustment process because the IS schedule depends on the exchange rate, and exchange rates are endogenous. The LM curve, however, does not shift during adjustment because, with no intervention, reserves are constant and the monetary base is a policy variable. Under fixed or pegged rates, the situation reverses. Exchange rates are exogenous, and the IS curve does not shift as part of the adjustment process. International reserves, however, become an endogenous variable. As a result, reserves and the monetary base shift as part of the adjustment process and so does the LM curve.

Employment

In the Keynesian paradigm, the economy is stuck inside the production possibility frontier. Output is limited by the level of aggregate demand, and employment is limited by the level of output. To determine the relationship between output and employment, we use a simple production function with two inputs, a fixed capital stock, K, and a variable labor input, N. As long as the price level is constant, we can equate nominal income, Y, and real income, y, by a judicious choice for the price index. Given this equality, we can write the production function as follows:

$$Y = y(N,K)$$

With the capital stock given and output determined by the intersection of the IS and LM schedules, the production function in a simple Keynesian model determines the level of employment, N.

Our Keynesian model for a small, open economy is complete. It is summarized by the production function and equations describing the IS and

LM schedules. This simple model is our tool for examining the Keynesian view of international adjustment. To illustrate the Keynesian approach, in the remainder of this chapter we consider the effects of monetary and fiscal policy under fixed exchange rates and monetary policy under flexible rates. The effects of fiscal policy under flexible rates are for you to work out on your own.

FIXED EXCHANGE RATES

A gold standard is one form of a fixed exchange rate, but it is not the only possibility. One example is the Panamanian currency called the balboa. The dollar and the balboa trade 1 for 1 and circulate side by side in Panama. Another is the fixed rate between dollars issued by different Federal Reserve banks in the United States. Whether we apply the model to a small country like Panama or small region within the United States, we need to start our analysis in equilibrium. For simplicity, we start with the simplest possible initial equilibrium.

Initial Equilibrium

Throughout this chapter and the next, we assume that in the initial equilibrium there is no net capital flow, and that exports equal imports. The initial equilibrium is depicted by the intersection of the *IS* and *LM* schedules in Figure 9.3, where the world interest rate is i_W and the level of income is Y_0.

It is instructive to look at this equilibrium from another perspective. Figure 9.4 shows the flow demand for and supply of credit generated by investment, government expenditure, and saving. Interest rates are measured along the vertical axis, and dollars per period are recorded along the horizontal axis. Since the United States hardly qualifies as a small country, we had better interpret these dollars as New Zealand or Australian dollars.

FIGURE 9.3 Initial equilibrium.

FIGURE 9.4 The domestic credit market.

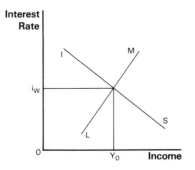

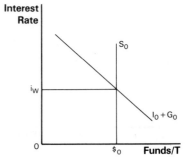

The schedule labeled $I_0 + G_0$ in Figure 9.4 shows how much investors and the government want to borrow at each alternative interest rate. This demand for funds is a supply of securities to domestic and foreign households and a demand for output. The saving schedule labeled S_0 in Figure 9.4 shows the quantity of credit supplied by households when income is Y_0. It is vertical because in this model interest rates do not affect consumption or saving. The supply of credit by households is a demand for assets, either domestic or imported. In the initial equilibrium there is no domestic excess demand for or supply of assets. The demand for credit, $I_0 + G_0$, in Figure 9.4 intersects the supply, S_0, at the given world interest rate, i_W, and there is no net capital flow. Since in equilibrium $I + G - S$ equals $IM - X$, imports also equal exports.

Fiscal Policy

Suppose government expenditure increases by \$100 from G_0 to G_1. By assumption, this expenditure is directed solely at domestic products, and it is financed by the sale of government bonds, which creates a capital inflow. Since there is unemployment and we are inside the production possibility frontier, the price mechanism does not convert the increased demand for domestic goods into a demand for imports, as it does in Chapter 1. Instead, with a constant exchange rate, a change in income acts as the transfer mechanism. Increased aggregate demand drives up income, and the rise in income reduces the capital inflow and increases imports.

The immediate effect of the increase in government expenditure is to generate a surplus on capital account. Figure 9.5 shows the credit market after the increase in government expenditure, but before the multiplier process has had a chance to work. The increase in government expenditure shifts the demand for credit to the right by \$100 to the broken line labeled $I_0 + G_1$, and the quantity of domestic assets sold rises from 0$\$_0$ to 0$\$_2$. Govern-

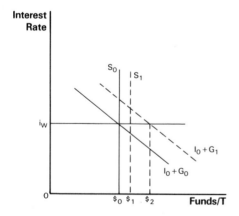

FIGURE 9.5
The immediate impact on the credit market of increased government expenditure.

ment spending increases income by \$100, and the saving schedule shifts to the right by the marginal propensity to save times the increase in income. The new saving schedule in Figure 9.5 is the vertical broken line labeled S_1. Since income rises by \$100 or $\$_0\$_2$ in Figure 9.5 and saving rises by $\$_0\$_1$, consumption must rise by $\$_1\$_2$.

At the world interest rate i_W, domestic firms and the government sell $0\$_2$ in assets, and domestic households buy assets worth $0\$_1$. The difference, $\$_1\$_2$, is exported and generates a surplus in the capital account. Since the marginal propensity to spend includes expenditures on both domestic and foreign goods, the increase in imports must be less than the rise in total consumption, $\$_1\$_2$. Given our small-country assumption, the excess of imports over exports must be less than the surplus on capital account. Aggregate demand exceeds output, there is a surplus in the balance of payments, and international reserves increase. (As country size increases, the capital inflow tends to fall and there can be an initial deficit.)

Now we let the multiplier process start to feed back into the system so that income begins to rise beyond the initial increase in government expenditure. The rise in income works to reestablish internal and external equilibrium. Rising income restores internal equilibrium because leakages through saving and imports imply that aggregate demand does not rise as rapidly as output. It works to reestablish external equilibrium by reducing the capital inflow and increasing the trade deficit. An increase in income reduces the surplus on capital account by increasing the domestic demand for assets. The saving schedule in Figure 9.5 moves to the right, reducing the gap between domestic sales and purchases of assets.

In addition, as income rises, imports increase and the deficit in the trade balance increases. Internal and external equilibria are restored and income stops rising when output has risen by enough so that the surplus on capital account just equals the deficit in the balance of trade. At that point, reserves stop increasing and aggregate demand equals output. This adjustment process is summarized in Figure 9.6 by the shift in the IS schedule from IS to $I'S'$. Given the constant world interest rate i_W, income must rise by the full amount of the simple multiplier—that is, from Y_0 to Y_3.

Wait a second! All we have talked about is the commodity market and capital flows. What about monetary equilibrium and the LM schedule? As long as income is below the new equilibrium level Y_3, the surplus on capital account exceeds the deficit in the trade balance and international reserves, R, rise. In the absence of sterilization, the rise in reserves increases the monetary base and shifts the LM schedule to the right. If the reserves accumulated during the transition to the new equilibrium level of income do not shift the LM schedule to $L'M'$, there are additional reserve and capital flows.

In Figure 9.7, the accumulation of reserves during the transition to the new equilibrium level of income is excessive, and the LM curve is too far to

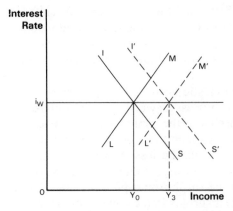

FIGURE 9.6
Fiscal policy under fixed exchange rates.

the right. Given the world interest rate i_W and equilibrium level of income Y_3, there is an excess supply of money.

In Keynesian models, an excess supply of money implies a decision to spend the excess balances on bonds. With income at Y_3, the trade balance just equals investment, I_0, plus government expenditure, G_1, minus saving, S_3. The decision to exchange money for bonds increases the demand for bonds, which reduces the surplus on capital account and generates a deficit in the balance of payments. As long as there are excess money balances and the *LM* curve is too far to the right, there is a deficit in the balance of payments, reserves decline, money balances fall, and the *LM* curve shifts to the left until it reaches $L'M'$. Of course, everything works in reverse if the *LM* schedule is too far to the left.

The new intersection between $I'S'$ and $L'M'$ at the world interest rate i_W shown in Figure 9.6 is the new equilibrium. The increase in government expenditure shifts the *IS* curve to the right to $I'S'$. Under a fixed exchange rate, the *LM* curve is endogenous, and it shifts to the right with the accumulation in reserves until the new *LM* schedule $L'M'$ intersects the new *IS*

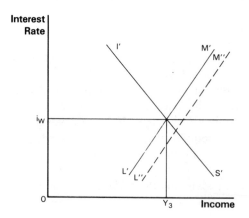

FIGURE 9.7
Excess money balances.

schedule $I'S'$ at the world interest rate i_W. In addition to increasing income, the increase in government expenditure causes a surplus in the capital account, a trade deficit, and an increase in international reserves.

Sterilization

We can use this model to illustrate how the sterilization we discussed in Chapter 7 short-circuits the adjustment process. Suppose the central bank sells bonds as it acquires reserves. The monetary base does not grow, and the LM curve does not shift to the right. The country is stuck with a persistent excess demand for money and a chronic surplus in the balance of payments. There are two solutions. Stop sterilization, or appreciate the currency by enough to shift the IS schedule back to its original position.

Monetary Policy

In Keynesian models for closed economies, expansionary monetary policy reduces interest rates, which spurs investment and increases aggregate demand. In our small, open economy, that sequence of events is ruled out because domestic interest rates cannot diverge from the exogenous world rate, i_W. Indeed, after an expansionary monetary policy, income cannot be higher in the new equilibrium than in the initial equilibrium. Any increase in income promotes saving and imports, which generate deficits in both capital and trade accounts. An increase in income therefore is inconsistent with equilibrium in the balance of payments. A small, open economy with a fixed exchange rate is caught in a kind of liquidity trap.

The solid lines in Figure 9.8 show the demand for money, D_0D_0, and supply of money, S_0S_0, in the initial equilibrium. An open market purchase by the central bank increases the monetary base, and the supply schedule shifts to the broken line labeled S_1S_1. The increase in the money supply puts downward pressure on interest rates. There is a capital outflow, a deficit in the balance of payments, and a loss of reserves. If there are both a temporary reduction in interest rates and an increase in investment and income, saving

FIGURE 9.8
Expansionary monetary policy and monetary equilibrium.

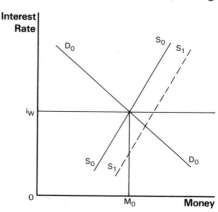

and imports increase. More saving adds to the capital outflow and more imports create a trade deficit. Any temporary increase in income therefore adds to the deficit in the balance of payments and the loss of reserves.

How long does this deficit persist? It lasts until the increase in the base generated by the open market operation is exactly offset by a reduction in reserves. If the central bank buys $1 million in assets, the country must lose $1 million in reserves, and there is no change in the stock of money.

Let's go through the same reasoning with the IS and LM schedules. The initial equilibrium is given by the solid IS and LM schedules in Figure 9.9. An open market purchase shifts the LM curve to $L'M'$. In a closed economy, equilibrium is reestablished where IS and $L'M'$ intersect, with a lower interest rate and higher income.

In our small, open economy, however, the interest rate cannot fall below the world rate, i_W. Since the exchange rate is fixed and there has been no change in exogenous expenditures, the IS schedule does not shift. Given the world interest rate, i_W, and the initial IS schedule, only one equilibrium level of aggregate demand and income is possible, Y_0. The LM schedule therefore must shift back to its initial position. That shift requires a fall in the monetary base equal to the original open market purchase. That is, the rise in the domestic assets of the central bank, D, must be matched by an equivalent decline in international reserves. There are two reasons for the loss of reserves. First, any temporary increase in income generates deficits in both trade and capital accounts. Second, even if income does not rise, any expansion of the money stock causes a net capital outflow because it puts downward pressure on domestic interest rates and/or creates an excess supply of money.

The new equilibrium looks exactly like the initial equilibrium. The IS and LM schedules are in their original positions, the stock of money is constant, and income is unchanged. As in the initial equilibrium, there is a zero balance in trade and capital accounts. The only difference is that in the

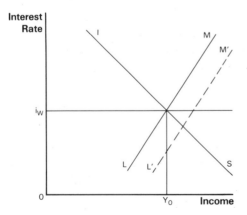

FIGURE 9.9
Monetary expansion under fixed exchange rates.

new equilibrium, the central bank is holding more domestic assets and fewer international reserves. The authorities cannot influence the stock of money; it is determined by demand. Open market operations simply change the composition of the central bank's portfolio. They do not alter the stock of money.

Suppose the central bank sterilizes the loss of international reserves by buying bonds as it loses reserves. In that case, the *LM* curve does not shift back to its initial position, and the country has a chronic deficit in the balance of payments.

Effectiveness of Alternative Policies

Monetary policy is completely ineffective for our small, open economy, but fiscal policy is highly effective. The multiplier response to an exogenous increase in aggregate demand is not stifled by rising interest rates because the domestic economy is fully integrated into the world capital market, which it is too small to influence. The inability to influence interest rates, however, works against monetary policy. In the Keynesian paradigm, monetary policy usually influences aggregate demand and output through its effect on interest rates. Here that channel is blocked because the country is too small to affect world interest rates. As we will see in the next section, flexible exchange rates open up another channel through which monetary policy can influence aggregate demand.

The advantage of the small-country model with perfect capital mobility is that it simplifies and magnifies the international linkages, which allows us to see them more clearly. Once we see how these linkages work, it is easier to interpret more sophisticated models in which the interaction is more complex. When we drop the small-country assumption the adjustment process becomes more complicated, but the basic story does not change. For a large country like the United States, the effects of an expansionary fiscal policy tend to be partially offset by rising world interest rates, but less so than for a closed economy. An expansionary monetary policy for a large country can increase income if the country can influence world interest rates. The effectiveness of monetary policy, however, tends to be reduced compared to a closed economy because it is more difficult to influence interest rates worldwide. The inertia in interest rates, however, is partially offset by increases in foreign income that spur domestic exports.

As we relax the assumption that domestic and foreign assets are perfect substitutes, the results also move closer to the closed-economy responses. With imperfect substitution, domestic and foreign interest rates can diverge. An expansionary monetary policy can lower domestic interest rates, increase investment, and raise income. An expansionary fiscal policy, on the other hand, pushes up domestic interest rates and slows down investment, which partially offsets the increase in government expenditure.

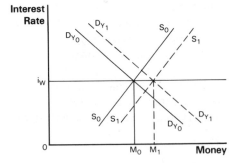

FIGURE 9.10
Monetary equilibrium and expansionary
monetary policy under flexible exchange
rates.

FLEXIBLE EXCHANGE RATES

Under fixed rates and perfect substitutability between domestic and foreign
assets, the equilibrium level of income for a small country is determined by
the position of the *IS* schedule and the level of world interest rates. The *LM*
schedule shifts with deficits or surpluses in the balance of payments until it
intersects the *IS* schedule at the world interest rate. With flexible rates, the
logic of the model reverses. The intersection of the exogenous world interest
rate with the *LM* schedule determines the level of income. Now changes in
the exchange rate shift the *IS* schedule until it intersects the *LM* schedule at
the world interest rate.

Consider an open market purchase of assets by the central bank. Domestic assets, D, and the monetary base both rise. The supply schedule for
money shifts to the right, and so does the *LM* schedule. These shifts are
depicted in Figures 9.10 and 9.11. The initial equilibrium described earlier is
shown by the solid schedules, and the new money supply and *LM* curve by
the broken lines S_1S_1 and $L'M'$.

An increase in the money supply creates excess money balances, puts
downward pressure on domestic interest rates, and generates a capital outflow. Without intervention in the foreign exchange market, the exchange

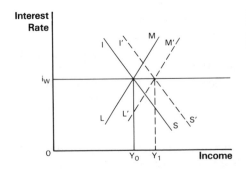

FIGURE 9.11
Expansionary monetary policy under
flexible exchange rates.

rate depreciates in order to generate a trade surplus to match the deficit in the capital account. Depreciation does what the interest rate cannot do. It increases aggregate demand, but by reducing imports and expanding exports rather than by increasing investment. How much must π increase and the exchange rate depreciate? By exactly enough to shift the IS schedule in Figure 9.11 to the right by enough so that it intersects the new LM schedule at the world interest rate, i_W. The increase in income to Y_1 shifts the demand for money to the right in Figure 9.10 to $D_{Y_1}D_{Y_1}$ so that it intersects the supply schedule $S_1 S_1$ at the world interest rate, i_W.

Under flexible rates and an exogenous world interest rate, monetary policy is effective. An increase in the stock of money creates a capital outflow, which causes depreciation. Depreciation, which increases exports and reduces imports, continues until income rises by enough to equate the demand for and the supply of money. In the new equilibrium, saving is higher because income is higher. The deficit in the capital account associated with more domestic saving is exactly offset by the trade surplus caused by depreciation. That is, $X - IM$ equals $S - (I + G)$. Aggregate demand equals output, and there is balance-of-payments equilibrium.

The new equilibrium in the capital account is illustrated in Figure 9.12. In the initial equilibrium, the saving schedule S_{Y_0} intersects the schedule describing investment and government expenditure, $I_0 + G_0$, at the world interest rate, i_W. Domestic purchases and sales of new assets equal $0\$_0$, and there is no capital flow. When income increases to Y_1, savings rises to S_{Y_1}. The quantity of new domestic assets sold each period remains at $0\$_0$, but households buy $0\$_1$. The difference, $\$_0\$_1$, is the capital outflow, which in the new equilibrium is exactly offset by the trade surplus. The new equilibrium, however, cannot normally be sustained, because it involves an accumulation of foreign assets. In Chapter 13 we consider how this accumulation of foreign assets can affect interest rates and exchange rates.

FIGURE 9.12
Credit market equilibrium and an expansionary monetary policy.

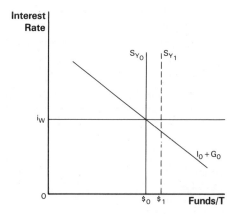

SUMMARY

An examination of how Keynesian models for open economies operate provides two kinds of insights. First, it shows how international integration influences the effectiveness of monetary and fiscal policy. Second, it illustrates the Keynesian vision of the transfer mechanism or the linkage between current and capital accounts.

Fiscal policy is highly effective under fixed rates because the upward pressure on domestic interest rates is dissipated in the world capital market, and the domestic money supply can rise with the increased demand for money. Monetary policy has no effect on income under fixed rates because the downward pressure on interest rates is lost in a capital outflow and reduction in international reserves. Monetary policy under flexible rates, however, is highly effective because equality between money demand and supply is restored entirely through a rise in income, rather than partly through a rise in income and a fall in the interest rate. Those of you who worked out the effects of fiscal policy under flexible rates know that it is ineffective with respect to employment because income cannot rise without an increase in the stock of money. The effects of expansionary fiscal and monetary policy are summarized in Table 9.1.

As for the Keynesian view of the linkage between current and capital accounts, that changes somewhat under fixed and flexible exchange rates. Under fixed rates, equality between trade and capital flows is achieved through changes in income. If the surplus in the capital account exceeds the deficit in the trade account, income rises, imports increase, and capital inflows fall until the international transfer of funds is converted into a transfer of commodities. Under flexible rates, both exchange rates and income work toward reestablishing the balance-of-payments equilibrium. Income operates exactly as it does under fixed rates. The exchange rate, however, works directly only on the trade balance, altering imports and exports. Its influence on the capital account is indirect through its effect on income.

If you stop and think about it, you will see that this chapter is an extension of the analysis we began in the first half of Chapter 5, where both the price level and real income were constant. Here we allow real income to

TABLE 9.1   Summary of Effects of Expansionary Monetary and Fiscal Policy

	FIXED RATES		FLEXIBLE RATES	
	MONETARY	FISCAL	MONETARY	FISCAL
Income	0	+	+	0
Capital account	0	+	−	+
Trade balance	0	−	+	−
International reserves	−	+	0	0

change, but retain the assumption of a constant price level. In the next chapter, we build on the approach we started in Chapter 6.

QUESTIONS FOR REVIEW

1. Why is there one *IS* curve but a whole family of *LM* curves when rates are fixed, and one *LM* curve but a whole family of *IS* curves when rates are flexible?
2. Assume a small, open economy with an interest rate that cannot diverge from an exogenous world interest rate. Consider the domestic response to each of the following shocks under both fixed and flexible exchange rates.
   a. An autonomous increase in imports like the one used in Chapters 5 and 6.
   b. An autonomous increase in the domestic demand for money.
   c. An autonomous increase in consumption matched by an equal reduction in desired saving.
3. Within the context of this chapter, compare and contrast the transfer mechanism under fixed and flexible exchange rates. Now compare and contrast this transfer mechanism with the one developed in Chapters 2 and 6. What is the crucial difference?
4. Explain why the level of imports in our Keynesian model depends on the exchange rate. Why do imports depend on domestic income, but not exports?
5. Drop the assumption of a constant price level. Assume instead an aggregate demand for labor that depends on the real wage, a rigid nominal wage rate, and an initial price level that yields a real wage above the market clearing wage. Now, work through the effects of fiscal and monetary policy for our small country under both fixed and flexible exchange rates.
6. Suppose domestic and foreign assets are not perfect substitutes. As an exercise, let international capital flows just close half the gap between the domestic interest rate for a closed economy and the world interest rate. If the domestic rate would rise from 4 to 6 percent without any change in capital flows, it rises to 5 percent with the new capital flow. Now work through the effects of domestic monetary and fiscal policy for a small country under fixed and flexible exchange rates.

ADDITIONAL READINGS

BAILEY, MARTIN J.   *National Income and the Price Level* (New York: McGraw-Hill, 1962).
MUNDELL, ROBERT A.   "Capital Mobility and Size." *Canadian Journal of Economics and Political Science* (August 1964).

————. "Capital Mobility and Stabilization Policy under Fixed and Flexible Exchange Rates." *Canadian Journal of Economics and Political Science* (November 1963). Reprinted in R. Caves and H. Johnson (eds.), *Readings in International Economics* (Homewood, Ill.: Irwin, 1968).

TAKAYAMA, AKIRA.   "The Effects of Fiscal and Monetary Policies under Flexible and Fixed Exchange Rates." *Canadian Journal of Economics* (May 1969).

APPENDIX
A Large-Country Model

This two-country model is based on Mundell's "Capital Mobility and Size" (see Additional Readings). The model allows us to drop the assumption of a small country and examine the adjustment mechanism for an economy that is large relative to the rest of the world. As a result, we can call the home country the United States and the other country the rest of the world.

We use the same behavioral equations and identities for the home country, now the United States, as we used in the chapter. The one exception is the export equation, where exports are now the domestic value of foreign imports.

$$S = a_0 - (1 - a_1)Y$$
$$I = b_0 - b_1 i$$
$$IM = n_0 + n_1 Y - n_2 \pi$$
$$X = \pi[\bar{x}_0 + \bar{x}_1 \bar{Y} + \bar{x}_2 \pi]$$
$$I + G - S = IM - X$$
$$M = kY - \lambda i$$
$$M = m_1 B + m_2 i$$
$$B = D + R$$

A similar model applies to the rest of the world, where overbars denote foreign variables or parameters:

$$\bar{S} = \bar{a}_0 - (1 - \bar{a}_1)\bar{Y}$$
$$\bar{I} = \bar{b}_0 - \bar{b}_1 i$$
$$\overline{IM} = \bar{x}_0 + \bar{x}_1 \bar{Y} + \bar{x}_2 \pi$$
$$\bar{X} = (1/\pi)(n_0 + n_1 Y - n_2 \pi)$$
$$\bar{I} + \bar{G} - \bar{S} = \overline{IM} - \bar{X}$$
$$\bar{M} = \bar{k}\bar{Y} - \bar{\lambda} i$$
$$\bar{M} = \bar{m}_1 \bar{B} + \bar{m}_2 i$$
$$\bar{B} = \bar{D} + \bar{R}$$

Measured in a common currency, the trade surplus of the United States equals the trade deficit of the rest of the world. If we continue the assumption of a zero trade balance in the initial equilibrium and choose our units judiciously so that π_0 equals unity, then we can write this condition simply as follows:

$$IM - X = \bar{X} - \overline{IM}$$

By appropriate substitutions, these 17 equations can be reduced to the following 4:

1. Domestic internal and external equilibrium:

$$b_0 - b_1 i + G + a_0 - (1 - a_1)Y$$
$$- [n_0 + n_1 Y - n_2 \pi - (\bar{x}_0 + \bar{x}_1 \bar{Y} + \bar{x}_2 \pi)] = 0$$

2. Foreign internal and external equilibrium:

$$\bar{b}_0 - \bar{b}_1 i + \bar{G} + \bar{a}_0 - (1 - \bar{a}_1)\bar{Y}$$
$$- [\bar{x}_0 + \bar{x}_1 \bar{Y} + \bar{x}_2 \pi - (n_0 + n_1 Y - n_2 \pi)] = 0$$

3. Domestic monetary equilibrium:

$$kY - \lambda i - [m_1(D + R) + m_2 i] = 0$$

4. Foreign monetary equilibrium:

$$\bar{k}\bar{Y} - \bar{\lambda} i - [\bar{m}_1(\bar{D} + \bar{R}) + \bar{m}_2 i] = 0$$

FLEXIBLE RATES

Under flexible exchange rates, we can differentiate and write the four equations in matrix notation as follows:

$$
\begin{bmatrix}
-(s + n_1) & \bar{x}_1 & -b_1 & (n_2 + \bar{x}_2) \\
n_1 & -(\bar{s} + \bar{x}_1) & -\bar{b}_1 & -(n_2 + \bar{x}_2) \\
k & 0 & -(\lambda + m_2) & 0 \\
0 & \bar{k} & -(\bar{\lambda} + \bar{m}_2) & 0
\end{bmatrix}
\begin{bmatrix}
dY \\ d\bar{Y} \\ di \\ d\pi
\end{bmatrix}
=
\begin{bmatrix}
-dG \\ 0 \\ dD \\ 0
\end{bmatrix}
$$

where s equals $(1 - a_1)$ and $\bar{s}$ equals $(1 - \bar{a}_1)$.

$$
\Delta_1 =
\begin{vmatrix}
-(s + n_1) & \bar{x}_1 & -b_1 & (n_2 + \bar{x}_2) \\
n_1 & -(\bar{s} + \bar{x}_1) & -\bar{b}_1 & -(n_2 + \bar{x}_2) \\
k & 0 & -(\lambda + m_2) & 0 \\
0 & \bar{k} & -(\bar{\lambda} + \bar{m}_2) & 0
\end{vmatrix}
$$

The term Δ_1 is positive because $b_1(n_2 + \bar{x}_2)\bar{k}k + (s + n_1)\bar{k}(\lambda + m_2)(n_2 + \bar{x}_2)$ is positive.

Under flexible rates, expansionary fiscal policy increases income at home and abroad. With the foreign money stock constant, a higher world interest rate reduces the foreign demand for money and requires a higher income. As a result, the exchange rate must change so that the increase in foreign exports exceeds the reduction in foreign investment by enough to restore monetary equilibrium.

$$dY/dG = (n_2 + \bar{x}_2)(\lambda + m_2)\bar{k}/\Delta_1 > 0$$
$$d\bar{Y}/dG = (n_2 + \bar{x}_2)(\lambda + \bar{m}_2)k/\Delta_1 > 0$$

An expansionary monetary policy increases domestic income, but reduces foreign income. With a fixed money stock and lower world interest rates, foreign income must decline to restore monetary equilibrium.

$$dY/dD = (n_2 + \bar{x}_2)[b_1\bar{k} + (\lambda + \bar{m}_2)\bar{s} + \bar{b}_1k]/\Delta_1 > 0$$
$$d\bar{Y}/dD = -(n_2 + \bar{x}_2)(\lambda + \bar{m}_2)s/\Delta_1 < 0$$

As expected, an expansionary fiscal policy raises world interest rates, and an expansionary monetary policy lowers them.

$$di/dG = (n_2 + \bar{x}_2)k\bar{k}/\Delta_1 > 0$$
$$di/dD = -(n_2 + \bar{x}_2)s_1\bar{k}/\Delta_1 < 0$$

An expansionary monetary policy always leads to depreciation. An expansionary fiscal policy, however, can result in appreciation or depreciation.

$$d\pi/dD = [(\bar{\lambda} + \bar{m}_2)(s\bar{s} + s\bar{x}_1 + n_1\bar{s}) + b_1\bar{k}n_1 + (s + n_1)\bar{k}\bar{b}_1]/\Delta_1 > 0$$
$$d\pi/dG = [(\lambda + m_2)n_1\bar{k} - \bar{b}_1\bar{k}k - (\bar{s} + \bar{x}_1)(\lambda + \bar{m}_2)k] \lessgtr 0$$

Comparable results hold for fixed rates.

FIXED RATES

When rates are fixed, reserves become endogenous, but there is a constraint on total reserves so that dR equals $-d\bar{R}$. As a result, we can write the model as follows:

$$\begin{bmatrix} -(s + n_1) & \bar{x}_1 & -b_1 & 0 \\ n_1 & -(\bar{s} + \bar{x}_1) & -\bar{b}_1 & 0 \\ k & 0 & -(\lambda + m_2) & -m_1 \\ 0 & \bar{k} & -(\bar{\lambda} + \bar{m}_2) & \bar{m}_1 \end{bmatrix} \begin{bmatrix} dY \\ d\bar{Y} \\ di \\ dR \end{bmatrix} = \begin{bmatrix} -dG \\ 0 \\ dD \\ 0 \end{bmatrix}$$

$$\Delta_2 = \begin{vmatrix} -(s + n_1) & \bar{x}_1 & -b_1 & 0 \\ n_1 & -(\bar{s} + \bar{x}_1) & -\bar{b}_1 & 0 \\ k & 0 & -(\lambda + m_2) & -m_1 \\ 0 & \bar{k} & -(\bar{\lambda} + \bar{m}_2) & \bar{m}_1 \end{vmatrix}$$

The term Δ_2 is negative because $-(s + n_1)(\bar{s} + \bar{x}_1)(\lambda + m_2)\bar{m}_1 - b_1(\bar{s} + \bar{x}_1)k\bar{m}_1 - \bar{x}_1 n_1(\bar{\lambda} + \bar{m}_2)m_1$ is negative.

Expansionary fiscal policy increases domestic income, but it can either reduce or increase foreign income. Higher domestic income decreases foreign exports, but higher world interest rates reduce foreign investment. The outcome depends on which factor dominates.

$$dY/dG = -[(\bar{s} + \bar{x}_1)m_1(\lambda + m_2 + \bar{\lambda} + \bar{m}_2) + \bar{b}_1 km_1]/\Delta_2 > 0$$
$$d\bar{Y}/dG = -[(\lambda + m_2 + \bar{\lambda} + \bar{m}_2)n_1 m_1 - \bar{b}_1 km_1]/\Delta_2 \gtreqless 0$$

Expansionary monetary policy increases both domestic and foreign income. Now the foreign money supply can increase, and both higher domestic income and lower world interest rates increase foreign aggregate demand.

$$dY/dD = -[\bar{x}_1 \bar{b}_1 m_1 - (\bar{s} + \bar{x}_1)b_1 m_1]/\Delta_2 > 0$$
$$d\bar{Y}/dD = -[(s + n_1)\bar{b}_1 \bar{m}_1 + b_1 n_1 \bar{m}_1]/\Delta_2 > 0$$

Once again, expansionary fiscal policy raises interest rates and expansionary monetary policy lowers them.

$$di/dG = -[(\bar{s} + \bar{x}_1)km_1 + n_1 \bar{k}m_1]/\Delta_2 > 0$$
$$di/dD = \bar{m}_1(s\bar{s} + s\bar{x}_1 + n_1\bar{s})/\Delta_2 < 0$$

If a country's currency depreciates (appreciates) under flexible rates, then under fixed rates it loses (gains) reserves.

$$dR/dD = [(\bar{\lambda} + \bar{m}_2)(s\bar{s} + s\bar{x}_1 + n_1\bar{s}) + b_1 \bar{k}n_1 + (s + n_1)\bar{k}\bar{b}_1]/\Delta_2 < 0$$
$$dR/dG = [(\lambda + m_2)n_1 \bar{k} - \bar{b}_1 kk - (\bar{s} + \bar{x}_1)(\bar{\lambda} + \bar{m}_2)k]/\Delta_2 \gtreqless 0$$

10

INTERNATIONAL ADJUSTMENT WITH FULL EMPLOYMENT

The objective of this chapter is to examine international adjustment when the price system works smoothly. In the last chapter, the invisible hand has a broken thumb and we are stuck inside the production possibility frontier. Here, there are no glitches in the price system. At times we may be inside the production frontier, but it is only a temporary situation until the price system reallocates resources from one sector to another. To simplify the analysis, we ignore transitional unemployment and use a model based on full employment and completely flexible prices.

First we build a simple macro model for a small, open economy with full employment. The following sections consider the effects of monetary and fiscal policy under fixed rates and monetary policy under flexible rates. Fiscal policy with flexible rates is left as an exercise.

MODEL

Output

We use the same aggregate production function as in Chapter 9 and retain the assumption of a fixed stock of capital, K.

$$y = y(N,K)$$

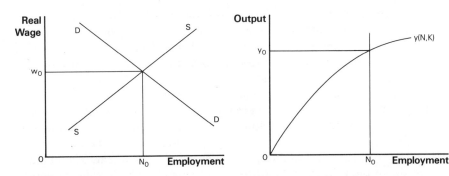

FIGURE 10.1 Demand for and supply   FIGURE 10.2 Output as a function of
of labor.   employment.

Here, however, the stock of capital is fully employed, and the level of output and real income, y, depend on the equilibrium level of employment.

The determination of the equilibrium level of output, employment, and the real wage is illustrated in Figures 10.1 and 10.2. Preferences between labor and leisure determine the aggregate supply schedule for labor, shown in Figure 10.1 as the solid line labeled SS. Given the capital stock, the marginal physical product schedule for labor derived from the aggregate production function describes the aggregate demand for labor, which is labeled DD. The intersection of the demand for and supply of labor determines the equilibrium real wage $0w_0$ and level of employment, $0N_0$. Figure 10.2 shows the relationship between output and employment. Given the equilibrium level of employment $0N_0$, the equilibrium level of output is $0y_0$.

In Keynesian models, output depends on aggregate demand. Here that dependence disappears because the price mechanism works. Output depends on preferences for leisure versus consumption, and the endowment of capital and other factors of production, but it does not depend on decisions such as saving versus consumption or the choice between domestic and foreign goods. Whatever happens in the rest of the model, the equilibrium levels for output, employment, and the real wage are, respectively, y_0, N_0, and w_0.

Aggregate Demand

In this approach we are interested in investment, saving, consumption, exports, and imports not because they influence output and employment, but because they determine the composition of output and the balance of payments. Our theoretical perspective is the one we developed in Chapters 1 and 2. In the absence of net capital flows, the demand for imports is a supply of exports. A capital outflow is a demand for future goods and a supply of present goods.

Imports and exports   If we ignore the choice between present and future goods, we are back to the pure theory of trade we reviewed in Chapter 1. An effective price mechanism implies that a demand for imports is a supply of exports. Figure 10.3 shows the production possibility frontier for our small, open economy, which is labeled *FF*. The terms of trade are determined in world commodity markets and they are reflected in the slope of the price line labeled *TT*. Given the terms of trade, the country produces at point *A*. The production of cloth is $0C_P$ and the production of wheat is $0W_p$. If we can summarize the country's preferences with the indifference curve *UU*, residents demand $0C_C$ in cloth and $0W_C$ of wheat. The country moves down the price line *TT* to the point *B*. At *B*, the demand to import C_PC_C cloth *is* a supply of W_CW_P wheat.

When there are nontraded goods the analysis is a bit more complicated, but the result is essentially the same. In this world, changes in preferences between foreign and domestic goods cannot cause a trade surplus or deficit. If residents of our small country demand more cloth, that increased demand for cloth is an increased supply of wheat. The volume of trade increases, but there is no trade deficit. This mechanism determines the composition of the trade account. In the rest of this chapter we ignore it and concentrate on the interaction between trade and capital accounts. That linkage is based on the Fisherian analysis we developed in Chapter 2.

Investment   For simplicity, real investment, *I*, is a linear function of the real interest rate. Since we assume there is no expected inflation, real and nominal interest rates are equal and we can use the same investment equation as in the last chapter:

$$I = b_0 - b_1 i$$

This equation describes a demand for present commodities that is financed by a supply of securities or claims on future goods.

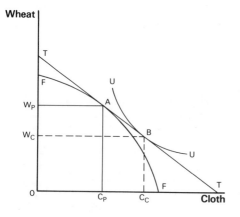

FIGURE 10.3
Composition of the trade account.

Saving   A Keynesian saving function is conceptually inconsistent with a Fisherian approach. In Chapter 2, saving represents a choice between present and future consumption. It depends on relative prices between present and future goods, or real interest rates, preferences, and the distribution of income over time. That is, real saving, S, depends on real income for this period, y_0, expected future real income, y_E, and the rate of exchange between present and future goods, i.

$$S = \alpha_0 y_0 - \alpha_1 y_E - \alpha_2 i$$

The signs for present income and the interest rate should seem reasonable, but the inverse relation between saving and expected future income may appear strange. The basic reasoning is illustrated in Figure 10.4, where present goods are measured along the horizontal axis and goods in the next period are measured along the vertical axis. For simplicity, we ignore production and begin with an initial endowment of present goods $0y_0$ and future goods $0y_1$. Given an interest rate i, which determines the slope of the price line ii, an individual with an endowment at point E has a level of wealth equal to $0W$. As a geometric convenience, we assume that at the initial equilibrium the individual consumes all current income, and saving is zero.

Now we increase expected income for next year from $0y_1$ to $0y_1'$ so that the endowment shifts from E to E' and wealth increases to $0W'$. Even though present income and the interest rate are constant, the increase in wealth induces the individual to increase consumption from $0y_0$ to $0C_0$. Instead of consuming more in just the next period when income is higher, our optimizing individual prefers to even out consumption over time. He or she sells claims on future goods to increase present consumption. Saving, which initially was zero, now becomes negative. It is this line of reasoning that leads us to write a saving function in which saving declines with increases in expected income.

FIGURE 10.4
Saving and the distribution of income over time.

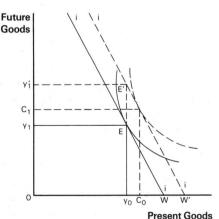

Given our saving function, we could derive a consumption function simply by subtracting saving from the level of current income, y_0. Since we have no need for a consumption function in the analysis that follows, we skip that exercise in subtraction.

Government expenditure   As in the last chapter, current government expenditure is financed entirely by sales of securities. Unlike the last chapter, however, government expenditure can influence saving through its effect on expected taxes.

Suppose this year the government borrows $10 billion to improve interstate highways. Next year the government must start paying interest on those bonds, which normally requires taxes. Those taxes reduce future disposable income. Better highways, however, increase future output. Which factor dominates depends on the productivity of government activities and the public's attitudes about future tax liabilities. For our analysis, we take the easy way out and assume that these two influences tend to offset each other. That assumption allows us to use a simple saving function that ignores government expenditure.

Credit Market

For those of you who are a little rusty on the Fisherian approach to the balance of payments, Figure 10.5 shows the domestic credit market for our small country. The investment schedule labeled *II* is a demand for credit and supply of bonds, and the saving schedule, *SS*, is a demand for bonds and supply of credit. At the world interest rate i_W, domestic firms sell $0N$ in securities, while domestic households purchase only $0M$. The difference, MN, is sold to foreigners in the world capital market. In other words, at the world interest rate of i_W, the desired capital inflow is MN.

In Figure 10.6 we look at this capital flow from another perspective. Future goods are measured along the vertical axis and present goods along the horizontal axis. The production possibility frontier is labeled *FF* and the initial endowment is at point *E*. Given the world interest rate i_W, wealth is

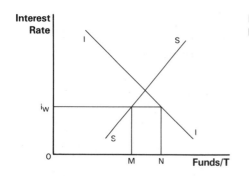

FIGURE 10.5
Domestic credit market.

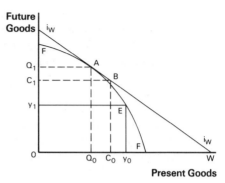

FIGURE 10.6
The link between capital and trade ac-
counts.

maximized by producing at point A, which involves investing $Q_0 y_0$ in order to produce $y_1 Q_1$ in future goods.

Given the optimal production at point A, society can choose its desired mix of present and future consumption from the alternatives described by the price line labeled $i_w i_w$. The equilibrium shown in Figure 10.5 corresponds to a point such as B in Figure 10.6. In Figure 10.6 the desired net import of commodities is $Q_0 C_0$. This desired import is made effective by a supply of $C_1 Q_1$ in future goods. The claims to these future goods take the form of securities whose present value is $Q_0 C_0$. This supply of securities appears as MN in Figure 10.5. The desired trade deficit corresponding to this desired capital inflow does not appear explicitly in Figure 10.5. To see that the supply of securities to foreigners *is* a demand for commodities from foreigners we have to go to Figure 10.6, which shows the analysis that underlies Figure 10.5.

Balance of Payments

As in the last chapter, the equilibrium condition for the balance of payments is that desired trade deficits equal desired capital inflows.

$$IM - X = I + G - S$$

In the Keynesian approach, there is no price theoretic link between trade and capital accounts. Balance-of-payments equilibrium must be achieved through changes in income and/or exchange rates. Here, full employment and an effective price mechanism imply that desired capital inflows are desired trade deficits. No changes in income or exchange rates are required to convert a capital flow into a transfer of commodities. When prices effectively allocate resources, there is no transfer problem.

Monetary Sector

This model reflects the classical dichotomy in which the real sector is independent from the monetary sector. Employment is determined by the demand for and supply of labor. Given the production function and existing capital stock, output depends on the equilibrium level of employment. An effective price mechanism ensures that there is sufficient aggregate demand to support output at full employment. With the interest rate determined in the world capital market, domestic investment and saving schedules determine the levels of real investment and saving, and the real balance in capital and trade accounts. The monetary sector has no influence on these real variables; it determines either the price level and exchange rate, or the level of international reserves. We begin our examination of the monetary sector with the supply of money, develop a demand for real money balances, and finish with purchasing power parity.

Money supply   The supply schedule for money is unchanged from the last chapter. The supply of nominal money balances depends positively on the monetary base, B, and interest rate, i.

$$M = m_1B + m_2i$$

As before, the monetary base equals the domestic securities, D, and foreign reserves, R, held by the central bank.

$$B = D + R$$

Money demand   The Keynesian tradition emphasizes the role of portfolio balance in the demand for money. In simple *IS-LM* models, the public chooses between holding bonds, a long-term asset, or money, a short-term asset. The monetarist approach stresses money's role as a means of payment. Money is demanded because it reduces the information and transaction costs associated with exchange. In a sense, money is more like a truck or lathe than it is like a Treasury bill. In this approach the public demands real, not nominal, money balances. Real money balances are nominal balances, M, deflated by the price level, P. The demand for real money balances, M/P, depends positively on real income, y, which is a proxy for the volume of transactions, and inversely on the interest rate, i. As in the last chapter, for simplicity we assume a linear relation.

$$M/P = ky - \lambda i$$

Monetary equilibrium   Monetary equilibrium is described in Figure 10.7. The interest rate is measured along the vertical axis and real money balances along the horizontal axis. Since there is only one equilibrium level for real income, y_0, there is only one demand schedule for real balances, which is labeled *DD*. Given this demand schedule and the exogenous world

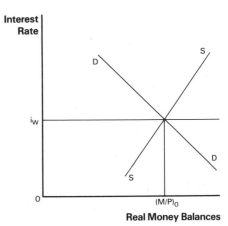

FIGURE 10.7
Demand for and supply of real money balances.

interest rate i_W, only one level of real balances, $(M/P)_0$, is consistent with full equilibrium.

With a fixed exchange rate, the domestic price level is determined by the world price level. In that case, international reserves must change until actual and desired real balances are equal. With a flexible rate, the monetary base is exogenous, and a given level of nominal balances is supplied at the world interest rate, i_W. In that case, the price level changes until desired and actual real money balances are equal.

Purchasing power parity   The basic premise of this chapter is that the price mechanism works. We therefore assume that international trade equates relative prices, and purchasing power parity holds.

$$\pi = \pi_0(P/\overline{P})$$

The equilibrium exchange rate in the new equilibrium π equals the equilibrium rate in the initial equilibrium π_0 times the ratio of the domestic price index P to the foreign price index $\overline{P}$. Since we are dealing with a small country, foreign prices are exogenous.

For simplicity, we assume that the price index used to deflate money balances and other nominal variables to obtain their real counterparts is an appropriate index for calculating purchasing power parity. As noted in Chapter 7, this assumption tends to distort the analysis by making the link between domestic and foreign price indexes too strong. The justification is that this distortion is a small penalty to pay for avoiding the complications introduced by two different domestic price indexes.

In this kind of model, money is simply a veil. Real capital and trade flows, the terms of trade, real income, and employment are all determined by endowments, tastes, and technology, independently of what happens in the monetary sector. Given these real outcomes, with flexible exchange rates the price level establishes monetary equilibrium and the exchange rate depends on relative price levels. With fixed exchange rates, the domestic price level for a small country is determined by the world price level, and monetary equilibrium is achieved through changes in international reserves.

Although this model is an extreme version of the monetarist approach, it does illustrate basic monetarist ideas about the nature of international adjustment. In particular, it reflects the view that exchange rates and balance-of-payments deficits are essentially monetary phenomena.

Initial Equilibrium

As in the last chapter, we assume that in the initial equilibrium there is a zero balance in trade and capital accounts. With no taxes, a balanced budget implies that government expenditure is zero and saving equals investment at the world interest rate i_W, as shown in Figure 10.8.

Figure 10.9 shows the initial equilibrium in the monetary sector. Given the level of real income y_0, the demand schedule for real balances is DD. With the interest rate determined in the world capital market at i_W, the equilibrium level of real money balances is $(M/P)_0$.

The determination of the stock of nominal money balances depends on the international monetary system. With flexible rates, the monetary base is exogenous and determines the position of the supply schedule for nominal balances shown in Figure 10.10. Given an exogenous monetary base B_0 and world interest rate i_W, the initial stock of money balances is $0M_0$. The initial price level P_0 is the one that converts this nominal money stock into the desired real stock $(M/P)_0$. The initial stock of real balances, therefore, is $(M_0/P_0)_0$. With flexible rates and exogenous world prices, the initial domestic price level determines the initial exchange rate π_0.

With fixed rates, the interpretation of the monetary sector changes. Real money balances are still demand-determined, but the domestic price

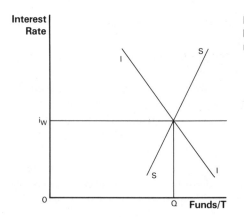

Interest
Rate

i_W

0   Q   Funds/T

FIGURE 10.8
Initial equilibrium in the domestic credit market.

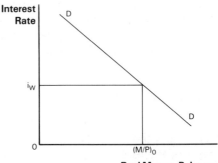

FIGURE 10.9
Initial equilibrium for real money balances.

level depends on the world price level. With a fixed rate, the monetary base and nominal money stock are endogenous. Given our assumption of purchasing power parity, the exogenous foreign price level determines the initial domestic price level, P_0. With a price level of P_0, only one stock of nominal balances, M_0, yields the desired level of real balances, $(M/P)_0$. Once again, the initial level of real balances is $(M_0/P_0)_0$, but now international reserves must adjust so that the supply schedule for nominal balances in Figure 10.10 shifts to the point where $0M_0$ in nominal balances is supplied when the interest rate is i_W.

Now that we know what the initial equilibria look like in the various markets, we can examine how the system responds to some exogenous shocks. As in the last chapter we consider fiscal and monetary policy under fixed rates and monetary policy under flexible rates. If you understand these three cases, you should have no trouble working out the effects of fiscal policy under flexible rates.

FIXED EXCHANGE RATES

We begin with fixed exchange rates. The market exchange rate is fixed at some level π_0 either through gold flows or intervention by the central bank.

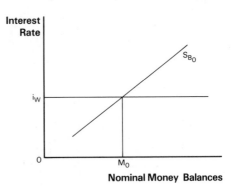

FIGURE 10.10
Initial equilibrium for nominal money balances.

The central bank, however, does not use sterilization to insulate domestic financial markets from the effects of reserve flows. As in the last chapter, for simplicity we assume that the exchange rate is fixed at an exact level π_0 rather than restricted to some narrow range around an official or par rate of exchange.

Fiscal Policy

Let's consider how an autonomous increase in government expenditure alters the initial equilibrium. We know that it does not affect employment or the level of real output because changes in relative prices maintain full employment for all factors of production. Constant real income implies that the demand schedule for real balances in Figure 10.9 is unchanged, so the equilibrium level of real balances remains $(M/P)_0$. With fixed exchange rates and a constant world price level $\overline{P}$, the domestic price level also remains unchanged. Given the initial price level P_0, only one level of nominal balances, the initial level M_0, yields the desired level of real balances, $(M/P)_0$. In terms of Figure 10.10, a constant stock of nominal balances implies a constant monetary base and unchanged international reserves.

The increase in government expenditure does not alter output, the price level, or the level of reserves, but it does change the composition of the balance of payments and increases the volume of trade in the foreign exchange market. We begin with the composition of the balance of payments.

Trade and capital accounts   The increase in real government expenditure is an increased demand for commodities financed by an increased supply of securities. The impact on the domestic capital market is illustrated in Figure 10.11. The initial supply schedule for securities, I, shifts to $I + G$. The rightward shift, which equals QN, represents the increased supply of securities measured in real terms. The excess supply of domestic assets is sold in the world capital market, creating a surplus on capital account equal

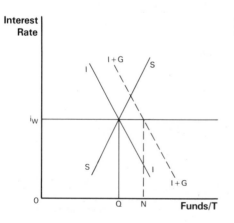

FIGURE 10.11
The real capital inflow.

to QN. In the last chapter, the transfer mechanism works through a rise in income, which reduces this surplus and creates a trade deficit. Here the transfer mechanism works through the price system. With an effective price system, the supply of securities is a demand for imports.

In order to illustrate what happens, let's take a simple case in which there are only three goods. There is an import, oil, an export, wool, and a third good, cement, which is not traded. To concentrate on the adjustment process, we assume that all the increased government expenditure is for concrete. This is consistent with our Keynesian analysis and gives us the simplest possible case where there is a change in the demand for only one product, concrete.

In the Keynesian model analyzed in the last section, an increased demand for concrete has no direct effect on exports or imports. Exports are determined by foreign income and the exchange rate. Imports are driven by domestic income and the exchange rate. With the exchange rate fixed, the only way imports can rise is through increases in income initiated by the increased demand for concrete. The reallocation of resources through changes in relative prices plays no role in the Keynesian model, but it lies at the heart of this approach. Here the increased demand for concrete tends to raise prices for concrete. Manufacturers of concrete bid capital, labor, and other factors away from domestic producers of cloth and wool. As resources are bid away, the supply schedules for these goods shift to the left. From the analysis of Chapter 1 we know that these shifts reduce exports and increase imports. With an effective price system, the deficit in the balance of trade is not generated by a movement toward the production possibility frontier, but by a movement along that frontier.

Given the production possibility frontier as an effective constraint, the increased production of concrete reduces the production of oil and wool. With domestic preferences for oil and wool unchanged and their prices determined in a world market this country cannot affect, imports rise and exports fall by the change in the domestic production of concrete. In this approach, the price mechanism creates a direct link between the increased demand for concrete and the balance of trade.

Foreign exchange market   What does this adjustment mechanism imply about the foreign exchange market? It implies that the rightward shift in the supply of pounds due to the export of securities is partially offset by a reduction in the supply of pounds as exports of wool decline. In addition, there is an increased demand for pounds as the import of oil increases.

The new equilibrium in the foreign exchange market is illustrated in Figure 10.12. The sale of QN in securities shifts the supply schedule from SS to $S'S'$. The reduction in commodity exports, however, shifts it back to $S''S''$. At the same time, the increase in imports increases the demand for pounds, and it shifts to $D'D'$. The surplus in the capital account of QN just equals the

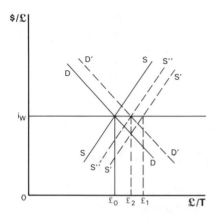

$/£

i_w

S S'' S'
D'
D
S'
S D'
S'' S' D

0   £_0 £_2 £_1   £/T

FIGURE 10.12
The market for foreign exchange.

deficit in the trade account, and the demand for pounds, $D'D'$, intersects the supply, $S''S'''$, at the official or par rate of exchange, π_0. All this adjustment is accomplished by the price system without any change in income.

Nontraded goods Did any of you catch the flaw in the argument we just went through? If you did, you deserve an A in the course. Concrete is a nontraded good. The increased demand for concrete increases the dollar price of concrete, while trade keeps dollar prices of oil and wool constant. For any price index containing concrete, the domestic price level rises. Purchasing power parity does not hold to the extent that prices for nontraded goods rise relative to those for traded goods. In addition, there must be a temporary balance-of-payments surplus so that nominal money balances can rise to accommodate the rise in the price level. (If this were a large country, in the rest of the world prices for wool and oil would tend to rise relative to the price of concrete.)

What kind of assumptions allow us to ignore this problem? One possibility is that changes in the patterns of demand associated with capital flows tend to be both random and broadly based, so that they introduce only a random error term into purchasing power parity. Another argument is that in the long run, everything is tradable either directly or indirectly. It may be prohibitive to ship concrete to New Zealand, but the machinery and some of the inputs used to produce concrete are tradable. In addition, substitutes such as steel, wood, and plastic are tradables. Another closely related argument is that in the long run, the production possibility frontier is quite flat. A very flat frontier implies that the production of concrete can rise substantially with only a very small change in relative prices.

It should be clear that the accuracy of purchasing power parity is *not* the crucial difference between the Keynesian and monetarist versions of how an economy responds to an exogenous real shock. The fundamental difference is the role of the price mechanism. The Keynesian paradigm rests on the assumption that the price mechanism fails. The monetarist position is based on the belief that the price mechanism allocates resources reasonably, quickly, and efficiently.

Transactions demand   There is another conceptual complication with this model that we might as well take up now. The demand for real balances is based on the idea that money is demanded because it reduces the transaction costs associated with exchange. The demand for real money balances is normally written as a function of real income, because real income is considered a useful proxy for the volume of transactions. For a closed economy that may be a reasonable assumption, but for an open economy there is a potential problem. In our example, domestic expenditure exceeds domestic income by the amount of the capital inflow. As a result, transactions tend to rise even though domestic income and output are unchanged. If the volume of transactions rises, so do the demand for real balances, the stock of nominal balances, and international reserves.

Monetary Policy

If you understand the response to fiscal policy, monetary policy is simple. Suppose the central bank buys government bonds. The immediate effect is to raise domestic assets held by the bank, and the monetary base increases by the same amount. This open market purchase has no impact on the equilibrium level of real income, which stays at y_0. It does not shift either real investment or saving, so the new equilibrium in the balance of payments looks just like the initial equilibrium. The trade balance is zero, and there is no net capital flow. With the initial level of real income and the world interest rate unchanged, the equilibrium level of real money balances is also unchanged. Given a constant price level due to a fixed exchange rate, nominal money balances and the monetary base also must be the same in the old and the new equilibrium. Since domestic assets have risen and the monetary base must return to the original level, international reserves must fall by as much as the initial increase in domestic assets held by the central bank.

In spite of their differences, with respect to monetary policy for a small country with capital mobility, the monetary and Keynesian models yield the same implications. Under fixed rates, an open market purchase leads to an equivalent loss of international reserves. The traditional monetarist story of how we get from the initial to the final equilibrium, however, is a little different from the usual Keynesian tale. For a monetarist, the open market purchase generates an excess supply of real money balances. Some of these excess balances are used to buy assets, which creates a temporary deficit in the capital account. Some of the excess balances are spent on commodities, which increases the demand for imports, reduces the supply of exports, and generates a temporary trade deficit. The deficit in capital and trade accounts persists as long as the monetary base is above the initial level and there are excess real money balances. During this transition, the rise in nominal aggregate demand generated by excess money balances may generate a temporary increase in the domestic price level relative to the foreign price level.

FLEXIBLE EXCHANGE RATES

Now we drop the assumption that the central bank fixes the exchange rate. Rates are flexible, there is no intervention, and international reserves are constant. The monetary base is a policy variable.

Monetary Policy

Suppose the central bank buys government bonds. Domestic assets, D, rise, and the monetary base rises, driving up nominal balances. As was the case with fixed rates, the open market purchase does not change the equilibrium level of real income or the composition of the balance of payments. The equilibrium level of real money balances is also unchanged. The rise in nominal balances therefore must be offset by a proportional increase in the price level that leaves real balances unchanged. If the initial level of real balances was $(M_0/P_0)_0$, it is now $(M_1/P_1)_0$.

The real demand for imports is unchanged, but the nominal demand rises proportionately with the rise in the domestic price level. This shifts the demand for foreign exchange in Figure 10.13 from DD to $D'D'$. The real supply for exports is also unchanged, but in nominal terms it shifts up (to the left) proportionately with the rise in the price level. The net result is that the real volume of trade is unchanged at $0£_0$, but the exchange rate in Figure 10.13 rises proportionately with the increase in the price level from π_0 to π_1.

Note that under both fixed and flexible exchange rates, monetary policy does not create the conceptual problems for PPP and the demand for

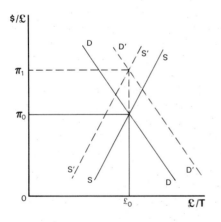

FIGURE 10.13
Demand for and supply of foreign exchange.

money generated by a real shock. There is no reason to presume that monetary policy affects either relative prices or the volume of transactions. As noted in Chapter 6, it is this kind of model that leads many monetarists to think of the price level as causing exchange rates, even though both are endogenous variables. Tastes, endowments, and the productivity of capital determine output and interest rates. The price level adjusts so as to equate desired and actual real money balances, and the exchange rate is driven by the price level, even though both are endogenous.

EFFECTS OF SIZE AND MOBILITY

If we drop the assumption of a small country, with fixed rates domestic monetary policy can affect the foreign money supply and the domestic price level. With flexible rates, the response to monetary policy is the same for large and small countries. With both fixed and flexible rates, domestic fiscal policy by a large country can influence interest rates. A change in interest rates alters the demand for and supply of money, which can alter price levels and create reserve flows or changes in exchange rates. The essence of the transfer mechanism, however, is the same for New Zealand and the United States. It relies on the pure theory of trade we reviewed in Chapter 1 and the Fisherian approach we developed in Chapter 2.

Imperfect capital mobility also does not change the basic story. If domestic and foreign assets are not perfect substitutes, an expansionary fiscal policy raises domestic interest rates relative to foreign rates. This shift in relative interest rates promotes a loss of reserves under fixed rates and depreciation under flexible rates, but it does not change the transfer mechanism. That mechanism still relies on a reallocation of resources through the price system.

SUMMARY

In the *IS-LM* model used in the last chapter, income, the composition of the balance of payments, and the exchange rate or international reserves are simultaneously determined in an interdependent system. With an effective price mechanism, this simultaneity begins to break down. The output sector determines the level of employment and production. Real aggregate demand does not affect output or employment, but it does determine the composition of output and the balance in trade and capital accounts.

The behavior of the monetary sector depends on the international monetary system. With fixed exchange rates, purchasing power parity implies that the domestic price level for a small country is driven by the world price level, and the monetary sector is cleared by changes in international re-

TABLE 10.1   Summary of Effects of Expansionary Monetary and Fiscal Policy

	FIXED RATES		FLEXIBLE RATES	
	MONETARY	FISCAL	MONETARY	FISCAL
Income	0	0	0	0
Capital account	0	+	0	+
Trade balance	0	−	0	−
International reserves	−	0	0	0
Price level	0	0	+	0

serves. With flexible exchange rates, changes in price levels clear the monetary sector, and the exchange rate is driven by relative price levels.

The effects of expansionary monetary and fiscal policies are summarized in Table 10.1. These results ignore any effect on relative prices between traded and nontraded goods or any increase in transactions associated with capital flows.

It is the inherent logic of this kind of model that leads many monetarists to think of exchange rates as being "caused" by relative price levels, even though price levels and exchange rates are both endogenous variables. As for the transfer mechanism, neither income nor exchange rates play an important role in the linkage between capital and trade accounts. A surplus in the capital account is converted into a deficit in the trade account by a movement along the production possibility frontier, not by a change in the exchange rate or a movement toward the production frontier.

The key role for purchasing power parity in this and other monetarist models tends to exaggerate its importance. This monetary approach to international adjustment does not stand or fall with purchasing power parity. The crucial issue is whether or not the price mechanism effectively reallocates resources. If it does, then this model provides a useful description of international adjustment whether or not PPP accurately predicts changes in exchange rates.

In the last two chapters we compared and contrasted the international adjustment to fiscal and monetary policy in Keynesian and monetarist models for a small, open economy. In the next chapter we continue this analysis by comparing and contrasting the effects of several other exogenous shocks.

QUESTIONS FOR REVIEW

1. In the model developed in this chapter, if a shock causes the country to lose reserves under a fixed rate, then that shock causes the country's currency to devalue under a flexible rate. Explain why.

2. In this chapter, imports are not a function of either income or the exchange rate. What is the relation here between real income, imports, and the exchange rate?

3. Compare and contrast the transfer mechanism with an effective price system under fixed and flexible exchange rates.

4. Given a small, open economy with perfect capital mobility and full employment due to an effective price mechanism, consider the internal and external adjustment to the following exogenous shocks:

   a. An autonomous increase in imports like the one used in Chapters 5 and 6.

   b. An autonomous increase in the demand for money.

   c. An autonomous increase in imports matched by an equal reduction in desired saving.

5. Compare and contrast your results for each of the shocks in the last question to the effects of the same shocks in a small, open Keynesian model.

6. Suppose domestic and foreign assets are not perfect substitutes. Because of political risk or transaction costs, international capital flows close just half the gap between the domestic and foreign interest rates that would exist in the absence of capital flows. Now use the model with an effective price mechanism to analyze the effects of domestic monetary and fiscal policy for a small country under fixed and flexible exchange rates. Compare these results to the ones you obtained for a similar exercise with the Keynesian model.

7. When a shock is monetary, Hume's price-specie-flow mechanism restores the initial relationship between domestic and foreign price levels. If a shock is real, PPP may fail and adjustment may require a change in relative price levels. Explain.

8. Suppose our small country with an effective price mechanism is forced to make a lump-sum reparations payment. It can raise the money by selling bonds and taxing future income or by taxing present income. For both options, explain how the debit in the unilateral account is converted into a matching surplus in other accounts in the balance of payments. Work through this exercise for both fixed and flexible exchange rates. (Remember, in this case the sale of government bonds is not associated with any increase in future income.)

9. Now work through the same problem again using the Keynesian approach developed in the last chapter and compare and contrast the two transfer mechanisms.

ADDITIONAL READINGS

CAVES, DOUGLAS W., AND EDGAR L. FEIGE. "Efficient Foreign Exchange Markets and the Monetary Approach to Exchange-Rate Determination." *American Economic Review* (March 1980).
COLLERY, ARNOLD. *International Adjustment, Open Economies, and the*

Quantity Theory of Money. Princeton Studies in International Finance, No. 28 (June 1971).

FRENKEL, JACOB, AND HARRY JOHNSON (EDS.). *The Monetary Approach to the Balance of Payments* (Toronto: University of Toronto Press, 1976).

JOHNSON, HARRY G. "The Monetary Approach to Balance-of-Payments Theory." *Journal of Financial and Quantitative Analysis* (March 1972). Reprinted in M. Connolly and A. Swoboda (eds.), *International Trade and Money* (Toronto: University of Toronto Press, 1973).

KREININ, MORDECHAI E., AND LAWRENCE H. OFFICER. *The Monetary Approach to the Balance of Payments: A Survey*. Princeton Studies in International Finance, No. 43 (November 1978).

APPENDIX
A Large-Country Model

Our large-country model assumes full employment at home and abroad so that we can treat output as though it were exogenous. Given this assumption, the interest rate and equilibrium composition of the balance of payments is determined by the Fisherian mechanism we analyzed in Chapter 2. Here we concentrate on how the monetary sectors determine the exchange rate or distribution of reserves.

MONETARY SECTORS

For simplicity, we use log linear versions of the demand and supply schedules for money. The domestic supply schedule for nominal balances now appears as follows:

$$M = m_1 B i^{m_2}$$

The foreign schedule has the same form:

$$\overline{M} = \overline{m}_1 \overline{B} i^{\overline{m}_2}$$

The demand schedules appear as follows:

$$M/P = kyi^{-\lambda}$$
$$\overline{M}/\overline{P} = \overline{k}\overline{y}i^{-\overline{\lambda}}$$

Bars again denote foreign variables or parameters. There is no bar over the foreign interest rate because there is no expected inflation, and capital flows equate real interest rates. Purchasing power parity holds.

$$\pi = P/\overline{P}$$

The base period exchange rate π_0 has been set equal to unity and eliminated by a judicious choice of units.

FLEXIBLE RATES

With flexible rates, we eliminate international reserves so that the base equals domestic assets, D or $\overline{D}$. By combining the demand and supply schedules in each country, we can obtain solutions for domestic price levels.

$$P = m_1 D i^{m_2}/kyi^{-\lambda}$$
$$\overline{P} = \overline{m}_1 \overline{D} i^{\overline{m}_2}/\overline{k}\overline{y}i^{-\overline{\lambda}}$$

Since the exchange rate equals $P/\overline{P}$, we can utilize these two equations to obtain a solution for the exchange rate.

$$\pi = \frac{m_1}{\overline{m}_1} \times \frac{D}{\overline{D}} \times \frac{\overline{k}}{k} \times \frac{\overline{y}}{y} \times i^{(m_2-\overline{m}_2)-(\overline{\lambda}-\lambda)}$$

The most interesting feature of this result is the implication for changes in the interest rate. With perfect capital mobility, there is no tendency for a country with increased investment demand to experience appreciation or depreciation due to rising interest rates. Which country depreciates depends on which has the relatively most interest-elastic demand for and supply of money. With imperfect capital mobility, there is more pressure on the price level of the country with increased investment, and depreciation of that currency is more likely.

FIXED RATES

To simplify the analysis under fixed rates, we assume the monetary base consists entirely of international reserves. This does not involve any serious loss of generality because we can interpret monetary policy as a change in reserve requirements that alters $\overline{m}_1$ or m_1. The domestic and foreign stock of international reserves just equals the world stock, G.

$$G = R + \overline{R}$$

Since price levels are equal under fixed rates, we can replace D with R, $\overline{D}$ with $\overline{R}$, and use the solution for prices to obtain a solution for the distribution of international reserves.

$$\frac{\overline{R}}{R} = \frac{m_1}{\overline{m}_1} \times \frac{\overline{k}}{k} \times \frac{\overline{y}}{y} \times i^{(m_2 - \overline{m}_2) - (\overline{\lambda} - \lambda)}$$

Any change, including a change in the interest rate, that would cause the domestic currency to depreciate under flexible rates leads to a redistribution of reserves away from the domestic country under fixed rates.

11

MORE
ON INTERNATIONAL
ADJUSTMENT

In the last two chapters we concentrated on the macro aspects of international adjustment to domestic shocks. The major objective of this chapter is to look at adjustment from a more micro perspective and to consider the response to foreign shocks. We will first analyze Keynesian and monetarist responses to an autonomous increase in imports. This exercise provides an introduction to our analysis of the OPEC oil shock in the next chapter. In the following sections we will examine the domestic effects of foreign fiscal and monetary policy with fixed and flexible rates. The chapter ends with a brief analysis of the effects of devaluation.

INCREASED IMPORT DEMAND

We retain our small-country assumption and restrict our analysis to three commodities. Once again there is an import, oil, an export, wool, and a nontraded good, concrete. In each case an increased demand for oil reflects a reduced demand for concrete. This assumption is consistent with most Keynesian analysis, and it highlights the differences in the two approaches. (If you want a little practice, consider the more general case in which an increased demand for oil reflects a reduced demand for concrete and wool.) We start by comparing and contrasting the two views for fixed rates and then shift to flexible rates.

Fixed Rates

To simplify the analysis, rates are fixed at an exact level rather than over some range. In addition, we exclude any sterilization. Initially there is a zero balance in both trade and capital accounts.

Keynesian   In the Keynesian paradigm, an increased demand for imports normally means a reduced demand for domestic output. Income falls because aggregate demand declines. As shown in Figure 11.1, for our small country the effects of this decline in aggregate demand are not mitigated by a fall in interest rates. Increased imports shift the IS schedule to the left from IS to $I'S'$, and output falls by the full multiplier from $0Y_0$ to $0Y_1$. The reduction in money demand due to lower income leads to a loss of international reserves, and the LM schedule shifts to $L'M'$.

Figure 11.2 shows the response of the capital account to the increased demand for imports. In the initial equilibrium depicted by the solid saving and investment schedules, there is no net capital flow. When income falls, saving declines from $0\$_0$ to $0\$_1$ and a net capital inflow of $\$_1\$_0$ emerges. At the new equilibrium level of income $0Y_1$, the surplus in the capital account equals the deficit in the trade account. This export of securities therefore pays for the trade deficit that remains after the decline in income to $0Y_1$.

Figures 11.3 to 11.5 show the adjustment process at a more micro level. Figure 11.3 shows the domestic oil market. With fixed exchange rates, the domestic price for oil, $0\overline{P}$, is set by the world oil price. At that price, in the initial equilibrium our country imports $0Q$ units of oil. The increased demand for oil shifts the import demand schedule out to $D'D'$, but the decline in income shifts the schedule back to $D''D''$. Imports therefore increase from $0Q$ to $0Q''$ rather than to $0Q'$. That is, part of the adjustment takes the form of a reduced demand for imports due to a fall in income.

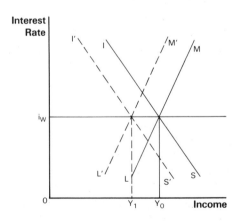

FIGURE 11.1
Effect on income of an increase in import demand.

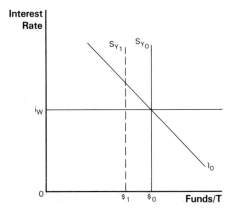

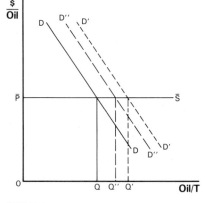

FIGURE 11.2 Effect on capital flows of an increase in import demand.

FIGURE 11.3 Effect on imports from an increased demand for oil.

The domestic market for concrete is shown in Figure 11.4. With unemployed resources, the domestic supply is infinitely elastic at the price $0P$. The demand schedule in the initial equilibrium is DD, and production is $0C$. The increased demand for oil reduces the demand for concrete to $D'D'$ and the fall in income reduces demand even further to $D''D''$. As a result, output falls to $0C''$. The resources released by the reduced production of concrete make no contribution to external adjustment. They simply become unemployed.

Given the exchange rate, exports are determined by foreign income, so they remain constant. Domestic exports are shown in Figure 11.5. The world

FIGURE 11.4 Effect on nontraded goods from an increased demand for oil.

FIGURE 11.5 Effect on exports from an increased demand for oil.

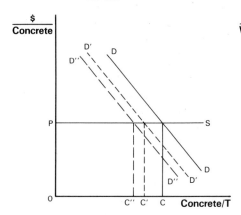

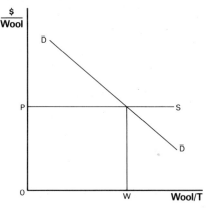

demand is labeled $\overline{DD}$. Given the infinitely elastic domestic supply at $0P$, domestic exports are $0W$. Since increased unemployment in the concrete industry does not lower the cost of wool production, domestic exports do not change.

In the Keynesian approach, the price mechanism fails and the increased demand for imports reduces income. The fall in income restores external equilibrium in two ways. First, it reduces the demand for imports, which makes the trade deficit smaller than it would have been at the original level of income. Second, it reduces saving and generates a capital inflow.

If we drop our assumption of a small country, the adjustment process becomes more complicated. It still works primarily through changes in income, but now both domestic and foreign income change. The increased domestic demand for imports raises foreign exports, and foreign income rises. The rise in foreign income increases domestic exports, and domestic income tends to fall by less than it would for a small country. Both the capital inflow and trade deficit also tend to be smaller.

For simplicity, the Keynesian model makes some implicit, but very important, assumptions. With respect to imports, it assumes that either oil is not produced domestically or, if there is domestic oil production, it is not the same as imported oil. A similar assumption arises on the export side. Our small country cannot export all the wool it can produce because domestic and foreign wool are not perfect substitutes. The Keynesian approach tends to emphasize product differentiation. Australian and New Zealand wools are not identical. Neither are California and French wine, nor U.S. and Canadian wheat. Given product differentiation, it makes sense for the exports of a small country to be limited by world aggregate demand.

Monetarist models tend to ignore product differentiation. As in the pure theory of trade, French and California wine are treated as though they were perfect substitutes. If domestic and foreign goods are identical and commodity arbitrage is effective, then purchasing power parity makes sense. With the monetarist approach, there is no reason to associate changes in exchange rates with changes in the terms of trade.

Monetarist   Given an effective price mechanism, shifts in the composition of aggregate demand alter the mix of output, but not the level of employment. Since the increased demand for oil is a reduced demand for concrete, neither the productivity of capital nor time preference change. Given our analysis in Chapter 2, investment and saving schedules do not shift, and there is no net capital flow in the new equilibrium. The increase in imports generates an increase in exports, just as it does in the pure theory of trade reviewed in Chapter 1. The adjustment process is illustrated in Figures 11.6 through 11.8.

The domestic oil market is depicted in Figure 11.6. The domestic oil price, $0\overline{P}$, is dictated by world oil prices and the fixed exchange rate. Given

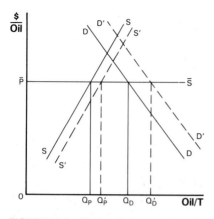

FIGURE 11.6   Change in imports due to increased demand for oil.

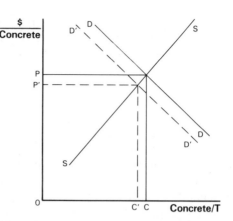

FIGURE 11.7   Change in price and production of concrete due to increased demand for oil.

the initial domestic supply, *SS*, and demand *DD*, domestic oil imports are Q_PQ_D. The increase in domestic demand to $D'D'$ increases imports, but they do not rise to Q_PQ_D'. The reduced demand for concrete releases factors of production. With more inputs available, domestic oil production rises.

The market for concrete is shown in Figure 11.7. As a result of the decline in demand for concrete from *DD* to $D'D'$, the price, output, and consumption of concrete fall. The reduction in output from $0C$ to $0C'$ releases resources that move into oil and wool production. In Figure 11.6 the supply schedule for oil shifts to $S'S'$, and domestic oil production rises from $0Q_p$ to $0Q_p'$. Part of the increased demand for oil is met by increased domestic production, and imports rise by $Q_DQ_D' - Q_pQ_p'$ rather than by the full shift in demand, Q_DQ_D'.

FIGURE 11.8
Change in exports due to increased demand for oil.

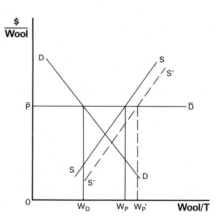

The fall in the relative price and output of concrete also shifts resources from the concrete industry into wool production, and the supply schedule for wool in Figure 11.8 shifts from SS to $S'S'$. With domestic demand for wool unchanged, exports increase by the increase in domestic production, W_pW_p'. If we drop the small-country assumption, the results are essentially the same except that the terms of trade change. The wool price of oil goes up.

In the Keynesian model, external equilibrium is restored by a fall in income, which generates a capital inflow and reduces the trade deficit by reducing oil imports. In this approach, the increased demand for imports does not create a trade deficit. As in the pure theory of trade reviewed in Chapter 1, the trade balance is restored entirely by a change in the composition of output—that is, by a movement along the production frontier rather than by a movement away from it. Concrete production falls, which increases oil and wool production. The increased production of oil reduces oil imports, and more wool production increases exports. In the end there are higher imports and exports, but no trade deficit.

If oil is not produced domestically, more resources shift into wool production, and the increased demand for oil is offset by an equivalent increase in wool exports. If oil is not the only import, domestic production of other imported commodities rises. In that case, higher oil imports are partially financed by a decline in other imports.

Once again purchasing power parity fails to hold exactly. For a small country, the prices for wool and oil remain constant because, with a fixed rate, they are determined in the world market. But the price of concrete falls, causing the domestic price level to fall relative to the world price level. Given the fall in the domestic price level, monetary equilibrium requires a reduction in nominal money balances to restore real balances to their original level. This reduction is achieved by a loss of international reserves during the transition to the new equilibrium.

Flexible Rates

For a monetarist, the adjustment mechanism is essentially the same with fixed and flexible rates. Under a Keynesian approach, with flexible rates the exchange rate rather than income bears the brunt of the adjustment.

Keynesian   Whether rates are fixed or flexible, an increased demand for imports reduces aggregate demand. With flexible rates, however, income does not fall when aggregate demand declines. Any reduction in income creates an excess supply of money, a capital outflow, and depreciation. To restore monetary equilibrium, the domestic currency must depreciate until

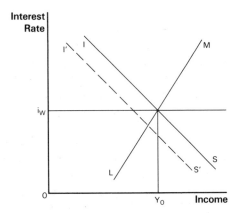

FIGURE 11.9
Effect on income of an increased demand
for imports with flexible exchange rates.

imports decline and exports rise by enough to restore aggregate demand to its original level. As in Chapter 5, the exchange rate restores equilibrium in the balance of trade. For now, we ignore any effects depreciation and higher oil prices might have on domestic prices. We will take up that complication in the next chapter.

The adjustment process is illustrated in Figure 11.9. In the original equilibrium, the solid *IS* and *LM* schedules intersect at the world interest rate i_W, yielding a domestic income of $0Y_0$. The increased demand for imports shifts the *IS* schedule to the left to $I'S'$. Income, however, cannot fall below $0Y_0$ in the new equilibrium because the *LM* schedule does not shift, and any decline in income implies monetary disequilibrium. The domestic currency therefore must depreciate by enough to shift the *IS* schedule back to its original position.

We see this adjustment process at a more micro level in Figures 11.10 through 11.12. Figure 11.10 shows the domestic market for oil. Given the

FIGURE 11.10
Effect on imports of increased demand for oil.

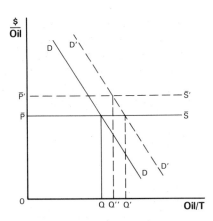

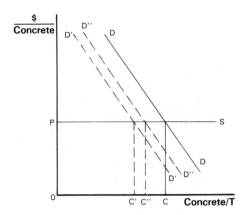

FIGURE 11.11
Effect on nontraded good of increased demand for oil.

initial exchange rate and world oil price, the domestic oil price is $0\bar{P}$, and oil imports are $0Q$. With the increase in demand, imports tend to rise to $0Q'$, but the increase in the exchange rate causes the price of oil to rise to $0\bar{P}'$, and imports fall back to $0Q''$.

The market for concrete is depicted in Figure 11.11. Given the domestic price, $0P$, and the initial demand, DD, output is $0C$. The increased demand for oil shifts the demand for concrete to $D'D'$. If the demand for oil is elastic, the rise in the exchange rate reduces expenditure for oil, and this shifts some aggregate demand back toward concrete. The net result is that demand for concrete in Figure 11.11 falls to $D''D''$ rather than $D'D'$, and domestic output falls to $0C''$ rather than $0C'$.

Figure 11.12 shows the domestic market for wool. The domestic supply is infinitely elastic at a price of $0P$. Given the initial exchange rate, foreign demand is $\bar{D}\bar{D}$, and exports are $0W$. Depreciation increases foreign demand, which shifts to $\bar{D}'\bar{D}'$, and exports rise to $0W'$. The rise in the value of wool

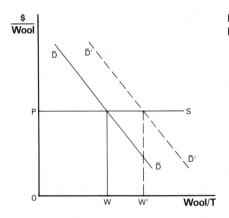

FIGURE 11.12
Effect on exports of increased demand for oil.

exports just matches the increase in the value of oil imports, which restores a zero trade balance. In addition, the decrease in concrete output is just offset by higher wool production.

If we drop the assumption of a small country, the adjustment mechanism does not change. Adjustment cannot take place through a rise in foreign income and a fall in domestic income, because that is inconsistent with monetary equilibrium. For both small and large countries, depreciation restores the trade balance after an increased demand for imports.

Monetarist   Now let the price mechanism work to maintain full employment. With no change in investment or saving, there is no change in the capital account. Indeed, whether the country is large or small, all the real adjustment goes through exactly as it did for a fixed rate. The relative price of concrete falls, and resources shift to oil and wool production. Oil imports rise by less than the increased demand for oil, and the value of wool exports rises by an amount equal to the rise in the value of oil imports.

The only difference between this and the fixed-rate case is how monetary equilibrium is restored. For a small country with fixed rates, the decline in the price level requires a reduction in the nominal money stock, and reserves fall. Here the money stock does not change because the monetary base is exogenous. Given constant desired real balances, the price level does not change. The fall in the relative price of concrete must be accomplished partly by a fall in the nominal price of concrete and partly by a rise in the nominal price of wool and oil. The rise in the nominal price of traded goods causes depreciation with a constant domestic price level. Here depreciation tends to be much less than in the Keynesian approach and it is the result, not the cause, of resource reallocation.

Summary Import Demand

Given our exogenous increase in import demand, whether rates are fixed or flexible, real international adjustment in the monetarist paradigm follows the pure theory of trade we reviewed in Chapter 1. With respect to the monetary sector, when rates are fixed, monetary adjustment takes place through reserve flows. If rates are flexible, prices and exchange rates adjust to restore monetary equilibrium. Nothing fundamental changes when we drop the assumptions of a small country or perfect capital mobility.

The Keynesian adjustment mechanism differs under fixed and flexible rates. With fixed rates, changes in income restore external balance. With flexible rates, the exchange rate plays the crucial role in restoring equilibrium. If we drop the simplifying assumptions of a small country or perfect capital mobility, the adjustment process becomes more complex, but the basic story remains. Equilibrium in the balance of payments is restored largely through changes in income and/or exchange rates.

Now that we have seen one example of adjustment at a micro level, we should be able to go back and apply a similar analysis to the exercises we carried out in Chapters 9 and 10. It would also be smart to do the micro-level analysis for the external shocks we take up next; that analysis would be an excellent exam question.

FOREIGN SHOCKS

Some advocates of flexible exchange rates argue that flexible rates tend to insulate a country from the effects of foreign shocks. From both a Keynesian and monetarist perspective, however, that insulation is quite limited. To analyze the effects of foreign shocks, we compare, from both a monetarist and a Keynesian perspective, the domestic effects of fiscal and monetary policy in the rest of the world with fixed and flexible exchange rates.

Fiscal Policy

We assume first that there is an expansionary fiscal policy in the rest of the world, or perhaps an increase in investment. We compare the effects of this shock with fixed and flexible rates from a Keynesian and then a monetarist point of view. For our purposes, we can think of the rest of the world as one very large country.

Keynesian   In a Keynesian model, expansionary fiscal policy in the rest of the world raises interest rates and drives up foreign income, just as it would in a closed economy. The rise in foreign income increases domestic exports. If exchange rates are fixed, income in our small country may rise or fall depending on whether the rise in exports due to higher foreign income is more or less than the fall in investment due to higher interest rates. But if rates are flexible, income rises because desired money balances fall.

The original equilibrium under fixed rates is shown by the intersection of the solid IS and LM schedules in Figure 11.13. Increased government or investment expenditures abroad raise foreign income, and the increased demand for money in the rest of the world drives up the interest rate. The interest rate in Figure 11.13 moves up from i_W to i_W'. The increase in foreign income also increases domestic exports, so the IS schedule shifts to the right to $I'S'$.

If the exchange rate is fixed, the new equilibrium is determined by the intersection of the new IS schedule, $I'S'$, and the new interest rate, i_W'. Figure 11.13 shows a slight decline in income from $0Y_0$ to $0Y_1$, but income can either rise or fall. Whether domestic income increases or decreases depends on a variety of factors. The greater the rise in interest rates and the

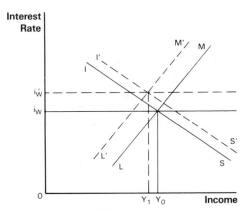

FIGURE 11.13
Effect on domestic income of an increase in foreign investment or government expenditure with fixed exchange rates.

flatter the domestic *IS* schedule, the more likely a fall in domestic income. The larger the rise in domestic exports, the more likely a rise in domestic income. In either case, international reserves change so that the *LM* curve shifts to restore monetary equilibrium. Whether income increases or decreases, there is a net capital outflow because investment falls relative to saving.

Under flexible rates domestic income must rise. The rise in interest rates from i_W to i_W' reduces desired money balances. Since nominal balances do not change, income must rise. In Figure 11.14, income rises to $0Y_1$, where the new interest rate i_W' intersects the original *LM* schedule. If the initial rightward shift in the *IS* schedule due to the rise in exports is insufficient to restore monetary equilibrium, households and firms respond to an excess supply of money by buying securities. These purchases contribute to a capital outflow and depreciate the domestic currency. Depreciation continues until the *IS* schedule moves to the right by enough so that it intersects the *LM* schedule where the interest rate is i_W'. If the rise in exports shifts the *IS* schedule too far to the right, appreciation moves it back. Since income and saving rise and investment falls, our small country must develop a net capital outflow.

FIGURE 11.14
Effect on domestic income of an increase in foreign investment or government expenditure with flexible exchange rates.

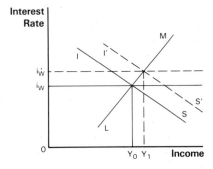

As one can see in the appendix to Chapter 9, the results are the same for large and small countries. For a Keynesian, neither fixed nor flexible rates insulate a country from foreign fiscal policy or changes in foreign investment as long as capital is mobile. As capital mobility declines, however, the interdependence under flexible rates declines. If capital were completely immobile, flexible rates would insulate a country from foreign fiscal policy and changes in foreign investment. In that case, the domestic interest rate would not change, and any change in domestic income would be inconsistent with monetary equilibrium. Foreign income and domestic exports would rise, but the domestic exchange rate would appreciate to restore the initial trade balance and level of income.

Monetarist The initial equilibrium in the domestic capital market is shown in Figure 11.15. The saving and investment schedules are labeled SS and II, and they intersect at the initial world interest rate i_W. For simplicity, the credit market is depicted in real rather than nominal terms. The increased sale of securities in the world capital market associated with the increased investment or government expenditure in the rest of the world drives the world interest rate up to i_W'.

Whether rates are fixed or flexible, real domestic investment declines, real saving increases, and the country develops a real net capital outflow equal to IS in Figure 11.15. Reduced domestic investment and consumption, however, generate an offsetting surplus in the trade account. Reductions in demand for export and import goods due to more saving and less investment decrease imports and expand exports. Decreased demand for nontraded goods shifts resources into the production of traded goods, further expanding exports and decreasing imports. In a similar way, increased foreign investment works toward increasing domestic exports and reducing domestic imports. As we saw in Chapter 2, we get essentially the same results when the country is large.

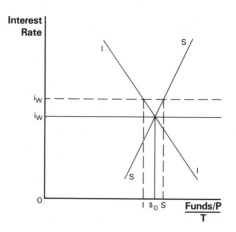

FIGURE 11.15
Effect of an increase in foreign investment or government expenditures on domestic capital flows.

The increase in interest rates reduces desired real money balances at home and abroad, and price levels rise whether rates are fixed or flexible. Under fixed rates, a small country can gain or lose international reserves. With flexible rates, the domestic exchange rate can appreciate or depreciate. If we ignore the complications introduced by changes in relative prices between traded and nontraded goods, then the change in exchange rates or international reserves depends primarily on the relative size of the interest elasticities of the demands for real money balances and supplies of nominal balances. (The result is the same for a large country; see the appendix to Chapter 10.) For example, suppose the interest elasticity for money supply is zero in both countries. In that case, if the interest elasticity for money demand is higher in our small country, under flexible rates the domestic price level rises relative to the foreign price level and the domestic currency depreciates. Under the same conditions and a fixed rate, our small country must lose international reserves, so domestic and foreign price levels rise proportionately.

As in the Keynesian model, flexible rates do not insulate a country from real external shocks. Although employment does not change, except during the transition, the composition of output and the balance of payments do change. Flexible rates do not even insulate an economy from the monetary consequences of foreign real shocks; the domestic price level rises under both fixed and flexible exchange rates.

Monetary Policy

Now we assume there is an expansionary monetary policy in the rest of the world. In the Keynesian approach, such a shock has real domestic effects under both fixed and flexible exchange rates. In our monetarist model, there are no real impacts under either regime, but under fixed rates the domestic price level rises.

Keynesian   The solid *IS* and *LM* schedules in Figures 11.16 and 11.17 show the initial equilibrium when the world interest rate is i_W. The expansionary monetary policy lowers world interest rates to i_W' and raises foreign income. The rise in foreign income boosts domestic exports and shifts the *IS* schedule to the right. Figure 11.16 shows the response of income when exchange rates are fixed.

The *IS* schedule shifts to the right to $I'S'$ because domestic exports rise as a result of the increase in world income. The decline in interest rates also stimulates investment, and income rises to $0Y_1$. As the country moves to the new equilibrium, there is a surplus in the balance of payments and the central bank accumulates international reserves. These additional reserves shift the *LM* schedule to $L'M'$.

When exchange rates are flexible, domestic income must decline to reestablish monetary equilibrium. Lower interest rates generate an excess

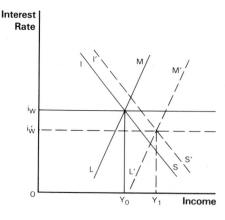

FIGURE 11.16
Effect on domestic income of an expansionary foreign monetary policy with fixed rates.

demand for money. Any increase in income reinforces this excess demand. The excess demand for money creates a capital inflow, and the domestic currency appreciates. Appreciation continues until the *IS* curve shifts far enough to the left so that the new *IS* schedule, *I'S'* in Figure 11.17, intersects the original *LM* schedule at the new lower interest rate, i_W'.

From a Keynesian perspective, the choice between fixed and flexible rates makes a difference in how foreign monetary shocks affect the domestic economy, but flexible rates do not insulate a country from such shocks. If we drop the assumption of a small country or perfect substitutability between domestic and foreign assets, it alters some of the details of our analyses, but it does not change the basic results. (For the large-country responses, see the appendix to Chapter 9.) In order for flexible rates completely to insulate a country from external monetary shocks, capital must be completely immobile so that domestic interest rates are not influenced by foreign yields.

Monetarist   In our monetarist approach, the expansionary open market operation by the foreign central bank has no real effects either at home or

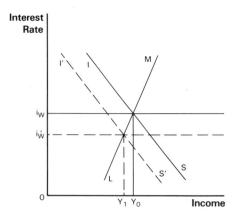

FIGURE 11.17
Effect on domestic income of an expansionary foreign monetary policy with flexible rates.

abroad because it does nothing to alter preferences or real endowments. The open market purchase simply increases the world price level. When rates are fixed, a rise in the world price level implies a proportional rise in the domestic price level. Since desired real balances are unchanged, that requires an increase in the stock of money through an accumulation of international reserves. If rates are flexible, not even the domestic price level changes. The domestic currency simply appreciates in proportion to the rise in the foreign price level. These results are the same when the domestic country is large and capital is immobile.

Insulation

In the monetarist approach, flexible rates can insulate a country from the purely monetary repercussions of foreign monetary policy. They cannot insulate a country from the real effects of real foreign shocks or even from the monetary effects of such shocks. For a monetarist, the choice between fixed and flexible rates depends largely on whether foreign or domestic monetary authorities are more likely to follow a sound monetary policy. If foreign authorities are more responsible, a fixed rate stabilizes the domestic price level. If the domestic central bank is more reliable, a flexible rate yields a more stable price level.

From a Keynesian perspective, the insulative abilities of flexible rates are also limited. Unless capital is immobile, they do not insulate a country from either foreign fiscal or monetary policy. From this perspective, however, flexible rates can insulate a country from some types of external shocks. Suppose a foreign country imposes a tariff or quota, and exports fall. With fixed rates, income falls; with flexible rates, the exchange rate adjusts to restore aggregate demand and employment. It is in the Keynesian response to autonomous changes in imports and exports that flexible rates can insulate a country from external shocks. When rates are fixed, income must change when there are autonomous shifts in imports or exports. Under flexible rates, these shocks alter exchange rates rather than income.

If autonomous imports and exports are unstable, flexible rates become attractive in a Keynesian framework. Of course, the same degree of insulation can be achieved by prompt and appropriate revaluation under a pegged rate. Insulation therefore may be a good Keynesian argument for preferring flexible to fixed rates, but it is not a strong argument in favor of flexible rather than pegged rates.

DEVALUATION

So far we have ruled out devaluation as a policy tool. But an adjustable peg is one of the international monetary systems we consider in the next chapter, so we need to examine alternative ideas about the effects of devaluation.

As in all the previous analyses, in the original equilibrium there is a zero balance in the current and capital accounts. The assumption of initial equilibrium is not realistic for cases of devaluation because devaluation is almost always the result of disequilibrium and a loss of international reserves. However, we cannot start our analysis in disequilibrium because then we need to know the source of the disequilibrium in order to determine how the disequilibrium is resolved. By assuming initial equilibrium, we can see what devaluation does without having to consider a variety of exogenous shocks. We start with a Keynesian view and then go to a monetarist approach.

Keynesian

The initial equilibrium is shown by the solid schedules in Figures 11.18 to 11.20. In Figure 11.18, the intersection of the solid IS and LM schedules determines the initial level of income, $0Y_0$. The bond market is described in Figure 11.19. Given the initial level of income Y_0, the investment schedule intersects the solid saving schedule at the world interest rate i_W, and there is no net capital flow. In Figure 11.20, the initial demand and supply schedules for foreign exchange intersect at π_0, and the pound value of both exports and imports is $0£_0$.

Devaluation shifts the exchange rate in Figure 11.20 to $0\pi_1$. Before there is any change in income, the pound value of imports falls to $0£_M$, and the pound value of exports rises to $0£_X$. (The fall in imports and rise in exports of course assume that both n_2 and x_2 in Chapter 9 are positive, which depends on the underlying elasticities of demand and supply for imports and exports.) The central bank acquires reserves at the rate of $£_M£_X$ per week. In dollars, the export surplus is $0\pi_1$ times $£_M£_X$. This export surplus increases aggregate demand, and the IS schedule in Figure 11.18 shifts to the right. The rise in income from $0Y_0$ to $0Y_1$ generates a capital outflow and

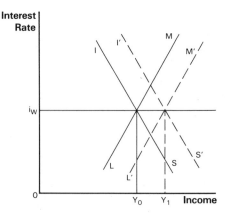

FIGURE 11.18
Effect of devaluation on income.

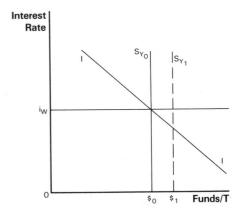

FIGURE 11.19
**Effect of devaluation on domestic capital
flow.**

reduces the surplus in the trade account. The accumulation of reserves during the transition to the new equilibrium shifts the *LM* schedule to *L'M'*.

In Figure 11.19, the increase in income shifts the saving schedule from S_{Y_0} to S_{Y_1}, and there is a net capital outflow equal to $\$_0\$_1$. In Figure 11.20, the increase in income increases the demand for foreign exchange in two ways. First, it increases imports. This increased demand is shown by the horizontal shift in the demand for pounds from D_0D_0 to D_1D_1. Second, it creates a deficit in the capital account. Higher income increases saving from S_{Y_0} to S_{Y_1}, and there is a capital outflow of $\$_0\$_1$ in Figure 11.19, which increases the demand for foreign exchange. The horizontal distance from D_1D_1 to $D_1'D_1'$ represents the pound value of this capital outflow.

The rise in income restores equilibrium to the balance of payments. At the new level of income $0Y_1$ and exchange rate $0\pi_1$, the trade surplus in dollars is $0\pi_1 \times \pounds_M'\pounds_X$ in Figure 11.20, which just equals the dollar value of the capital outflow.

Except for a decline in domestic interest rates, the effects are essentially the same when we drop the assumption of perfect substitutability

FIGURE 11.20
**Effect of devaluation on the market for for-
eign exchange.**

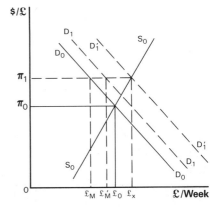

between domestic and foreign assets. The analysis also remains essentially the same when we drop the assumption of a small country. In that case, however, devaluation tends to reduce foreign aggregate demand and income, which reduces domestic exports. A change in the exchange rate that encourages domestic exports and discourages imports does just the opposite for foreign countries. As a result, devaluation is a policy of "beggar thy neighbor" because it exports unemployment.

In the Keynesian paradigm, devaluation is a powerful tool of economic policy. It can be used to influence both employment and the composition of the balance of payments. In a monetarist world, however, devaluation has no real effects; it simply leads to an accumulation of international reserves.

Monetarist

The basic reasoning underlying the monetarist view of devaluation is identical to the analysis we went through for an expansionary monetary policy in Chapter 10. Devaluation raises the exchange rate in Figure 11.21 from $0\pi_0$ to $0\pi_1$, which generates a balance-of-payments surplus equal to $£_D£_S$. This surplus increases the monetary base, and the domestic supply of money increases. Since we are at full employment, desired real balances are unchanged, and the rise in nominal balances implies a higher price level.

According to purchasing power parity, the demand and supply schedules for foreign exchange in Figure 11.21 shift upward in proportion to the rise in the domestic price level. As they shift, the accumulation of reserves slows. Reserves stop rising when the money stock and price level have risen by the same proportion as the increase in the price of foreign exchange. At that point, the demand for and supply of foreign exchange in Figure 11.21 are $D'D'$ and $S'S'$, and there is equilibrium in the balance of payments.

These results do not change if we drop the assumptions of a small country or perfect substitutability for securities. The only modification in the

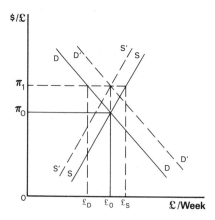

FIGURE 11.21
Effects of devaluation when full employment and purchasing power parity hold.

large-country case is that some of the adjustment takes place through a fall in foreign international reserves and prices.

The difference in views about the effects of devaluation should not come as a surprise. In the Keynesian paradigm, the exchange rate is related to the terms of trade, and changes in it have real effects. In the monetarist paradigm, the price mechanism works, and the exchange rate is essentially a monetary variable. Given that perspective, it is hardly surprising that in the monetarist model devaluation alters only the price level and international reserves.

SUMMARY

The analysis of the effects of four shocks—an increase in imports, changes in foreign monetary and fiscal policies, and devaluation—reinforces the basic theme of the last two chapters. In the Keynesian paradigm, the price mechanism fails and international adjustment works through income and/or exchange rates. In the monetarist approach, the price system works. Exchange rates and international reserves respond to monetary influences, and real adjustment works through resource reallocation.

An increased demand for imports in the Keynesian model reduces income and generates a capital inflow when exchange rates are fixed. If rates are flexible, depreciation restores the initial level of output by reducing imports and expanding exports. With an effective price mechanism, whether rates are fixed or flexible, we are back to the pure theory of trade: An increased demand for imports increases domestic production of both imports and exports, which eliminates the trade deficit.

With respect to insulation, from a Keynesian perspective flexible rates do insulate a country from shocks to the trade balance, but not from shocks to the capital account. In the monetarist paradigm, the price mechanism integrates the country into the world economy whether rates are fixed or flexible. As a result, there is no way to avoid the domestic effects of foreign real shocks. Flexible rates, however, can insulate a country from the purely monetary effects of foreign monetary shocks.

In a Keynesian world, devaluation is a powerful tool for economic policy. Because the price mechanism fails, devaluation can influence both income and the composition of the balance of payments. From a monetarist perspective, devaluation can stem a loss of international reserves, but it has no permanent real effects.

QUESTIONS FOR REVIEW

1. Assume a small, open economy with perfect capital mobility. From both a Keynesian and monetarist perspective, analyze the microeconomic effects of the following shocks under both fixed and flexible exchange rates:

    a. An expansionary domestic fiscal policy.
    b. An expansionary domestic monetary policy.
    c. A contractionary foreign fiscal policy.
    d. A contractionary foreign monetary policy.

2. From a monetarist perspective, how and to what extent do flexible rates insulate a country from foreign shocks? Does this insulation provide a strong argument for flexible rates?

3. From a Keynesian perspective, how and to what extent do flexible rates insulate a country from foreign shocks? Does this insulation provide a strong argument for flexible rates?

4. Why is devaluation an effective policy tool in our Keynesian model, but not in our monetarist model?

5. Why are the microeconomic responses to an increase in import demand so different in the monetarist and Keynesian models?

6. Suppose the law of one price held for every good in the Keynesian model. Would this change the Keynesian view of the international adjustment mechanism in any fundamental way?

7. Suppose we have to reject the theory of purchasing power parity. Would this change the monetarist view of the international adjustment mechanism in any fundamental way?

8. A Keynesian is likely to argue that depreciation causes inflation. A monetarist will claim that inflation causes depreciation. Explain both positions.

9. "The establishment of an effective European monetary system or any system with truly fixed rates requires national monetary and fiscal policies that are highly coordinated." Evaluate this statement first from a Keynesian and then from a monetarist perspective.

10. "The difference between the Keynesian and monetarist views of international adjustment is based on a fundamental disagreement about microeconomics." Do you agree? If so, why? If not, why not?

ADDITIONAL READINGS

BRANSON, WILLIAM H. "Monetarist and Keynesian Models of the Transmission of Inflation." *American Economic Review* (May 1975).

DORNBUSCH, RUDIGER. "Monetary Policy under Exchange-Rate Flexibility." In J. Artus et al. (eds.), *Managed Exchange-Rate Flexibility* (Boston: Federal Reserve Bank of Boston, 1978). Reprinted in R. Baldwin and J. D. Richardson, *International Trade and Finance: Readings,* 2d ed. (Boston: Little, Brown, 1981).

JOHNSON, HARRY G. "Elasticity, Absorption, Keynesian Multiplier, Keynesian Policy and Monetary Approaches to Devaluation Theory: A Simple Geometric Exposition." *American Economic Review* (June 1976).

12

POLICY
ALTERNATIVES

All rational decisions, whether they are political, economic, or personal, are based on theory. Without some kind of theory, life is a jumble of unrelated events and rational decisions are impossible. Since theory is the mechanism through which we interpret the world, it follows that our choices and decisions depend on our theories or ideas about how events are related.

In this chapter, we use the ideas developed in earlier chapters to examine the debate over alternative international monetary systems. We concentrate on three alternatives: fixed, pegged, and flexible rates. We first analyze the debate within our Keynesian model; then we shift to a monetarist approach. Finally, we use the ideas developed in Chapters 9, 10, and 11 to look at the choice between pegged and flexible rates in a historical context, the OPEC oil crunch of 1973–1975.

A KEYNESIAN VIEW

In this section, we consider the pros and cons of fixed, pegged, and flexible exchange rates from our Keynesian perspective, where the primary concern is restoration and maintenance of full employment. Price stability and equity are desirable, but the major criterion for judging alternative institutions is their contribution to full employment.

Fixed Rates

Pro   The rapid expansion of trade and capital flows under the gold standard in the late 1800s and early 1900s suggests that stable exchange rates promote international trade and capital flows. The obvious advantages of a single currency within a large country like the United States reinforce this conclusion. A major argument in favor of fixed rates, therefore, is that they promote international trade and capital flows.

A belief in destabilizing speculation further reinforces this argument. It also suggests that, as opposed to a flexible rate, a fixed rate tends to stabilize output and employment. Destabilizing speculation amplifies short-run fluctuations in exchange rates. In Keynesian models, those fluctuations alter exports and imports by changing the terms of trade. Fluctuations in imports and exports influence aggregate demand and change employment and output. Fixed rates therefore avoid unnecessary fluctuations in employment due to destabilizing speculation.

Con   One argument against fixed rates is that they reduce the effectiveness of monetary policy. In Chapter 9, monetary policy is completely ineffective for a small, open economy with a fixed rate. An ineffective monetary policy can be a serious handicap because fiscal policy is often difficult to implement quickly.

Once the decision to expand is made, open market operations can be started immediately. Increased government expenditures, however, often involve a political debate. Not only must legislators decide how much to spend, they must also decide how to spend the money. Should we build a dam in Arizona or an airport in Michigan? In addition, many projects require long lead times and take years to build. By the time construction on a dam starts, the problem could have switched from unemployment to inflation.

The major Keynesian argument against fixed rates, however, is that they force a country to put external objectives above full employment. As we saw in Chapters 7 and 9, a truly fixed rate cannot survive prolonged sterilization. A country that is steadily losing international reserves and has high or rising unemployment must eventually devalue or allow the domestic money supply to decline. In the face of high and rising unemployment, it must follow a contractionary monetary policy or abandon fixed rates. In such a situation, how can one defend a fixed exchange rate if it contributes to human suffering?

Pegged Rates

Pro   Given a Keynesian perspective, pegged exchange rates make a lot of sense. The stability of rates promotes stable employment and encourages trade and capital flows. This argument is particularly strong if one believes speculation is destabilizing. Even more important, pegged rates allow a country to place employment above the balance of payments. With a pegged rate, a country facing reserve losses and high unemployment can sterilize reserve losses and even follow an expansionary monetary policy to fight unemployment. If the fight against unemployment creates a fundamental disequilibrium in the balance of payments, then the appropriate response is devaluation, not contractionary monetary policy and more unemployment.

Con   The major arguments against pegged rates are based on our experience with them during the 1950s and 1960s. We discussed most of these problems in Chapter 7. A major objective of pegged rates is to promote trade and capital flows. In practice, however, the system often discourages trade and capital flows because countries impose trade and capital controls to defend inappropriate exchange rates.

The lack of an adjustment mechanism is another argument against pegged rates. With the link between reserves and money broken, there is no automatic adjustment mechanism, and the political process is apparently unable to handle the burden. It is difficult in practice to determine whether or not a loss or increase in reserves is temporary and should be financed or reflects a fundamental disequilibrium and requires revaluation. Even if the disequilibrium appears to be fundamental, there are strong political pressures working against revaluation. Depreciation is an admission of failure by the party in power, and it tends to contribute to inflation. Appreciation increases imports and decreases exports, which creates unemployment and can devastate industries that have relied for a long time on the indirect subsidy of an undervalued currency.

Pegged rates prevent destabilizing speculation, but they create their own form of perverse speculation, the one-way option. Under normal circumstances, a speculator must risk a substantial loss to obtain an expected profit. Under pegged rates, situations arise in which, in the short run at least, the exchange rate can move in only one direction. For a country with a large and prolonged loss of international reserves, there is a high probability of a large devaluation, but almost no chance of significant appreciation. For a country with ever-mounting reserves, there is a strong possibility of appreciation, but no chance of an immediate devaluation. Both speculators and ordinary businesspeople respond to these one-way options and in doing so often precipitate an international financial crisis.

Large reserve flows generated by one-way options and the lack of an automatic adjustment mechanism compound another serious problem: no satisfactory mechanism for reserve growth. During the era of pegged rates, the U.S. dollar was the major reserve currency, and the dollar was tied to gold. Given a fixed dollar price for gold and inflation, gold production dwindled. The monetary gold stock in the United States declined, and the U.S.

commitment to foreign central banks to redeem dollars for gold at a fixed price became questionable. Raising the dollar price of gold might solve the problem in the short run, but it could never supply the steady increase in international reserves required by a system that allows persistent inflation and is committed to financing prolonged deficits.

Insufficient international cooperation contributed to all the other problems. Pegged rates require extensive international cooperation, but the necessary level of cooperation was never achieved. Surplus and deficit countries argued over who was at fault and should bear the burden of adjustment. Should the surplus country follow an expansionary monetary policy or the deficit country pursue a tight monetary policy? These disagreements delayed adjustment, promoted speculation, and increased the need for international reserves.

Supporters of pegged rates argue that none of these problems is inherent in the system. With international cooperation, they all can be resolved. Gold can be replaced by other reserve assets, perhaps SDRs (Special Drawing Rights) at the IMF. Rules can be developed to resolve the problem of the burden of adjustment, and mechanisms can be established to promote prompt revaluations. Opponents respond that this is all pie in the sky: There is no reason to believe that countries are any more cooperative now than they were in the 1950s and 1960s.

Flexible Rates

Pro   One argument for flexible rates is that they provide some insulation from foreign shocks. As we saw in the last chapter, with flexible rates an increase in imports or a decline in exports results in depreciation rather than unemployment.

The major support for flexible rates, however, comes primarily from rejection of the alternatives. Fixed rates subordinate full employment to the exchange rate and balance of payments. From a Keynesian perspective, that is a gross distortion of priorities. Theoretically, pegged are preferable to flexible rates, but pegged rates failed and there is little hope they will work in the future. By a process of elimination, that leaves flexible rates as the feasible alternative.

Given the second-best status of flexible rates, it is not surprising that someone with our Keynesian perspective would prefer a managed float. Official intervention moves the system toward pegged rates, and sufficient intervention can effectively restore a pegged rate. A managed float is particularly attractive to those who believe in destabilizing speculation.

Con   The standard argument against flexible rates is that they reduce trade and capital flows and contribute to domestic unemployment. Uncertainty about future rates increases risk, and traders require higher profit margins. Price differentials increase, and the volume of trade in commodities and securities decreases.

Temporary fluctuations in exchange rates affect output in two ways. At the micro level, they cause unnecessary transitional unemployment as resources first move out of export industries as the price of foreign exchange falls and then move back into those industries as exchange rates rise. At the macro level, exchange rate fluctuations alter aggregate demand, disrupt domestic output, and can contribute to inflation. A belief in destabilizing speculation reinforces both problems.

With respect to insulation, it is very limited. Flexible rates do not protect a country from the employment effects of capital flows or the inflationary effects of depreciation. In addition, insulation may be an argument for flexible over fixed rates, but it is not an effective argument for flexible versus pegged rates. Prompt devaluation with a pegged rate can insulate a country from foreign shocks just as well as depreciation under a flexible rate.

A final argument against flexible rates is that they only appear to reduce the need for international cooperation. Effective demand management requires international cooperation whether rates are fixed, pegged, or flexible. Indeed, the illusion of independence under flexible rates can reduce cooperation and make stabilization policy even more difficult.

Summary

From a purely theoretical point of view, the Keynesian view that we developed in Chapters 9 and 11 tends to support pegged exchange rates. Unlike fixed rates, pegged rates allow the authorities to concentrate on domestic objectives. At the same time, they avoid the misallocation of resources and destabilizing influence on aggregate demand created by flexible rates.

The case for flexible rates rests primarily on the restrictions of fixed rates and the failure of pegged rates. Compared to fixed rates, flexible rates may reduce trade and capital flows and contribute to unemployment, but at least they do not tie the hands of the authorities in their struggle to restore and maintain full employment. In addition, the harmful effects from destabilizing speculation can be reduced by adopting a managed float.

Flexible rates may be inferior to an ideal system of pegged rates, but in practice pegged rates failed. In the absence of convincing evidence that countries are prepared to cooperate and resolve the practical problems associated with pegged rates, flexible rates appear to be the best achievable alternative.

When we move to our monetarist model, the policy debate shifts. Fixed rates become more attractive, and the theoretical support for pegged rates disappears. The debate now revolves around fixed versus flexible rates, and it hinges more on political than on economic issues.

A MONETARIST VIEW

In the Keynesian paradigm, the primary policy issue is unemployment. In our monetarist framework, shocks generate transitional unemployment, but the price mechanism quickly reestablishes full employment. In this approach, price stability replaces unemployment as the major criteria for judging alternative institutions. Price stability is desirable both for its own sake and because it helps minimize transitional unemployment created by monetary instability.

Pegged Rates

Pro   There essentially is no argument for pegged rates in our monetarist framework because there is no need for stabilization policy. The market mechanism restores full employment. Monetary policy primarily affects the price level or international reserves. Fiscal policy alters the composition of output and the balance of payments, but it does not alter employment. Given the monetarist model, about all devaluation can do is remove the economic distortions created by an inappropriate exchange rate and stem a loss of international reserves.

Con   All the practical arguments against pegged rates discussed earlier still hold. They tend to promote controls and reduce trade. Delayed revaluations generate one-way speculation and greatly expand the need for international reserves, a need the system cannot fulfill partly because of inadequate cooperation.

Given the absence of any theoretical support for pegged rates in our monetarist approach and the problems with the system in practice, it is hardly surprising that very few monetarists advocate pegged rates. For monetarists, the debate tends to be over fixed versus flexible rates, and the dividing line is often very thin. Many supporters of flexible rates prefer some ideal form of fixed rate, but they support flexible rates as a politically feasible second best.

Fixed Rates

Pro   One argument for fixed rates is the same as in the Keynesian approach: They promote international trade and capital flows. The other major argument is that they constrain domestic monetary authorities.

Over the centuries monarchies, dictatorships, and democracies have abused their right to create money. Faced with large deficits, governments have repeatedly turned to the printing press to fill the gap between expenditures and taxes. A fixed exchange rate severely limits such abuses. As we saw in Chapters 7 and 10, any attempt to use the printing press is limited by the loss of international reserves. If there is an expansionary monetary policy, the central bank loses international reserves. If the expansion goes too far, reserves fall so low that there is a serious threat to convertibility. At that point, commitment to a fixed rate forces an end to monetary expansion.

Given the track record of governments when monetary policy is not restrained, it is hardly surprising that many people support fixed rates as a mechanism for avoiding inflation. Unfortunately, as we will see shortly, the issue of price stability is a bit more complicated than simply fixed versus flexible rates.

Con   Since the arguments against fixed rates are essentially the arguments for flexible rates, we can ignore the con side of the debate and turn to flexible rates.

Flexible Rates

Pro   Most supporters of flexible rates recognize that they could reduce trade and capital flows. Advocates, however, point out that there is no impressive body of empirical evidence to support the argument that flexible rates reduce trade and capital flows. Apparently forward markets and other mechanisms for reducing risk due to uncertainty about exchange rates effectively offset the effects of flexible rates.

As for speculation, the evidence from foreign exchange and other financial markets is much more consistent with rational expectations than it is with destabilizing or other forms of perverse speculation. Even if speculation at times is destabilizing, such behavior is an argument for a managed float rather than a reason to adopt fixed exchange rates.

In this context, the major arguments for flexible rates are more political than economic. They are concerned with the politics of monetary policy. First, governments are not willing to surrender control over domestic monetary policy, which is an absolute prerequisite for a fixed rate in our monetarist model. Second, unless fixed rates are based on a gold standard or some other mechanism for limiting the growth in international reserves, fixed rates can become a mechanism for international inflation.

Many, if not most, supporters of flexible rates would prefer a system of truly fixed rates under which international reserves grow steadily and slowly. They advocate flexible rates because they do not believe such a system is politically feasible. Countries are not willing to relinquish control over domestic monetary policy, and neither an international central bank nor a gold standard is likely to provide for the slow and steady increase in international reserves that would promote growth and be necessary for price stability.

The failure of various attempts to create a European monetary union illustrates these problems. Almost everyone agrees that the members of the

European Common Market would benefit from a single currency, just as the United States benefits from one monetary system. It might be called marks in Germany and pounds in the United Kingdom, but as long as the currencies traded at absolutely fixed rates, they would be effectively the same money.

In spite of the obvious benefits, there still is no European monetary union because the countries are not willing to surrender control over domestic monetary policy. France, for example, is not willing to surrender French monetary policy to a supranational central bank that it cannot control. Neither is Germany, England, or any of the other countries involved. As a result, rather than a system of truly fixed rates between all the countries, there is only a system of pegged rates between a few members of the Common Market.

The problem is not European, it is universal. Let's try a historical illustration. Suppose, like the Articles of Confederation, the United States Constitution allocated the control of money to each individual state. Each state would have its own central bank and its own currency. Given different political and financial pressures, some states would follow a conservative monetary policy and have price stability. Others would go on occasional monetary binges. Exchange rates between the various states would change over time because price levels would not move together. There would be a tremendous incentive to set up a central monetary authority. Imagine having to buy foreign exchange for a trip from Boston to New York or from Los Angeles to Las Vegas. Nevertheless, what state would voluntarily surrender such an important function to the federal government, particularly when it increases the state's ability to spend? You might as well ask politicians to stand on their heads and spit nickels. Fourth of July speeches never mention a central monetary authority as one of the great blessings of the U.S. Constitution, but they should.

Even if a country, or state, were prepared to sacrifice control over monetary policy to a fixed rate, it is not necessarily wise to do so. A fixed rate is not a guarantee of price stability. Indeed, price stability can be an argument for flexible rates. Wait a second. What is this? How can price stability be an argument for both fixed and flexible rates? Another look at the European Common Market shows how it is possible to work both sides of this argument.

Consider West Germany first. Over the years since 1950, Germany has had inflation, but much less than almost any other potential member of a monetary union. If a monetary union were established, fixed rates would require monetary coordination. That almost certainly means some form of central monetary authority. Since Germany cannot expect to dominate such an authority, it is only reasonable to assume that the policy followed by this supracentral bank would be closer to the policies followed by other countries than to the monetary policy of Germany. If so, then a fixed rate probably means more inflation, not less, for Germany. Now let's look at the issue from the perspective of Italy. Over the years, Italy has suffered a series of inflationary spurts. An Italian quite reasonably might expect a supracentral bank to moderate some of the domestic political pressures for monetary expansion and create a more stable price level for Italy.

In other words, whether or not fixed rates promote price stability depends largely on two factors. One is the domestic commitment to price stability; the other is the political mechanism for controlling international reserves. Since price stability tends to be the crucial issue in a monetarist framework, whether one advocates fixed or flexible rates often depends on attitudes about these essentially political issues.

Summary

In the monetarist approach we developed in Chapters 10 and 11, the rationale for pegged exchange rates disappears. The exchange rate is essentially a monetary variable, and income stabilization is not the primary policy objective. In addition, most monetarists believe that speculation is not perverse and that flexible rates do not seriously inhibit trade and capital flows. The policy debate therefore tends to focus on price stability both as an objective in its own right, and as a way to moderate business cycles. As a result, for most monetarists the debate over fixed versus flexible rates generally turns on which system contributes most to price stability.

OPEC

In spite of some talk about returning to a gold standard, any major reform of the present managed float will be a move toward pegged rather than fixed exchange rates. Let's therefore take another look at the debate over pegged versus flexible exchange rates. The first OPEC oil crunch provides an excellent framework.

From 1973 to 1975, the Organization of Petroleum Exporting Countries, commonly known as OPEC, drove up world oil prices dramatically. The average annual price for Saudi crude was $3.29 in 1973; by 1975, it was $12.73. The shock was felt throughout the world. Inflation jumped, and industrial production fell.

Table 12.1 shows the annual rate of increase in the price of domestic output for five industrialized countries. From 1972 to 1975, the average annual rate of inflation more than doubled, rising from 5.9 to over 12 percent. The annual rate of change in industrial production for these same countries appears in Table 12.2. In 1973, industrial production rose by an average of 8.5 percent, but it fell in 1974 and 1975, first by 1.4 and then by 7.5 percent. The sharp rise in inflation and unemployment set off a heated policy debate. In the remainder of this chapter, we consider the general debate, but concen-

TABLE 12.1   Annual Rates of Inflation for GNP Deflators

YEAR	FRANCE	GERMANY	JAPAN	U.K.	U.S.A.*	AVERAGE
1966	4.3%	3.7%	5.0%	4.4%	3.2%	4.1%
1967	3.2	1.4	5.8	2.9	3.0	3.3
1968	4.2	1.8	5.2	4.2	4.4	4.0
1969	6.6	3.5	4.8	6.2	5.1	5.2
1970	5.6	7.3	7.3	6.6	5.4	6.4
1971	5.8	7.7	5.2	9.3	5.0	6.6
1972	6.2	5.6	5.2	8.6	4.2	5.9
1973	7.8	6.0	11.9	7.0	5.7	7.7
1974	11.1	6.9	20.6	15.0	8.9	12.5
1975	13.4	6.7	7.8	26.9	9.3	12.8
1976	9.9	3.3	6.4	14.7	5.2	7.9
1977	9.0	3.8	5.7	14.0	5.8	7.7
1978	9.5	3.7	4.6	10.9	7.3	7.2
1979	10.1	3.8	2.3	15.0	8.5	8.0

* GNP deflator.
Source: *International Economic Conditions,* Federal Reserve Bank of St. Louis (June 1982).

trate on the role of the international monetary system. We start with a Keynesian perspective and then shift to a monetarist interpretation of the OPEC oil shock.

Keynesian Response

From a Keynesian perspective, the unemployment is a result of insufficient aggregate demand and the inflation is driven by increased factor costs.

TABLE 12.2   Annual Rate of Change in Index of Industrial Production

YEAR	FRANCE	GERMANY	JAPAN	U.K.	U.S.A.	AVERAGE
1966	4.5	1.3	13.1	1.6	8.9	5.9
1967	2.9	-3.8	19.6	1.1	2.2	4.4
1968	4.2	9.3	17.0	6.4	6.3	8.6
1969	10.7	13.4	16.0	2.7	4.5	9.5
1970	4.8	6.5	13.8	0.1	-3.0	4.4
1971	5.7	1.0	2.6	0.1	1.7	2.2
1972	5.4	4.0	7.3	2.2	9.2	5.6
1973	7.2	4.8	14.9	7.4	8.4	8.5
1974	2.9	-1.8	-4.0	-3.9	-0.4	-1.4
1975	6.5	-6.5	-11.0	-4.9	-8.9	-7.5
1976	8.0	8.0	11.1	2.0	10.8	8.0
1977	1.9	1.9	4.1	3.8	5.9	3.5
1978	1.8	2.7	6.2	3.7	5.7	4.0
1979	4.5	5.3	8.3	2.6	4.4	5.0

Source: *International Economic Conditions,* Federal Reserve Bank of St. Louis (June 1982).

The appropriate policy is to stimulate aggregate demand, if possible without aggravating inflation.

The value of oil imports rises as world oil prices rise because the demand for oil is inelastic. Higher spending on imported oil reduces expenditures on other goods, and domestic aggregate demand declines. In Chapters 9 and 11, for simplicity we held domestic prices constant. Now domestic prices rise as output falls because prices are forced up by the increase in factor costs. Even with higher unemployment, prices for labor and other domestic inputs do not fall significantly. Oil, however, is a major input for products from fertilizer to plastics, and those prices rise dramatically. If exchange rates are fixed, output falls because of the decline in aggregate demand. If rates are flexible, depreciation aggravates the inflation and output falls because of the increased demand for money.

The effect of the OPEC price increase is illustrated in Figure 12.1, where we now measure real income along the horizontal axis. The solid *IS* and *LM* schedules show the initial conditions, where $0Y_0$ represents full employment. If exchange rates are fixed, more imports shift the *IS* schedule to the left to $I'S'$. The rise in domestic prices due to higher oil prices also shifts the *LM* schedule to the left. For a given interest rate and real income, desired nominal balances rise as prices increase. Since these shifts are taking place in all oil-importing countries, interest rates can either rise or fall. In Figure 12.1, the typical *LM* schedule shifts to $L'M'$ and interest rates remain constant, but output falls to $0Y_1$.

The outcome is quite similar when exchange rates are flexible. Higher prices shift the *LM* schedule to the left, and more imports also shift the *IS* schedule left. Depreciation, however, cannot restore income to its original level. Depreciation aggravates the inflation and shifts the *LM* schedule farther to the left. In addition, among oil-importing countries, which includes almost all industrialized countries, depreciation is a zero-sum game. The dollar cannot depreciate against the German mark and the mark also depreciate vis à vis the dollar.

Depreciation in terms of the currencies of oil-exporting countries might help restore aggregate demand, but OPEC set oil prices in dollars, and

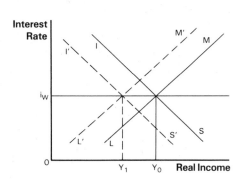

FIGURE 12.1
Effects of OPEC oil crunch.

countries like Saudi Arabia and Kuwait have relatively small populations that account for only a small part of world trade. At least initially, most of the increased oil revenue is saved rather than spent. As a result, there is a major shift in the world away from consumption to saving. In oil-importing countries, prices rise as world aggregate demand declines and output falls.

Under these conditions, neither fixed, flexible, nor pegged exchange rates can insulate countries from the effects of the shock. From a Keynesian perspective, however, a pegged exchange rate can contribute to price stability and the management of aggregate demand because it gives the authorities an additional policy tool, the exchange rate, that they do not have under either flexible or truly fixed exchange rates.

We must be quite clear, however, that monetary policy, fiscal policy, and the exchange rate are not independent tools. Given the objective of restoring full employment, the choice of any two influences the third. For example, suppose a country, perhaps the United States, responds to the oil shock with expansionary monetary and fiscal policies. Given these policies and similar policies in other countries, the new equilibrium exchange rate does not depend primarily on whether exchange rates are pegged or flexible. If a combination of policies implies depreciation under flexible rates, then external balance with pegged rates ultimately requires a similar devaluation. The alternative is a different monetary or fiscal policy.

If oil-importing countries were able to coordinate fiscal and monetary policies, exchange rates could be quite stable even though they were flexible. Without coordination, exchange rates are likely to take an unnecessary ride on a roller coaster. These fluctuations complicate demand management and can contribute to inflation.

For simplicity, let's assume that the industrialized countries follow monetary and fiscal policies that ultimately leave exchange rates among them essentially unchanged. Implementation of these policies, however, is not fully coordinated. Great Britain, for example, has a parliamentary system, and the government can alter both monetary and fiscal policy relatively quickly. In the United States, the Federal Reserve can change monetary policy very quickly, but major tax and spending changes must be passed by both houses of Congress and approved by the president. This can take a long time, particularly if the party of the president does not dominate both houses of Congress. For our example, therefore, we assume that most other countries use a balanced monetary and fiscal policy throughout, but the United States relies first on an expansionary monetary policy and then on an expansionary fiscal policy.

With flexible rates, our analysis in Chapter 9 implies that first the dollar depreciates under the influence of an expansionary monetary policy and then appreciates due to fiscal policy. The initial depreciation exports U.S. unemployment and contributes to domestic inflation. If resistance to wage and price cuts introduces a ratchet effect into the price level, depreciation causes a permanently higher domestic price level. (If the authorities do not ratify the higher wages and prices with an expansionary monetary policy, there is more unemployment.) When the currency begins to appreciate due to fiscal policy, the rise tends to offset the domestic expansionary effects of monetary policy and can contribute to foreign inflation. If speculation is destabilizing, it amplifies this swing in exchange rates, which reinforces inflationary pressures and makes income stabilization even more difficult.

From our Keynesian perspective, pegged exchange rates allow monetary and fiscal policies to operate without transient effects on exchange rates. Unlike under a fixed rate, the initial loss of international reserves due to an expansionary monetary policy is sterilized, and the money stock is maintained at its new higher level. This may be less effective for employment than a flexible rate, but it is more desirable than a fixed rate and avoids the inflationary effects of depreciation. As fiscal policy takes hold, the loss of reserves disappears. At this point, pegged rates prevent appreciation from reducing the effectiveness of fiscal policy and contributing to foreign inflation.

Given our Keynesian approach, a pegged rate appears to offer the best of both worlds. If a shock such as the oil crunch ultimately requires devaluation, pegged rates permit an orderly and timely change. If not, the deficit can be financed to avoid the destabilizing effects of unnecessary fluctuations in exchange rates. Given these theoretical arguments for pegged rates, the strong support that exists for them is not surprising even after their collapse in the early 1970s.

The Keynesian paradigm makes pegged rates look good. But in our monetarist framework, the oil shock requires real adjustments and a pegged rate is useless because it cannot contribute to those adjustments.

Monetarist

In both monetarist and Keynesian approaches, a major increase in oil prices leads to higher expenditures on imports, reduced spending on domestic goods, and unemployment. From that point on, however, the two paradigms part company. The Keynesian approach stresses the fall in domestic output due to reduced demand and the ripple effects generated by the multiplier. Monetarists concentrate on the reallocation of resources required by higher oil prices. For them, unemployment is a painful but necessary part of this adjustment process.

In the monetarist view, the increase in oil imports requires a major reallocation of resources. Gas stations close and automobile production falls, but oil exploration increases and so does the installation of solar heating units. At the same time, capital flows smooth out consumption paths over time. This shift in resources requires transitory unemployment. For the unemployed the experience is devastating, but from this perspective the alternative is an inefficient economy and an even greater reduction in welfare.

Given this view of the world, microeconomic policies might be appropriate, but not expansionary monetary or fiscal policies. Increased unemployment insurance can contribute to a more equitable sharing of the burden of adjustment, and retraining programs might help speed up the transition. But expansionary monetary and fiscal policies are likely to distort price signals and delay readjustment. Even more important, in this framework there is absolutely nothing macroeconomic policy can do about the basic problem. Increased real oil prices reduce domestic real income and wealth even with full employment.

So far we have only mentioned the role of capital flows in the adjustment process. Now let's take a closer look. Since adjustment to sharply higher oil prices takes time, current output falls relative to future output. Given the Fisherian analysis we developed in Chapter 2, we would expect households in the United States and other oil-importing countries to smooth out their consumption streams by consuming a higher proportion of current income and a smaller proportion later when output is higher. In other words, in the short run part of the domestic adjustment to higher oil prices is an export of securities. For the Saudis and other OPEC countries, the sudden rise in income is like a windfall, and a large proportion is saved. As a result, they want to exchange present oil for claims on future goods. In time, however, the windfall effect wears off, and expenditure by OPEC countries rises to meet income.

The net result is that, during the transition to the new equilibrium, oil-importing countries pay for oil imports partly through a net capital inflow. Once adjustment is complete, the capital inflow disappears and we start to pay off the loan. For the United States, that means lower net income on foreign investments and a smaller trade deficit. Other countries tend to develop a trade surplus.

All this adjustment takes place through the price mechanism. The primary responsibility of government here is to provide an institutional framework that promotes adjustment. One may debate the relative merits of fixed and flexible rates, but it is almost impossible to make a strong argument for pegged rates. Here the exchange rate is basically a monetary variable, and devaluation cannot contribute to the necessary real adjustment. Sterilization, however, delays adjustment, and threats of devaluation can distort trade and capital flows more than market-driven changes in exchange rates, particularly if speculation is reliably anticipatory or rational.

LONG RUN VERSUS SHORT RUN

One last point on the policy debate. Like the debate over macro policy in general, the debate over the international monetary system often hinges on our interpretation of the terms long run and short run. Almost all economists believe that the price mechanism is effective in the "long run," but the long run can have very different interpretations. If the long run is measured in years or even decades, the Keynesian model becomes relevant for policy. In that case, the exchange rate is an important tool for stabilization, and a pegged exchange rate is theoretically very attractive. If the long run is measured in months or perhaps a year or two at the most, then policy must be formed in an essentially monetarist world. In that case, the exchange rate is primarily a monetary variable, and the debate centers on whether fixed or flexible rates promote price stability.

SUMMARY

Within the context of the ideas developed in Chapters 9, 10, and 11, the debate over pegged rates on the one hand and fixed or flexible rates on the other hinges primarily on economic issues. The role of speculation and the effect of exchange risk on trade and capital flows are important elements, but they are not the key issue. The fundamental issue is the efficacy of the price system in maintaining and restoring full employment. Pegged rates are attractive when the price mechanism is ineffective, and exchange rates are an important tool in the struggle to maintain full employment. Under those conditions, there is a strong theoretical case for pegged exchange rates. The failure of pegged rates in practice, however, forces many potential advocates to support flexible rates or a managed float.

Our analysis also suggests that the debate over fixed versus flexible rates takes place largely between monetarists and is on two levels: economic and political. On the economic level, the debate tends to center on the role of speculation and the effect of exchange rate uncertainty on trade and capital flows. Since monetarists generally view speculation as at least reliably anticipatory and a managed float can moderate exchange risk and reduce the influence of perverse speculation if it does exist, the crucial issues tend to be political.

One argument for flexible rates is that coordination of monetary policy is not politically feasible. Another is that policy coordination is not desirable. An independent monetary policy can yield more stable prices and require less internal adjustment than subordination to a fixed exchange rate.

Supporters of fixed rates must assert the opposite of both arguments. Coordination of monetary policy is possible, and it will provide more stability than an independent monetary policy. Perhaps it is the need to accept both claims that helps explain why there are so few supporters of truly fixed rates, even among monetarists.

QUESTIONS FOR REVIEW

1. The United States has a common currency. As a result, there is a fixed exchange rate between the various regions of the United States. This system has operated admirably enough to constitute irrefutable evidence

against the adoption of flexible rates and for pegged rates between countries. Do you agree? If so, why? If not, why not?

2. Evaluate the following statement. "A system of fixed rates will not work unless there is a high degree of coordination between domestic and foreign monetary policy; but if that level of coordination exists, rates will be stable, even though flexible."

3. Do expectations about the source, magnitude, and nature of exogeneous shocks have any relevance to the choice of an appropriate international monetary system? If so, how? If not, why not?

4. No international monetary system is perfect. Fixed, pegged, and flexible rates, either clean or managed, all have their drawbacks. Describe the empirical evidence you would like to have in order to make a rational choice among these alternatives.

5. Assume the Keynesian model describes the short-run responses to contractionary shocks and the monetarist model shows the long-run responses. Given both fixed and flexible rates, describe how you would expect the U.S. economy to respond over time to another shock like the OPEC oil shock in the early 1970s. Do you see any viable role for pegged rates and devaluation in this scenario? If so, why? If not, why not?

6. Did you explicitly include the effects of rational or reliably anticipatory expectations in your answer to question 5? If not, how would they change your answer?

ADDITIONAL READINGS

CHOUDHRI, EHSAN U., AND LEVIS A. KOCHIN. "The Exchange Rate and the International Transmission of Business Cycle Disturbances: Some Evidence from the Great Depression." *Journal of Money, Credit and Banking* (November 1980).

BLACK, STANLEY W. *Floating Exchange Rates and National Economic Policy* (New Haven, Conn.: Yale University Press, 1977).

HOOPER, PETER, AND STEVEN KOHLHAGEN. "The Effect of Exchange Rate Uncertainty on the Prices and Volume of International Trade." *Journal of International Economics* (November 1978).

JOHNSON, HARRY G. "The Case for Flexible Exchange Rates, 1969." In G. N. Halm (ed.), *Approaches to Greater Flexibility of Exchange Rates* (Princeton, N.J.: Princeton University Press, 1970).

LANYI, ANTHONY. *The Case for Floating Exchange Rates Reconsidered.* Princeton Essays in International Finance, No. 72 (February 1969).

PIPPENGER, JOHN. "The Case for Freely Fluctuating Exchange Rates: Some Evidence." *Western Economic Journal* (September 1973).

THE ASSET APPROACH

13

After the system of pegged exchange rates established at Bretton Woods broke down in the early 1970s, fluctuations under flexible rates appeared large compared to changes in relative price levels. The asset approach discussed here represents an attempt to explain these fluctuations.

In Chapters 5 and 6, the exchange rate is determined in a market for flows of foreign exchange. These flows are derived primarily from the import and export of goods and services, which are flows. In the asset approach, exchange rates are the price of an asset, foreign money, and asset prices are determined in markets for stocks.

What makes the shift from flow to stock analysis attractive is that asset prices typically fluctuate more than corresponding commodity prices. For example, the price of General Motors stock on the New York Stock Exchange fluctuates more on a day-to-day basis than does the sticker price for a new Pontiac. The reason asset prices fluctuate so much is that they are driven by expectations. The price of a share in General Motors does not depend on past or even present profits. It depends primarily on expectations about interest rates and future profits. Any news or information that affects these expectations alters the price. Since markets are continually bombarded with news, asset prices change frequently and occasionally even wildly.

No consensus asset model for exchange rates has emerged. Instead, there are a number of different approaches using a variety of simplifying assumptions. Some of the more important assumptions concern relative speeds of adjustment, the degree of substitutability between assets, the role of wealth, country size, and the nature of expectations.

Most asset models assume that financial markets clear rapidly compared to markets for commodities. Markets for stocks and bonds clear minute by minute, but on a day-by-day basis neither commodity prices nor production respond rapidly to excess demand or supply. A theoretical rationale for this assumption is that information and transaction costs tend to reduce the number and frequency of transactions, which slows down the speed of adjustment. Since stocks and bonds are homogeneous goods for which information and transactions costs are relatively low, markets for stocks and bonds tend to clear relatively quickly.

Spreads between bid and ask or buy and sell prices reflect one form of transaction costs. At any moment you might be able to buy a given amount of Ford stock for $10,100 and sell the same amount for about $10,000. But if you buy a new Ford Capri and try to sell it just a few minutes later, you could easily lose $1,000.

All asset models implicitly assume a large amount of substitution between securities to reduce the number of markets and simplify the analysis. If two assets are perfect substitutes, their relative price is constant and they can be combined into a single security using Hicks's aggregation theorem. Some approaches, however, stress differences between remaining assets; others concentrate on money. The former models normally emphasize the role of wealth as measured by the portfolio of financial assets, whereas the latter often ignore it.

The assumption of a small country greatly simplifies the analysis, and most approaches adopt it. All the models we consider in this chapter are for a small country.

As mentioned earlier, expectations dominate prices in asset markets. Some asset models of the foreign exchange market assume static expectations, but most use some variant of rational expectations. We will see examples of both.

Our first model is based on the portfolio approach. It emphasizes imperfect substitution between domestic and foreign assets. The second concentrates on the role of covered arbitrage, and the last stresses the effects of inflationary expectations. The appendix discusses some variations for the portfolio and arbitrage models.

PORTFOLIO BALANCE MODEL

Portfolio models for foreign exchange rates are direct descendants of the portfolio approach in macroeconomics developed by James Tobin. Like Tobin's models, they assume financial markets clear rapidly compared to commodity markets so that, for purposes of very short-run analysis, we can take prices and output as given. They also follow Tobin in stressing the role of wealth and imperfect substitutability between assets. These models help explain the observed variability of exchange rates because they usually imply that some shocks cause the exchange rate to overshoot. An expansionary monetary policy, for example, can cause the domestic currency to depreciate and then partly recover its initial value. Our particular portfolio model, which is based on the work of William Branson, implies this type of overshooting.

The Branson model describes a small country where expectations are static. Domestic residents cannot affect foreign interest rates, and they expect the future to be like the present. Wealth is measured by the stock of financial assets rather than by the discounted value of expected future income. Domestic residents hold three kinds of financial assets: a noninterest-bearing domestic money, M; a domestic bond, B, with a yield of i; and a foreign bond, F, that earns $\bar{i}$. Due to either political risk or information and transaction costs, domestic and foreign assets are imperfect substitutes. As a result, domestic interest rates can change relative to foreign yields. For simplicity, domestic bonds, B, are short term, so that changes in domestic interest rates do not affect the value of the existing stock of financial assets. Foreigners do not hold domestic assets. The domestic value of domestic holdings of foreign bonds, πF, depends on the stock of foreign bonds, F, which is fixed in the very short run, and on the domestic price of foreign exchange, π.

The demand for each asset varies directly with its own yield and inversely with other interest rates. In the very short run, the domestic holdings of each asset are constant and the aggregate portfolio of financial assets, W, is fixed. As the stock of assets increases, the demand for all three assets increases. For a given level of wealth, an increase in nominal income, Y, increases the demand for money and decreases the demand for domestic bonds, but it does not affect the demand for foreign bonds. In other words, changes in the transactions demand for money do not affect the demand for foreign assets.

LM Schedule

Before we develop a model with foreign assets, let's get a feel for the portfolio approach by deriving the *LM* schedule for a closed economy with only domestic money and bonds. It simplifies the analysis if these "bonds" are very short term so the value of the portfolio does not depend on interest rates. This approach is consistent with standard *IS-LM* models, which tend to ignore the wealth effects of changing interest rates.

Wealth, W, is the sum of money, M, and bonds, B:

$$W = B + M$$

The demand for money depends positively on wealth, W, and income, Y, and inversely on the interest rate, i.

$$M = M(i,W,Y)$$

The demand for bonds depends positively on the interest rate and wealth, and inversely on income. As ways of holding wealth, money and bonds are substitutes, but any increased demand for money for transactions purposes reduces the demand for bonds.

$$B = B(i,W,Y)$$

There are two important restrictions implied by our equilibrium conditions and the portfolio constraint that W equals B plus M. The first is that any increase in wealth must be allocated to the two assets. For example, if wealth increases by 1 dollar, then desired stocks of both bonds and money rise and the combined increase must equal 1 dollar. The other condition is that, for a given level of wealth, an increase in the demand for one asset must be offset by a decreased demand for the other. For example, suppose a rise in the interest rate increases the demand for bonds by 1 dollar; then it must also decrease the demand for money by 1 dollar. A similar restriction applies to the effects of a change in income for a given level of wealth.

If we take the stock of bonds and money as fixed at any point in time, these three equations describe an LM schedule such as the one drawn in Figure 13.1. For each alternative level of income there is an interest rate for which the demand for and stock of bonds are equal and the demand for and stock of money are equal. In order to see this, assume that at an interest rate of $0i_0$ and a level of income $0Y_0$ in Figure 13.1, both the bond and money markets are in equilibrium. Now consider a higher level of income, $0Y_1$. The rise in income increases desired money balances and reduces desired bond holdings by the same amount. Since a given rise in the interest rate reduces desired money balances and increases desired bond holdings by the same

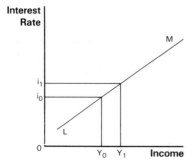

FIGURE 13.1
Derivation of LM schedule from portfolio model.

amount, there is some rise in the interest rate that restores equilibrium in both markets. In Figure 13.1, that interest rate is $0i_1$.

As in Chapter 1, where there were two commodities, wheat and cloth, if one market is in equilibrium, then by Walras's law, the other also is in equilibrium. If, as in the next model, there are three assets and two are in equilibrium, then the third market also must be in equilibrium.

Domestic and Foreign Assets

With two assets, our model determines one relative price, just as it does with two commodities in Chapter 1. When there are three assets, the analysis determines two relative prices, an interest rate and the exchange rate.

The model takes the following form. The stock of money, M, equals the demand for nominal balances, $M(i,\bar{i}, W, Y)$, at the given level of income, Y:

$$M = M(i,\bar{i},W,Y)$$

An increase in either interest rate decreases the demand for money, and an increase in wealth or income does the opposite.

The stock of domestic bonds, B, equals the domestic demand for those bonds, $B(i,\bar{i},W,Y)$.

$$B = B(i,\bar{i},W,Y)$$

An increase in the domestic yield, i, or portfolio, W, increases the demand for domestic bonds; an increase in $\bar{i}$ or Y does the opposite.

The stock of foreign bonds valued in domestic currency, πF, equals the domestic demand for those bonds, $F(i,\bar{i},W)$.

$$\pi F = F(i,\bar{i},W)$$

An increase in $\bar{i}$ or W increases this demand, and an increase in i does the opposite.

The financial portfolio, W, is the sum of the three assets:

$$W = M + B + \pi F$$

At each instant, the existing stocks of the three assets are fixed and the exchange rate and domestic interest rate must adjust so that these stocks are held willingly. That is, prices adjust so that actual and desired stocks are equal.

As in the domestic version, the portfolio constraint imposes important restrictions on the model. First, the increased demand for one asset due to a change in its interest rate must exactly equal the reduced demand for the other two assets. Second, any increase in wealth must be absorbed by the three assets. If wealth increases by 1 dollar, the combined demand for money plus domestic and foreign bonds also must rise by 1 dollar. The assumption that domestic rather than foreign bonds absorb changes in transactions demand for money implies that a 1-dollar increase in the transactions demand for money due to a rise in income reduces the demand for domestic bonds by 1 dollar and leaves the demand for foreign bonds unchanged.

Figure 13.2 describes an initial equilibrium. Unlike the *LM* schedule, income is constant. There are two endogenous prices, the exchange rate, π, and domestic interest rate, i. These prices adjust so that all three markets are in equilibrium. The exchange rate is measured along the vertical axis and the interest rate along the horizontal axis. For simplicity, each asset is assumed to be a linear function of the two prices.

The schedule labeled *MM* describes the combination of exchange rate and interest rate for which, at a given level of income, the demand for and stock of money are equal. The schedule slopes up and to the right. Given the existing stocks of the assets M, B, and F, an increase in the exchange rate, π, increases wealth, which raises desired money balances. The domestic interest rate therefore must rise to reduce desired balances and restore monetary equilibrium.

The *BB* schedule in Figure 13.2 describes the combinations of exchange rate and interest rate for which there is equilibrium in the market for domestic bonds. This schedule must slope downward from left to right. For a given level of income, an increase in the exchange rate increases wealth and the demand for bonds. Bond yields must therefore fall in order to make domestic bonds less attractive and restore equilibrium.

The *FF* schedule describes equilibrium in the domestic market for foreign bonds. This schedule also slopes down and to the right. A rise in domestic interest rates decreases the desired stock of foreign assets, and the

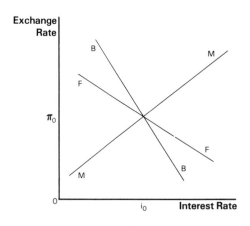

FIGURE 13.2
Initial portfolio equilibrium.

price of foreign exchange must fall in order to reduce the domestic value πF of the given stock of foreign bonds, F. In order for the system to be stable, the FF schedule must be flatter than the BB schedule. This condition appears reasonable. If the demand for money is sensitive to the interest rate, given the wealth constraint, a rise in domestic interest rates must increase desired holdings of domestic bonds by more than it reduces the demand for foreign assets. As a result, as long as the demand for money responds to wealth, a larger decline in π is needed to restore equilibrium in the domestic than foreign bond market.

In Figure 13.2, the FF and BB schedules intersect at π_0 and i_0, where both markets are in equilibrium. Since two of the three asset markets are in equilibrium, we know that the third is also. The MM schedule therefore must pass through the intersection of BB and FF at π_0 and i_0.

Now that we know what an equilibrium looks like, it is time to see how the exchange rate responds to fiscal and monetary policy. We consider fiscal policy first, and then monetary policy.

Fiscal Policy

Fiscal policy usually means financing government expenditure by selling bonds over time rather than instantaneously. In this context, that kind of fiscal policy would not yield a useful experiment. Our fiscal policy therefore takes the form of an instantaneous increase in the stock of domestic bonds.

Given an increase in the stock of bonds, the demand for bonds rises due to the wealth effect, but this rise in demand is less than the increase in the stock of bonds, because some of the wealth effect spills over into money and foreign bonds. Domestic interest rates must rise to restore equilibrium in the bond market at the original exchange rate. An increase in the stock of bonds therefore shifts the BB schedule to the right.

The wealth effect of the increase in bond holdings also shifts the FF curve to the right. A larger portfolio increases the demand for foreign assets. At the initial exchange rate π and stock of foreign assets F, the domestic yield must rise to offset the increased demand for foreign assets generated by the wealth effect of the increase in domestic bonds. The MM schedule shifts to the right for the same reason. The wealth effect increases the demand for money. With the stock of money fixed, at the original exchange rate the interest rate must rise in order to restore monetary equilibrium.

Since all three schedules move to the right, the domestic yield must rise. The change in the exchange rate, however, is ambiguous. The change in the exchange rate depends on the substitutability among the three assets. If domestic and foreign bonds are better substitutes in portfolios than domestic bonds and money, the substitution effect dominates and the domestic price of foreign exchange, π, declines as people shift out of foreign assets into domestic bonds. If the opposite holds, the wealth effect dominates the demand for foreign assets, and the price of foreign exchange rises as people attempt to increase their holdings of foreign bonds.

We can illustrate this point by taking two polar cases. In the first, domestic and foreign bonds are close substitutes in the sense that any increased demand for domestic bonds due to higher domestic interest rates takes the form of a reduced demand for foreign bonds. This assumption implies that domestic interest rates do not affect the demand for money. In the second case, money and domestic bonds are close substitutes. An increase in domestic yields reduces the demand for money by the same amount that it increases the demand for domestic bonds, which implies no response in the demand for foreign bonds.

Case 1   As the interest elasticity of the demand for money approaches zero, the *MM* schedule becomes flat. Given the initial stock of assets, M, B, and F, and constant income, Y, only one level of wealth and therefore one exchange rate is consistent with monetary equilibrium. In Figure 13.3, this exchange rate is π_0 and the *MM* schedule is horizontal at that exchange rate. Since we can delete one market, we drop the *FF* schedule and show the *BB* schedule. Given the initial solid *MM* and *BB* schedules, the equilibrium exchange rates and interest rates in Figure 13.3 are π_0 and i_0, respectively.

An increase in the stock of bonds shifts the *BB* schedule in Figure 13.3 to B_1B_1. The wealth effect of this increase forces the *MM* schedule down. In this case, higher interest rates cannot restore monetary equilibrium because money demand is insensitive to interest rates. The exchange rate must fall by enough to eliminate the effect of the increase in wealth on the demand for money. That is, the value of the domestic portfolio must fall back to the original level. Since the *MM* schedule shifts down and the *BB* schedule shifts right, the exchange rate must fall and the interest rate rise. In Figure 13.3, the exchange rate falls to π_1, and the interest rate rises to i_1. In this case, there is no change in wealth. The substitution effect dominates, and the demand for foreign bonds falls as domestic interest rates rise. The price of

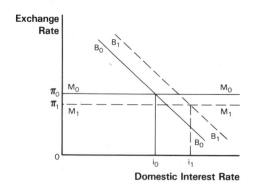

FIGURE 13.3

Effect of an exogenous increase in domestic bonds as the interest elasticity of money demand approaches zero.

foreign exchange declines because people try to sell foreign bonds as domestic yields rise.

Case 2   As the substitutability between foreign and domestic bonds decreases and the substitutability between domestic bonds and money as ways of holding wealth increases, the downward pressure on exchange rates declines. For example, suppose the demand for foreign bonds becomes totally insensitive to domestic yields. In that case, the *FF* schedule becomes flat. Given the stock of assets M, B, and F, only one exchange rate is consistent with equilibrium in the domestic market for foreign bonds. This exchange rate is consistent with any domestic interest rate, and the *FF* schedule is horizontal.

In Figure 13.4, the initial situation is described by the solid *BB* and *FF* schedules. Given these schedules, the exchange rate is π_0, and the interest rate is i_0. An exogenous increase in bond holdings shifts the *BB* schedule to the right to B_1B_1. The increase in wealth also increases the demand for foreign bonds, and the *FF* schedule shifts to F_1F_1. A rise in interest rates alone cannot restore portfolio equilibrium. With F fixed and the demand for foreign bonds insensitive to domestic yields, equilibrium in the market for foreign bonds must be achieved by an increase in the supply πF, and exchange rates rise. An increase in the exchange rate restores equilibrium to the market for foreign bonds because the domestic value πF of the fixed stock F rises faster than the increased demand generated by the wealth effect of the rise in the exchange rate. In this case, the wealth effect of fiscal policy on the demand for foreign bonds dominates, and the interest rate and exchange rate both rise. In Figure 13.4, they rise to i_1 and π_1.

Summary   An instantaneous exogenous increase in the stock of bonds tends to increase wealth, reduce bond prices, and raise interest rates. The increase in wealth raises the demand for foreign bonds, which tends to drive up the domestic price of foreign exchange. The increase in domestic interest rates, however, reduces the demand for foreign bonds, which lowers

FIGURE 13.4
Effects of an exogenous increase in domestic bonds as the interest elasticity of demand for foreign bonds approaches zero.

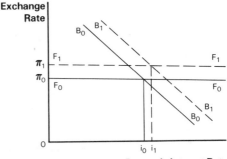

the price of foreign exchange. Whether the exchange rate rises or falls as the result of the expansionary fiscal policy depends on which factor dominates. In Figure 13.3, where the price of foreign exchange falls, the interest rate effect dominates because domestic and foreign bonds are close substitutes. In Figure 13.4, where the price of foreign exchange rises, the wealth effect dominates because the demand for foreign bonds does not respond to domestic interest rates.

Monetary Policy

An expansionary monetary policy is a more straightforward intellectual experiment. For the purposes of this analysis, an open market purchase is an instantaneous increase in the stock of money and an equivalent reduction in holdings of domestic bonds. The immediate response is devaluation and lower interest rates. The initial equilibrium is shown by the solid BB, FF, and MM schedules in Figure 13.5. The original interest rate and exchange rate are i_0 and π_0.

The reduction in the stock of bonds due to the open market purchase shifts the domestic bond schedule in Figure 13.5 to the left, to B_1B_1. The increase in the stock of money shifts the schedule describing monetary equilibrium to the left from M_0M_0 to M_1M_1. With no change in wealth, at the original exchange rate the domestic interest rate must fall in order to restore equilibrium for both money and bonds. Since the open market operation does not shift the FF schedule, the intersection of the MM and BB schedules must move up and to the left along the FF schedule, which implies devaluation and lower interest rates.

The open market purchase drives down domestic interest rates, which increases the domestic demand for foreign bonds. As people try to buy foreign bonds, they drive up the domestic price of foreign exchange. Depreciation increases the domestic value of the existing stock of foreign bonds and restores equilibrium in the market for foreign bonds.

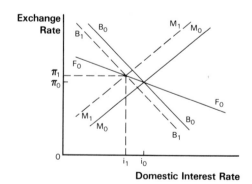

Exchange Rate

π_1
π_0

i_1 i_0

Domestic Interest Rate

FIGURE 13.5
Instantaneous effect of an expansionary monetary policy.

Transition to Steady State

So far we have restricted our analysis to instantaneous responses, but the portfolio approach also provides an explanation for the new steady-state equilibrium where stocks and flows have had time to adjust. A precise description of the time path to the new equilibrium, however, requires assumptions about dynamic responses of production and prices. Since we have no solid empirical base for making such assumptions, we restrict our analysis to a general description of the adjustment process.

We start in steady-state equilibrium where stocks and flows are mutually consistent. For simplicity, there is full employment and no growth. The trade deficit measured in foreign currency, X_0, just equals the income from domestically held foreign assets, $\bar{i}F$. As a result, there is a zero balance in both the current and capital accounts., Whether or not purchasing power parity holds in the initial equilibrium is an issue we sidestep for now, but will return to later. Like the foreign interest rate, the foreign price level is exogenous and constant. To keep the analysis as simple as possible, there is no domestic investment and no government deficit, so that the stock of domestic bonds does not change between the initial and final steady state.

We concentrate on monetary policy and start our analysis of the transition where Figure 13.5 stops. The solid schedules in Figure 13.6 show the equilibrium immediately after the open market purchase. The exchange rate is π_1, and the domestic interest rate is i_1. In the instantaneous response, the trade balance does not have time to adjust, so the exchange rate must rise by enough to eliminate any incipient capital outflow. Since the price level also needs time to adjust, the instantaneous rise in the exchange rate drives the actual exchange rate up relative to the exchange rate consistent with purchasing power parity. This rise in the real exchange rate encourages exports and discourages imports, and the country develops a surplus in the current account. With flexible rates, this surplus must be matched by a deficit in the capital account, and the stock of foreign assets increases. As the stock of

FIGURE 13.6
The adjustment to a new steady-state equilibrium.

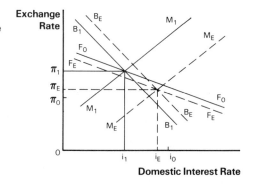

foreign assets, F, rises, the FF schedule in Figure 13.6 shifts down and to the left toward $F_E F_E$.

The trade surplus and decline in interest rates associated with the open market purchase increase aggregate demand. With full employment, prices rise. The increase in nominal income drives up the demand for money and reduces the demand for domestic bonds. The increase in the portfolio due to the capital inflow reinforces the rise in money demand and moderates the fall in the demand for bonds. The MM schedule shifts to the right. As long as the income effect on the demand for bonds exceeds the wealth effect, the BB schedule also shifts to the right. Relative to i_1 and π_1, interest rates tend to rise and the exchange rate appreciates as the economy responds to the initial shock.

Rising interest rates, appreciation, and inflation all work toward restoring equilibrium. Appreciation and higher prices reduce the trade surplus. Higher interest rates and a falling trade surplus reduce aggregate demand, and the pressure on prices declines. A smaller trade surplus also reduces the deficit in the capital account, and the accumulation of foreign assets slows down.

Full equilibrium is restored at the original full employment level of output when prices, interest rates, and the exchange rate all adjust to eliminate the current account surplus and import of foreign assets. The new steady state is described in Figure 13.6 by the $M_E M_E$, $F_E F_E$, and $B_E B_E$ schedules that yield π_E and i_E as the new steady-state exchange rate and interest rate.

Exchange rates must overshoot. The initial rise in the exchange rate to π_1 generated by the increased demand for foreign assets is partially reversed as the current account surplus increases the stock of foreign assets. In Figure 13.6, the expansionary monetary policy causes the initial depreciation to overshoot the ultimate depreciation by $\pi_E \pi_1$.

Interest rates tend to rise after the initial shock because higher income and more foreign bonds increase the demand for money. The price level rises proportionately less than the increase in the stock of money. Both a larger portfolio and the decline in interest rates from i_0 to i_E increase the demand for money and reduce the rise in nominal income required to restore monetary equilibrium.

The role for purchasing power parity depends on one's view about the adjustment process for the balance of payments. The accumulation of foreign assets implies that real interest income from those assets rises, which requires a larger deficit in the trade account in order to achieve a zero balance in the current account. The issue is this: With constant real output, what increases the real trade deficit?

William Branson uses an essentially Keynesian argument. Given the level of output, the trade balance depends on the actual exchange rate relative to the rate implied by purchasing power parity. In the initial equilibrium there is a trade deficit. Given the level of output, this deficit is associated with some relationship between the actual rate, π_0, and the initial parity rate implied by relative price levels. A larger trade deficit at a constant level of output requires a fall in the actual exchange rate relative to the parity rate—that is, a fall in the real exchange rate, in order to spur imports and discourage exports. Inflation must exceed depreciation. We are back to the Keynesian view of the balance of payments we analyzed in Chapter 9. The trade balance and exchange rates are interdependent.

Trade theory and Fisherian capital theory suggest an alternative interpretation. As long as we are in a true steady state, there is no growth and saving is zero. All income, whether from domestic production or interest on foreign assets, is spent on commodities. Real domestic expenditure therefore exceeds real domestic output by the income from the new stock of foreign assets, $\bar{i}F_E$. This "excess demand" generates an equivalent trade deficit through the price mechanism along the lines discussed in Chapters 1 and 11. From this perspective, it is natural to assume that purchasing power parity holds, and the exchange rate rises proportionately with the rise in domestic prices.

Since domestic and foreign assets are not perfect substitutes in this model, covered interest rate arbitrage is not relevant. In the next model, domestic and foreign assets are perfect substitutes and arbitrage eliminates net covered yields.

ARBITRAGE AND EXPECTATIONS

Rudigar Dornbusch and others have developed an asset approach based on restrictions implied by covered arbitrage and rational expectations about exchange rates. It stresses close substitutability between domestic and foreign securities and concentrates on monetary equilibrium. Like the last model, this approach implies that exchange rates tend to overrespond to monetary shocks, but the reasoning is different.

Once again, our economy is small and foreign interest rates and prices are exogenous. Financial markets also clear rapidly compared to markets for commodities. Purchasing power parity holds in steady state, but not during the transition from one steady state to another.

Dornbusch Model

In this model, domestic and foreign assets are perfect substitutes given a proper forward premium or discount to offset anticipated changes in exchange rates. In other words, the equilibrium condition for covered interest rate arbitrage from Chapter 5 holds continuously. If π_F is the forward exchange rate, then using the notation from the last model, π_F/π always equals $(1 + i)/(1 + \bar{i})$.

The assumption that net covered yields are always zero highlights expectations and imposes strong restrictions on the analysis. Unlike the portfolio model, here any interest rate differential must be offset by expected changes in exchange rates. Suppose an open market purchase depresses domestic interest rates. A decline in domestic interest rates relative to foreign yields must be offset by expectations that the domestic price of foreign exchange will fall. It is this feature that forces the spot rate to overrespond to an expansionary monetary policy.

Expectations about future spot rates can be formed in many ways. One analytically convenient and reasonable assumption is that expectations are rational in the sense that they reflect the implications of the model. If expectations are rational and forward rates equal expected future spot rates, then forward rates are unbiased estimates of future spot rates. In terms of the notation we used in the last section, the forward rate, π_F, which refers to the new steady-state equilibrium equals the new steady-state equilibrium exchange rate, π_E, plus a random error term with zero mean. If we ignore the random error, we can rewrite our covered arbitrage equation as follows:

$$\pi_E/\pi = (1 + i)/(1 + \bar{i})$$

The expected change in the exchange rate is π_E/π, and it equals the interest rate differential, $(1 + i)/(1 + \bar{i})$.

To keep the analysis as simple as possible, we assume full employment and a demand for real money balances that depends on real income, y, and domestic interest rates, i. Unlike in the last section, the demand for money does not depend on wealth or foreign interest rates:

$$M/P = y^k i^{-\lambda}$$

This demand for money is simply a log linear version of the equation we used in Chapter 9. A log linear version simplifies some of the analysis later in this chapter.

In this approach, changes in interest rates restore monetary equilibrium in the short run, but in the long run monetary shocks have no influence on interest rates. Monetary equilibrium is reestablished in the long run entirely by changes in the price level. Consider, for example, a 10 percent increase in the stock of money. In the shortest of the short runs, commodity prices are fixed and output is constant. If monetary equilibrium is continuous, the interest rate must fall by whatever is necessary to maintain monetary equilibrium. But when the exchange rate reaches its new long-run equilibrium, the expected change in the exchange rate is zero, and domestic interest rates must again equal the exogenous foreign interest rate. With real income and domestic interest rates unchanged from initial to final steady-state equilibrium, the price level must rise by 10 percent to restore real money balances to their original level.

Monetary Policy

Now we are ready to analyze the effects of an unanticipated expansionary monetary policy. Initially, domestic and foreign interest rates are equal. Then an open market purchase by the central bank increases the nominal money stock. With output and commodity prices given in the shortest of short runs, the interest rate falls in order to restore monetary equilibrium.

The decline in domestic yields implies a forward discount. In order to accept lower yields on domestic assets, residents must anticipate the same lower yield from foreign assets. Given the fixed yield in terms of foreign currency on foreign assets, $\bar{i}$, the only way the expected domestic yield on foreign assets can fall is for there to be an expected decline in the domestic price of foreign exchange. That is, π must rise by more than π_F. If expectations about the new steady-state exchange rate are rational, the only way there can be expected appreciation is for the instantaneous rise in the spot exchange rate to exceed the ultimate increase. That is, the spot exchange rate, π, must overshoot its new long-run equilibrium value, π_F, as shown in Figure 13.7.

Up to time zero, the price level is constant and the exchange rate in Figure 13.7 is π_0. At time zero, the central bank engages in an open market purchase that instantaneously increases the money stock by 10 percent. The new steady-state and expected equilibrium exchange rate, π_E, is now 10 percent higher than the original rate, π_0, but the expected decline in the domestic price of foreign exchange, π_E/π_0', must just equal the new interest rate differential required to restore monetary equilibrium. For example, suppose monetary equilibrium implies that the yield on domestic assets of one year's maturity falls from 10 to 9 percent. If the new equilibrium is expected to be restored in one year, then π_0' in Figure 13.7 must be 1 percent larger than π_E. That is, the instantaneous rise in the exchange rate overshoots the long-run rise by 1 percent.

FIGURE 13.7
The dynamic response of the exchange rate to an open market purchase.

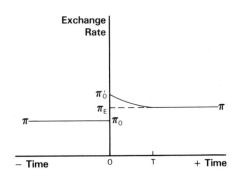

As in the previous model, purchasing power parity does not hold in the short run because portfolio equilibrium dominates the exchange rate. Here, however, PPP does hold in the long run. Prices ultimately rise by 10 percent, and the exchange rate depreciates by 10 percent.

Both portfolio and arbitrage-expectations models implicitly assume underlying price stability. They are not designed to explain the behavior of exchange rates in inflationary environments. Our next model is designed for inflation.

INFLATION

Relatively high transaction costs are the economic rationale for sluggish adjustment in commodity markets. Inflation, however, imposes serious costs on firms and households that respond slowly to monetary shocks. For example, if you own a shoe store and you do not raise your shoe prices promptly when your suppliers raise their prices, you sell shoes for less than their replacement cost. That is a sure-fire formula for bankruptcy.

Inflationary Model

The major change in this model is to drop the assumption that asset markets clear rapidly compared to markets for commodities. Here inflation promotes rapid price responses in all sectors, and purchasing power parity holds even in the very short run. We are in a world where the analysis developed in Chapter 10 holds even in the short run.

By a judicious choice of units, we can set the initial exchange rate equal to unity and write the purchasing power parity equation simply as follows:

$$\pi = P/\overline{P}$$

As in the last model, there is full employment, and the demand for real money balances, M/P, depends on real income, y, and nominal domestic interest rates, i.

$$M/P = y^k i^{-\lambda}$$

Now, however, we must distinguish between real interest rates, r, and nominal interest rates, i. For simplicity, we adopt the usual approximation that nominal rates equal real rates plus the expected rate of inflation, $\dot{P}^E$.

$$i \approx r + \dot{P}^E$$

This form ignores the interaction term $r\dot{P}^E$, but it is close enough for our purposes.

Domestic and foreign assets are perfect substitutes and, as in Chapter 2, exchange equates real yields. Foreign yields, both real and nominal, are exogenous. As a result, domestic real interest rates are determined in the world capital market.

Expectations

Under these conditions, inflationary expectations directly affect price levels and exchange rates. Take some initial money stock, real income, real interest rate, and inflationary expectations. Monetary equilibrium implies some price level, and PPP implies an exchange rate. Now let the public expect an increase in the rate of monetary expansion so that inflationary expectations rise. The anticipated cost of holding real balances rises, and desired real balances fall. Given nominal balances, lower real balances imply a higher price level and more depreciation. As we we will see in the next section, this response creates a different form of overshooting.

Monetary Shock

Let's start with a steady-state rate of inflation and depreciation of 10 percent. Real income is constant. The nominal money supply is rising 10 percent per year, and real balances are constant. Foreign and domestic real interest rates are 10 percent, and so is the expected rate of inflation and depreciation. The domestic nominal interest rate is 20 percent, 10 percent real and 10 percent due to inflation.

Without warning, the monetary authorities step up the rate of increase in the stock of money from 10 to 20 percent. The situation in the new steady state is easy enough to describe. There is 20 percent inflation and depreciation. The real interest rate is 10 percent, and the nominal rate is 30 percent. Real income is unchanged, but real balances fall because nominal yields rise.

During the transition, however, the rate of inflation and depreciation must exceed the new steady-state rate of inflation and depreciation because desired real balances fall. Figure 13.8 shows a reasonable path for real money balances. Before the rise in monetary expansion at time zero, desired real balances are constant at $(M/P)_0$. The increase in inflationary expectations raises nominal interest rates and reduces desired real balances. In the new steady state, desired real balances in Figure 13.8 are $(M/P)_E$.

Given a 20 percent rate of increase in nominal balances, a decline in actual real balances requires a temporary rate of inflation of more than 20 percent. The behavior of the rate of inflation is illustrated in Figure 13.9. In the initial steady state it is 10 percent, and in the new steady-state inflation it is 20 percent. But during the transition from time zero to the new steady

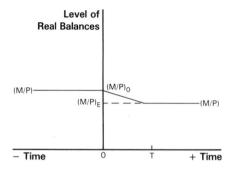

FIGURE 13.8
The dynamic response of real balances to an increase in the rate of monetary expansion.

state at time T, both the rate of inflation and depreciation are greater than 20 percent.

In this approach, the level of the exchange rate does not overshoot; at no time does the exchange rate fall in this sequence of events. Instead, during the transition the rate of inflation and depreciation overshoot the rate of increase in the stock of money. Doubling the rate of increase in nominal balances temporarily causes more than twice the rate of inflation and depreciation.

So far we have concentrated on monetary expectations, but any expectations that influence money demand alter the price level and exchange rate. For example, suppose the public becomes more optimistic about real income and expects real income to rise. Other things being equal, higher income implies that the price level does not rise as rapidly as previously expected. The change in expectations about real income reduces the cost of holding real balances, and desired real balances rise before income increases. The major lesson here is that changes in expectations about any of the factors that influence the demand for or supply of money alter current price levels and exchange rates.

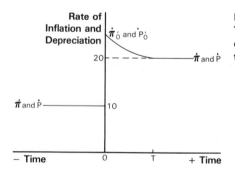

FIGURE 13.9
The dynamic response of the rate of depreciation to an increase in the rate of monetary expansion.

SUMMARY

All the asset models have one characteristic in common. In the short run, asset equilibrium drives exchange rates. There are, however, an almost infinite variety of variations on that basic theme.

The portfolio model pushes expectations into the background, stresses differences between domestic and foreign assets, and concentrates on the portfolio balance approach reviewed in Chapter 2. In that model, the exchange rate is essentially another asset price that must change in order to restore instantaneous portfolio balance after some exogenous shock. This change in exchange rates and yields alters aggregate demand, output, and the balance of payments. As these flows change, they feed back into the portfolio until a new equilibrium in both asset and commodity markets is established. If the initial shock is monetary, exchange rates overshoot their long-run equilibrium levels.

The arbitrage-expectations approach stresses substitutability between domestic and foreign assets, concentrates on one asset, money, and develops the implications of effective covered arbitrage with rational expectations. Instantaneous monetary equilibrium requires that interest rates fall in response to an expansionary monetary shock. Covered arbitrage and the decline in domestic yields imply that the instantaneous rise in the spot rate must overshoot the long-run movement in the spot rate even though expectations regarding exchange rates are rational.

The first two models implicitly assume an environment of monetary stability. The third model provides an essentially monetarist explanation for the determination of exchange rates with monetary instability. This approach stresses the role of expectations in determining exchange rates.

In an inflationary environment, commodity prices tend to adjust rapidly and purchasing power parity can hold even in the very short run. Since inflation imposes a cost on holding real money balances, any change in expectations that alters expected inflation also affects present desired real money balances and current prices. If purchasing power parity holds even approximately in the short run, these changes in expectations also affect current exchange rates.

QUESTIONS FOR REVIEW

1. Explain why the *MM* schedule in Figure 13.2 slopes up and to the right.
2. Explain why the *BB* and *FF* schedules in Figure 13.2 slope down and to the right.
3. How does a rise in foreign interest rates shift the *MM*, *BB*, and *FF* schedules? How does the maturity of the foreign bonds affect these shifts?

4. Compare and contrast the effects on the exchange rate of an expansionary monetary policy in the portfolio balance model with the effects of the same policy under flexible rates in Chapters 9 and 10.

5. In both the portfolio balance and arbitrage-expectations models, the exchange rate overshoots in response to an expansionary monetary policy. Compare and contrast these two explanations for overshooting.

6. Given the arbitrage-expectations model, describe the dynamic response of the exchange rate to an increase in foreign interest rates.

7. Given the inflationary model with price flexibility, compare and contrast the effects of an open market purchase of securities when the purchase is fully anticipated and when it is completely unanticipated.

8. Are any of the models we developed in this chapter applicable to fixed rates? If a model is applicable to fixed rates, describe the effects of an expansionary monetary policy under fixed rates. If a model is not applicable to fixed rates, explain why it is not.

ADDITIONAL READINGS

BRANSON, WILLIAM H. "Asset Markets and Relative Prices in Exchange Rate Determination." *Sozialwissenschaftliche Annalen* (June 1980). Reprinted by International Finance Section, Department of Economics, Princeton University, as Reprints in International Finance, No. 20.

DORNBUSCH, RUDIGER. "Expectations and Exchange Rate Dynamics." *Journal of Political Economy* (December 1976).

DRISKILL, ROBERT. "Exchange Rate Overshooting, the Trade Balance, and Rational Expectations." *Journal of International Economics* (August 1981).

FAMA, EUGENE F., AND ANDRÉ FARBER. "Money, Bonds and Foreign Exchange." *American Economic Review* (September 1979).

FRANKEL, JEFFREY A. "On the Mark: A Theory of Floating Exchange Rates Based on Real Interest Differentials." *American Economic Review* (September 1979).

FRENKEL, JACOB A., AND CARLOS A. RODRIGUEZ. "Portfolio Equilibrium and the Balance of Payments: A Monetary Approach." *American Economic Review* (September 1975).

LEROY, STEPHEN F. "Expectations Models of Asset Prices: A Survey of Theory." *Journal of Finance* (March 1982).

MURPHY, ROBERT G., AND CARL VAN DUYNE. "Asset Market Approaches to Exchange Rate Determination: A Comparative Analysis." *Weltwirtschaftliches Archiv* (Issue 4, 1980).

MUSSA, MICHAEL. "A Model of Exchange Rate Dynamics." *Journal of Political Economy* (February 1982).

———. "Empirical Regularities in the Behavior of Exchange Rates and Theories of the Foreign Exchange Market." In *Policies for Employment, Prices, and Exchange Rates,* supplementary volume 11, *Journal of Monetary Economics* (1979).

APPENDIX
A Monetarist Critique and Reinterpretation
of Portfolio and Arbitrage-Expectations Models

In the first two models developed in this chapter, interest rates clear the monetary sector, which is consistent with a liquidity preference view of interest rates. The third model reflects a more monetarist approach in which the price level clears the monetary sector. Here we discuss some of the problems with and develop more monetarist versions of the portfolio and arbitrage-expectations models. These alternatives do not imply overshooting, which is more consistent with the empirical evidence that freely flexible exchange rates essentially perform a random walk.

ARBITRAGE EXPECTATIONS

In spite of the emphasis on the monetary sector, the arbitrage-expectations model retains an important Keynesian element: Fluctuations in interest rates maintain continuous monetary equilibrium. When monetarists describe the adjustment process, they usually refer to "excess money balances." Such references implicity reject the notion of continuous monetary equilibrium. This attitude is consistent with the monetarist emphasis on money as a means of payment; money serves as the primary buffer stock between receipts and payments. That function requires that at times actual money balances diverge from what our typical equations describe as desired balances. Whether we want to call these divergences "disequilibria" or "transitional equilibria" has more to do with how we want to use the term "equilibrium" than it does with the underlying economic concept. With either interpretation, we cannot use the monetary sector to determine the interest rate and so we must look for another mechanism.

A Reinterpretation

The arbitrage-expectations model assumes that domestic and foreign assets are perfect substitutes. A natural way to reinterpret that assumption is that real yields are identical on domestic and foreign assets. If domestic and foreign real yields are equal, then the domestic nominal yield, i, depends on the exogenous real foreign interest rate, $\bar{r}$, and expected domestic inflation, $\dot{P}^E$.

$$(1 + i) = (1 + \bar{r})(1 + \dot{P}^E)$$

We now can write the arbitrage equation as follows:

$$\pi_F/\pi = \frac{(1 + \bar{r})(1 + \dot{P}^E)}{(1 + \bar{r})(1 + \bar{\dot{P}}^E)} = \frac{(1 + \dot{P}^E)}{(1 + \bar{\dot{P}}^E)}$$

As in Chapter 7, the forward premium π_F/π equals the difference between expected rates of domestic $\dot{P}^E$ and foreign inflation $\bar{\dot{P}}^E$. With foreign price stability, the forward premium depends only on expected domestic inflation:

$$\pi_F/\pi = (1 + \dot{P}^E)$$

Monetary Policy

Let's start with an initial equilibrium where domestic and foreign real yields are both 10 percent and there is no expected inflation. Then an open market purchase increases the nominal money stock by 1 percent, which causes the public to expect the price level to rise by 1 percent over the next year. The domestic price of foreign exchange is also expected to rise by 1 percent.

The arbitrage-expectations model implies that nominal yields fall in order to restore monetary equilibrium. Given effective covered arbitrage and rational expectations about the steady-state exchange rate, the decline in domestic nominal yields requires an instantaneous rise in the spot rate that overshoots the steady-state depreciation. In that interpretation, however, either real rates fall by more than nominal yields or expectations are rational with respect to exchange rates but not prices. Here real rates are constant, and the open market operation affects expectations about exchange rates and prices symmetrically. As a result, the forward premium and domestic nominal yields both rise by 1 percent.

Suppose initially all nominal and real yields are 10 percent, and both spot and one-year forward rates are 1 dollar per pound.

$$\frac{\$1/£1}{\$1/£1} = \frac{1 + 0.10}{1 + 0.10}$$

Then the open market purchase generates actual and expected rates of inflation over the next year of 1 percent. The expected spot rate and one-year forward rate both rise to \$1.01/£1. Since domestic and foreign securities are perfect substitutes, domestic real yields are constant and nominal yields rise. With "sticky" commodity prices, there are excess money balances because the open market purchase increases actual real balances and reduces desired real balances.

The open market purchase has no instantaneous effect on the spot exchange rate. The one-year forward rate is \$1.01/£1, and the interest rate differential is 1 percent $(1 + 0.10)(1 + 0.01)/(1 + 0.10)$. Only one spot rate, $1/£1, is consistent with a zero net covered yield.

$$\frac{\$1.01/£1}{\$1.00/£1} = \frac{(1 + 0.10)(1 + 0.01)}{(1 + 0.10)}$$

There is no instantaneous depreciation and no overshooting.

If an open market purchase can temporarily reduce real yields on domestic securities relative to foreign securities, then effective covered interest rate arbitrage implies that the rise in the spot rate matches the decline in domestic real yields. Suppose the open market purchase temporarily drives down real yields on domestic securities from 10 to 9.5 percent. In that case, with 1 percent expected inflation, the domestic nominal yield rises to 10.5 percent. There is a one-year interest rate differential of 0.5 percent and a one-year forward rate of $1.01/£1. To eliminate profitable arbitrage, the spot rate must rise from $1/£1 to about $1.005/£1 so that the forward premium equals the interest rate differential. And still there is no overshooting.

In order for the spot rate to overshoot and rise by more than 1 percent, real domestic yields must fall by more than the expected rise in prices. With a 1 percent expected rate of inflation, the domestic real yield must fall below 9 percent in order for the nominal rate to fall below 10 percent, which is what is required for overshooting.

REVISED PORTFOLIO MODEL

In the revised portfolio model, domestic residents again hold domestic bonds, B, with an endogenous yield of i; foreign bonds, F, with an exogenous yield of $\bar{i}$; and domestic money, M. All three assets are imperfect substitutes. Bonds remain short term. The domestic value of foreign bonds, πF, still depends on the domestic price of foreign exchange. As in the standard portfolio model, expectations are static. Here, however, there is a foreign exchange market and an explicit mechanism to determine exchange rates. For simplicity, all foreign exchange dealers are domestic residents, and they hold a stock of foreign exchange, £.

Standard portfolio balance models implicitly assume that, when the public sells securities to the central bank, households or firms plan to purchase other assets. Here a decision to sell securities can reflect a planned purchase of either assets or commodities.

In this model, all assets for which there are markets are in continuous equilibrium. There is, however, no market for money. It is the other side of all other markets, including commodity markets. As a result, money demand and supply may not be equal. For simplicity we assume that, if part of the securities sold to the central bank reflect a planned purchase of commodities, the immediate effect is to generate an equivalent excess supply of money. Any planned purchase of other assets is executed immediately. In other words, any excess supply of money is an excess demand for commodities, and all other assets clear continuously.

Before we develop a formal model, let's go through the basic reasoning of how the system responds to an open market purchase. Interest rates are determined in the bond market. Since an open market purchase reduces the stock of domestic bonds, it reduces domestic yields. The fall in domestic yields increases the desired stock of foreign bonds. With instantaneous arbitrage between domestic and foreign capital markets, the domestic price of foreign bonds depends on the exogenous foreign price of those bonds and the domestic price of foreign exchange.

The domestic price of foreign exchange is not determined in the domestic market for foreign bonds. As in Chapter 4, foreign exchange dealers set that price in response to market pressure. As domestic yields fall, investors switch to foreign bonds and start to bid up prices for those bonds. Arbitragers respond by buying foreign exchange in order to import foreign bonds; foreign exchange dealers raise the dollar price of foreign exchange as their holdings fall.

In this scenario, both the domestic value of a foreign bond and the stock of foreign bonds increase. The domestic value rises because foreign exchange dealers push up the exchange rate as their inventory of foreign exchange declines. The domestic stock of foreign bonds, F, increases because arbitragers use the foreign exchange they buy from dealers to import foreign bonds.

Model

Now that we have a feel for how things work, let's look at a formal model. The demand for domestic and foreign bonds is the same as in the standard model:

$$B = B(i,\bar{i},W,Y)$$
$$\pi F = F(i,\bar{i},W)$$

There is, however, a difference in interpretation. For each equation, there is now an implicit market mechanism that determines the relevant interest rate or price. Even though for simplicity we have excluded changes in domestic bond prices, intuitively we might think of bond dealers that raise bond prices as their inventories decline.

We assume that the stock of foreign exchange demanded by dealers, £, depends only on the current exchange rate. Even with static expectations, this is a gross simplification. The main advantage is that it allows us to develop schedules similar to those used in Figures 13.1 through 13.4.

$$£ = £(\pi)$$

As in the other two asset markets, dealers adjust prices instantaneously to maintain continuous equilibrium.

This model describes the instantaneous response before any deficit or surplus can develop in the current account. As a result, the total holdings of foreign assets, K, is fixed in terms of the foreign currency:

$$K = £ + F$$

When foreign bonds are imported, the foreign exchange held by dealers falls by an equivalent amount.

The standard portfolio approach equates wealth with the portfolio of financial assets. Here wealth is the discounted value of an expected future income stream. Wages aside, these are essentially two ways to view the same thing. As we will see shortly, however, the Fisherian approach forces us to ask some questions we are not likely to raise with a portfolio perspective.

Given a transactions view of money, the demand for real money balances depends on interest rates and real income, but not real wealth. If a shock increases wealth but does not change interest rates or the productivity of money in reducing information and transactions costs associated with exchange, it does not alter the demand for real money balances:

$$M = M(i,\bar{i},Y)$$

Regardless of the interpretation of wealth, the financial portfolio no longer serves as a constraint that allows us arbitrarily to drop one asset. We must drop money. Monetary equilibrium is not continuous, and if we delete any other asset, we also implicitly eliminate the mechanism for setting the price for that asset.

Given linear demand functions, Figure 13A.1 describes the initial equilibrium. As in the standard portfolio model, the BB schedule shows the combination of exchange rate and domestic interest rate for which there is equilibrium in the domestic bond market. This schedule has essentially the same interpretation as in the original portfolio model. The line labeled KK is the counterpart to the FF schedule in that model. It shows the combinations of interest rate and exchange rate for which there is equilibrium in the domestic market for foreign assets. Since K equals $£$ plus F, we can express the domestic stock of foreign bonds, F, as follows:

$$F = K - £(\pi)$$

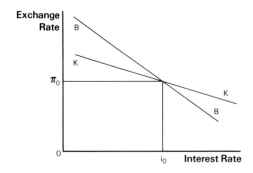

FIGURE 13A.1
Initial equilibrium in revised portfolio model.

When we replace F with $K - £(\pi)$ in the description of the domestic market for foreign securities

$$\pi F = F(i,\bar{i},W)$$

we obtain an equation that describes the combinations of interest rates and exchange rates for which the actual and desired stocks of foreign assets are equal:

$$\pi[K - £(\pi)] = F(i,\bar{i},W)$$

This equation describes the KK schedule in Figure 13A.1. The slope of the KK schedule depends on the elasticity of demand for foreign bonds with respect to domestic interest rates and how rapidly foreign exchange dealers raise the exchange rate as their inventory of foreign exchange falls. As with the FF schedule in the standard model, stability requires that the KK schedule be flatter than the BB schedule. In general, that condition will hold for essentially the same reasons that the FF schedule is flatter than the BB schedule.

Monetary Policy

In the initial equilibrium shown by the solid schedules in Figure 13A.2, there is full employment. Both output and the price level are constant. Given tastes, technology, and resource endowments, actual and desired wealth are equal and there is no saving. Investment is also zero, and the stock of domestic bonds is constant. There is a zero balance in current and capital accounts, and the stocks of foreign exchange, $£$, and foreign securities, F, are constant. The BB and KK schedules are B_0B_0 and K_0K_0 so that the initial exchange rate and interest rate are π_0 and i_0, respectively.

Now there is an open market purchase which shifts the BB schedule to the left to B_1B_1. The instantaneous effect is to increase the money stock, reduce the stock of bonds, and drive down domestic interest rates. The fall

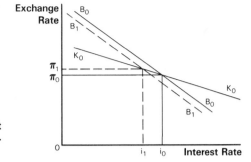

FIGURE 13A.2
Effect on exchange rates and interest rates of an expansionary monetary policy.

in domestic yields increases the demand for foreign securities. Importation of foreign securities lowers dealers' holdings of foreign exchange, and they raise the domestic price of foreign exchange. As a result, the immediate response to the open market purchase is a fall in domestic yields to i_1 and a rise in the exchange rate to π_1.

Real interest rates fall because domestic and foreign assets are not perfect substitutes. Nominal interest rates fall because expectations are static. As in the original portfolio approach, the current price level is expected to persist indefinitely even though the open market purchase eventually raises prices.

Over time, the interest rate tends to rise to the initial level, and prices rise in order to reduce the level of real balances and restore monetary equilibrium. Depending on the initial response, the exchange rate can rise or fall during this transition. The lower the domestic interest elasticity of demand for foreign bonds and the less dealers raise exchange rates as their inventories fall, the less likely the exchange rate is to overshoot.

If we can ignore any distributional effects, the open market purchase does not alter either domestic time preference or the productivity of capital. The open market operation, therefore, not only drives the real yield on domestic securities down relative to real yields on foreign securities, but also drives that yield below the return from domestic physical assets such as factories and refrigerators. The usual assumption is that such a gap leads to investment, a larger capital stock, and more wealth in the new steady state. But from a Fisherian perspective, if wealth was at its steady-state equilibrium level before the open market purchase and neither productivity nor time preference has changed, domestic interest rates, the domestic stock of real assets, and total wealth in the new steady state must be the same as in the original steady state. The restoration of steady-state portfolio equilibrium cannot involve an increase in wealth, as it does in the standard portfolio model.

Since interest rates and real income are the same in the initial and final steady states, the price level must rise in the same proportion as the increase in the stock of money in order to restore the original level of real money balances. With real wealth and the real stock of domestic assets unchanged, there is no increase in the domestic holdings of foreign assets.

In this model, the price mechanism works and the open market purchase does not change real endowments, tastes, or productivity. Distribution effects aside, all relative prices are the same in the new and old steady states. In order for that to be true, the domestic price of foreign exchange must rise by the same proportion as the rise in the domestic price level. Purchasing power parity holds.

The open market operation, however, redistributes wealth in at least two ways. First, it reduces interest income for some households and presumably reduces taxes for everyone. Second, the rise in prices transfers wealth from holders of bonds to the owners of firms that issue bonds. We do not ignore the effects of these transfers because there is a strong presumption that they are unimportant, but because we have no idea about their effects. They could, for example, cause the exchange rate to rise by either more or less than the rise in the domestic price level.

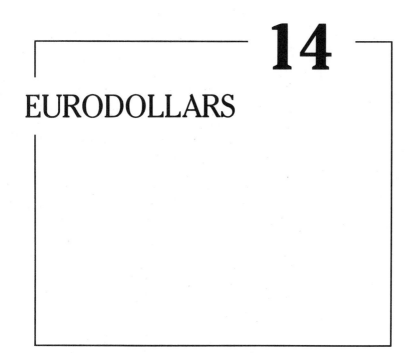

EURODOLLARS

14

This chapter discusses the market for Eurodollars and other Eurocurrencies. The first step is to understand what Eurodollars are. Next we examine the development of the market. Then we look at how it operates and how Eurodollars are created. Finally, we consider the debate over regulating the market for Eurocurrencies.

DESCRIPTION

Deposits

The Eurodollar market consists of banks in Europe and Britain that borrow and lend U.S. dollars. By convention, dollar loans to these banks are called Eurodollar deposits. The deposits, however, are not savings or checking accounts: You do not write checks on Eurodollar deposits, and they are not like a savings account—you cannot go in and draw out your money whenever you want it. Perhaps the closest analogy is a certificate of deposit or CD. With a certificate of deposit you lend a bank, say, $10,000 for perhaps 90 days. At the end of 90 days you get back your $10,000 plus accrued interest.

Eurocurrencies

Dollars are not the only currency borrowed and lent by Eurobanks; there is a market for almost every major European currency. Banks in Britain, for example, are willing to borrow or lend German marks, Swiss francs, or Italian lire. There are banks in Paris, Frankfurt, and Geneva that borrow and lend pound sterling. These transactions are part of the market for Eurocurrencies because they take place outside the jurisdiction of the country whose currency is borrowed and lent.

Other Locations

The original Eurocurrency markets in Europe and Britain were so successful that similar institutions developed in Asia and the Caribbean. Now banks in Singapore and the Grand Caymans borrow and lend U.S. dollars and other currencies. The term *Eurodollar* is commonly used to refer to all these markets for borrowing and lending dollars; the term *Eurocurrency* is used in the same way.

Functions

Eurocurrencies serve four important functions. (1) They finance international trade. (2) They provide an important interbank market. (3) They replace domestic intermediation. (4) Eurocurrency banks also act as intermediaries between deficit and surplus countries.

Finance trade   In the example used in Chapter 4, the contract to import wine from France might call for payment in dollars on delivery. One option for the French exporter, who wants the money when the wine is shipped, is to borrow dollars from a French bank at time of shipment and use these dollars to buy francs. The amount and timing of the loan is arranged so that the dollars paid by the U.S. importer pay off the loan from the French bank. The net result is that the Eurodollar market finances the goods in transit, and neither the importer nor the exporter faces any risk of loss due to changes in exchange rates.

Interbank   The Eurodollar market provides an important interbank market that allows banks to match the maturities of their assets and liabilities. Later in the chapter we will see how banks use the interbank market to balance their portfolios. The interbank market also helps banks cover forward exchange obligations undertaken for their nonbank customers and, in the process, generates a form of covered interest rate arbitrage.

Domestic intermediation   The Eurodollar market replaces transactions that would have taken place in domestic financial markets. For example, funds that would have been lent by a firm in Cleveland to a bank in New

York and then relent to a company in Pittsburgh are lent by the firm in Cleveland to a bank outside the United States and then borrowed in the Eurocurrency market by the firm in Pittsburgh. In the next section we see why this shift in location can be beneficial for the nonbank borrower and lender.

International intermediation The market acts as an intermediary between surplus and deficit countries. Governments or investors in surplus countries find it convenient and profitable to invest short- or medium-term funds in Eurodollars. These deposits are an excellent source of short- and medium-term loans for deficit countries. This last function became particularly important after the first OPEC oil shock. After the increase in oil prices, OPEC countries had about $100 billion to invest, and oil-importing countries were scrambling to find the financing needed to avoid drastic reductions in other imports due to higher expenditures on oil. (We will return to OPEC and petrodollars later.)

EVOLUTION

Now that we know what Eurodollars are and what the Eurodollar market does, let's see how and why the market developed. Although central bank decisions, the Cold War, and OPEC all contributed to the early development of the Eurodollar market, our story starts with the sterling crisis of 1957.

Sterling Restrictions

After World War II, London began to reestablish itself as a major center for international finance, and British banks resumed financing trade between third parties. They might lend sterling to a German importer to finance a shipment of wheat from Argentina to Germany. The sterling crisis of 1957 threatened to eliminate these operations because the authorities tried to defend an inappropriate exchange rate by placing restrictions on sterling loans to nonresidents.

At the same time, European restrictions on dollars were rapidly disappearing, and the financing of third-party trade shifted from sterling to dollars. Since only *sterling* loans to nonresidents were restricted, some British banks tried to recoup their business by lending dollars to finance trade. From there it was only a very short and logical step for these banks to seek dollar deposits actively. The Eurodollar market was born.

U.S. Regulations

Given the switch to dollars, New York should have replaced London as the major center for trade financing. London was able to survive and the Eurodollar market grew there primarily because regulations in the United

States restricted the development of New York as an international financial center. The Interest Equalization Tax (1963) put restrictions on short- and long-term capital outflows. The Voluntary Foreign Credit Restraint Program (1965) and the requirement that American multinationals raise funds outside the United States for foreign direct investments also discouraged international loans by U.S. banks. In addition, as we will see shortly, Regulation Q diverted funds from U.S. banks to Eurodollar banks. Perhaps most important of all, unlike the Bank of England, the Federal Reserve insisted on reserve requirements for deposits in foreign currencies.

Russian Gold Sales

In the early 1960s the Eurodollar market was given a boost by the Soviet Union. The Russians needed wheat, and they sold gold on the London bullion market to finance their imports. These sales were spread over time to avoid pressure on gold prices. As a result, the Soviets wanted a place to invest their funds until they used them to buy wheat.

Neither sterling nor European currencies were very attractive because of possible revaluations and currency restrictions. Since they paid dollars for the wheat, it was the natural currency for their short-term investments. The Cold War, however, was still a threat, and the Soviets apparently were afraid of retaliation in the form of currency restrictions or even confiscation if they held assets in the United States. Their solution was to make dollar deposits in British and French banks. This solved their problem and gave them a nice capitalistic interest rate as a bonus.

Regulation Q

The Federal Reserve provided the next big boost to Eurodollars. In the 1930s Congress gave the Fed authority to set maximum interest rates paid by banks. In the alphabet soup of Federal Reserve regulations, this one is known as Regulation Q. Before the mid-1960s the maximum rates set by Regulation Q for certificates of deposit were above market rates, and the regulation had no effect. But as we approached the 1970s, inflation reared its ugly head. Interest rates began to rise, and Regulation Q became an effective constraint.

Table 14.1 illustrates what happened. The first column shows the maximum yield allowed by Regulation Q for 90- to 179-day deposits of $100,000 and over. That corresponds to the maximum rate on large CDs. The second column shows the market yield on prime commercial paper. Prime commercial paper is a close substitute for large CDs. The third column shows the difference between the limit under Regulation Q and market yields.

In the mid-1960s yields on commercial paper were below the maximum rates banks could pay on large CDs, so Regulation Q was ineffective. Market rates, however, were rising, and in 1966 the yield on commercial paper was

TABLE 14.1   Prime Commercial Paper Rates and Regulation Q Ceiling Rates for 90- to 179-Day Deposits for Amounts of $100,000 or over

	REGULATION Q CEILING	PRIME COMMERCIAL PAPER, 4 TO 6 MONTHS	REGULATION Q MINUS YIELD ON PRIME COMMERCIAL PAPER
1964 Jan.	4.50%	3.97%	0.53
June	4.50	4.00	0.50
1965 Jan.	5.50	4.25	1.25
June	5.50	4.38	1.12
1966 Jan.	5.50	4.82	0.68
June	5.50	5.51	−0.01
1967 Jan.	5.50	5.73	−0.23
June	5.50	4.65	0.85
1968 Jan.	5.50	5.60	−0.10
June	6.00	6.25	−0.25
1969 Jan.	6.00	6.53	−0.53
June	6.00	8.23	−2.23
1970 Jan.	6.75	8.78	−2.03
June	6.75	8.21	−1.46
1971 Jan.	6.75	5.11	1.64
June	6.75	5.45	1.30
1972 Jan.	6.75	4.03	2.72
June	6.75	4.60	2.15
1973 Jan.	6.75	5.78	0.97
June	—	7.99	—

Source: Federal Reserve *Bulletin,* various issues.

above the maximum rate banks could pay on large CDs. The Fed raised the maximum rate in 1968 and again in 1969, but market rates also rose and remained above the maximum rates under Regulation Q. In early 1970 market rates began to decline and fell below the limits imposed by the Fed, but then they started a sharp rise in 1972. In early 1973, as market rates once again rose sharply, the Fed suspended the restriction on yields for large certificates of deposit.

Banks are financial intermediaries. They are in business to borrow and relend. The rise in market rates relative to what U.S. banks could pay severely restricted the ability of U.S. commercial banks to function as intermediaries because they could not borrow at competitive interest rates. One result was that large lenders withdrew their funds from U.S. banks and opened deposits in Eurodollar banks. Some large banks in the United States encouraged this movement of funds into the Eurodollar market.

These banks had subsidiaries or branches in Europe or Britain, and they used these facilities to avoid Regulation Q. Suppose we hold a $1 million CD with Last City National Bank. It is maturing, and we want to roll it over for two more weeks. If Last City can roughly match yields on prime commercial paper, we are more than willing to roll it over with them. Regulation Q, however, prevents Last City National from giving us a competitive yield. We start to think about commercial paper or T-bills. Then our phone rings. A vice-president at Last City has a suggestion. The bank, he explains, has a branch in London. If we would be willing to make a two-week deposit there, we would get a return slightly above market rates in New York. Of course Last City would take care of all the details; just don't withdraw the money. If we go along, the bank is back in business. As soon as our million is transferred to its branch in London, the home office borrows the funds from the London branch and lends them to a customer in Camden.

Last City actually comes out ahead! If we hold a CD, the bank must hold reserves against it. That means it cannot lend out the full amount. There are no reserve requirements in the Eurodollar market, and up to 1969 there were no reserve requirements when a bank borrowed funds from a foreign branch or subsidiary. As a result, Last City can lend out the full amount of the deposit. It didn't take other banks long to realize the advantages of this game, and a number of U.S. banks quickly made arrangements that allowed them to use the Eurodollar market to avoid Regulation Q.

The Fed eventually realized what was happening and reacted. In October 1969, the Fed established Regulation M, which imposed a 10 percent reserve requirement on liabilities to foreign branches in excess of the amount outstanding as of May 1969. The reserve-free base was gradually eliminated, and the required reserve ratio was raised to 20 percent between January 1971 and June 1973. After that, the reserve requirement was gradually reduced until it was eliminated in 1978.

OPEC

The next major contribution to the Eurodollar market came from the Saudis and other OPEC countries. By 1975, OPEC countries had acquired about $100 billion that they wanted to invest. These countries, particularly Saudi Arabia, wanted liquidity while they decided on more long-term investments. A large amount of these petrodollars found their way to the Eurodollar market. From 1973 to 1976, OPEC countries' deposits in the Eurocurrency market rose from $10.0 to 45.2 billion (see Table 14.7).

Deposit Growth and Composition

The result of all these and other factors is illustrated in Table 14.2, which shows the growth of Eurodollars and other Eurocurrencies. The figures are for Britain and Europe. Like all data on Eurocurrencies, these should be regarded as approximate. The high level of interbank relending and absence of strict reporting associated with very little regulation makes accurate data collection almost impossible.

TABLE 14.2 Foreign Currency Liabilities of Banks in Reporting European Counties (In billions of U.S. dollars)

YEAR	DOLLARS			OTHER FOREIGN CURRENCIES						
	TOTAL	NONBANKS	OFFICIAL MONETARY AUTHORITIES	TOTAL	NONBANKS	OFFICIAL MONETARY AUTHORITIES	DEUTSCHE MARK	SWISS FRANC	STERLING	YEN
1966	14.77	4.13	N.A.*	3.57	0.51	N.A.	0.97	1.22	0.71	N.A.
1967	18.12	4.68	N.A.	4.15	0.47	N.A.	1.67	1.40	0.80	N.A.
1968	26.87	6.24	N.A.	6.60	1.04	N.A.	3.01	2.29	0.80	N.A.
1969	46.20	10.46	N.A.	10.17	1.32	N.A.	4.64	4.03	0.81	N.A.
1970	58.70	11.24	N.A.	15.87	2.32	N.A.	8.08	5.72	0.94	N.A.
1971	70.75	9.98	N.A.	26.98	2.75	N.A.	14.63	7.76	2.11	N.A.
1972	96.73	11.81	N.A.	35.20	3.62	N.A.	19.54	8.81	2.21	N.A.
1973	131.38	17.47	N.A.	69.96	5.63	N.A.	32.02	17.16	4.56	N.A.
1974	155.69	23.11	N.A.	64.34	8.08	N.A.	34.22	18.25	3.56	N.A.
1975	189.47	24.28	N.A.	69.20	6.69	N.A.	39.94	15.29	3.14	N.A.
1976	230.04	29.55	N.A.	80.61	8.97	N.A.	47.23	15.88	3.98	N.A.
1977	278.84	34.33	49.25	117.36	12.23	17.97	68.68	22.72	6.87	2.67
1978	348.59	44.34	48.90	162.22	16.57	27.02	93.08	27.89	10.32	6.19
1979	436.63	64.19	66.74	229.20	22.48	41.62	127.94	40.71	15.18	10.33
1980	548.36	83.90	69.65	252.14	27.48	41.49	125.26	51.62	23.82	11.24
1981	631.52	116.11	61.92	259.97	29.74	31.24	117.13	68.11	18.33	16.18

* N.A. Not Available.

Source: Bank for International Settlements, Annual Report for 1981–82.

In spite of these limitations, Table 14.2 tells an interesting tale. The most impressive is the growth in Eurocurrency operations. Measured in U.S. dollars, total Eurocurrency deposits rise from about $18 billion in 1966 to almost $900 billion by 1981. Over the same period, nonbank deposits grew proportionately. The data also illustrate the importance of the interbank market. For both Eurodollars and other currencies, total deposits are four to six times larger than nonbank deposits. Each nonbank deposit appears to be relent four to six times to other banks before it is loaned out to a final user. Even though data for official monetary authorities does not start until 1977, it suggests that for Eurodollars this source is becoming progressively less important.

Table 14.2 clearly demonstrates the dominance of U.S. dollars. In 1981, nonbank dollar deposits are almost four times as large as nonbank deposits of all other currencies combined. Total deposits in marks and Swiss francs, the two next most important currencies, are less than one-fifth as large as total deposits in dollars.

Permanence

Exchange control, the Cold War, OPEC, and Regulation Q may have been the midwives for the Eurocurrency market, but now it can stand on its own because it is efficient. Two major factors make the market efficient. First, it is a wholesale market that specializes in large transactions between highly reputable firms. This specialization keeps the cost of transactions to a minimum, which promotes relatively narrow spreads between borrowing and lending rates. The other factor is the absence of reserve requirements. These requirements impose a cost on domestic banks that widens the spread between borrowing and lending rates.

For simplicity, let's consider a one-year deposit for $1 million. Suppose there are no reserve requirements, and the market rate is about 10 percent. If the bank pays the depositor 9.9 percent and lends the funds out at 10.1 percent, it makes about 0.2 percent on the transaction, which comes to $2,000. Given a competitive market, the imposition of reserve requirements should not materially affect this profit. If so, then what would the bank have to pay and charge on this transaction if the reserve requirement were, say, 5 percent? With a 5 percent reserve requirement, it must hold $50,000 of the $1 million as a nonearning asset such as cash or a deposit at the central bank. That leaves $950,000 to lend out. With only $950,000 to lend, the bank needs a spread of about 0.7 percent in order to earn $2,000 on the transaction. For example, if it lowers the yield for the depositor to 0.97 percent, it pays $97,000 in interest. In that case, it must raise the interest rate to the borrower to slightly over 10.42 percent in order to receive $99,000 and earn a profit of $2,000. Without the reserve requirement, the spread is 0.2 percent. With a 5 percent reserve requirement, the spread rises to over 0.7 percent. Under these conditions, for a $1 million loan, the lender and borrower combined would save $7,000 by using the Eurodollar market rather than a local bank.

OPERATION

In this section we look at the operation of the market for Eurocurrencies. First we consider our options as a depositor, and then we look at the factors determining the interest rate if we are a borrower. We next examine the operation of the interbank market, and then see how Eurodollars are created and analyze the issue of a Eurodollar multiplier.

Deposits

Suppose we have $1 million we want to invest in Eurodollars. We have essentially two options. We can deposit the money in a Eurobank for a fixed period of time, from one day to several years. The alternative is to invest in a negotiable certificate of deposit, or NCD. The main advantage of an NCD is that there is a well-organized secondary market where we could sell the instrument if we wanted our money before maturity. The same options apply to other currencies, except that there is no active secondary market for NCDs in other currencies. The yield on our deposit is determined primarily by the London interbank bid rate, LIBBR and the maturity of the deposit. Eurobanks accept deposits well below $1 million, but smaller amounts, say $100,000, have lower yields.

Loans

What if we want to borrow a million dollars for one year? The cost of the loan depends on four factors. One is the commitment fee. This is a per annum fee or interest rate we must pay on any of the loan commitment we do not use. For example, we might use $750,000 immediately to finance some imports, but not require the rest for a month or so. We still pay the bank a fee or interest rate on the unused $250,000 because this commitment reduces the liquidity of the bank. Obviously this fee cannot substantially exceed the spread between our borrowing rate and what we could get by lending these funds short term. If it did, we would take the rest of the loan and reinvest it elsewhere until we needed it. There also is some up-front money. This fee is expressed as a percentage of the loan and is usually paid shortly after signing for the loan. It helps cover the bank's transactions costs. The third element is the London interbank offer rate (LIBOR). This is the rate at which name banks and a very few highly reputable firms lend funds in the interbank market. It determines the marginal cost of funds to a Eurobank.

The final factor is the spread. The interest rate we pay on the part of the loan we use depends on LIBOR and our credit rating. If our name is first rate and we have an excellent credit rating, we might pay only one-half percent over LIBOR. If there is the least shadow of doubt about us, the spread might rise to 2 or even 3 percent. The total cost of the loan therefore depends on the commitment fee, how fully we utilize the commitment, the up-front money, LIBOR, and the spread.

One factor we did not consider is the maturity of the loan. We might pay a smaller spread for a six-week than a six-month loan, but the spread probably is not significantly influenced by a longer loan. The reason is that loans for over six months usually have a floating rate. In our case, that means we pay the current LIBOR plus the agreed spread for the first six months and then pay the LIBOR (plus the original spread) that holds when the loan is rolled over for another six months. In other words, our loan has a variable rate that is adjusted every six months according to the change in the London interbank offer rate. Most Eurocurrency loans have a floating rate, and three, six, or nine months are the most common intervals for re-adjustment.

Interbank

Interbank operations integrate the different Eurobanks into a single market. The interbank market also provides for a form of covered interest rate arbitrage.

Arbitrage   Suppose a Eurobank enters into a forward contract to sell French francs for dollars in 90 days. The most direct way to cover this obligation is to buy 90-day French francs in the foreign exchange market, but that may not be the most profitable option. The bank also can borrow dollars for 90 days in the Eurodollar market, convert them to francs in the spot market for foreign exchange, and lend the francs to another Eurobank for 90 days. At the end of the 90 days, the first bank uses the proceeds from the franc loan to supply francs to its client and it uses the dollars it receives from the client to pay off the Eurodollar obligation.

Each dollar the bank borrows in the Eurodollar market costs the bank $(1 + i_{US})$ dollars in 90 days, where i_{US} is the 90-day borrowing rate (not annualized) for dollars in the interbank Eurodollar market. Each current dollar buys $1/S$ in spot francs, where S is the spot dollar price of the franc. At the end of 90 days, these francs grow to $(1/S)(1 + i_F)$ francs, where i_F is the 90-day lending rate (not annualized) in the interbank market for Eurofrancs. The cost in terms of dollars due in 90 days of obtaining future francs in this way is $(1 + i_{US})/[(1/S)(1 + i_F)]$, which we can write more simply as follows:

$$\frac{S(1 + i_{US})}{(1 + i_F)}$$

If this cost is higher than the forward price of the franc, this bank and other banks buy forward francs directly and pay the forward rate, F. If it is cheaper to borrow dollars and lend francs, our bank and other banks do that instead. That decision reduces the demand for forward francs, increases the demand for spot francs, raises Eurodollar interest rates, and lowers Euro-franc interest rates. This pressure continues until F and $S(1 + i_{US})/(1 + i_F)$ are approximately equal.

In case you haven't seen it, F equals $S(1 + i_{US})/(1 + i_F)$ is simply another way of writing the equilibrium condition for covered arbitrage we developed in Chapter 5. If

$$F = \frac{S(1 + i_{US})}{(1 + i_F)}$$

then

$$\frac{F}{S} = \frac{1 + i_{US}}{1 + i_F}$$

When banks look for the cheapest way to cover their forward commitments, they engage in a form of covered interest rate arbitrage, or perhaps a better description would be covered exchange rate arbitrage. Whatever we call it, their profit motive works toward equating forward premiums and interest rate differentials.

Table 5.3 in Chapter 5 shows evidence of large and persistent net covered yields for Treasury bills between the United States and Canada and the United Kingdom. Covered arbitrage between Eurocurrency deposits, however, is much more effective. Table 14.3 shows estimates for net covered yields between the United States and United Kingdom using both Treasury bill rates and Eurocurrency deposit rates. For the three months from May 1982 to July 1982, the net covered yield for T-bills is as high as 2.68 percent per annum and never falls below 1.46 percent. During the same period, the net covered yield for Eurodeposit rates never is larger than 0.72 percent. Given unavoidable measurement problems and transaction costs, net covered yields in the Eurocurrency markets appear to be effectively zero. Indeed, covered arbitrage is so effective that Eurobanks often use the spot rate and interest rate differential as the basis for quoting forward rates.

Interbank operations also integrate the various Eurobanks into a single market. In order to see how, let's take a simple example. Two firms want to borrow $1 million. One wants a six-week loan and the other a one-year loan. Both are prime names. Two other companies want to invest $1 million each in Eurodollars, one for six weeks and the other for a year.

TABLE 14.3   Weekly Net Covered Yields between the U.S. Dollar and Pound Sterling, 1982

DAY	3-MONTH FORWARD PREMIUM	3-MONTH T-BILLS U.K.	3-MONTH T-BILLS U.S.	3-MONTH EUROCURRENCY DEPOSITS STERLING	3-MONTH EUROCURRENCY DEPOSITS DOLLARS	NET COVERED YIELDS IN FAVOR OF U.K. T-BILLS	NET COVERED YIELDS IN FAVOR OF U.K. EURO-DEPOSITS
May 7	1.55	13.62	13.51	13.16	14.44	1.66	0.27
May 14	1.68	13.54	13.66	13.19	14.66	1.56	0.21
May 21	0.98	13.62	12.52	13.53	14.37	2.08	0.14
May 28	1.34	13.62	12.64	13.50	14.44	2.32	0.40
June 4	1.94	13.48	13.21	13.44	14.66	2.21	0.72
June 11	1.92	13.11	13.14	12.90	14.87	1.89	−0.05
June 18	3.23	12.98	13.91	13.03	15.94	2.30	0.32
June 25	3.64	13.05	15.23	13.06	16.56	1.46	0.14
July 2	3.14	13.11	13.68	13.06	16.00	2.57	0.20
July 7	3.60	12.90	13.82	12.66	15.94	2.68	0.30
July 16	2.23	12.48	12.61	12.50	14.56	2.10	0.17
July 23	1.11	12.05	11.29	12.06	12.75	1.87	0.42
July 30	1.45	11.85	11.32	11.87	13.00	1.98	0.32

Source: Bank of England *Quarterly Bulletin* (September 1982).

Search   The interbank market reduces search costs. Suppose the six-week lender opens a Eurodollar deposit with First International Bank, but the six-week borrower goes to Fourth International Bank for a loan. With an interbank market, Fourth International can make the loan because it can borrow the funds from First International. Without the interbank market, our six-week borrower would have to search for the bank that had six-week funds to lend. The interbank market reduces search costs and, from the perspective of the nonbank public, effectively consolidates the Eurobanks into a single market.

Portfolio balance   The interbank market also contributes to portfolio management by the banks. Consider the following example. The six-week lender makes a deposit at First International bank, and the one-year borrower goes to that bank for a loan. At the same time, the one-year lender makes a deposit at Fourth International and the six-week borrower applies for a loan there. In this case, both banks have money to lend and a potential borrower. The problem is that the maturities do not match.

With a one-year deposit, Fourth International can always relend the funds after the initial six-week loan matures, but it would take a loss if interest rates fall. The bank, for example, might earn only 8 percent on subsequent loans while paying 10 percent on the one-year deposit. First International faces the opposite problem. The yield on its loan is fixed for six months before it is adjusted. If interest rates rise after six weeks, it might have to pay 12 percent to get the funds needed to support a one-year loan that yields only 10 percent for the first six months.

Without an interbank market, both banks would be faced with risk because the maturities of their assets and liabilities are not matched. They would charge for this risk in the form of a spread between borrowing and lending rates. The interbank market, however, allows both banks to balance the maturities of assets and liabilities more closely than they could in isolation. In this example, Fourth International makes a one-year loan to First International and at the same time borrows funds for six weeks from that bank. The maturities of assets and liabilities at both banks match exactly. Neither bank requires a risk premium, and the spread between borrowing and lending rates is narrower than it would be without an interbank market. Banks avoid risk, but the major beneficiary is the nonbank public. It gets higher yields and pays lower interest rates with an interbank market.

Maturity Distribution

The real world is not as simple as our last example. Lenders typically want liquidity, while borrowers want to be certain they will have credit when they need it. As a result, in the absence of inflation, interest rates usually rise as term to maturity increases. Banks take advantage of this difference in interest rates by lending for longer maturities than those at which they borrow. For the system as a whole, there is relatively little risk because the vast majority of short-term deposits are rolled over as they mature. If, on the average, a one-month deposit is rolled over six times before it is withdrawn from the system, then one-month deposits normally can finance six-month loans with little risk.

The threat to the system as a whole is that depositors might switch out of Eurodollars into commercial paper or Treasury bills. The floating rate on loans provides substantial protection to the Eurobanks, but if such a movement ever started, it could cause some banks to fail. That would encourage a flight out of Eurodollars and, in the absence of a lender of last resort, could cause the system to collapse.

The maturity transformation in Eurocurrency markets is illustrated in Table 14.4, which shows the maturity distribution of nonsterling assets (loans) and liabilities (deposits) of all Eurobanks based in the United Kingdom. The table is divided into two parts. The left-hand side shows claims on and liabilities to other banks, including non-Eurobanks. The right-hand side shows Eurobank loans to and borrowings from the nonbank public. For maturities of less than one year, claims on and liabilities to other banks are fairly closely matched. As a whole, assets exceed liabilities by less than 1 percent. For one year and longer, however, loans are almost three times larger than deposits. Between banks and nonbanks, the pattern is even

TABLE 14.4   Maturity Structure of Nonsterling Loans and Deposits of U.K.-Based Euro-banks (In millions of U.S. dollars, May 19, 1982)

	BETWEEN BANKS			WITH NONBANK PUBLIC		
	ASSETS	LIABILITIES	NET	ASSETS	LIABILITIES	NET
Less than 8 days	76,740	83,909	−7,169	13,179	28,768	−15,589
8 days to less than 1 month	82,511	77,243	5,268	13,702	19,641	−5,939
1 month to less than 3 months	117,727	112,176	5,551	17,218	23,382	−6,164
3 months to less than 6 months	79,427	73,324	6,103	11,147	13,456	−2,309
6 months to less than 1 year	24,900	24,098	802	9,196	4,607	4,589
1 year to less than 3 years	16,188	8,751	7,437	17,011	1,703	15,308
3 years and over	20,658	4,738	15,920	51,939	2,621	49,318

Source: Bank of England *Quarterly Bulletin* (September 1982).

stronger. The public is lending short and borrowing long. At the very short end, Eurobank deposits exceed loans by over 2 to 1. For the longest maturities, loans exceed deposits by almost 20 to 1.

These figures tend to exaggerate liquidity creation for at least two reasons. First, almost all loans for more than one year have variable rates. A two-year loan is actually a short-term loan that the bank guarantees to roll over every three, six, or nine months for two years. Second, most Eurocurrency intermediation replaces similar activity in domestic markets. The net liquidity creation by Eurobanks therefore depends on the maturity transformation in the markets they displace. Suppose a domestic bank borrows for 90 days and lends the funds for one year. The depositor then shifts the 90-day deposit to a Eurobank that also lends the funds for one year, but with a rollover at the end of six months. In that case, Eurobanks are lending long and borrowing short, but their net contribution is to slightly reduce liquidity because the one-year loan is now a six-month loan that is rolled over.

Credit Creation

Similarities between Eurocurrency and domestic commercial banks led many early observers to apply a money multiplier analysis to Eurodollars. Because Eurodollar banks hold almost no liquid reserves, this approach suggests that an initial deposit in a Eurobank creates several dollars in bank loans and deposits just as an additional dollar of high-powered money generates 2 to 3 dollars in loans or investments by domestic banks.

That view, however, has been rejected. Shifts in deposits from domestic to Eurobanks tend to have multiple effects, but the multiplier is small and Eurocurrency markets in this regard are no different from, say, the commercial paper market. The source of the multiple effect is not the Eurocurrency market itself, but rather the difference in reserve requirements between domestic and Eurocurrency banks.

Domestic bank   In order to see the effects of differential reserve requirements, we start with a shift from demand to time deposits within the domestic banking system. For simplicity, we ignore differences in reserve requirements between banks and combine all domestic banks into a single bank called Consolidated National Bank, or CNB. We also assume there are no competing credit markets. The only three financial assets are currency, demand deposits, and time deposits.

Table 14.5 shows a simplified T account for the bank. In the initial equilibrium, the bank has $10 million in demand deposits or checking accounts. These are labeled DD. An equal amount is deposited in time accounts and labeled TD. For our simple example, we assume that desired and required reserve ratios are the same. The required reserve ratio is 20 percent for demand deposits and 5 percent for time deposits. That is, for each $100 of demand (time) deposits, the bank must hold $20 (5) dollars in legal reserves. Legal reserves are deposits at the central bank and currency on the premises.

Under these conditions, the bank is in portfolio equilibrium in step 1 of Table 14.5. It holds $2 million as reserves for $10 million in demand deposits, and $500,000 in reserves against $10 million in time deposits. The remainder of the bank's liabilities, $17.5 million, are invested. Given the preferences of the nonbank public and economic factors such as the level of interest rates, the deposits held by the bank also reflect portfolio equilibrium for the nonbank public.

Now we conduct an experiment. Preferences of the nonbank public change, and they shift $1 million from demand to time deposits. This shift is shown in step 2 of Table 14.5. At this point, the public is in portfolio equilibrium, but not the banking system. The $1 million increase in time deposits raises required reserves by $50,000, but the same reduction in demand deposits reduces required reserves by $200,000. As a result, the bank has $150,000 in surplus reserves, and its portfolio is in disequilibrium. Profit is the objective, and it attempts to restore equilibrium by investing immediately. As the bank buys bonds and makes additional loans, bank assets and demand deposits expand.

If the nonbank public refused to increase its demand deposits and converted any additional deposits into time deposits, earning assets and total

TABLE 14.5   Effect on Domestic Banking System of a Switch from Demand to Time
Deposits

	STEP 1		
	A	L	
(Reserves)	2,500,000	10,000,000	(DD)
(Loans)	17,500,000	10,000,000	(TD)
(Total)	20,000,000	20,000,000	
	Actual reserves	2,500,000	
	Required reserves	2,500,000	
	Surplus reserves	0,000,000	

	STEP 2		
	A	L	
(Reserves)	2,500,000	9,000,000	(DD)
(Loans)	17,500,000	11,000,000	(TD)
(Total)	20,000,000	20,000,000	
	Actual reserves	2,500,000	
	Required reserves	2,350,000	
	Surplus reserves	150,000	

	STEP 3		
	A	L	
(Reserves)	2,465,000	9,200,000	(DD)
(Loans)	19,235,000	12,500,000	(TD)
(Total)	21,700,000	21,700,000	
	Actual reserves	2,465,000	
	Required reserves	2,465,000	
	Surplus reserves	0,000,000	

deposits would have to rise by $3 million in order to restore portfolio equilibrium at CNB. With a 5 percent required reserve ratio and $150,000 in surplus reserves, earning assets and time deposits would have to rise by $3 million in order to increase required reserves by $150,000.

Three million is an upper bound. Deposits and earning assets expand by less because demand deposits rise and there is some loss of reserves as deposits are converted into cash. Demand deposits rise and bank reserves fall for two reasons. First, when the public switches $1 million from demand to time deposits, it represents a new desired composition for the assets in its financial portfolio: a higher proportion of financial assets in time deposits, a lower proportion of demand deposits, and the same proportion in currency. As the bank increases earning assets and the financial assets of the public increase, portfolio balance requires an increase in all three types of assets—demand deposits, time deposits, and currency.

In addition, as the bank buys bonds and makes new loans, it tends to reduce interest rates. When yields on earning assets fall, the bank lowers yields on time deposits. Lower yields on time deposits alter the desired composition of the public's portfolio. Time deposits become relatively less attractive, while demand deposits and currency become more attractive. The public reduces the proportion of time deposits and increases the proportion of demand deposit and currency in its portfolio.

Step 3 in Table 14.5 illustrates one possible effect of the shift in $1 million from demand to time deposits. The public withdraws $35,000 in currency, and bank reserves fall to $2,465,000. The rise in the public's portfolio and the fall in interest rates cause demand deposits to rise from $9 million to $9.2 million. Time deposits rise from $11 million to $12.5 million. The net result of the shift in $1 million from demand to time deposits therefore is as follows: (1) Bank reserves fall and currency in the hands of the public rises. (2) Demand deposits fall, but not by the full $1 million. (3) Time deposits rise by more than $1 million. (4) Interest rates decline. (5) Bank loans or other earning assets expand.

The reason the shift raises total deposits, reduces interest rates, and expands bank loans and other earning assets is that demand and time deposits have different reserve requirements. If banks' required reserves per dollar deposited were the same for demand and time liabilities, a shift from one type of deposit to another would not drive a wedge between required and actual bank reserves that can be resolved only by a change in interest rates and the level of earning assets and deposits. Exactly the same reasoning applies to shifts from domestic banks to Eurobanks.

Eurodollar multiplier   In the last section we considered the effects of a switch from demand to time deposits within the domestic banking system. Here the experiment is that the nonbank public has a change in preferences, and it switches $1 million from a domestic time deposit to a Eurodollar deposit of the same maturity. As in the last example, the domestic banking system is represented by a single bank, Consolidated National Bank. The Eurodollar system is also combined into a single bank, Consolidated Euro Bank or CEB. Once again there are three financial assets: currency, time deposits, and demand deposits.

Step 1 in Table 14.6 shows the initial situation. In order to keep the balance sheets simple, the entries are restricted to the $1 million TD held by an American corporation that shifts to a Eurodollar deposit and the offsetting items. For the domestic banking system, the corresponding items are

TABLE 14.6 Effect of a Shift in Time Deposits from a Commercial to a Eurodollar Bank

STEP 1

CNB

A		L	
(Reserves)	50,000	1,000,000	(TD)
(Loans)	950,000		

CEB

A		L	

PUBLIC

A		L	
1,000,000	(TD)	950,000	(Loan)
		50,000	(Net worth)

STEP 2

CNB

A		L	
(Reserve)	50,000	50,000	(DD)

CEB

A		L	
50,000	(DD)	1,000,000	(TD)
950,000	(Loan)		

PUBLIC

A		L	
1,000,000	(TD)	950,000	(Loan)
		50,000	(Net worth)

STEP 3

CNB

A		L	
(Reserve)	50,000	50,000	(DD)

CEB

A		L	
50,000	(Reserves)	1,000,000	(TD)
950,000	(Loan)		

PUBLIC

A		L	
1,000,000	(TD)	950,000	(Loan)
		50,000	(Net worth)

STEP 4

CNB

A		L	
(Reserves)	49,000	95,000	(DD)
(Loans)	646,000	600,000	(TD)

CEB

A		L	
1,000,000	(Loan)	1,000,000	(TD)

PUBLIC

A		L	
1,000,000	(TD)	1,000,000	(Loan)
95,000	(DD)	646,000	(Loan)
600,000	(TD)	50,000	(Net worth)
1,000	(Currency)		

$50,000 or 5 percent in legal reserves and a $950,000 loan to a German firm that is importing wheat from Nebraska. The T account for the nonbank public shows the time deposit as a $1 million asset. The loan from the bank is a liability, and there is a net worth item of $50,000.

Now the American Corporation shifts the $1 million deposit to a Eurodollar bank. CEB now has a $1 million claim on CNB which it converts into a demand deposit in order to make a loan. The shift from a time to demand deposit makes surplus reserves negative, and CNB contracts earning assets. For purposes of exposition, we assume that it does not renew the $950,000 loan to the German importer. CEB, however, is looking for business, and it takes up the German loan. Step 2 in Table 14.5 shows the situation after the German importer uses the $950,000 loan from CEB to pay off the loan to the American commercial bank. At that point, CNB has $50,000 in reserves and a $50,000 demand liability to a Eurodollar bank. Eurodollar banks have a $1 million fixed-maturity liability to an American corporation, which is balanced by a $50,000 demand deposit at CNB and a $950,000 loan to a German importer. As for the nonbank public, it now has a claim on and liability to a Eurodollar bank rather than an American commercial bank.

Step 3 illustrates what would happen if Eurodollar banks had to maintain the same reserve requirements as U.S. commercial banks. In that case, CEB would, in effect, write a check on its deposit at CNB and deposit the check in its account at the Federal Reserve Bank in New York. The Fed would collect the check by transferring $50,000 from CNB's account at the Fed to CEB's account there. At that point, all portfolios are back in equilibrium. CNB has $1 million less in time deposits and $50,000 less in legal reserves; so actual and required reserves are equal. CEB has $1 million more in time deposits, but it is fully loaned up and holds exactly the $50,000 in additional legal reserves it needs to back up that deposit. The nonbank public now has claims on and liabilities to a Eurodollar bank rather than a domestic commercial bank.

However, since there are no reserve requirements for Eurodollar deposits, we have to go back to step 2 to see what actually happens. In that step, the public is in portfolio equilibrium, but both groups of banks want to expand earning assets. With a $50,000 demand deposit and $50,000 in reserves, CNB has $40,000 in surplus reserves. CEB has a demand deposit that is not earning any interest, which it wants to loan out. As the banks expand their loans and other earning assets, they tend to drive down interest rates, which alters the portfolio composition desired by the public. Without detailed information about portfolio preferences of both the banks and the public, we cannot know exactly what the new equilibrium looks like.

Step 4 in Table 14.6, however, illustrates the general nature of the final equilibrium. The fall in interest rates and increase in financial assets held by the public increase its desired holdings of currency and demand deposits.

Step 4 shows a $1,000 currency drain from commercial banks to the public, and the public also converts $95,000 of time deposits into demand deposits. Both responses reduce the expansion of U.S. commercial banks' earning assets. Compared to step 1, earning assets fall by $304,000 and total deposits fall by $305,000. In addition, there is likely to be some reduction of deposits in Eurobanks because the expansion of Eurobank loans and contraction of loans by U.S. commercial banks as compared to step 1 tend to reduce Eurodollar deposit rates relative to yields on time deposits at U.S. commercial banks. Depositors respond to relatively lower yields by switching some of their deposits back to the United States. This effect, however, is balanced by a desire to expand Eurodollar deposits as the financial portfolio expands. In Table 14.6, Eurodollar deposits remain at $1 million, reflecting the assumption that these two influences just offset each other. The balance sheet of the nonbank public shows the biggest change. On the asset side, time deposits at Eurodollar banks rise to $1 million and at U.S. commercial banks they fall to $600,000. Demand deposits, however, rise to $95,000, and currency holdings increase by $1,000. On the liability side, the public owes Eurodollar and commercial banks $1,000,000 and $646,000, respectively.

Table 14.6 may not be easy to follow, but it is worth spending some time on because it illustrates almost all the important issues concerning the creation of Eurodollars. First, a shift in deposits from U.S. commercial banks to Eurodollar banks does tend to expand total deposits at and earning assets of the entire banking system. Eurodollar loans and deposits rise, but this rise is partially offset by a fall in loans and deposits at U.S. commercial banks. Second, if there is a Eurodollar multiplier, it is small. The expansion of the public's portfolio works toward increasing Eurodollar deposits beyond the initial level, but the likely fall in relative yields works in the opposite direction. Third, and most important of all, there is nothing special about the way the Eurodollar market works. It is like any credit market where there are no reserve requirements. If our American corporation withdrew $1 million from a commercial bank and invested it in the commerical paper market where there are no reserve requirements, exactly the same kind of expansion would take place. But no one refers to or is concerned about a commercial paper multiplier.

International Intermediation

In our last example, Eurodollar banks borrow funds from an American corporation and relend them to a German firm. The market serves as an important mechanism through which governments, firms, or even individuals in one foreign country lend to individuals, governments, or firms in another foreign country.

So called petrodollars are an excellent example. After the rapid rise in oil prices from 1973 to 1975, OPEC countries had about $100 billion to invest, and many firms and governments wanted to borrow dollars in order to cover deficits caused by higher oil prices. OPEC countries, particularly Saudi Arabia, could have lent funds directly to these countries, and to some extent they did, but they also made large Eurodollar deposits. These deposits were then relent to a variety of foreign governments and firms.

Table 14.7 illustrates the role of the Eurodollar market as a financial intermediary for loans between foreign countries. In 1973 OPEC was only a small net lender, less than $7 billion. By 1977, OPEC and related oil-exporting countries were lending over $38 billion net. Indeed, the United States and OPEC are the only two major net lenders to the market. Europe and Offshore Banking just about break even, and the unallocated areas are small lenders. All other areas are net borrowers from the Eurocurrency markets.

Eurobonds

Eurobanks make intermediate and even some longer-term loans, but these normally have interest rates that are adjusted every three, six, or nine months. In recent years, however, intermediate and long-term Eurobonds have appeared. These bonds are issued primarily by American corporations and sold through banks in Europe and the United Kingdom. Most are denominated in dollars, but some other currencies also are important. As with Eurodollar deposits, the attempt to avoid domestic restrictions is a major incentive.

The Securities and Exchange Commission, for example, has regulations covering the issuance of bonds by large corporations. If a corporation wants to float an issue quickly, these regulations can slow it down. The Eurobond market is not regulated, so a corporation is not faced with what it views as unnecessary red tape.

From the point of view of the investor, Eurobonds have several interesting features. For example, they are likely to have a slightly higher yield than comparable bonds issued domestically. In addition, Eurobonds often are bearer bonds. That means no records are kept of the owners or interest payments, which makes them ideal for tax evasion.

The Eurobond market is still very small. Probably not much over $15 billion worth of new issues are floated per year. The gradual elimination of bearer bonds issued in the United States, however, is likely to create renewed interest in Eurobonds. Indeed, this feature may eventually allow large corporations to pay a lower interest on these bonds than comparable registered bonds sold in the United States.

REGULATION

The existence of essentially unregulated Eurocurrency markets raises an important policy issue. Should these markets be regulated? That debate seems to revolve around two main issues: safety, and the role of Eurocurrency markets in domestic monetary policy. Let's consider safety first.

TABLE 14.7 Estimates of the Sources and Uses of Funds by Region in the Eurocurrency Markets (In billions of U.S. dollars)

END OF DECEMBER	REPORTING EUROPEAN AREA	UNITED STATES	CANADA AND JAPAN	OTHER DEVELOPED COUNTRIES	EASTERN EUROPE	OFFSHORE BANKING CENTERS*	OPEC COUNTRIES†	DEVELOPING COUNTRIES	UNALLOCATED	TOTAL
Uses										
1973	49.0	13.5	12.7	14.7	-7.4	18.7	3.3	11.0	1.7	132.0
1974	61.5	18.3	18.2	20.4	10.1	26.7	3.5	15.7	2.7	177.0
1975	63.0	16.6	20.2	25.8	15.9	35.5	5.3	19.5	3.2	205.0
1976	75.1	18.3	21.6	33.0	20.8	40.7	9.6	24.7	3.2	247.0
1977	110.4	21.3	18.7	30.8	25.7	43.9	15.7	30.3	3.2	300.0
1978	136.0	24.6	24.6	34.7	31.4	55.0	24.3	40.1	4.3	375.0
1979	171.3	36.7	33.0	40.5	36.0	67.5	30.4	55.1	4.5	475.0
1980	216.4	39.7	45.1	52.1	38.9	73.0	33.8	71.0	5.0	575.0
Sources										
1973	50.8	9.5	9.8	17.7	3.7	12.5	10.0	14.6	3.4	132.0
1974	67.8	11.9	8.7	18.5	5.1	17.8	29.1	15.5	2.6	177.0
1975	79.5	15.4	8.3	19.9	5.4	21.8	34.6	16.2	3.9	205.0
1976	87.6	18.8	10.5	21.3	6.4	30.1	45.2	21.3	5.8	247.0
1977	117.3	25.4	8.4	18.8	7.0	33.4	54.5	29.6	5.6	300.0
1978	142.5	37.0	13.0	26.2	8.8	45.4	54.7	39.8	7.6	375.0
1979	174.0	50.5	15.2	31.7	13.0	52.8	81.0	47.8	9.0	475.0
1980	211.0	59.7	22.1	33.5	12.8	68.0	109.8	46.6	11.5	575.0

* Bahamas, Barbados, Bermuda, Cayman Islands, Hong Kong, Lebanon, Liberia, Netherlands, Antilles, Panama, Singapore, Vanuaaty and other British West Indies.

† Also includes Bahrain, Brunei, Oman, Trinidad, and Tobago.

Source: *Annual Report*, Bank for International Settlements, various issues.

Safety

From the perspective of safety, the argument for regulation runs something like this. Federal and state agencies regulate domestic commercial banks and savings and loan institutions. This regulation restrains banks from making unwise loans, which reduces failures and promotes confidence. In addition, the government provides insurance to depositors up to $100,000. This insurance protects depositors and reduces the possibility of a run on the banking system and widespread bank failures. Perhaps even more important, as part of its regulatory obligation the Fed accepts its responsibility as the lender of last resort to banks in an emergency. All these factors stand as a bulwark against a financial collapse like the one in the United States during the early 1930s that contributed to the Great Depression.

The argument against regulation is that it is unnecessary, ineffective, and makes the market less efficient. It is unnecessary because, in order to attract sophisticated depositors, Eurobanks must be prudent. Prudence means lending to the best names and avoiding illiquidity by closely matching the maturities of assets and liabilities. As we saw earlier, reserve requirements make the market less efficient by increasing the spread between borrowing and lending rates. Other forms of regulation also increase operating costs and have a similar effect.

The effect of imposing reserve requirements illustrates the ineffectiveness of regulation. Reserve requirements force banks to hold more highly liquid assets than is "optimal." The natural response to this "excess" liquidity is to increase the maturity of loans relative to deposits, the exact opposite of the intention of the regulators.

Policy

For most monetarists, Eurocurrencies are not a serious threat to monetary policy because they interpret monetary policy in terms of the money stock, not interest rates. Eurocurrency deposits are loans, not a means of payment. The Eurodollar market is no more a threat to control of the domestic stock of money than the market for municipal bonds or commercial credit.

There is, of course, always the possibility that Eurodollar deposits might be used as a means of payment. Their acceptance, however, almost certainly would be limited to very large or international transactions. Given the problems associated with cashing an out of town check, it seems unlikely that our local grocery store would accept a check written on a bank in London or Paris.

For Keynesians, Eurocurrency markets are a serious threat to domestic monetary policy. In the Keynesian paradigm, monetary policy affects output and prices primarily through its influence on interest rates. The Eurodollar market affects the Fed's ability to influence domestic interest rates in two ways. First, it tends to integrate domestic credit markets more fully into world capital markets. This integration makes it more difficult for central banks to influence domestic interest rates. It is one thing for the Fed to move the yield on U.S. Treasury bills 50 basis points. It is quite another to also move Canadian, British, French, and German Treasury bills by, say, 20 or 30 basis points.

The existence of a Eurodollar market also limits the Fed's regulatory powers over domestic credit. The application of Regulation Q to large CDs is a case in point. As mentioned earlier, the rise in interest rates above the limits set by Regulation Q was a major cause of the early expansion of the Eurodollar market. It also gave banks with foreign subsidiaries or branches an advantage over purely domestic banks because they could get around Regulation Q by having their customers convert large CDs into deposits at a branch in London or Paris. The Fed was placed in a position where it either had to abolish Regulation Q for large CDs or permit a few large banks to capture almost all the CD market through their Eurodollar branches. As a result, in 1973 the Fed eliminated restrictions on interest payments for large certificates of deposit.

The basic problem of regulation, however, goes beyond Regulation Q. It is very difficult, if not impossible, to regulate any market if there is a parallel market that is unregulated. If restrictions are imposed in one market, they simply drive sophisticated participants into the other market. What makes the Eurodollar market a greater threat than, say, domestic money market funds is that the Fed can ask for and probably receive congressional authority to regulate money market funds, if that appears to be necessary. Congress cannot give the Fed authority over foreign banks located in other countries.

SUMMARY

Eurodollar deposits are dollar loans to banks located outside the jurisdiction of the U.S. government. Eurodollar and Eurocurrency markets in general serve four important functions: They finance trade, serve as an interbank market, replace domestic intermediation, and act as an intermediary between deficit and surplus countries.

The Eurodollar market began with restrictions on sterling in 1957. Russian gold sales, Federal Reserve regulations, and OPEC all contributed to its growth. In the absence of heavy regulation, the efficiency of Eurocurrency markets will ensure their continued existence.

Deposit and loan rates to nonbank customers are determined primarily by the return on and cost of funds in the interbank market. This interbank market is four to six times as large as the market between banks and nonbanks. It helps banks cover their forward exchange commitments, reduces search costs for nonbank customers, and helps banks balance their portfolios. Eurocurrency markets probably do increase liquidity, but it is very difficult to tell by how much. Any Eurocurrency multiplier, however, is almost certainly small—close to unity.

The primary policy question is whether or not the market should remain unregulated. The major arguments for regulation are that it would reduce the likelihood of a financial collapse and, from a Keynesian perspective, improve monetary policy. On the other hand, for a monetarist, Eurocurrencies have little to do with the stock of money, and therefore regulation is not important for monetary policy. With respect to safety, supporters of an unregulated market argue that regulation is not needed and in fact reduces efficiency.

QUESTIONS FOR REVIEW

1. Discuss the functions of Eurocurrency markets.
2. What were the major factors contributing to the establishment of Eurodollars?
3. Is the market for Eurocurrencies likely to survive? If so, why? If not, why not?
4. The interest rate Eurobanks charge for loans depends on LIBOR and three other factors. Discuss these four elements of the lending rate.
5. How do interbank operations benefit the nonbank customers of Eurobanks?
6. Do Eurocurrency markets increase liquidity? If so, how? If not, why not?
7. Do Eurocurrency markets increase the amount of bank credit? That is, is there a Eurocurrency multiplier? If so, why is there a multiplier? If not, then why not?
8. Discuss the arguments for and against regulating Eurocurrency markets.
9. What effect would regulation of Eurocurrency markets, such as the imposition of reserve requirements, have on these markets? Are the effects any different if the regulation is imposed by one country, such as Britain, or all countries?

ADDITIONAL READINGS

BHATTACHARYA, ANINDYA K. *The Asian Dollar Market* (New York: Praeger, 1977).
EINZIG, PAUL. *The Euro-Dollar System,* 5th ed. (New York: St. Martin's Press, 1973).
FRYDL, EDWARD J. "The Debate over Regulating the Eurocurrency Markets." Federal Reserve Bank of New York, *Quarterly Review* (winter 1979–80).

GRABBE, J. ORLIN. "Liquidity Creation and Maturity Transformation in the Eurodollar Market." *Journal of Monetary Economics* (July 1982).

STEM, CARL H., JOHN H. MAKIN, AND DENNIS LOGUE (EDS.). *Eurocurrencies and the International Monetary System* (Washington, D.C.: American Enterprise Institute, 1976).

MCKINNON, RONALD I. *The Eurocurrency Market*. Princeton Essays in International Finance, No. 125 (December 1977).

INDEX

Bank(s):
  commercial, 296
  domestic, 293–95
  world, 141
Bank Charter Act of 1844, 120–21
Banker's acceptance, 60
Bank of England, 120–21
Barter, 20
Basic balance, 46, 48
Belgium, spot exchange rates, 65
"Below the line," 45
Bond(s):
  export of, 43
  import of, 42
  substitutability of, 259
Bookkeeping, double-entry, 36
Branson, William, 253, 262
British Exchange Equalization Account, 165
Buffer stock facility, 154
Burden of adjustment, 146

C

Capital, Fisherian theory of, 13–18
Capital controls, 86–87
Capital flows, 42–43, 75–76
  Bank of England and, 120
  devaluation and, 231
  nominal, 20–21
  offsetting, 119–20
  with political risk, 25–27
  reinforcing, 119
  Tobin-Markowitz model and, 31
Capital outflow, 41
Chile, spot exchange rates, 65
Closed economy, 174–75
Committee of Twenty, 159–60
Commodities, 116–19
Commodity equilibrium, 173
Comparative advantage, 9
Compensatory funding, 154
Covered arbitrage, impediments to, 84–87
Covered interest rate arbitrage, 80–83
Credit instruments, 59–60
Credit market, 198–99
Credits and debits, 36–37
Cross-rate arbitrage, 78–79

D

Debits and credits, 36–37
Demand, excess, 7–9
Demand and supply, 4–6
  exchange rates and, 79–80
Demand schedule for foreign exchange, 68–69
Depreciation:
  of gold standard, 130
  OPEC and, 245–46
Devaluation:
  flexible rates and, 239
  gold standard and, 130
  international adjustment and, 229–33
Dirty float, 113–14
"Disequilibria," 271
Diversification, incentives for, 32

Dollars:
  excess of, 133–34
  shortage of, 146
Domestic assets, 255–57
Domestic bonds, 255
  exogenous increase in, 258
Dornbusch, Rudiger, 171, 263
Draft, 59

E

Economy, closed, 174
Efficient market, 91
Employment, 178–79
  and international adjustment, 194–210
Equilibrium:
  balance of payments and, 173
  commodity, 173
  credit market, 187
  of exchange rate, 81–82
  initial, 179–80
    portfolio, 256
  interpretation of, 24
  steady state, 261–63
Eurobanks:
  arbitrage, 288–89
  liquidity of, 292
  safety of, 301
Eurobonds, 299
Eurocurrencies, 280
  composition of, 284–86
  deposit growth of, 284–86
  function of, 280
  maturity transformation of, 291
  policy, 301–2
  regulation of, 299–302
Eurodollar multiplier, 295–98
Eurodollars:
  arbitrage and, 288–91
  composition of, 284–86
  credit creation, 292–98
  deposit growth of, 284–86
  deposits, 279, 287
  domestic banks and, 293–95
  domestic intermediation of, 280–81
  evolution of, 281–87
  interbank, 280, 288–91
  international intermediation of, 281, 298–99
  liquidity and, 291
  loans in, 287–88
  maturity distribution and, 291–92
  money multiplier analysis, 292
  OPEC and, 285
  operation, 287–99
  permanence, 286
  policy, 301–2
  portfolio balance and, 290–91
  regulation of, 299–302
  Regulation Q and, 282–84
  Russian gold sales and, 282
  safety, 301
  sterling restrictions of, 281
  trade finance and, 280
  U.S. regulation of, 281–82
European Monetary System, 157
European Recovery Program, 151